3/9/11
$28.00
I

A5
14day

3/11

THE SHADOWS OF YOUTH

THE SHADOWS OF YOUTH

The Remarkable Journey of the
Civil Rights Generation

ANDREW B. LEWIS

Hill and Wang
A division of Farrar, Straus and Giroux / New York

Hill and Wang
A division of Farrar, Straus and Giroux
18 West 18th Street, New York 10011

Distributed in Canada by D&M Publishers, Inc.
Printed in the United States of America
First edition, 2009

Library of Congress Cataloging-in-Publication Data
Lewis, Andrew B., 1967–
    The shadows of youth : the remarkable journey of the civil rights
    generation / Andrew B. Lewis. — 1st ed.
        p.   cm.
    Includes bibliographical references and index.
    ISBN: 978-0-8090-8598-9 (hardcover : alk. paper)
    1. African Americans—Civil rights—History—20th century.   2. African American civil rights
workers—Biography.   3. African American college students—Biography.   4. Student Nonviolent
Coordinating Committee (U.S.)—Biography.   5. African American political activists—Biography.
6. African Americans—Biography.   7. Student Nonviolent Coordinating Committee (U.S.)—History.
8. Civil rights movements—United States—History—20th century.   9. United States—Race
relations—History—20th century.   10. Southern States—Race relations—History—20th century.
I. Title.

E185.615.L47755 2009
323.1196′073—dc22

                                                                                    2009009980

Designed by Abby Kagan

www.fsgbooks.com

10   9   8   7   6   5   4   3   2   1

For Mom and Dad

This world demands the qualities of youth: not a time of life but a state of mind, a temper of the will, a quality of the imagination, a predominance of courage over timidity, of the appetite for adventure over the love of ease . . . It is young people who must take the lead.

—ROBERT KENNEDY,
Cape Town, South Africa, 1966

CONTENTS

THE SHADOWS OF YOUTH

Raleigh, North Carolina, Good Friday 1960

Even now, more than forty years later, Charles McDew can close his eyes and summon a clear memory of Easter weekend 1960—the cramped and sweaty auditorium, the worn-out dorm room he bunked in for the weekend, the poor institutional food he ate. He came to join other young African Americans at Shaw University in North Carolina for a summit about the sit-in protests that he and others had begun to conduct at the lunch counters of the South. The result was the founding of the Student Nonviolent Coordinating Committee (SNCC). No one attending could have predicted how much SNCC would contribute to the successes of the civil rights movement—or, more simply, the movement—how directly it would take up epoch-making causes like the antiwar protests and the women's movement, how it would end up making history.

It was also the moment when the civil rights movement tapped the energies—the careless expectations and raw idealism—of its own youth, becoming the potent force that would finally topple legal segregation during the next five years. In the wake of the Supreme Court's 1954 decision against segregated schooling in *Brown v. Board of Education of Topeka* and the 1955 Montgomery bus boycott, a civil rights movement seemed ready to take off. But during the nearly three years following the bus boycott's conclusion in 1956, civil rights activism had sputtered and stalled. The student-led sit-ins revived the movement, harnessing mass protest as an effective weapon, providing every black American with a sense of involvement, reaching into the farthest corners of the South, and tugging at the conscience of the nation.

The sit-ins that swept the South in the winter and spring of 1960 marked the political awakening of the baby boom generation. Many of those at Shaw were born just before World War II, before the boom, but they set the generational tone in terms of rhetoric, style, and ideas. In one way or another baby boomers would shape the politics of the rest of the twentieth century; their values, black and white, were formed in places like Shaw in the early 1960s. This was when they grasped for the first time that the world of their parents was theirs to take, and to remake.

When the leaders of the fledgling sit-in effort arrived at Shaw University, a small, little-known black school, they numbered just a hundred or so, but their cause had swept across the South in the ten weeks since the first sit-in demonstration on February 1. The uncertain leaders of what suddenly seemed like an authentic movement had come to Shaw to share tactics, to refine strategy, to swap stories, and simply to meet one another for the first time.

Charles McDew had no idea where the movement was heading; all he knew was that this was about the most exciting thing he had done in his entire life. Like many of the delegates, McDew had stumbled into political protest. In 1960, he was a nineteen-year-old burly ex-football-playing freshman from Massillon, Ohio, nearing the end of his first year at South Carolina State in Orangeburg. He'd had trouble moving from the relatively liberal world of Massillon to the segregated world of the small-town South. Once during a traffic stop, a local cop demanded that McDew call him sir, asking, "They never taught you that up North?" When McDew made the mistake of actually answering, the cop responded by smacking him across the face with his nightstick, breaking his jaw.[1]

McDew encountered racism in more intimate ways as well. When none of the local white churches allowed him in to worship during Religious Emphasis Week, he converted to Judaism because the rabbi welcomed him with open arms, and Judaism led McDew into the movement. Shortly after the first sit-ins in North Carolina, he stumbled on the following passage in the Talmud, the Jewish compilation of rabbinical knowledge: "If I am not for myself, who will be for me?

If I am for myself only, what am I? If not now, when?" At that moment McDew realized that the injustices he faced went beyond any personal experience and he had a moral obligation to join the protests. When the Orangeburg students held their first sit-in on February 25, they picked Charles McDew as their leader. In the six weeks since then, more than five hundred students had been arrested, beaten by policemen, drenched with fire hoses in the freezing cold of winter, and jailed in a chicken coop. Though they had not yet succeeded in integrating the lunch counters of Orangeburg, the students did not waver in their commitment.[2]

A year later McDew's friend Bob Moses perfectly captured the young activist's spirit: "McDew, a black by birth, a Jew by choice, and a revolutionary by necessity, has taken the deep hates and loves of America, and the world, reserved for those who dare to stand in a strong sun and cast a sharp shadow." Moses's words revealed the crosscurrents that pulled at the young activists: some things they chose, other things were thrust upon them, but most important was their participation in the movement, the simple choice to stand up and claim their due as American citizens.

Few of the young men and women gathered at Shaw knew then that becoming civil rights activists would define the arc of their lives. Far from being confined to a few dramatic years in the early 1960s, the story of SNCC and the influence of the civil rights generation stretches from World War II to Barack Obama's election. But at Shaw, the young protesters only vaguely understood how the powerful forces of economic development, migration, and youth culture unleashed by World War II had created the conditions that made the sit-ins possible. Nor could they have predicted that SNCC would become for a brief period the center of the civil rights movement, or that their own milestones over the next few years—from the Freedom Rides to Freedom Summer—would define a key passage in American history, or that by the 1970s they would be big-city mayors, members of Congress, organizational leaders, and policy experts who shaped national debate. For what was to remain of the American Century, other baby boomers would measure their own influence against the standard set by SNCC, and SNCC veterans would measure the rest of their lives against the standards they set in their youth.

.   .   .

In April 1960, the movement was fresh and the future unwritten. The students were flush with excitement at the power of the sit-ins, at their sheer newness. The Good Friday air crackled with anticipation as students from all over the South began arriving at Shaw. As one participant recalls: "There was no SNCC, no ad hoc committees, no funds, just people who did not know what to expect but who came." As people filtered onto the campus that Friday night to introduce themselves, it was a bit like a revved-up version of the first day of college. Here everyone had already done something brave and fantastic. "You began to meet these people from all these different sit-in places," one participant from Atlanta remembers, "and you said, 'Oh yeah, I remember reading about what you all did there.' The idea began to seep in that we might be real hell-on-wheels."[3]

As McDew looked around the room, he spied in one corner Ezell Blair, Franklin McCain, David Richmond, and Joseph McNeil. They were the four North Carolina Agricultural and Technical State University freshmen who staged the first sit-in, just ten weeks earlier at a Woolworth's in Greensboro, seventy-five miles to the northwest. They were a bit shy, probably even more overwhelmed than McDew. Theirs had been a spontaneous protest. They had had no idea it would mushroom into a political movement. Though none would again take a leading role, they inspired curiosity, and admiration for what they had set in motion.

More impressive still was the contingent from Nashville, site of some of the largest demonstrations yet. McDew found the group intimidating. "There were these very eloquent people from Nashville," he remembered, "who understood the philosophy, who understood the reason behind, who could talk about a redemptive community." Among themselves, the other students referred to them as the "Nashville All-Stars."[4]

One of the first people who caught McDew's eye was Nashville's Diane Nash. John Lewis, also from Nashville, recalled the first time he met her: "The first thing anyone who encountered her noticed— and there was no way *not* to notice—is that she was one of God's beautiful creatures, just about the most gorgeous woman any of us had seen." Nash had, in fact, won several teenage beauty pageants back in her native Chicago. She was a prototypical 1950s teenager— she looked like she had stepped out of an African-American version of *Father Knows Best*. She was the kind of woman that college boys tripped over themselves to be near. It was rumored that more than one fellow joined the sit-ins in the hope of getting closer to Diane Nash.[5]

But physical beauty was just the first thing that one noticed about Diane Nash. There was something about her, something distant in her eyes, that made men even more eager to pursue her. Partially it arose from the seriousness with which she approached her work in the civil rights movement. Long before many of the other young activists, Nash had grasped that ending segregation meant more than simply having blacks and whites sitting next to each other at restaurants and bus stops; it would profoundly change the way Americans related to each other, how they thought about their country, what it meant to be a citizen.[6]

Nash's comrade John Lewis did not make the trip to Raleigh. He had volunteered to stay behind in Nashville to monitor the ongoing sit-ins, but he would soon emerge as one of SNCC's most important leaders. At that early stage, Lewis was still easy to mistake for the painfully shy, socially awkward kid from the woods of Carter's Quarters, Alabama, who had arrived in Nashville three years earlier with just a battered secondhand trunk and a hundred dollars to his name. On the surface, he seemed pretty unsophisticated. His country roots, evident in his manners, thick accent, and neat but simple Sunday-best minister's suits, made Lewis feel like a rube lost in the city. What he did bring to the table was a deep religious conviction in the immorality of segregation and an absolute certainty that nonviolence represented not simply a tactical innovation but a new way of living one's life. Increasingly, these attitudes would propel him to a position of high visibility in the movement and, eventually, in American politics. But in 1960 he still felt insecure in the presence of what he thought were his more articulate, better-dressed, and more outwardly sophisticated peers.[7]

For his part, his fellow Nashville activist twenty-four-year-old Marion Barry, a self-assured graduate student of chemistry, was eager to make the trip to Raleigh that Easter weekend. Barry was a few years older than most of the others at Shaw, and this translated into an extra dose of confidence. To John Lewis, Barry was tall, lanky, and "cool, very cool." Lewis envied Barry's ability to look completely at ease in any social situation. Barry instantly impressed Julian Bond, an Atlanta activist, as a charismatic leader. He was a good listener, easily connecting with all types of people, and he was a good debater, glib and quick-talking. Indeed, Barry had a hipster's swagger, honed on the streets of Memphis, where he shopped in the same Beale Street stores frequented by a young truck driver named Elvis Presley. Barry's nicely pressed shirts and sleek calf-length socks intimidated Lewis and the other protesters from humbler, more rural backgrounds. Few of them had traveled much outside of the South. Barry, they whispered, had actually been to California.[8]

After the Nashville contingent, the other big group came from Atlanta, home to the most prosperous black community in the South. *Fortune* magazine had recently called Auburn Street, the heart of the city's black neighborhood, the "richest negro street in America." Atlanta was also home to Morehouse College, the "black Harvard." (Martin Luther King, Jr., was a Morehouse man.) To McDew, nobody better exemplified the sophisticated manners of Atlanta than Julian Bond. Tall, thin, and stylishly preppy, Bond had the boyish good looks and cool self-assurance of a movie star. If Marion Barry was Elvis, then Bond was James Dean. He had grown up in the rarefied world of the black intelligentsia. His father, Horace Mann Bond, had been the first black president of Lincoln University, the oldest private college for African Americans in the United States. As a high school student, Julian had attended the elite George School outside Philadelphia. But he was also a bit of a rebel and an artist. Instead of the professional career his parents imagined for him, Bond dreamed of being a writer and composed poetry in his spare time. While his parents fretted that he did not study enough, he joined the swimming team, wrote for the literary magazine, and acquired something of a reputation as a ladies' man.[9]

The students eyed each other warily. They knew one another only by reputation—Nashville was disciplined, Atlanta was wealthy, Montgomery and Orangeburg had faced great physical danger. To some extent, they were all cocky. For the students, the past three months had been intoxicating stuff—running their own protests, conferring with the South's most prominent black citizens, and challenging white power. Now they wondered how to bring it all together and under whose vision.

At Shaw that Easter in 1960, the students who gathered—most of them under age twenty-two—had no idea what the future would bring, and few could imagine how they would transform themselves into a coherent group, a wedge, a lever, a force for social change. They were, after all, still young, still raw, and still strangers; the combination of moral conviction, political awakening, and sudden camaraderie—all filtered through the heady medium of youth itself—was combustible but unpredictable.

They came to Raleigh because "Miss Ella" issued the invitations. Ella Baker was the executive director of the Southern Christian Leadership Conference, the group founded by Martin Luther King, Jr., following the Montgomery bus boycott, and already a legend in civil rights circles for her three decades of activism. She had badgered King into allotting eight hundred dollars of the SCLC's money to bring together the different sit-in leaders, and then she'd convinced her old school, Shaw University, to host the group. As McDew recalled, "In rural South Carolina we didn't know what this SCLC was about, but everybody we knew trusted Ella Baker."[10]

Baker was the kind of woman often overlooked by casual observers, who perhaps would mistake the dark-skinned middle-aged woman in the neatly tailored business suit and pillbox hat for a schoolteacher. Even the students at Shaw thought she had a plain appearance. As one attendee said, she was "pleasingly prim and benignly schoolmarmish"; she was "very much your mom." She was also a microcosm of the tragedy of segregation, her intelligence and skills discounted by the wider world because of the color of her skin and her understated appearance.[11]

But Ella Baker was emphatically *not* like most people's mothers. Born and raised in Norfolk, Virginia, she graduated from Shaw as valedictorian in 1927, at a time when opportunities for women, let alone black women, were limited. She ended up in New York City, where she fell in love with the excitement, cultural ferment, and social freedoms of Harlem during the Roaring Twenties. She plunged into activism, spending the next decade involved in a variety of reform causes—organizing worker co-ops, volunteering at different trade unions, and working for the Works Progress Administration during the Great Depression. In 1941, she joined the NAACP, quickly rising to director of branches. She spent the next five years traveling around the South starting new branches, getting to know black activists in every nook and cranny of the region. But Baker was frustrated by the unwillingness of NAACP leaders to launch a bottom-up mass movement.

Instead, the organization cultivated influence in Washington, challenging segregation in the nation's courts and legislatures. It was, Baker concluded, an elitist organization. Disappointed, she resigned her position in 1946.

In January 1958, Martin Luther King recruited Baker to head up the fledging SCLC's voter-registration efforts in the South. Four months later the executive director, John Tilley, resigned, and Baker took over his job. It was a rocky relationship from the start. She had misgivings about the personality cult King nurtured around himself; instead, she argued for a "group-centered leadership." If the SCLC depended solely on King's charisma and popularity, it would never become a self-sufficient organization. Baker clashed with the young Baptist ministers who formed the core of the SCLC's leadership. King's confidant, the Reverend Andy Young, confessed that Baker reminded the ministers of the "strong Mommas they were trying break free of." They resisted taking orders from her. Four months after the Shaw meeting, she left the SCLC.[12]

More than any other adult activist, Ella Baker grasped the significance of the sit-ins. She had long hoped that ordinary black southerners would one day take charge of their own destiny. This is how Jim Crow would be brought down—on the streets and at the lunch counters of the South, not in the courts. She knew, though, that these young people would need guidance to turn the scattered sit-ins into a cohesive force. The Shaw conference filled her with excitement at the idea that these students could become leaders in the civil rights movement. "This may only be a dream of mine," she confided to a friend, "but I think it can be made real." Ella Baker would become SNCC's most important mentor, resolving disputes, suggesting staff to hire, and shaping the direction of protest. She was part den mother, part strategic adviser, and part kindred spirit.[13]

"Where do we go from here?" Ella Baker asked in her invitations to the meeting at Shaw. From her perspective, the sit-ins were just a foreshadowing of much bigger things to come; in a sense, the press clippings from ten weeks of demonstrations outweighed the actual accomplishments. The spread of the sit-ins clearly put pressure on southern merchants, but it was not certain if the pressure could be sustained or if the sit-in movement would fizzle out before achieving real gains. Certainly many white businessmen believed all they needed to do was hold the line until the school year ended; the protests would fall apart as the students dispersed. From a broader per-spective, it was unclear whether even successful protests could be translated into substantial changes in the everyday lives of southern blacks. The most recent civil rights victories were not necessarily en-couraging precedents. The *Brown* decision declaring segregated schools illegal was already six years old, and still only a very few African-American children attended school with white children. In the three years since the Montgomery bus boycott ended, its influence had not extended beyond eliminating the color bar on many southern city buses.[14]

Where do we go from here? Baker's question was on everyone's mind as they gathered in Raleigh. In fact, it was not one question but many questions intertwined. Could young people really run their own or-ganization? Would the ideas of nonviolence and civil disobedience prove to be an effective rallying point for the entire South—rich and poor, urban and rural, young and old, even black and white? Could such simple ideas really bring down as powerful an institution as seg-regation? Shaw was an eye-opener, for Bond, the first time he had considered these larger questions. "I knew that racial problems ex-tended far beyond lunch counters. But I didn't see us doing anything" bigger until Shaw.[15]

The task at Shaw was to begin to sort out these questions, to figure out how to transform an initial blow against injustice into a sustained and effective movement, a cause to be reckoned with. Theirs was heavy thinking and heavy work. During the day, the students broke up into smaller groups to trade their experiences from the sit-ins and to strategize about the next step. At night, older delegates shared their advice in speeches to the whole group. James Lawson, the Nashville minister who had trained students in nonviolent protest, gave one of the speeches; Martin Luther King, the most recognized civil rights activist in America since his emergence during the Montgomery bus boycott, would give the keynote address on Saturday night. Even though the students were still feeling their way forward, even though their working group conversations were often tentative, uncertain, and disjointed, they knew they stood on the precipice of something transformative.

Lawson's opening-night speech was energizing. He criticized the NAACP for relying too heavily on the courts and extolled the ne-glected power of the black masses, the possibilities of which the sit-ins only hinted at. Most important, the speech tapped into the students' sense that the sit-ins were a turning point for the movement, calling out to the restive nature of their youth:

> The nonviolent movement is asserting "get moving." The pace of social change is too slow. At this rate it will be at least another generation before the major forms of segregation disappear. All of Africa will be free before the American Negro attains first-class citizenship. Most of us will be grandparents before we can live normal lives.[16]

Those from outside Nashville, hearing Lawson speak for the first time, found his words electric. As Bond listened, he could see the people around him getting stirred up, and he thought Lawson's "dynamite" speech made him a legitimate challenger to King for the students' allegiance. After all, Lawson was closer in age to them than King and, like them, was still a student (albeit a graduate student). In his absolute belief in nonviolence, Lawson was more radical than King. While King seemed to have abandoned activism for a perpetual speaking tour, Lawson had spent the last few years in the trenches with the students in Nashville. A palpable energy flowed through the participants as they filtered out of the evening meeting, and many voiced the need for the students to chart their own course.[17]

These rumblings of independence bewildered the adult observers. Martin Luther King had visions of turning the students into the SCLC's youth wing. On Saturday morning, he summoned Ella Baker to meet with him and his inner circle. The men grilled her: Where was the conference going? What were the students' intentions? How can we control them? Baker was incredulous. All they cared about was controlling the students. That they would succeed was her biggest fear.[18]

Furious, Baker stormed out of the meeting. To affiliate with one of the established organizations would take away the students' unique, if raw, idealism, their capacity to imagine new methods, to press the cause of impatience and idealism against the ossified complacency and pragmatism of their elders' campaigns. They brought a new energy to the struggle for civil rights. Their youth alone managed to dissolve—almost immediately—the wariness based on regional and temperamental difference. This was a new path, and Ella Baker believed the students needed to go off on their own. Quietly and in secret, she talked to the students, urging them to consider setting up a separate organization.

On Saturday night, with everyone gathered in Shaw's gymnasium, King delivered the main address to close the meeting. But before he took the podium, Ella Baker spoke about the significance of the recent protests. She told the students to remember that the sit-ins were about "more than a hamburger or even a giant-sized Coke." They were not even only about obtaining "first-class citizenship" for black Americans. The campaign for civil rights had implications for the whole world; it could be a beacon of hope to oppressed people everywhere, a symbol of the transformative power of human rights. She told the students that their "group-centered leadership" offered a new model of leadership, one that gave young African Americans the chance to take the civil rights movement in a new direction.

Then King spoke. After Baker's and Lawson's stirring addresses, King's speech fell flat. Bond recalled it "left no real impression" on him and many others. Rejecting King and the NAACP, the students embraced Baker's vision and voted to set up their own separate organization, christening it the Temporary Student Nonviolent Coordinating Committee.[19]

Someone started to sing "We Shall Overcome," an old gospel song that had been picked up during the Depression by the folksinger Pete Seeger and recast as a protest song. Everyone joined in what was soon to become the anthem of the civil rights movement. The lyrics filled the room: "We are not afraid . . . We are not alone . . . The whole wide world around . . . We shall overcome someday." People linked arms, swayed to the music. The old gym pulsed with energy. "It was inspiring because it was the beginning, and . . . it was the purest moment," one participant recalled. "I am a romantic . . . I call this moment the one."[20]

PART ONE

Qualities of Youth

1. SURE BUGS ME

THE CIVIL RIGHTS GENERATION AND THE FAILURES
OF THE 1950s

When fourteen-year-old John Lewis opened the paper on May 16, 1954, the headline stunned him: the Supreme Court had declared segregated schools unconstitutional. He could not believe it. Separate schools were one of the cornerstones of southern segregation. He felt his world "turned upside down." He was sure he would be attending an integrated school that coming September, a mere four months away. But Lewis's hopes would be dashed by a school desegregation process that saw only about one in one hundred black students enter white schools by 1960. Lewis's broken dream captured in a microcosm how the 1950s teased young African Americans with the unrealized promise of racial change.[1]

The Supreme Court decision that shocked Lewis was actually the culmination of a twenty-year legal odyssey begun by Charles Hamilton Houston, the chief architect of the NAACP's legal strategy and the former dean of Howard University's law school. At the NAACP Legal Defense Fund, Houston built a fraternity of shrewd and courageous lawyers that included Thurgood Marshall, his best student at Howard. During the 1930s and 1940s, Legal Defense Fund lawyers had attacked the soft underbelly of segregation—the failure of white southerners to make separate truly equal—through a series of lawsuits. Starting with the most glaring examples of discrimination in higher education, NAACP lawyers chipped away at Jim Crow. First they forced the establishment of separate graduate programs for African Americans and then the admission of blacks into white programs.

Next they tackled inequality in grade schools, forcing southern states to spend millions of dollars to provide the same pay to all teachers regardless of race and to raise the quality of black facilities. The equalization campaign was so successful, in fact, that by 1950 the NAACP took only cases that challenged segregation directly.[2]

Smart lawyers and creative legal thinking were only part of the story, however; good lawyers needed good clients. Concerned that a loss would do more to reinforce the legality of segregation than ten wins would do to undermine it, they avoided many cases, especially those originating in rural areas where white resistance was strongest.

So when Barbara Johns, a determined sixteen-year-old who led her classmates at the all-black high school in Prince Edward County on a strike for better schools, asked Oliver Hill, the chief NAACP lawyer in Virginia, to take their case, he was not optimistic. The rural county was known for its strong support of segregation. Still, he agreed to meet with them and, impressed by their passion and determination, agreed to take the case on the condition that the students scrapped their demand for better schools and attacked segregation head-on. Less than one month later, on May 23, 1951, Hill filed suit challenging segregated education in Prince Edward County, and it would soon be combined with the *Brown* case in Topeka and three others to make up the five different suits consolidated into *Brown v. Board of Education* for the Supreme Court hearing.[3]

Almost three years to the day later, the nine justices of the Supreme Court announced their decision in *Brown*. The unusually brief opinion strongly denounced school segregation. It argued that education was the most important function of state and local governments, central to a democratic society and the "foundation of good citizenship." To exclude young African Americans from white schools was more than simply a violation of equal protection; segregated education generated "a feeling of inferiority" that permanently scarred their "hearts and minds."[4]

The Court's rhetoric may have been strong, but its actions were tempered. Instead of ordering the immediate integration of the South's segregated schools or even the immediate integration of the schools involved in *Brown*, the Court postponed any action for a year to allow the South time to adjust. Acceptance was crucial for Chief Justice Earl Warren; he believed the mechanics of integration would come relatively easily once southerners accepted the idea that segregation was unconstitutional.[5]

One year later, on May 31, 1955, the Supreme Court enshrined caution as law. *Brown* II, as the implementation decree is usually called, was again brief and to the point. Federal judges would consider desegregation requests on a community-by-community basis. The Court offered no specific guidance on how long the process of ending segregation should take; nor did it set an end date. Instead, the Court instructed white officials "to make a prompt and reasonable start toward" ending school segregation and advised judges to make sure it happened "with all deliberate speed." Any delays should clearly benefit the public and be in the spirit of "good faith" compliance with the *Brown* decision.[6]

"All deliberate speed" robbed black activists at the local level of the issue of school desegregation in important ways. Courts were slow. Courts were abstract. Hearings were long and boring. The Supreme Court had made the implementation of the basic constitutional rights of African Americans a negotiated process overseen by lower federal courts; black rights would be balanced against white anxiety in designing desegregation plans. By keeping the issue in the courts, school desegregation could not become the focal point of mass protest. Except for a few dramatic incidents that punctuated the years after *Brown*, school desegregation played a surprisingly peripheral role during the heyday of the movement in the 1960s.

Julian Bond was both less surprised by and less excited about the *Brown* decision than John Lewis. He saw the Supreme Court decision as ratifying the positive parts of his experience at George, the integrated private school he attended in Pennsylvania, and as confirming his optimistic hope that racial differences were becoming less important. His parents were doubtful about the speed of change when they discussed the decision at the dinner table. But as 1954 gave way to 1955 and then 1956, Bond became unsure about the ability of the American democratic system to reform itself. He saw how the Court's decision had deferred action and emboldened white southerners. As the only black student at an all-white prep school, he understood how wide the gap between the rhetoric and the reality of American democracy could be.

The slow pace of change also frustrated Lewis as he searched in vain for news of Alabama's desegregation plans. In some ways more naïve than Bond, Lewis really believed that desegregation was around the corner. But state officials never announced a plan for integration. In fact, no school desegregation of any kind would occur in Alabama until the 1963–64 school year, when 21 of a possible 293,476 black students attended their first classes with whites. In the late summer of 1955, fifteen-year-old John Lewis came across a story in the newspaper that had a much more immediate and depressing impact on his life.[7]

As the summer of 1955 wound down, two fourteen-year-old cousins, Emmett Till and Wheeler Parker, begged their parents to let them go to Mississippi for a vacation. Their hometown of Chicago had been mercilessly hot, and the boys were itching to get some fresh air, to fish along the Tallahatchie, to just get outside. After much pleading, their parents agreed they could spend the last two weeks of the summer in Mississippi at their great-uncle Moses Wright's farm.[8]

Till and Wheeler's trip was not unusual. Many northern blacks sent their children back down South to visit relatives during the summer. Both of Emmett Till's parents had been reared in the South. Louis Till, Emmett's father, had died in Europe during World War II. Having emigrated to Chicago, Mamie Till Bradley made a good living as a civilian employee of the air force, and she and Emmett lived a comfortable middle-class life on the South Side.[9]

Emmett Till was a study in teenage contradictions. His mother described him as well mannered, polite, and good-natured; his friends saw him as spirited, boastful, and rambunctious. While his mother talked about his church attendance, his friends mentioned his drive to be the center of attention. Childhood polio had left him with a slight stutter. Still, Emmett was confident and something of a dandy; on one pinky he sported a gold signet ring with the initials *LT* in honor of his father. In short, he was a typical fourteen-year-old, basically a good kid but still trying to sort out who he was, to walk that fine line between pleasing his mother and fitting in.[10]

On August 24, only a few days after arriving in Mississippi on the train, Till, his cousin, and a few other local kids were doing what American teens have done since the invention of the automobile— cruising aimlessly, trying to gin up a little fun on a quiet summer night. The group pulled up in front of the Money General Store, a little store that served a mostly black clientele and was a popular place to hang out. Money, Mississippi, was not much of a town, really just a post office, a gas station, and a cotton-ginning station. When their car pulled up, a dozen kids, mostly boys, were already milling about in front.[11]

As they sat outside in the hot summer air, the joking and the bragging went around fast and furious. Till bragged about his white girlfriend back in Chicago, but the teens were skeptical. Someone in the group dared him to prove his story by talking to the white woman working behind the counter. Caught in the web of his own boasts, Emmett did what any brash teenager would do: he went inside.

No one knows exactly what happened next. The most repeated version of events comes from Carolyn Bryant, the woman behind the counter that night. Till bought two cents' worth of bubble gum. He then grabbed Bryant's hand, asking "How about a date, baby?" As she tried to back away, Till grabbed her by the waist. "Don't be afraid of me, baby. I ain't gonna hurt you. I've been with white girls before." At that point, someone in the group outside—they had been watching through the window—rushed in to grab Till. Bryant went for a gun in her sister-in-law's car behind the store. As Till's friends hustled him out, he said "Bye, baby" and possibly wolf-whistled, though others in the group dispute this.

The racial code of the Deep South was such that what had actually happened mattered less than local perceptions. When the story spread, Bryant's tenuous position in the community was at stake. The Bryants were at the bottom of white society, just eking out a marginal income at the store selling small goods and food to local blacks. As Roy Bryant admitted later, he needed to "whip the nigger's ass" or other whites would think he was a coward or a fool.

Bryant recounted how he and his brother-in-law J. W. Milam went over to Moses Wright's place and hauled Till out of bed.

"You the nigger who did the talking?"

"Yeah," answered Till.

"Don't say 'Yeah' to me. I'll blow your head off," Milam said.

He ordered Till to get dressed. Till even started to put on his socks before Milam stopped him.

Bryant and Milam put Till in the back of the pickup and drove off. They intended to whip Till "and scare some sense" into him by dangling him over a cliff that dropped one hundred feet into the Talla-hatchie River. But they got lost, driving around in circles for three hours, and returned to Milam's house.

They took Till out to a toolshed in back and started pistol-whipping him with Milam's old army .45-caliber gun.

Till stood up to the men. "You bastards, I'm not afraid of you. I'm as good as you are. I've 'had' white women. My grandmother was a white woman."

Milam was dumbfounded. "'Chicago boy,' I said, 'I'm tired of your kind coming down here to stir up trouble. Goddamn you, I'm going to make an example of you—just so everybody can know how me and my folks stand.'"

They put Till back in the truck and drove over to a cotton-gin company to grab a discarded gin fan that weighed seventy-four pounds. They made Till put it in the back of the truck, and then they drove to a deserted spot on the Tallahatchie River where Milam sometimes hunted. The men ordered Till to strip naked.

"You still as good as I am?" Milam asked.

"Yeah."

"You still had white women?"

"Yeah."

Bang. Milam shot Till in the head at point-blank range. He was probably dead before he hit the ground. They tied the body to the gin fan with barbed wire and rolled him into a deep part of the river. It was just before seven a.m. on Sunday.

Three days later a fisherman saw two feet poking out of the water and reeled in a bloated, distended body. It would have been impossible to identify it as Emmett Till if not for the telltale gold signet ring on one pinky inscribed *LT*.

To this point, the story is a depressingly familiar tale from the Deep South. The abduction and murder of a young African-American man was not an uncommon occurrence, and from time to time the bodies of unknown African Americans bobbled up from the South's swamps and rivers. In fact, if Milam and Bryant had done a better job disposing of the body, the local sheriffs would have dismissed his disappearance as simply that of a young boy who ran away; his family would never have learned what happened to him, and few people would ever have heard the name Emmett Till.

But the murder of Emmett Till became a national sensation. The potent cocktail of sex, race, and death in Till's lynching reinforced the nation's image of the Deep South as a gothic and sinister place out of step with national norms. Mixed with lurid speculations about the facts of the case were condemnations of the South's violence and cries for justice.

On September 2, Emmett Till's body arrived back in Chicago in a casket nailed shut at the insistence of Mississippi authorities. Mamie Till Bradley dropped to her knees to pray: "Lord take my soul, show me what you want me to do, and make me able to do it." Bradley told the funeral director that if he did not help her open the box, she would take a hammer to open it herself. As the coffin was pried open, the horrible odor of river water and rotting flesh flooded the room. "I was forced to deal with his face," his mother said. "I saw that his tongue was choked out. I noticed that the right eye was lying midway on his cheek, I noticed that his nose had been broken like somebody took a meat chopper and chopped his nose in several places." The mortician told Till's mother that he could fix up the body for public viewing. "No, Mr. Rayner, let the people see what I've seen," she told him.

Over the next three days, perhaps as many as fifty thousand people came to the funeral home for the wake and viewed Emmett's body. The crowds were so thick that mourners filed past four abreast, and the doors stayed open until two in the morning. One of Emmett's classmates recalls filing past the glass-covered casket and being shocked that his friend looked "like a monster."[12]

A week after the funeral, *Jet*, a magazine for black readers, published photos of Till's mutilated corpse. A few days later, so did the *Chicago Defender*, the city's black paper, followed by other papers. It's hard now to convey the sensation created by those photographs or to overestimate their impact. Just as the Abu Ghraib prison photos in 2004 turned an abstract story about military abuse in Iraq into a national scandal, the photos of Till turned the hidden and abstract problem of white violence in the South into a tangible story easily grasped by most Americans. By moving the question of lynching out of the South, Till's death forced northerners, white and black, to pay attention to what was going on in the ex-Confederate states.

White Mississippians could not ignore the calls for justice. In early September, Bryant and Milam were indicted for Till's murder. Despite

Moses Wright's dramatic courtroom identification of the killers, the jury took just one hour and seven minutes to return a verdict of not guilty. Later, Mississippi officials declined to prosecute the two men for kidnapping—the one crime they had actually confessed to committing.

On the heels of the acquittal, the two men sold their story to a reporter from *Look* magazine for about four thousand dollars in the hope of countering the sympathetic coverage of Mamie Bradley. Their Emmett Till was impudent to the end, which suggests that if only Till had known his place, he would still be alive. The dueling media stories—Mamie Bradley's in *Jet*, the two men's in *Look*—set in place a pattern that would recur throughout the subsequent struggle for racial justice. Civil rights activists used the media deftly, segregationists awkwardly and ineffectively. Rather than making northerners more sympathetic to the men—and by extension to segregation—the story simply reinforced the brutality of the crime. The more exposure Americans had to segregation, the more they disliked it.[13]

Till's lynching punctured the optimism of young African Americans. To this day, Julian Bond's memories "are exact and parallel those of many others my age—I felt vulnerable for the first time in my life—Till was a year younger," and Bond believed "that this could easily happen to me—for no reason at all." John Lewis had the same thought, "that it could have been me . . . at the bottom of the river." It deflated any enthusiasm he had for the *Brown* decision. "It didn't seem that the Supreme Court mattered. It didn't seem that the American principles . . . I read in beat-up civics books mattered . . . They didn't matter to the men who killed Emmett Till."

On the streets of Stokely Carmichael's white Bronx neighborhood, his neighbors did not talk about the case; he first learned about it by listening to the gossip at his Harlem barbershop. Cleveland Sellers, who would become one of Carmichael's best friends in SNCC, remembers finding out the same way in his little South Carolina town. "For weeks after it happened . . . it was impossible to go into a barber shop or corner grocery without hearing" talk about the murder. The case haunted Sellers as he tried to imagine how he would have responded to Bryant and Milam on the banks of the river; other times he would get angry dwelling on how the killers had escaped punishment.[14]

Parents worried about Till's lynching, not because they feared for their own safety, but because it destroyed the illusion of safety they had created for their children. In Chicago, Diane Nash's parents lectured her more forcefully to be careful and watched her more strictly in the months after the murder. They would not let her see Till's body, but she remembers how the story hung over her home and neighborhood, shattering the illusion that middle-class blacks in the North were insulated from southern racism. Nash and her friends, who usually paid little attention to current events, followed the Till story closely. No one wanted to discuss the murder directly, but it came up all the time.

Bond's parents, Nash's parents, Carmichael's parents, had all convinced themselves that middle-class prosperity and exposure to white society could insulate their children from the harshest aspects of American racism. The Till murder shattered that illusion. Soon after the murder, Carmichael's mother reacted with alarm when she saw her son walking home from Sunday school in a group that included white boys and white girls. With increasing anxiety, she told him to forget about white women like "a bullfrog forgot his tail."[15]

For young African Americans, especially those entering into the emerging mainstream of the new youth culture and middle-class consumerism, Emmett Till overshadowed everything else that happened during the 1950s. It scared them, erasing the distance between the violence of Jim Crow and their lives, pushing the nominal gains of *Brown* to the sidelines. The murder hung over the rest of their youth, a bad memory that would not go away. If it scared them, it also made them more aware. They subtly came to understand something that Martin Luther King would articulate eloquently a few years later: "Injustice anywhere threatens justice everywhere."[16]

Even the stirring emergence of Martin Luther King, Jr., onto the national stage just five months after Emmett Till's funeral did not fully shake the unease of young African Americans. It did, however, provide a counterpoint to the failures of *Brown* and the horrors of Till's death. The Montgomery bus boycott that thrust King into the spotlight was the first great organized protest of the southern civil rights movement; it foreshadowed the effectiveness of collective action in the fight against segregation and made King, just twenty-six years old, internationally famous.

The idea of a bus boycott had been percolating in Montgomery for some time. Both the head of the local branch of the powerful Brotherhood of Sleeping Car Porters union and the head of the Women's Political Council suggested protesting the treatment of black riders on the city's buses. The Women's Political Council had been particularly active since its formation in 1949, registering so many new African-Americans voters that they were now the swing constituency between two nearly equally divided white factions. Black leaders saw the boycott as a bargaining chip, demonstrating the growing economic and political power of the city's African-American residents.[17]

Rosa Parks was deeply enmeshed in Montgomery's black politics. She had been a member of the local NAACP branch since 1943 and was an acquaintance of Ella Baker. In the summer of 1955, she attended a conference at the Highlander Folk School in Tennessee, a little institution that had a hand in training just about every important movement activist during the 1940s, 1950s, and 1960s. So when Rosa Parks decided not to give up her bus seat on December 1, 1955, it may have been a spur-of-the-moment decision; it was not, however, a random one.[18]

The idea of a boycott quickly coalesced. The Women's Political Council staged a one-day boycott on December 5, and the next day a coalition of black leaders formed the Montgomery Improvement Association (MIA) to continue the boycott. Divisions among the city's blacks, especially between union activists and clergy, threatened to undermine their unity. As a compromise, King, newly appointed pastor of the Dexter Avenue Baptist Church, was picked to head the group. No one had any real inkling of King as a leader; he just had not been in Montgomery long enough to make many enemies.[19]

At the beginning of the boycott, African Americans' tactics and strategy remained unsettled. With King's selection, the clergy took a central role in the boycott. Because black preachers play such a prominent role in the mythology of the movement, it is easy to assume that was inevitable. In fact, secular organizations like the NAACP, the Brotherhood of Sleeping Car Porters, and the Women's Political Council had been the principal engines of civil rights activism.

The initial black demands were cautious, seeking to make segregation fairer, not to eliminate it, reflecting a belief that the end of segregation would be a gradual process of negotiation, worked out through politics, not through a quick strike of protest. The boycotters wanted more courtesy from drivers, the hiring of a few black drivers, and the use of the "Mobile plan" for seating. In Montgomery, the line between the black and white sections shifted depending on the number of white passengers, humiliating African Americans by requiring them to give up their seats. In Mobile, Alabama, blacks sat from the back to front and whites from front to back; once seated, an African-American rider would not have to give up a seat to a white.[20]

When King stepped up to the pulpit of the Holt Street Baptist Church on the evening of December 5, 1955, he found the building jammed to the rafters and an overflow crowd looking in through the windows. Montgomery's ordinary African Americans were impatient. King acknowledged their impatience and urged them toward nonviolence. "There comes a time when people get tired of being trampled over by the iron feet of oppression," he intoned. Only the combination of nonviolence, Christianity, American democracy, and black unity could make the boycott a success and inject "new meaning into the veins of history."[21]

The boycott quickly became a grassroots effort. Black people had made up such a high percentage of riders that the bus company quickly teetered on the edge of bankruptcy. When city leaders threatened to arrest black cabdrivers for charging less than the legal minimum fare, more than 150 people volunteered their cars for an ad hoc carpool. Reverend Ralph Abernathy, King's close friend, liked to tell the story of the old African-American woman who walked during the boycott, declining rides. "My feets is tired," she would say, "but my soul is rested."[22]

Ironically, legal action and not the boycott resolved the question of bus segregation. From the very beginning, the NAACP's national leaders told the MIA that they would support the boycott only if it also directly challenged bus segregation in federal court. On February 1, 1956, about three months into the boycott, the MIA filed *Browder v. Gayle*, which challenged the constitutionality of bus segregation, and by late 1956 the case was before the Supreme Court. On November 13, 1956, the Supreme Court issued a simple one-sentence decision upholding a series of lower court decisions invalidating Montgomery's bus segregation.[23]

Even though the boycott did not by itself bring an end to bus segregation, it hinted at the power of grassroots activism to challenge Jim Crow. Though black activism had been on the rise for more than a decade and there had been similar, though smaller, boycotts in other cities, nothing captured the national spotlight like the Montgomery boycott. It humanized the emerging civil rights movement, moving it from the abstractions of the legal system to the real world of ordinary people. To both black and white southerners, it demonstrated—really for the first time—that mass protest by African Americans could be an effective weapon against segregation.

As he was thrust into the national spotlight, King became the subject of complimentary profiles in *Time* and *The New York Times Magazine*. His celebrity began to overshadow the mass protest at the heart of the boycott. The establishment of the Southern Christian Leadership Conference (SCLC), with King as its first president, in January 1957 only reinforced the move away from mass protest. The SCLC was an organization of organizations, with membership offered to groups like the MIA but not to individuals. Very quickly it seemed as if the main purpose of the SCLC were to promote King, even as he struggled to re-create the success of the boycott. The December 1957 Prayer Pilgrimage in Washington, D.C., drew about thirty thousand people and featured a widely covered address by King, but did nothing to build the sustained grassroots organizing that worked so well in Montgomery.[24]

Ella Baker, for one, had urged King to develop the SCLC into a mass organization. She dreamed of an organization that combined the strategies of the boycott with the size of the NAACP. But King disregarded her advice. He not only lacked Baker's faith in the power of the masses, but he could not envision the eagerness of ordinary young African Americans to participate in protest.[25]

No one was more excited about King than John Lewis. The debates about the structure of the SCLC meant little to him. King's example reinforced his childhood dream of being a minister. The way King linked Christianity, civil disobedience, and civil rights changed Lewis's thinking, and he viewed the young minister from Montgomery as a role model. "Without question," Lewis thought, "the Montgomery bus boycott changed my life more than any other event before or since."[26]

Marion Barry's initial reaction paralleled Lewis's but faded when he sought practical lessons from the boycott. Barry was already a college sophomore, and King's inspiration led him to join the campus NAACP. But a subsequent incident revealed the limits of that inspiration. A policeman denied Barry and his friends entrance to the white Tennessee State Fair. They wanted to protest, but "we didn't know what to do." King and the bus boycott did not provide a good model for responding to this sort of racism, and "that sort of left us with an empty feeling." The fairground incident led Barry to conclude that the pulpit distanced ministers from the yearning of all African Americans to participate in protest. "My friends [and I] were frustrated as to what we could do. We always wondered, what can we do?"

As he followed the boycott during 1956, Bond found himself drawn to King. King seemed bold, daring, and close in age to him—especially in comparison to the older generation of cautious black ministers his parents were acquainted with. Two years later, when he had the chance to take a philosophy course taught by King, the preacher made so little an impression on Bond that he cannot now recall anything specific he learned from that semester. Rather, he was struck by King's caution and concern with public attention. To Bond, King was "a nice fellow" with "a flair for publicity" who had failed to capitalize on his earlier success.[27]

King's well-publicized example, however, was transformative for many. Before the boycott, Bob Zellner—a white junior at Huntingdon College, a small Methodist school in Montgomery, Alabama—had never thought much about the inequities of segregation even though he had lived his whole life in the most racially conservative part of a racially conservative state. His grandfather was a Klansman, as were his father and many other members of his family. Both his father and mother graduated from Bob Jones College (now Bob Jones University), a deeply religious, conservative institution that would not admit blacks until 1971. But Zellner's father, unlike other men in the family, broke with the Klan and instilled in his son an open-mindedness unknown to his forebears.

After he had read about the boycott in the newspapers, Zellner set about trying to meet King as part of a sociology project involving writing a paper about race in the South. He and four other students told the professor that they wanted to go over to the MIA offices to interview Martin Luther King and Ralph Abernathy. The teacher suggested they instead go to the library. When they continued to badger him about doing field research, he directed them to the white citizens' council and the Klan. The students pointed out that scholars from all over the world were coming to the MIA offices, and as students they would be derelict in not exploring *both* sides of the problem. The professor cut them off by saying, "That won't be necessary."

Disobeying their teacher, they met with students from the all-black Alabama State University and visited the MIA's offices. Their intellectual curiosity made local whites anxious. Zellner's friends looked at him like he was crazy when he started speaking approvingly of King. "Don't let anybody hear you say that," they told him. "We know you're crazy. But somebody, those other people [in Alabama], will hurt you." He was threatened with expulsion. The Klan burned crosses in front of the dorm. The Alabama attorney general summoned Zellner and the other four to his office and accused them of being Communists. They stuck to their guns, and the incident calmed enough for Zellner to graduate a few months later in the spring of 1961. But the way his rights were so casually violated by the college made Zellner even more sympathetic to the plight of black southerners, whose oppression he came to understand also threatened the freedom of whites.[28]

As King struggled, over the four years following the successful boycott, to regain the SCLC's momentum, the attention of young black southerners shifted to the fight over school desegregation in Little Rock, Arkansas. What fascinated young people about Little Rock was the nine black teenagers at the center of the story. For the first time, teenagers saw their peers in important roles in a civil rights battle, and by galvanizing the imagination of several other black teenagers scattered around the country, all paying close attention, Little Rock would prove decisive in reigniting the civil rights movement.

The Little Rock Nine were extensively covered by both the mainstream media, like *The New York Times* and *Time* magazine, and African-American publications such as *Jet* and *Ebony*. More important, less prestigious black publications such as *Sepia* and *Colored*—the kind of stuff you might read only at the barbershop—breathlessly followed the story. The six girls and three boys who made up the Little Rock Nine were easy to idolize. All of them came from good middle-class families. Their parents had jobs as salesmen, teachers, or postal workers or at the local Veterans Administration hospital. The nine teens did not apply as a group to integrate Central High, but they all knew one another from church, Sunday school, and Horace Mann, the city's black high school.

Each was cast in a distinctive role. Ernest Green, the only senior, knew several white kids from his work at the mostly Jewish Westridge Country Club; soft-spoken Jefferson Thomas had been one of the best athletes at Horace Mann but wanted to attend a better high school like Central to fulfill his dream of moving to the West Coast; tall and lanky Terrence Roberts was a jokester, quick to defuse any tension with humor.[29]

Minnijean Brown, Melba Pattillo, and Thelma Mothershed were all friends. Thelma's two sisters were among the first African Americans to attend their respective colleges. She wanted to follow in their footsteps, but a heart condition often left her pale and short of breath. Melba and Minnijean were particularly close and, like typical teenage girls, loved to sing and swooned over Nat King Cole and Johnny Mathis. Gloria Ray, quiet and determined, dreamed of being an atomic scientist. Perky fourteen-year-old Carlotta Walls was the baby of the group, but she seemed as prepared as any of them for the challenge of integrating Central High, having grown up in an integrated neighborhood. Finally, there was quiet, deliberate Elizabeth Eckford, who debated all summer whether to attend Central.[30]

That Little Rock erupted in a crisis just three years after the first *Brown* decision reflected both the flaws in the Supreme Court's cautious logic and the post–World War II evolution of the urban South. The 1940s had been a productive decade for Little Rock's black activists. A general loosening of the rigidity of segregation was evident across the city. Activists had fought hard to win equal salaries for African-American teachers and a park for blacks, and they had quietly desegregated the city library. The two major papers stopped referring to African Americans by just their last names, adding courtesy titles like "Mr." and "Mrs." The changes may seem minor in retrospect, but they gave the city of Little Rock and the state of Arkansas reputations for racial tolerance.[31]

In keeping with the state's and the city's relative moderation but under pressure from black activists, the Little Rock school superintendent Virgil Blossom announced in September 1954 that the city's three high schools (two white, one black) would adopt putatively color-blind geographically based attendance zones designed to reduce integration to a bare minimum by relying on existing patterns of residential segregation. At the state level, Arkansas was split between the relatively moderate northwest and urban areas and the Deep South–oriented, strongly segregationist southern and eastern sections. Since his election as governor in November 1954, Orval Faubus had given contradictory answers to the question of school desegregation, sometimes emphasizing defiance and other times moderation. In 1956, a challenge from a strongly segregationist candidate forced Faubus into a more defiant position. He faced another election in 1958, still worried about a challenge from a segregationist.[32]

In August 1957, the nine African-American students were assigned to the city's all-white Central High School. Many more had applied to attend Central, but through rigorous academic screening, personality testing, and outright arm-twisting, Superintendent Blossom had whittled the list down to just the nine. Black activists argued that Blossom's manipulation of the transfer process abused *Brown* II's requirement of "good faith" by white officials. Blossom countered by likening his efforts to Branch Rickey's careful selection of Jackie Robinson to desegregate baseball.[33]

With desegregation approaching, a vocal minority of white segregationists rallied to prevent it. Several groups filed lawsuits, hoping the courts would uphold a series of new laws passed by the state legislature guaranteeing white students the right to attend segregated schools. The lawsuits stood little chance of success, but one shrewd group, the Mothers' League of Central High, created a spectacle by forcing Governor Faubus to appear as a witness. Faubus now chose to hitch his political future to the segregationist cause. On the stand, the governor repeated rumors circulating around the city that white and black citizens were arming themselves, and he ominously predicted violence if black students entered Central High School.[34]

Faubus's prediction of violence became a self-fulfilling prophecy. On the night before the scheduled opening of Little Rock's schools, he surrounded Central High with the Arkansas National Guard, arguing that the only way to avoid violence was to stop the next day's "forcible integration" and to operate Central High as it had "been in the past." Black leaders kept the nine away from Central High on September 3, the first day of school. Finally at 2:30 on the morning of September 4, they decided the nine students would go escorted to school the next morning; black leaders phoned all the students except Elizabeth Eckford, whose family did not have a phone.[35]

Oblivious to the plan, Elizabeth Eckford set off for school by herself the next morning. As she approached from the city bus stop, Elizabeth saw a mob of about four hundred people out in front and headed for a side entrance. The National Guard soldier at the side door made her go back around to the front. The white mob was caught off guard by the appearance of a lone black girl and let Eckford pass quietly, but the soldier at the entrance would not let her in.[36]

Suddenly, the crowd came alive. Cries of "Lynch her!" rang out. Someone else yelled "Nigger bitch!" and "Get out of here!" With tears streaming down her face, the young girl ran the block back to the bus station as the mob pursued her. Luckily, Grace Lorch, one of the two whites in the Little Rock NAACP, saw what was going on. She sheltered Eckford with her arm and scolded the mob: "Six months from now you will hang your heads in shame." Unfortunately for the Little Rock Nine, what happened to Elizabeth Eckford that morning was a preview of their entire school year.[37]

It would be three more weeks before the nine students started classes. During that time, Governor Faubus continued to stir up the white population, flouted the authority of the Court, and ignored President Eisenhower's private pleas. Finally, Eisenhower could not tolerate such a blatant disregard of federal authority. He federalized the Arkansas National Guard and called up the 101st Airborne Division to protect the Little Rock Nine. On September 25, they entered Central High as a white mob, held back at bayonet point by the soldiers, jeered and hollered.[38]

School proved to be anything but a sanctuary from the mob outside. Throughout the year, white students harassed the new black students in ways large and small. Packs of whites chanting "Nigger, nigger, nigger" often followed them around. Other whites tried to push them down the main stairs or into the fountain in the lobby. In early October, a pair of whites attacked Terrence Roberts and Jefferson Thomas in the boys' locker room as other students simply looked on.[39]

Despite the danger, the nine felt a sense of adventure and retained an essential optimism, taking hope in the belief that because law and morality were on their side, they would prevail. Like teenagers everywhere, the Little Rock Nine still found time to worry about their clothes, fret about their homework, and joke with each other. They never lost sight of the absurdity of the situation. Often on the ride home—they were chauffeured back and forth in army vehicles—they would break the day's tension by cracking each other up, trying to come up with over-the-top descriptions of their day voiced in the driest monotone and mock gravity of a reporter.[40]

Things worsened in early November when Eisenhower withdrew all but six soldiers from inside the school. On the very next morning, two white boys jumped Jefferson Thomas right in the middle of a main hallway, knocking him out cold. The continual harassment took a toll on the nine students, and some of their sense of humor disappeared. Instead, their conversations increasingly focused on trading information on what hallways to avoid or which white students were particularly hostile. One senior boy secretly befriended Melba Pattilo, playing the role of double agent. After hanging out with other white students to learn about their plans, he would feed her advance information about possible attacks. No one else knew what he was doing. He certainly did not tell his parents, who were committed segregationists, and she never told the other eight she had a secret white source. He, however, was the exception.[41]

In December, Minnijean Brown retaliated against the harassment by dumping a bowl of chili on several boys. White students looked on in stunned silence, shocked that a black student had finally retaliated. The all-black cafeteria staff, however, broke out in hearty applause. But by retaliating, Minnijean only made herself more of a target. In early February, a girl kicked Brown and called her a "black bitch," and Minnijean responded by calling the girl "white trash." Later that same day, a boy threw a bowl of soup on Minnijean. The principal suspended the boy for three days, but because Brown had been involved in several incidents, Blossom expelled her. Such actions only emboldened white students; some wore buttons that said "One down and eight to go."[42]

For the Little Rock Nine, it was a surreal time. Attacked in school, they were celebrated elsewhere. The school day, especially in the beginning, was often followed by an afternoon press conference. Reporters barraged them with questions that ranged from serious ones about the situation to frivolous ones about music, clothes, and dating. *The New York Times* asked if it could run excerpts from their diaries. On a trip to Washington, they got a private tour of the White House and posed for a photograph with Thurgood Marshall on the steps of the Supreme Court. The NAACP awarded them the Spingarn Medal, the organization's highest honor. Still, they got used to being the most famous black teenagers in America, seeing their pictures in *Life*, or *Time*, or *Sepia*.[43]

A tough year came to a close on May 25, 1958, with the graduation of Ernest Green, the one senior. It was a bittersweet moment. Green had "cracked the wall" of segregation, but at the expense of the normal senior activities—being in the school play, going to the prom, getting his yearbook signed by friends—that he would have enjoyed had he stayed at the black high school. On the other hand, no other teenager in America had Martin Luther King, Jr., sitting with his parents at graduation. Also in attendance were 125 soldiers and scores of Little Rock police. When school officials called Green's name and he crossed the stage to collect his diploma, the normal cheers and claps died down to just his few friends and family.[44]

White segregationists did not give up the fight after Green's graduation. At the start of the next school year, they took advantage of new state laws to hold a referendum on desegregation. Citizens voted almost three to one to close the high schools under court-ordered desegregation. They remained closed for the entire 1958–59 school year, and the battle over school desegregation became an internecine white struggle between those who would abandon public education entirely and those who would accept some small amount of integration to preserve public schools. African Americans were pushed to the sideline of this fight. By the spring of 1959, having lived with the consequences of a year without school for the city's teenagers, white moderates regained control of the school board from the die-hard segregationists; they reopened the schools on an integrated basis and quashed any dissent.[45]

For young African Americans, the important lesson of the Little Rock crisis was that they could play an important, decisive, even heroic role in the struggle for civil rights. The Little Rock Nine proved the perfect idols—they were photogenic, bright, and articulate, but also never seemed like anything other than the ordinary teenagers they were. In turns, they were quiet and dignified, reflective and articulate, bold and defiant. Because of the size of the group, every young African American could identify a role model. Collectively, the nine expressed the complex emotions that black teenagers felt about integration, the pressure to behave perfectly to win over fearful whites, and the desire to fight back against violence. As the Little Rock story unfolded, eager young African Americans across the South began to imagine themselves at the forefront of the struggle for civil rights.

The events of the 1950s hinted at the promise of change. The *Brown* decision, the Montgomery bus boycott, and the integration of the Little Rock schools all suggested that segregation was weakening and that a new day was coming. In the few years from 1954 to 1959, African Americans had made more headway against segregation than in the previous fifty. Black and white children attended class together in a few public schools, in parochial schools, and in many colleges and universities. Some southern cities, like Nashville and Atlanta, had elected black city councilmen and hired black policemen. The seating on public buses in most major cities now occurred without regard to race, and black patrons were welcomed as customers in downtown department stores.

But young African Americans found the 1950s frustrating as well. For all the great promise of the time, change seemed to happen at an achingly slow pace. Precious few African Americans attended schools with whites, and white leaders seemed willing to dismantle the entire system of public education simply to satisfy their prejudices. The publicity the Montgomery bus boycott generated brought about little actual desegregation beyond the bus systems of the South's biggest cities. Most chilling of all was the murder of Emmett Till, someone just about their own age. How much had segregation really changed if whites could still kill black teenagers without fear of going to jail?

For those African Americans who were in high school during the 1950s, the glass seemed half full and the cautious, legalistic approach of older generations inadequate. They had been excited about the appearance of Martin Luther King, but he had squandered the momentum of Montgomery and failed to use his personal popularity to engage ordinary African Americans in the process of change. The NAACP was a slow-moving bureaucratic organization caught up in a legal system that was abstract and remote. Most important, the NAACP's approach depended on whites' good-faith compliance with court rulings. Little Rock demonstrated that whites responded only to a crisis. By the end of the 1950s, young African Americans across the South had come to the same conclusion: if the civil rights movement was really going to succeed, it needed bold new tactics and dynamic leaders ready to challenge segregation head-on.

Few anticipated the potential generational gap in the offing. In 1957, E. Franklin Frazier, the distinguished African-American sociologist, published *Black Bourgeoisie*, a scathing indictment of the growing African-American middle class and its romance with mass consumption, which made him pessimistic about its commitment to social justice. In particular, Frazier singled out college students for being "less concerned with the history or the understanding of the world about them than with their appearance at the next social affair . . . Money and conspicuous consumption are more important than knowledge." Frazier believed that prosperity had bred only political indifference, apathy, and materialism among the young. Yet just a few years later Bond, Barry, Lewis, Nash, and others in this generation would lead the sit-ins. Why was Frazier so wrong about the civil rights generation? How had prosperity bred a shared frustration rather than complacency and individualism?[46]

THE CIVIL RIGHTS GENERATION AND THE PROMISE
OF THE 1950s

The world that John Lewis grew up in, the world of Pike County, Alabama, was instantly recognizable to most Americans of the time. It was at once familiarly reassuring to white southerners and sadly anachronistic to northerners. Pike County was isolated and rural, a place of large landowners and small tenant farmers, of better-off whites and poorer blacks. The biggest town in the county was not much more than a few run-down small stores, mostly a place for farmers to pick up supplies, catch up on the news, and gossip. Its landscape and rhythms were dictated by cotton, that staple of the southern economy. It was a place where church met just once per month because the travel took so long. It was an insular world where everyone seemed to be related either by blood or marriage.

Eddie Lewis, John's father, was a cotton farmer, which was as tough a way to make a living as you could pursue. At the beginning of spring planting season, Eddie Lewis hitched the mule to the plow and drove a furrow a hundred yards or more long. The work was physically demanding; John would not be big or strong enough to plow until he was twelve. Yet no matter how hard the work, the sense of hope and renewal that accompanied the start of spring made planting his favorite chore. Picking, which began in late August, was his least favorite. Since the cotton stalks were only about waist high, pickers had to bend over to pull the cotton puffs off each stalk while the sharp ends of the stalks cut at their hands. A good picker might pick two hundred pounds of cotton in one day, which would sell for about seventy cents. But Eddie Lewis would rarely see any of that money. As a tenant farmer, he owed half to the white family that owned the land. Out of the other half would come what the family owed for the furnishings—seed, fertilizer, equipment—supplied at the start of the season. In good years there might be some money left over; in bad years, they might still owe the landlord.[1]

Lewis's life in Carter's Quarters conjures up a world that the twentieth century seemed to have passed by. The Lewis family lived in a shotgun shack—so named because one could fire a shotgun through the front-to-back central hallway—without running water or insulation. The bathroom was an outhouse that stank in summer and froze in winter. Their main connection to the outside world was an old battery-powered radio on which they listened to a mix of country (WLAC out of Nashville) and gospel music (WRMA out of Montgomery). The family grew or raised much of what it ate—vegetables, chickens, fruits for pies and jams—and purchased staple goods like flour and sugar from the "Rolling Store Man" who drove through regularly in an old truck. When they could afford them, bigger items often came in the mail from the Sears catalog, or the "wish book," as the Lewis family called it.[2]

For rural southerners, the shiny promise of the postwar consumer's life could seem as exotic as a foreign country. When he was eleven, Lewis got an eye-opening chance to visit it. In 1951, he spent the summer in Buffalo, New York, living with an uncle and aunt who had moved north some years before. When Lewis arrived in the northern metropolis after a seventeen-hour drive, he felt like he had stepped onto "a movie set." He was awed by the hustle and bustle of the city, the paved streets, the shiny department stores with the incredible moving staircases, the candy counter overflowing with treats he had never seen, and his uncle's house, which had white neighbors on either side.[3]

As the trip to Buffalo tantalized Lewis, events closer to home reinforced his desire to leave Carter's Quarters. Following the events of the emerging civil rights movement closely—from *Brown* to the Montgomery bus boycott, to the integration of the University of Alabama, to the Little Rock school crisis—made Lewis eager to participate. He dreamed not just of becoming the first person in his family to attend college but of enrolling in Morehouse, the alma mater of his hero,

Martin Luther King, Jr. But when he got the brochure in the mail, he was heartbroken: there was no way his family could afford the tuition. He despaired, convinced that he would never be able to attend college.[4]

Then one day his mother brought home a brochure from American Baptist Theological Seminary that she had found in the orphanage where she did laundry. Lewis could see that ABTS was no Morehouse, but two things got him excited: it was located in a big city, Nashville, Tennessee, and students worked jobs on campus in exchange for tuition. So in September 1957, John Lewis boarded a bus for Nashville, a city he had never visited, to attend American Baptist Theological Seminary, a school he had never seen, in pursuit of an education and a chance to participate in a civil rights movement he had only read about.[5] And with that bus trip, Lewis crossed an important generational Rubicon.

Carter's Quarters was the stereotypical South, but by the 1950s, Lewis's experience in the rural South had become the exception. Places like Nashville and Buffalo—vibrant, urban, middle-class, and consumer oriented—had become the crucible of the civil rights generation. Cities, even southern cities, insulated young African Americans from the harshest realities of race, offered unparalleled educational opportunities, and exposed them to new ideas.

Most important, the postwar boom and material abundance of urban America pulled African Americans closer to the social and economic mainstream than at any other point in the nation's history. No group felt the tug of the "affluent society" more than the civil rights generation, as they grew up in a relative prosperity previously unknown to African Americans. They were also part of the first generation to self-consciously think of themselves as teenagers and to see themselves as part of a distinct youth culture. Crucial to this definition of youth, reinforced by a bombardment of targeted advertising for jeans and movies and music, was that generation mattered more than race, that youth itself cut across all the other divisions in American life. What mattered, they were told, was not who you were or what color you were but how old you were, what you bought, what you listened to, what you watched.

As African-American teens internalized the image of themselves as first-class consumers, they became increasingly frustrated with their second-class citizenship. The New Deal generation had worked hard to provide their children with things and opportunities that they had missed out on; their success, however, had opened a generational gap in experience and in expectations of what the world offered. The resulting friction between the lure of the good life and the reality of Jim Crow laid the groundwork for the younger generation's involvement in the civil rights movement.

In 1941, twenty-three-year-old Mattie Barry—sick of her husband's drinking, his physical abuse, and the economic vulnerability of share-cropping—left Itta Bena, Mississippi, a little town in the Deep South surrounded by cotton plantations. With her three children in tow, including her youngest child and only boy, Marion, she headed for Memphis, hoping to raise enough money to move on to Chicago. But the work was good in Memphis, so Mattie, Marion, and the other children stayed there.

The great exodus of African Americans out of the rural South shuffled the population in unpredictable ways. Mostly we think of it as a journey from south to north, but Mattie Barry's journey ended in Memphis. By 1940, nearly two-thirds of urban blacks in the North had migrated from other urban areas, suggesting that internal migration, rural to urban, within the South was a powerful propellant for the great migration nationally. Like the Mississippi River, the great wave of migration that propelled so many black southerners up north also deposited them like sediment along the route, especially in Memphis.

Memphis joined two images of the South—old rural plantations and the newer industrial cities. In 1935, the writer David Cohn famously observed that "the Mississippi Delta begins in the lobby of the Peabody," the city's grandest hotel. "If you stand near the fountain in the lobby, where ducks waddle and turtles drowse, ultimately you will see everybody who is anybody in the Delta." What was true for the planters, bankers, and businessmen at the top was also true for ordinary southerners. African Americans making their way out of little towns of the Delta with names like Itta Bena, Money, and Ruleville converged on the city to catch the *City of New Orleans* train that ran from New Orleans through Memphis and on to Chicago, with African Americans embarking and disembarking at all the cities on the route.[6]

Nineteen forty-one turned out to be a good year to arrive in Memphis, as the city's population and economy swelled in anticipation of war. In 1940, the War Department had relocated the headquarters of the Second Army to the city. Pearl Harbor was still several months off, but Allied demand for supplies was already creating new jobs as companies that produced arms, ammunition, and aircraft opened plants near the new army base. In just three years, the number of manufacturing jobs in the city doubled. And the population, which nearly doubled between 1920 and 1940, jumped another hundred thousand to 396,000 by 1950.[7]

Mattie Barry worked in a slaughterhouse cleaning newly killed cows and hogs, reflecting both the opportunities and the boundaries facing African Americans during the war boom. It was tough physical work: the smell of the slaughterhouse was wretched, and she was often covered in animal blood. But compared to farming, the conditions seemed good. It was easier than bending over for hours on end picking cotton. Best of all, the forty dollars a week she made was a fortune compared to the meager returns of sharecroppers. Though wartime Memphis confined African Americans to the least desirable jobs, it offered them a better living than they found in the rural South.[8]

After the war, Mattie remarried. Marion's stepfather, Dave Cummings, made a good living as a butcher at the packing plant, while Mattie worked as a maid to spend more time with her children. Marion had two full sisters, three stepsisters, and two half sisters in the house with him. (Yes, he was the only boy.) The family lived in a ramshackle shotgun house in the predominantly black neighborhood of South Memphis. Because there were only two bedrooms—one for the parents, one for the girls—Marion slept on a couch in the living room.

Between her work and her husband's job, they made a comfortable income, enough to support a family of eight children but with little to spare. Marion had just three sets of clothes: Sunday best, school, and play, and if his mother caught him fooling around in his school clothes, she'd give him a good spanking. As Barry recalled later, the family had meat on the table, but his clothes were either old and frayed or a couple of sizes too small, or sometimes both.[9]

The family's story was typical, but how blacks viewed their circumstances depended on how recently and from where they had moved. Many lived better than ever before, but segregation was pervasive, and the signs of racial demarcation were everywhere—from the dual drinking fountains in public buildings to the real estate agents who steered black customers to certain neighborhoods, to the nearly all-white police force. Migrants were attuned to the social and cultural freedoms allowed by a large urban black population, to the relative absence of violence, and most of all to the economic opportunities. Many African Americans had grabbed the bottom rung of the working middle class in Memphis and were determined to stay there.

Barry's happy and carefree childhood reflected the freedom of city life. He spent his days riding bikes, roller-skating, and playing down by the Mississippi River (which ran past his South Memphis neighborhood). He loved the outdoors—camping, hiking, and swimming—so much that he joined the Boy Scouts and stayed long enough to become one of Tennessee's first black Eagle Scouts. The pursuit of Eagle Scout merit badges brought out Barry's best qualities—his diligence and drive—while the Scout's clear path forward appealed to his desire for order and neatness. "Some people are destined and some are determined," he has observed, "and I am determined."[10]

Barry had a bit of Tom Sawyer in him as well. In the fourth grade, he made himself three or four extra sandwiches each day to sell to other kids for a nickel or a dime. When the principal needed volunteers to walk a couple of miles to pick up the meat supplies for the cafeteria, Barry always raised his hand because the kids who volunteered were rewarded with extra hot dogs and hamburgers. In high school, he bagged groceries, worked at a drive-in restaurant, and waited tables at a downtown white businessmen's club.

Race was never far below the surface. When he and his friends were about ten, they liked to go to the movies on Saturdays. Forced to sit in the balcony, they occasionally poured drinks and threw cups on the unsuspecting white patrons below. When young Marion set his sights on winning first prize in a delivery contest for paperboys—an all-expenses-paid trip to New Orleans—the paper told him that the trip was for white carriers only. So Barry led a strike of the black paperboys until the paper modified the rules and offered them an equal prize.[11]

Unlike his rural cousins still in Itta Bena, Barry discovered that the twin evils of poverty and race were not insurmountable hurdles to those blacks who got a good education in Memphis. At Booker T. Washington High School (one of just two black high schools in the city), Barry played basketball, boxed, and studied. Known more for his drive than for his raw intelligence, he still managed a B-plus average and membership in the National Honor Society. And yet for most of high school, the idea of going to college never crossed his mind. Neither of his parents had advanced beyond high school, and the guidance counselors never really brought up the subject. They pushed him toward a vocational track, and Barry took shop classes with an eye to becoming a plasterer. He was terrible at it, hating the dust, the mess, and most of all the physical labor.[12]

A friendship struck up in church inspired Barry to see college as a realistic—and fun—possibility. William Hawkins, a freshman at LeMoyne, a small African-American college in the city, enthralled Barry with stories about fraternity life and impressed him with the sophistication he'd gained from a couple of semesters of college. Suddenly Barry started thinking that college looked pretty neat, even if he was not sure exactly what it was about. Most important, college would free him from the manual labor that was the future of many African-American youths—and by eighteen, if he was sure of anything, it was that he wanted a different future.

Barry's aversion to manual labor shaped his college choice. He was lucky enough to get accepted to several colleges, even earning a scholarship to Morehouse, probably the best black college in America. However, the scholarship required him to pull tobacco during the harvest. Barry took one look at the admissions packet, which included instructions to bring boots and gloves for working in the tobacco fields, and decided that no matter how prestigious Morehouse was, he was not going to attend any college that sent him back to the fields. From other scholarships and part-time work, and with a little help from his parents, Barry scraped together enough money to enroll at LeMoyne. To young African Americans, a college education—any college education at all—offered a clear shot at the middle class, and the social and economic changes of the 1950s meant that many more young blacks like Barry had the chance at one.[13]

LeMoyne nurtured Barry's middle-class ambitions and broadened his horizons. No one exerted more influence than his freshman chemistry professor, Samuel Massie. A pioneering black chemist who received his doctorate from Iowa State, worked on the Manhattan Project, and had been awarded a patent for a breakthrough in the fight against gonorrhea, Massie mentored a generation of black scientists by arguing that scientific rigor, knowledge, and hard work could trump racial prejudice.[14] Massie also encouraged Barry to expand his interests beyond chemistry, to become interested in current events and the world around him, and especially civil rights—all things he had never paid attention to before. He joined the campus NAACP, becoming chapter president in his senior year.

Barry became the central player in a huge campus civil rights controversy. A city bus company had hired Walter Chandler, a former mayor and a white LeMoyne trustee, to defend its segregated seating policy; Chandler then made a condescending remark about African Americans. Barry wrote LeMoyne's president urging Chandler's resignation—and cannily sent a copy to the city's two major newspapers. The publication of the letter created an uproar. In the 1950s, black colleges depended on white trustees to act as patrons and foster smooth community relations; Barry had clearly violated the etiquette of the black college–white trustee relationship. Whites wrote in to the local paper criticizing Barry for speaking out. LeMoyne's other white trustees issued a statement saying they would resign as well if Chandler left the board. Some trustees even tried to have Barry expelled. Only the presence of a few calmer voices on the board of trustees and the support of the school president saved Barry.[15]

Barry was invited to join Alpha Phi Alpha, the most prestigious black fraternity. For a working-class kid from South Memphis, membership in APA was the the surest sign of his growing middle-class status. Its alumni ranged from W.E.B. Du Bois to Jesse Owens to Martin Luther King to Thurgood Marshall: even today Barry's voice swells with pride at its mention. But in order to join such company, he had to submit to the fraternity's legendarily harsh hazing. The most notorious test came when the pledges were stripped to their underwear, driven out to the countryside, and told to find their way home. Barry had no intention of being dumped in the rural South in just his boxers. Anticipating the prank, Barry taped a dime to his crotch (figuring correctly that the brothers wouldn't search there), so that when he was dumped on the side of the road, he could just call a friend to pick him up.[16]

"Shep" Barry—a nickname derived from his unusual middle name, Shepilov—ran with a group of friends who thought of themselves as sophisticated college men, carrying their books in briefcases, smoking pipes, and drinking Schenley's whiskey. They bought nice clothes along Beale Street, wide-legged suits that they thought made them look suave when they hung out to pick up dates at the Beale Street clubs, which were at the center of the emerging rock-and-roll dance craze.

Shep and a friend made plans to hitchhike across the country to California after graduation, but at the last minute he backed out of the trip to attend graduate school. Barry was motivated in part by the example of Sam Massie, but equally important was his fear of being drafted if he gave up his educational deferment. The army represented everything Barry hated—the arbitrary power of authority figures and the backbreaking work of manual labor. The closer he got to graduation, the more Barry wanted to avoid the draft. So in the fall of 1958, he packed up his belongings and moved to Nashville to enroll in Fisk University's doctoral program.[17]

The basic stories of Mattie Cummings and Marion Barry were repeated over and over again by hundreds of thousands of African Americans during the 1930s and 1940s. The journey from the world of Itta Bena to the world of Memphis was not the only route that black Americans took to the civil rights movement, but Barry's experiences are representative of the generational shifts among young African Americans—from rural to urban, from working class to middle class, from manual labor to professional aspirations.

Diane Nash's family made the same journey out of the Delta, but Carrie Bolton, Nash's maternal grandmother, had yearned for something more than the circumscribed opportunities of segregated Memphis. As a young girl in turn-of-the-century Memphis, she worked as a maid for a prominent white doctor and his family, and their home, filled with books and culture, fascinated her. She eavesdropped on the family's conversations, which she found far more interesting than the servants' gossip and crude sexual banter. Seeing her interest, the family, especially the doctor, reciprocated by introducing her to the arts and culture. They encouraged Bolton to believe that she could achieve anything she wanted to, but she also internalized their belief that the road to success lay in assimilating into white culture.

With the doctor's encouragement, Bolton moved to Chicago, the terminus of the Great Migration. For African Americans who ended up in Chicago—which saw its black population nearly double between 1940 and 1950 and then nearly double again by 1960—the main route was the Illinois Central Railroad, which originated in New Orleans, then wound northward through the Delta and Memphis.[18]

Carrie Bolton passed on to her daughter Dorothy the lessons she had learned in Memphis. And for seven years after Diane was born, Bolton was her caretaker while Dorothy worked to support them. Carrie instilled in Diane an appreciation of art and culture, a love of learning, and the expectation that she would go to college. Most important, she told her granddaughter she could do anything she wanted, could be anybody she imagined, unhindered by race. But the other side of this message of uplift was a romanticization of white culture and an implication that getting ahead meant conforming to it.

Diane Nash enjoyed a conventional middle-class childhood in Chicago. After the war, Dorothy Nash remarried. Her new husband, a Pullman waiter, which in the 1940s and 1950s was considered a good middle-class job for an African American, provided a good life. Train workers were often community leaders because their jobs came with membership in the Brotherhood of Sleeping Car Porters, the powerful and militant black union headed by A. Philip Randolph, and the extensive travel encouraged a broad cosmopolitan worldview.[19]

The heart of Chicago's African-American community—and the area Carrie Bolton and Diane Nash called home—the South Side was a sprawling city within a city, nicknamed "the Black Metropolis." It included department stores, banks, movie houses, and hotels, many of which were owned by African Americans. The *Chicago Defender*, the black newspaper with the largest readership in the South, had its headquarters there. Because Chicago's pervasive residential segregation confined African Americans to the South Side, everyone from janitors to doctors, from factory workers to corporate executives, lived close together. The South Side had a number of poor blocks and public housing projects, but what often surprised white observers was the substantial wealth of its middle-class neighborhoods. A writer for *Fortune* magazine driving through these areas was surprised at the size of the mansions, the number of sports cars and Cadillacs in the driveways, and the glitz of the debutante balls. Joe Louis, the boxing champion, lived on the South Side, as did William Dawson, one of only two black congressmen. Nash grew up in Hyde Park, the most integrated section of the South Side and the home of the University of Chicago.[20]

In the broad middle class at the heart of the South Side, Nash enjoyed a childhood remarkable for its ordinariness. Her Roman Catholicism reinforced the distinctiveness of her integrated youth. She attended parochial school until she entered high school. She loved the ritual and rhythm of mass and even dreamed of becoming a nun. The order that ran her school, the Sisters of the Blessed Sacrament, was founded in 1891 specifically to provide schools and help to African Americans and Native Americans; in fact, her school enrolled only minority students. Nash soaked up their Social Gospel message of a church engaged in the problems of poverty, injustice, and war. But even at a young age, she was acutely aware of the condescension that some nuns brought to this mission. She still recalls the sting she felt when one of the nuns told her that the Sisters served "the least of God's children."

Her parents tried to shield her from the harshness of the world. Nash moved from the parochial school to Hyde Park High School, one of the city's best and most integrated. It had a student body that was 60 percent white and 40 percent black. Here she never really thought about race and never really felt limited by it. For her parents, the decision to live in Hyde Park and to send their daughter to an integrated high school was an extension of Carrie Bolton's belief in moving in the white world.

Nash knew about Emmett Till, the lynching victim; after all, he, too, came from the South Side of Chicago and was just three years younger. But her parents avoided the spectacle of his viewing and funeral. While they talked about Till and the *Brown* decision at the dinner table, mostly her parents avoided race, focusing instead on the importance of a good education.[21]

Nash's life centered on the typical concerns of teen girls in the 1950s—boys, clothes, and makeup. She and her friends went downtown to shop and eat in the coffee shops in and around the department stores. She dreamed of college and a quiet, conventional future as an English teacher. She even wanted to be a beauty queen, getting as far as runner-up in one of the regional contests leading to the Miss Illinois Pageant. Nash's interest in beauty pageants reveals the broad influence of her relatively integrated world and the powerful shadow of her grandmother. In the 1950s, beauty queens were the apotheosis of womanhood, portrayed as beautiful, smart, and talented—all the things black women were imagined not to be. In the world of these pageants, beauty meant white beauty.[22]

As a freshman in high school, to help herself in the pageants, she enrolled in a modeling agency's charm school. On the phone, the owner did not realize she was black until she gave her address.

"My dear, are you by chance colored?"

"Yes," she said.

"Dear, we don't have a facility for colored students."[23]

That it had never really occurred to Nash that her race might matter to the modeling agency just underscores the gap between the experiences of black teenagers in the 1950s and those of their parents and grandparents.

When she moved to Washington, D.C., in the fall of 1957 to attend Howard University, Nash began to understand how sheltered her childhood had been. Although Washington was on the edge of the South, she found it liberating. The combination of a large African-American population and the federal government (which had long ago desgregated its buildings and museums) allowed her to stretch her wings both personally and intellectually, visiting museums and art exhibits, attending concerts and cultural events; she immersed herself more in a cultured African-American world. But her Howard experience soured (even today she's reluctant to say exactly why), and after two years she returned to Chicago and enrolled in the University of Illinois–Chicago.[24]

After the freedom of Washington, living at home seemed stifling, and Nash was restless. In the fall of 1959, she transfered to Fisk University in Nashville, despite some hesitation from her parents about her going south. Still, Fisk was one of the premier African-American colleges, and she thought it would reproduce the best parts of her Howard experience in a new location. Instead, she found Nashville provincial. It had few of the concerts, museums, and art shows that she had enjoyed in Washington. Perhaps naïvely, she was even less prepared for the city's pervasive segregation. "I really started feeling unjustly limited by not being able to go downtown with a girlfriend and have lunch, even at someplace like Woolworth's or Walgreens, and not being able to attend a movie theater."

Even more suprising to her was the way her fellow classmates seemed to accept the racial inequality. The first time she encountered segregation, really encountered it, was when she attended the Tennessee State Fair soon after arriving. There she saw the "white" and "colored" signs on the restroom doors. When she asked about it, the other students shrugged and told her that that was just the way the world worked. "I came to the depressing conclusion," she recalled, "that Fisk students were really apathetic." Everything about the situation was at odds with her own experience: the rank discrimination, the limited social and cultural life, and, most important, her peers' willingness to let others define them as inferior. Within weeks of her arrival, Nash started looking for people on the Fisk campus who were just as outraged as she was.[25]

To follow Stokely Carmichael on one of his regular jaunts from his home in a white Bronx neighborhood to the all-black Harlem business district for a haircut shows why New York was the one city that challenged Chicago as the center of African-American life. At the intersection of Seventh Avenue and 125th Street, he listened to an infinite variety of black political speakers standing on stepladders, making their pitches. For the young Carmichael, this was an education. He loved the cadences and rhythms of their speech, so different from what he heard in the Bronx.

And the politics were a revelation. His favorites were the aging supporters of Marcus Garvey, the Pan-African leader from the 1920s who celebrated the independence movements in Africa and spun visions of a renewed Pan-African movement. For the first time, Carmichael got a sense of the "roaring storms of revolution" sweeping black people in the Caribbean and Africa after World War II, stories that rarely penetrated his white neighborhood in the Bronx.[26]

Harlem's vibrant political culture was a product of its polyglot population, just as the tangled movements of Stokely Carmichael's family were part of the black diaspora that stretched from Brazil to Harlem. His grandparents were part African, part Irish, and part Caribbean, having moved from Tobago to Antigua, from Montserrat to the Panama Canal Zone; Carmichael's mother was born in the Canal Zone, making her an American citizen. When Carmichael was three, his mother moved to New York to earn more money. Two years later Carmichael's father jumped ship in New York Harbor to sneak into the United States to reunite with his wife. They left Carmichael and his two sisters in the care of their grandmother in Port of Spain, the capital of Trinidad. Despite his parents' absence, it was an idyllic time for Carmichael. But in June 1952, his eleven-year-old world turned upside down when his grandmother died and he was reunited with his parents in New York.[27]

What started out in his imagination as a great adventure to the "magic carnival" of New York City quickly became a disappointing reality. The endless stream of cars zooming by at breakneck speeds made his head spin. The weather bothered him so much that he wore his winter overcoat in August, even though his father mocked him for it. His parents would not let him wander free as he had in Trinidad; for their first summer, he and his sisters were forbidden to step beyond the sidewalk in front of their apartment building.[28]

But he was soon just another American kid. Television—not available in Trinidad—bridged the gap. He became obsessed with Superman; one time he was even going to "fly" over the courtyard on the laundry-line pulley strung across it. Luckily, a neighbor spied him through the window and stopped him before he plunged to his death.

His mostly Italian neighborhood in the Bronx influenced his development so much that he thought of himself as a "pint-size paisano in blackface." His friends were mostly kids with names like John DiMillo and Cookie Delappio, and he absorbed their love of spaghetti and pizza, their ability to curse in Italian, and their suspicion of the federal government. (As a boy, he thought that FBI stood for Forever Bugging Italians.) His friends welcomed him into their world by nicknaming him "Sichie," short for Sicilian, in honor of his darker skin.[29]

Still, Carmichael felt he did not really fit in. Partly it had to do with religion. Sure, his church, Methodist United, was all white, but it was still worlds away from the Catholic Church of his friends. More important, his parents hardly socialized with their neighbors; they were in, but not of, the neighborhood. On weekends and holidays, the Carmichaels traveled across the city to Brooklyn, Queens, and Harlem to socialize with other Caribbean immigrants.[30]

For the young Carmichael, Harlem was more than just another stop on the Caribbean community's social circuit. It was where he went to get his hair cut properly, where he met up with his cousin Inez and her black friends, where he first heard about Marcus Garvey, and where he learned about the *Brown* decision and Emmett Till. It was where he came to understand his blackness.

His parents had moved to Morris Park because they thought a white neighborhood would feature a better class of people, reflecting a middle-class black ethos that overvalued white culture. Carmichael, for one, found his friends in the new neighborhood rough and undisciplined. They invited him into their neighborhood gang, the Morris Park Dukes. Most of what they did was harmless, young boys playing at being tough, but sometimes their pranks veered in dangerous directions. Once they dared Carmichael to join them in breaking into a local store to steal the change left in the register, never more than twenty dollars. They had been doing this for a while, but Carmichael had always wiggled out of participating. He took the dare, but halfway through it, he was overcome with guilt at the thought of disappointing his parents if he got caught. He hid his nervousness from his friends but never again joined in on one of their robberies.[31]

When Carmichael and his friends were assigned to different high schools, the gap between them widened into a chasm. Carmichael was the only one in his neighborhood to gain admittance to one of the city's elite entrance-exam high schools, the Bronx High School of Science. Looking back, Carmichael was unsurprised that their paths split. Whereas almost none of his neighborhood friends went on to college, his parents had always expected him to do so. West Indian culture placed a high value on education and success; his maternal uncle, a medical doctor, made him take Latin as preparation for a career in medicine or law.[32]

So, in September 1956, fifteen-year-old Stokely Carmichael left the cozy confines of Morris Avenue to make the short walk to his new school at the corner of Creston Avenue and 184th Street, little aware of how much he was leaving behind. His first new friendship came about because of a fluke of the alphabet; Gene Dennis had the assigned seat next to Carmichael in all his classes. At first, he found himself intimidated and more than a little put off by Dennis, who boasted of having read Karl Marx and John Steinbeck. Carmichael's reading rarely ventured beyond *Readers' Digest* or Hardy Boys mysteries. But they bonded when they both made the freshman soccer team. Carmichael liked Dennis because he was smart and funny, irreverent and easygoing, thoughtful and full of life.[33]

But something set Gene Dennis apart from his classmates: he was a Communist, and not just any Communist but the son of the head of the American Communist Party. To Carmichael, Dennis seemed just a normal fifteen-year-old boy, even if he was one of the few whites living in Harlem. Only when another classmate attacked him for befriending a Commie did he learn about his friend's politics. Carmichael felt torn by the news. The autumn of 1956 was only slightly removed from the high-water mark of McCarthyism, and he had been taught to believe that Communists were the enemy. On the other hand, Dennis was his best friend. Carmichael's parents, who liked Gene, nevertheless worried that the friendship might jeopardize his future. In the end, Carmichael rejected the demonization of some classmates and stuck with Gene.

Carmichael did more than just stay friends with Dennis. His friend became his guide to New York's left-wing politics. He read Marx; he went to meetings of the Young Communist League; he attended rallies and conferences and even camping trips organized by Communists and socialists. Though he never officially joined the Young Communist League or the Socialist Party, it was through these groups that he developed a worldview, learned to consider the broader structural forces that shaped society, and grasped the underappreciated role of class in America. And of course the Communist suspicion of government power just reinforced the street wisdom Carmichael had picked up in his Italian-American neighborhood.[34]

Carmichael's left-radical politics are more suprising to modern observers than they would have been to contemporaries. Even as McCarthyism blossomed in the 1950s, far-left political activism in New York City remained vibrant. Many people in in the city's large immigrant population came from countries with strong leftist political traditions, and the high rate of unionization fostered a left-leaning politics. Finally, state electoral laws permitted electoral fusion—for example, allowing a Democratic Party candidate to also appear on the ballot as a Socialist Party candidate. Together these things allowed left-leaning political groups to retain a measure of political influence even at the height of McCarthyism.

Harlem was the other pillar of Carmichael's political and cultural education. He made the crosstown journey there every few weeks, since none of the white barbers in his neighborhood had any idea how to cut his kinky black hair. He treasured the time he spent in the barbershop waiting for his turn, staring at the pictures of black heroes on the wall, listening to the rhythms of black speech, picking up tidbits of black history and news. The barbershop became the way in which he absorbed African-American culture and an African-American worldview.

The only other place he found black culture was on the radio. When he was thirteen, he began sneaking the radio into his bedroom so he could listen to Jocko Henderson's nighttime show. With a distinctive rapping style ("eat the yock / this is the jock / back on the scene / with mah record machine"), Henderson was one of the most popular black disk jockeys of the 1950s; from him, Carmichael got his education in gospel, jazz, and rhythm and blues. Until he left for college in August 1960, falling asleep to Jocko was a nightly ritual.[35]

Throughout high school, music became the place where he connected with African Americans his own age. During the summers, he worked at his cousin Stephen's Atlantic City record shop. Like Harlem, Atlantic City was a melting pot for different groups of African Americans, in this case for blacks who had migrated from the Deep South. From new migrants who came in seeking the rhythm and blues, gospel, and soul music of their native South, he absorbed everything from gospel groups like the Soul Stirrers and jazz greats like Louis Armstrong to new rock stars like Little Richard. By the summer of his junior year, he essentially ran the store. One day he set up a turntable and speakers outside the shop to play new records as a way of attracting customors. Pretty soon it was the hot gathering spot for teens to hang out, listen to music, and dance. Seeing at first hand that record companies aimed more and more of their material at young people, Carmichael marveled at how inexpensive new technology—in this case, the cheaper and more durable vinyl 45 rpm singles that replaced 78 rpm records—fueled the pop culture that was transforming his generation.[36]

Carmichael hardly thought about civil rights during his high school years. Among the mainly white young Communists and socialists he associated with, civil rights was just one of the many issues that concerned them. They organized sympathy marches for Little Rock and other school integration fights in the South but also ban-the-bomb and peace rallies. For Carmichael, concern for civil rights was embedded in a larger liberal worldview concerned about the militarization of American life and the general fate of civil liberties.[37]

A fortuitous encounter, during his senior year of high school, at a Washington rally against the work of the House Un-American Activities Committee set him on a new path focused on civil rights. Here he met a group of young African-American activists about his age. At first, he thought they were just another group of young socialists.

When he went up to introduce himself, he was surprised to learn that they were from Howard University and called themselves the Non-violent Action Group (NAG). Carmichael had never seen a group of exclusively black activists his own age who were so politically engaged. He was so excited that he told his parents that Howard was the only college for him. He wanted to be part of NAG.

Julian Bond grew up in a world that showcased the increasing cosmopolitanism of middle-class African Americans. Horace Mann Bond, his father, was a well-respected professor and college administrator who, when Julian was born, had just become president of Fort Valley College, a black college in rural middle Georgia. Bond, however, was delivered in Nashville: his mother was nervous about the quality of medical care available to African Americans near the college. When Bond was five, his father accepted the presidency of Lincoln University in Chester County, Pennsylvania, about an hour outside Philadelphia. In part, Horace Bond took the job so Julian and his older sister, Jane, would have access to better schooling.[38]

The Bond household revolved around education. Their home overflowed with books, and a steady stream of African-American scholars passed through its doors. When W.E.B. Du Bois and E. Franklin Frazier, probably the two best-known black scholars of their generation, visited Lincoln University, they held a mock induction into the "Estate of the Scholar" for Julian and Jane, complete with diplomas and photographs. In the ceremony Julian pledged that he would "all his life diligently seek the truth, and worthily set himself to communicating truth to his fellow man."[39]

For high school, the Bonds enrolled Julian in the George School, a Quaker boarding school not far from Lincoln. His parents saw him following in his father's footsteps and hoped a rigorous environment would focus his attention. They also believed that George would help their son move comfortably in a majority-white world. During one visit, they spied Julian approaching with his two best friends on either side, his arms casually draped over the shoulders of the white boys. "Look, Horace, he has his arms around *them*—they don't have their arms around him," Bond's mother whispered to her husband.

Still, as the only black student at George, Bond felt the casual racism around him. He lived in one of the faculty houses, a much-coveted honor usually reserved for the top students because it came with more freedom; he realized that the school probably put him there (even though he did not have the grades) to avoid any controversy about having a black student in the dorms. But the school was liberal enough not to make much of a fuss when Bond dated a white student. Like many a high school student in the 1950s, Bond's prize possession was his letterman's jacket, worn (in the fashion of the day) with collar flipped up and the bottom button open. The jacket cost Bond the princely sum of thirty-five dollars, but it was required wearing for the school's cool crowd.[40]

Bond loved that jacket. It was a symbol that he fit in. He wore it everywhere—until school officials firmly told him not to wear the jacket when he went into town on Saturdays with his white girlfriend. They were afraid of what local residents would say. That stark and sudden reminder of Bond's difference from his fellow students struck him hard; it "was like somebody just stopping you and slapping you in the face."[41]

Bond in his late teens was something of a Holden Caulfield–like figure, and like the hero of Salinger's 1951 novel *The Catcher in the Rye*, he seemed to have mastered a youthful pose of detachment and skepticism toward the values of the older generation—a pose captured in the prototypical youth attitude of 1950s cool. He certainly looked the part, having adopted the shabby preppy look of his boarding school peers—beat-up loafers, wrinkled oxford shirt, and a sport coat most notable for its ugliness and casual insouciance. With his good looks, he had little trouble attracting girls. Good fortune seemed to follow him. Early in college he stumbled into a lucky break when he got cast in a Pepsi-Cola ad.[42]

During high school, his great vice was *American Bandstand*, the rock-and-roll dance program hosted by Dick Clark that started in Philadelphia as *Bandstand* before going national on ABC in August 1957. The show was a huge hit among teenagers, featuring the biggest pop stars, both black and white. The teenage dancers—all Philadelphia-area high school students—became famous in their own right. Bond loved the music, and he identified more with the show because it featured a couple of black dancers. But he also chafed at the fact that *Bandstand* had only one African-American boy and girl on each week, and they were allowed to dance only with each other.[43]

When the family moved to Atlanta in 1957—Bond to attend college at Morehouse, his father to take a new job at Atlanta University—he rarely ventured beyond his West Atlanta neighborhood. The black business district near his house had everything he needed, and he rarely encountered segregation. The five African-American colleges in West Atlanta (Clark, Morris Brown, Atlanta University, Spelman, and Morehouse) and the large black population that lived in the surrounding neighborhoods ensured an abundance of grocery stores, shops, restaurants, dance halls, and coffee shops catering to students and local residents. Perhaps once or twice a year, he would go with his mother to one of the white-owned department stores downtown for school clothes, but otherwise he spent most of his time near the campus. Because the economic vitality of West Atlanta meant that Bond rarely experienced the humiliations of legal segregation in his daily errands, his world did not differ much from that of northern teens.[44]

A poem Bond wrote in the late 1950s captures the way pop culture promised to include African-American teens in broader American society but also made them acutely aware of their second-class status:

> I, too, hear America singing
> But from where I stand
> I can only hear Little Richard
> And Fats Domino.
> But sometimes,
> I hear Ray Charles
> Drowning in his own tears
> Or Bird
> Relaxing at Camarillo
> Or Horace Silver doodling
> Then I don't mind standing a little longer[45]

The first line riffs on Langston Hughes's poem of the same title, which itself riffed on Walt Whitman's "I Hear America Singing." All three writers used the popular culture of their times to emphasize their essential American identity. But Hughes and Bond, in so doing, challenged the way segregation pushed blackness to the margins of American identity. With its echoes of Allen Ginsberg's *Howl* and Jack

Kerouac's *On the Road*, the poem reinforced pop culture's deep influence on Bond. His references to Little Richard and Fats Domino had a double meaning as well. Bond slyly reminded the reader of the important African-American contributions to the 1950s youth culture while underscoring the similarity of influences across racial lines. By deftly blending the newly popular idea of teenagers as alienated figures with allusions to Langston Hughes, the poem echoes W.E.B. Du Bois's famous essay on the "double consciousness" of African Americans.

But there was something of the bohemian in Bond as well. After his freshman year in college, he spent the summer in Boston with a cousin at Harvard, where he spent considerable time in the beatnik coffee shops of Harvard Square composing poetry. He memorialized the experience in another poem:

> *I know you Cambridge beard-town of New England*
> *I have sat all night in Hayes-Bickford in Harvard Square*
> *I have gamboled along the grassy slopes of the Charles-bank*
> *And I have been refused service in the Paradise Bar*
> *When rain comes in on little hippo feet*
> *Mewling and wetting my body, I have sneezed in Cambridge*
> *Damn . . . I have stolen books from you, Widener, and you, Lamont*
> *You saw me with my little green bag and smiled*
> *I have ferried the river (by the Brattle Street Bridge)*
> *And ventured onto Beacon Hill, where I danced*
> *With wild and woeful wenches from B.U. My hair grew long in*
> *Cambridge*
> *(shave and haircut—$2.50) and my belly thin*
> *when I could not pilfer pastries pastily from Schrafft's and the*
> *Widener book-*
> *guards wondered at my coat on summer days*
> *Several roads diverge at Harvard Square; I took the one most*
> *   Traveled by*
> *I sojourned in P-town, that haven for misguided males, get ye*
> *back to Fire*
> *Island. A Bard girl, thinking me sweet, comforted me. I asked her*
> *with my*
> *Eyes to ask again, yes, yes, ask again, yesyesyes I will have a*
> *   Danish*

I rescued her from a pimply Yalie. P-town, O'Neillian fools
      Simpering on the
Beach, like an ostrich, New England has its head in the sand.
      (heard in a Boston coffee-house)
         SODOMY IS A SUMMER FESTIVAL
Sweet Cindy, who had never been south of New Haven, can you
      Believe it?
See you later, educator, after a while, bibliophile
You can bet your sweet life you can and will ball in Cambridge.[46]

Bond's idle dream seems a far cry from Martin Luther King's more famous 1963 dream about racial unity, but it is no less important to understanding the history of the civil rights movement. His fanciful recounting of the summer weaves race and youth together, beautifully illuminating the dual consciousness of the African-American teenager. Ironically, Bond's carefree summer was possible only because of the booming American economy and the growth of a new black middle class. But his youthful wit and insouciance are not simply the voice of an indulged and apathetic teen; rather, his is the ironic, wary tone of someone caught between his generation's expectations of affluence and the racial divisions that haunted American life.

At every step, young African Americans demonstrated their expectation that they would have the same opportunities as other middle-class teenagers. They tested the system not of out of a sense of alienation and exclusion (at least, no more than normal teenagers did), or out of radicalism. They tested the system because they saw themselves as typical middle-class teenagers entitled to participate in American life. The more they were confronted with the truth of their constricted freedom, however, the more they chafed, and the more primed they were to rebel. These African-American teens were thus the embodiment of a youth culture that promised inclusion yet nurtured alienation.

African-American teens like Barry, Nash, Carmichael, and Bond were the most visible signposts of the geography of the new African-American middle class, itself an important element of the consumer spending that fueled the booming American economy of the 1950s and 1960s. In the 1930s, African Americans had accounted for only a small proportion of overall consumer spending, far below their roughly

10 percent share of the population. Barely 1 percent of spending on cars and 3 percent on new clothing came from African-American wallets. By the 1950s, these numbers had risen exponentially. The rise in the disposable income of black consumers meant that they now accounted for more than 3 percent of auto spending and 6 percent of clothing purchases. Overall, African-American spending in the mid-1950s totaled $15.25 billion, or about the yearly value of American exports at the time. By then black America represented to American companies a consumer market as large as Canada's and twice the size of Australia's.[47]

The rise in black consumer spending mirrored the broader increase in the country as a whole. By the 1950s, Americans increasingly identified the American Dream with consumer spending, as shopping and the good life were linked together. In the decade following World War II, the American economy doubled in size, propelled by the pursuit of the visible symbols of prosperity—televisions, refrigerators, washing machines, and cars. The United States was now a "Consumers' Republic."[48]

Teenagers, the children of the Eisenhower years, were uniquely poised to take advantage of the promise of that republic. Too young to have experienced the hardships of the Great Depression, they actually benefited from their parents' eagerness to compensate for those old deprivations. As the percentage of teens attending high school surpassed the number working, and as demographically specific magazines like *Seventeen* debuted, the idea of the teenage years gained popular currency. With Elvis signing a record contract with RCA and James Dean dominating the box office in *Rebel Without a Cause*, teenagers were clearly a full-blown cultural phenomenon. *Newsweek* touted "The Dreamy Teen-Age Market: It's Neat to Spend," and *Life* reported that teenagers spent nearly $10 billion a year.[49]

The new youth culture was more than the sum of its purchases. The messages that teenagers received were also important. As embodied by Jim Stark, Dean's character in *Rebel Without a Cause*, teenagers learned that adults did not really understand their hopes and dreams and aspirations. Adults, moreover, could not understand teens, *Rebel* suggested slyly; teens were the only authentic people in the movie, the only ones true to their feelings, the only ones willing to challenge convention. But even as the idea of teenage alienation became mainstream, young people heard a message of generational unity in news reports about the power and importance of the baby boomers and in advertising campaigns that told kids to fit in, to be part of "the Pepsi Generation."

The youth culture of the 1950s presented two contradictory messages—alienation and the power of unity—that especially appealed to black teenagers, who, more than any others, felt these tensions in their everyday lives. And they recognized that this new youth culture had roots in African-American culture. R&B groups like Little Anthony and the Imperials, the Drifters, and the Miracles easily found white fans, and white artists such as Elvis Presley appeared often on the black-oriented R&B charts. The crossover nature of pop music suggests that feelings of alienation stemming from youth and race drew from the same artistic well. By conflating teen angst and racism, integrated pop music reinforced the marketing message of generational unity to black teens and signaled to white teens that black culture was hip.

The writer Norman Mailer recognized the allure of black hipness in a 1957 essay, "The White Negro." Mailer's "hipness" was equal parts black culture, sex, and existentialism. He rooted the relationship between black music and sex in the daily dilemma of African Americans: either act deferentially or court danger for being uppity. This dilemma caused African Americans to embrace life more fully, to be existentialists in the most basic sense—deeply aware of the world they lived in and searching for meaning. Black culture was the erotically and morally charged opposite of the dominant culture of white teens. Mailer suggested that the African-American dilemma was now that of white youth, in an age shadowed by nuclear annihilation and stultifying conformity. Hipness offered both a release from the danger of modern life and a model for finding one's authentic self.[50]

African-American teens did more than just inspire this new youth culture; they were immersed in it. Across regions and classes, teenagers came to have similar tastes in fashion and music. Even poverty was not necessarily a barrier, particularly in cities. Many of the outward symbols of youth culture—clothes and music, most notably—were relatively affordable. Even those at the economic margins often had part-time jobs that provided extra spending money. Because a higher proportion of black teens worked and spent about the same proportion of their income on recreation as did whites, they could purchase the outward symbols of generational inclusion.[51]

The increasingly powerful and targeted consumer messages around them linking the acquisition of material goods with the good life and the American dream implied that even equality could be purchased. But the reality of the everyday lives of black teens belied these seductive messages. Middle-class African-American teens spent like first-class consumers but usually found themselves treated like second-class citizens. The more young African Americans saw themselves in a national context, part of a generation of teenagers, the more they chafed at the contradictions they encountered every day in stores, trains, and restaurants. More than their parents, black teens felt the sting of the gap between first-class spending and second-class citizenship.

Julian Bond's poetry beautifully captured the dual consciousness of black teens, the friction between generational inclusion and continued racial exclusion. The irony of Bond's alienation was that it was made possible only by his generation's relative affluence. Without the postwar boom and the resulting consolidation of youth itself as a category of marketing and demographic targeting (and later of political activism), the civil rights movement as we know it would not have happened. The number of African Americans like Bond, Barry, Nash, Carmichael, and even Lewis was still small in absolute terms. In relative terms, though, their multiplying numbers help explain why the civil rights movement took on a new urgency with the sit-ins.

HOW THE MOVEMENT GOT ITS GROOVE BACK

The first sit-in happened spontaneously. Like freshmen everywhere, Franklin McCain, David Richmond, Ezell Blair, and Joseph McNeil often stayed up late into the night talking in their dorm
rooms at North Carolina A&T. Their bull sessions centered on the injustices of segregation. In January 1960, McNeil was still smarting
from an incident that had happened only a few weeks before: on his
way back from Christmas vacation, none of the restaurants in the bus
terminal would serve him food. All four had suffered the indignities
of Jim Crow, but now they were gathering the seeds of resistance.
They had heard about nonviolent protest: Ezell Blair had recently
seen a television documentary about Gandhi. They admired the courage of the Little Rock Nine. They were reading an anthology of stories
about heroic black Americans. Inspiration was all around them, though
in the years afterward they could never put a finger on the specific
incident that triggered their decision to act.[1]

As their frustrations fed off one another, their conversation turned
more serious. They resolved to challenge the system by sitting at a
whites-only lunch counter downtown until they were served. They
chose Woolworth's because it had the double standard common to
many national chains—its lunch counters were integrated everywhere but in the South. On the spur of the moment, they decided to
stage their protest the next day.[2]

On February 1 the four met outside the campus library at three
p.m., getting a late start because McCain had to attend an ROTC class.

(He was still wearing his uniform.) On the short walk from campus, they stopped to tell Ralph Johns, a white merchant sympathetic to the black quest for civil rights, what they were planning and asked him to phone a local reporter.

Once at Woolworth's, they split into pairs and bought some tooth-paste and school supplies to emphasize the inconsistency of the way Woolworth's treated of them. Then they sat down at the lunch coun-ter and tried to order coffee. An African-American busboy behind the counter thought they must be out-of-towners, because local blacks knew the rules. The white waitress refused to serve them, and the manager asked them to leave. But the students stayed. When an el-derly white woman approached them to say she was proud of them and wished they had tried this sooner, their spirits soared. Curly Har-ris, the store manager, wanted the police to stop the sit-in. The chief told him that, as long as the four behaved, he could do nothing. After about an hour of watching the young men just sit there, a flustered Harris decided to close the store in the hope that the problem would go away.

On the way walk back to campus, the four were elated. They had done something; they had struck a blow against segregation. "I prob-ably felt better that day than I've ever felt in my life," said McCain. "I felt as though I had gained my manhood."[3]

The A&T campus buzzed with talk about the sit-in. The next day more than twenty-five students staged another one at lunchtime. The day after that, they filled sixty-three of the sixty-six seats at the Wool-worth's counter. On Thursday, the demonstrations spilled over to the Kress department store down the block, with several white students from the local women's college participating. On Friday, the number of demonstrators topped three hundred. On Saturday, several hun-dred students—including the A&T football team—were harassed by white mobs clutching Rebel flags. Tensions mounted as the white toughs tried to prevent new protesters from relieving those at the counter, and the football players used a flying wedge to barrel them through. When bomb scares forced both Woolworth's and Kress to close, the students peacefully returned to campus. That night sixteen hundred students voted to halt the protests momentarily for a period of "negotiation and study."[4]

The sit-ins leaped across the South like wildfire. A week after the first one, black students in Durham held their own sit-in. The next day there was a sit-in in Charlotte, then one in Portsmouth, Virginia, and on February 13, in Nashville and Tallahassee. By the end of the month, African-American students in more than thirty communities had staged sit-ins. In March, they did so in another forty communities, including Atlanta, Miami, Houston, Little Rock, and Birmingham. By mid-April, when the last southern state, Mississippi, experienced its first sit-in, more than fifty thousand people had participated. These were staggering numbers. It was not just the largest black protest against segregation; it was the largest outburst of civil disobedience in American history.[5]

African Americans, of course, had been protesting segregation since whites first imposed it after the Civil War. In the twentieth century, an alphabet soup of organizations—the NAACP, CORE, the Urban League—led organized protests. The NAACP, founded in 1909, won its first lawsuit against segregation in 1917. Every day individual African Americans challenged the system in their own way, often pushing the challenge to the edge of arrest or white retaliation. Even the idea of a sit-in was not original. Labor unions had perfected the technique in the 1930s as a strike tactic. NAACP youth groups in Oklahoma and Kansas briefly tried it in 1958. But something was different this time: now historical conditions and small, determined action on the part of a few individuals conspired to change the course of events.[6]

The sit-ins changed everything by rewriting the rules of protest. Where the *Brown* decision had relied on lawyers and court orders and the Montgomery bus boycott had relied on an elite leadership for a highly coordinated and legal campaign, the sit-ins explicitly broke the law to challenge the legitimacy of segregation. Unlike even the Montgomery bus boycott, which was more economic in nature, they were a true act of civil disobedience. But the sit-ins were more than just a tactical innovation; they represented a profound ideological shift in the nature of protest. They were radically democratic and egalitarian. Anybody could sit in, and sit-ins were easily replicable. All one needed was a commitment to a few easy-to-learn principles of nonviolence. Each person became the leader of his or her own protest. The distance between leader and follower collapsed. To a young generation whose hopes had been raised but not fulfilled by recent civil rights victories, the sit-ins put them in control of their own destiny, giving them a chance to act. Finally.

The sit-ins drew inspiration from a variety of sources. King's emergence during the bus boycott spurred an interest in the idea of nonviolence. Many of the students had at least a passing familiarity with Gandhi's tactics and Thoreau's essay "Civil Disobedience." Many were influenced by the wave of decolonization that had swept through Africa since the end of World War II. The choice of a department store drew attention to the friction that young African Americans felt between the promise of generational unity symbolized by the clothes they wore and the music they listened to, and the reality of racial exclusion in the segregated South.[7]

At their core, the sit-ins were rooted in the same optimism that had led black teenagers to believe that racial change was right around the corner. The students were convinced that if they exposed the evil that was segregation to Americans of goodwill, then change would happen. The sit-ins elegantly fused the dominant strands of American liberalism, bringing together the New Deal's emphasis on an activist, engaged, caring federal government with World War II's emphasis on human rights and democracy. In this way, the sit-ins were an appeal to creed and commonwealth, to the belief that America's ideals and America's government endorsed their cause. Far from repudiating the American creed, the students insisted they were its true adherents. The rightness, the bright moral simplicity, of their cause would bring them victory in the land of the free.

The most prominent demonstrations happened in the South's major cities. In Nashville, a small group of students had already been earnestly planning to hold sit-ins when the Greensboro students acted first. They had been meeting since September 1959, recruiting members and holding nonviolence workshops to prepare their way. During the Christmas shopping season, they had even conducted a quiet series of test sit-ins to gauge local reaction. They were planning a full-scale assault later in the spring when the Greensboro students jumped the gun.[8]

The organizer of the Nashville group was a thirty-two-year-old Vanderbilt University divinity student named Jim Lawson, who had come to Nashville in 1958 to battle segregation. In a bit of serendipity, Lawson came from Massillon, Ohio, the hometown of Chuck McDew. Lawson's father was pastor of a local Methodist church and a founder of the town's NAACP branch. Jim Lawson's activist leanings expanded when he enrolled at Baldwin-Wallace College, intending to follow in his father's footsteps and become a pastor. But after joining the Fellowship of Reconciliation, a leading peace group, Lawson became a committed pacifist, even spending a year in jail as a conscientious objector to the Korean War. After his release in 1952, he traveled to India as a missionary, where he became well versed in Gandhi's doctrine of nonviolent protest.[9]

Soon after returning to the United States in 1956, Lawson met Martin Luther King: the young minister came to give a speech at Oberlin, where Lawson was enrolled as a graduate student. After Lawson introduced himself, the two fell fast into conversation. When King mentioned that he would like to go to India someday, Lawson said that when he finished school, he would like to fight segregation in the South like King. Before he could finish his thought, King interrupted: "Don't wait! Come now! We don't have anyone like you down there. We need you right now. Please don't delay. Come as quickly as you can." So in 1958 Jim Lawson moved to Nashville as the Fellowship of Reconciliation's new southern field secretary.[10]

Arriving in Nashville, Lawson hosted workshops on nonviolence at First Baptist, the city's most prominent black church. By the fall of 1959, his Tuesday-night workshops regularly attracted two dozen participants. In particular, he drew students from Nashville's four black colleges: Fisk University, Meharry Medical College, Tennessee A&I, and American Baptist Theological Seminary.[11]

Some were drawn to Lawson's workshops because of their religious beliefs. John Lewis had wanted to be a preacher. When other kids were outside playing, he was coaxing his siblings into playing preacher and congregation. Sometimes he practiced on the family chickens, performing mock rites on the fowl—chicken weddings, chicken sermons, chicken funerals. Most of all Lewis had a deep spiritual sense; one of his teachers called him "pure of heart." He embraced the idea of the "beloved community," the notion that human history was about building community, about coming together. The beloved community would be an earthly realization of the Christian vision of a just and fair society. Those, like Lewis, who embraced the idea of the beloved community believed it was their moral duty to use nonviolence to struggle against those forces—greed, revenge, power—that stood in the way of its realization.[12]

• • •

They were a motley bunch who gathered at the First Baptist Church to attend Lawson's workshops. All were outsiders in one way or another: Diane Nash, the sophomore transfer student; Marion Barry, the graduate student; and John Lewis, along with his friends Bernard Lafayette and James Bevel, the poor kids from the Bible college.

The gap between Lewis's American Baptist Theological Seminary and Fisk University could not have been greater. Only thirty-five years old and tolerated without enthusiasm by its sponsor, the Southern Baptist Convention—one of the South's whitest and most conservative denominations—the unaccredited seminary scraped by on a limited budget and threadbare facilities. Most of the students were like Lewis—poor kids from the rural South who were the first in their families to go to college and who chose American Baptist because they had no other options. To them, Fisk seemed as remote as Vanderbilt and other segregated undergraduate colleges. It had a history that stretched back to the days after the Civil War, famous alumni like W.E.B. Du Bois, grand buildings, and the only Phi Beta Kappa chapter on a black campus.

The one thing that stood out to Barry about these early workshops was the conspicuous absence of Fisk men. He thought it an interesting window into the class divisions among Nashville's black college students. Barry had been a big man on campus at LeMoyne College—an athlete, a student government leader, a fraternity man. Now, as a Fisk graduate student, he brought an outsider's eye to understanding the school's social hierarchies. The higher up in Fisk's pecking order you were because of money, or athletic accomplishment, or fraternity involvement, Barry thought, the less likely you were to show up for Lawson's workshops at First Baptist. It was the same thing Diane Nash had noticed when her dates from Fisk shrugged off the indignities of segregation. When she asked these young men about civil rights protests, their answers revealed their cautious, conventional outlook. It was illegal, they said; or an arrest would undermine their career prospects; or protesting was futile.[13]

The class divisions Barry noticed, however, were not clear-cut. To a degree, all of Lawson's protégés were products of the long economic boom in black America that went back to the start of World War II. Black college students may have been divided, but the greater gap was between the very small number of American blacks who attended college at all and the vast majority who did not. The gap between rural and urban African Americans was just as great: those who lived in the cities were better educated, made more money, and had more freedoms than their country cousins. Whatever the young protesters' ambivalence about the black middle class, it was precisely the growing economic and political independence of the South's urban blacks that would help make the civil rights movement possible.

At first, the students were skeptical of Lawson. Soft-spoken and cerebral, he spent a lot of time going over the historical and philosophical roots of nonviolent protest. The plight of African Americans was not unique, he wanted them to understand; at other times and in other places, groups had faced similar challenges. Lawson had them read Thoreau and Gandhi, Reinhold Niebuhr, Chinese philosophers, anything that would give them a better understanding of social struggle and nonviolent theory. At first, Nash thought, "This stuff is never going to work." To the students, the workshops seemed slow, almost contemplative. They wanted passion; they wanted action. Lawson seemed to offer neither.[14]

Gradually, though, he won them over. He got them to see that nonviolence was more than a tactic—it was a way of life. Compared to Lawson's approach, King's discussion of nonviolence, which focused on the mechanics of protest, seemed superficial. Lewis saw that nonviolence shaped how you approached life, from the curt store clerk to the state trooper beating you during a protest. In his own quiet way, Lawson convinced the students that the moral clarity of a nonviolent approach would draw people to their cause.

Just attending the workshops gave the students new confidence. The months of discussion and training brought them together, creating camaraderie. They gained a better appreciation for the historical and intellectual forces behind their movement. And they learned another lesson, a hard one for college students but one that would serve them well over the next couple of years. They learned the importance of subsuming individual differences to the power of collective action.[15]

The Greensboro sit-ins caught the Nashville group off guard and prompted much debate about what to do next. While they were still planning, others were acting. Barry, Nash, and the other students wanted to accelerate their timetable, to start their own demonstrations right away. Lawson tried to slow the students, raising practical questions they had not considered: Would the students be arrested? Who would bail them out? Was there enough money for bail? Who would defend them? Worse, would they be beaten? In a sense, Lawson's hesitancy reflected all the things that had slowed the struggle for civil rights over the last decade. The older generation's caution, its obsession with legalisms, and its lack of faith in the power of collective action undermined its good intentions. The students chafed at Lawson's advice, eager to seize the opportunity provided by Greensboro.[16]

On an unusually quiet Saturday—a rare winter storm had left eight inches of fresh snow on the ground—groups of students set out from each of the city's four black colleges, converging at First Baptist Church before heading to the downtown shopping district to begin sit-ins at several department stores. It was February 13, twelve days after the first Greensboro sit-in.[17]

Diane Nash was nervous. The night before, she had sat in her dorm room alone, nearly overwhelmed with fear. She was going to break the law. However much they had talked in the workshops of the potential power of nonviolent protest, however much she thought segregation was wrong, it was still the law. And obedience to the law was one of the earliest and most powerful lessons Diane Nash had been taught. Segregation was not just the law of the land—it was an institution so deeply ingrained in the psyche of every southerner, white and black, that in many places signs to remind blacks to sit in one place, whites in another, were not necessary.[18]

At the same time on the other side of the city, John Lewis was having similar fears as he, too, sat in his dorm room. He worried about the possible consequences. He might be jeopardizing his future, or be thrown out of college. But the next morning, like Nash, Lewis got up, dressed in neat, respectable clothing, and went to First Baptist. As the group headed downtown, he drew sustenance from his faith and, most important, courage from the camaraderie and fellowship of the group. Making the snowy walk to the city's downtown department stores, they were comforted by the knowledge that they were not alone. They were doing this *together*.[19]

The students sat down on the shiny chrome stools at the long linoleum Woolworth's lunch counter, laid out neatly with napkin holders and straw dispensers and saltshakers. Big glass and steel holders were

stuffed with cakes and pies. Along the back wall printed signs advertised ham and cheese sandwiches (fifty cents), pumpkin, apple, and
cherry pie (fifteen cents), and hot coffee (ten cents). A long mirror running the length of the counter reflected their nervous faces.

The nervousness of the whites surprised Nash; it never had occurred to her that the white customers and employees might be more
jittery than she was. One waitress was so rattled that she kept dropping dishes and then unthinkingly grabbing another dish off the pile,
only to drop it as well. Nash and her fellow protesters glanced at one
another, suppressing giggles. The scene reminded Nash of something
out of a cartoon. They wanted to laugh but realized it would be disrespectful in the middle of such a serious protest.[20]

The first day was relatively quiet. When the group asked for service, one waitress told them, "We don't serve niggers here." Another
employee then put out a hand-lettered "Counter Closed" sign. They
turned off the lights. Still, the students stayed; just enough light filtered in for them to continue studying. Small crowds of whites
gawked, and occasionally someone yelled "Niggers go home!" but
there was no violence. One observer thought it looked like a scene
from a 1950s science fiction movie, in which a city was mutely paralyzed by an alien invasion.[21]

By the fourth day of their sit-in, the threat of violence hung in the
air and drained any humor from the situation. Nashville's white residents were recovering from their initial shock, and the defenders of
Jim Crow were beginning to stir. The students heard rumors of groups
planning to attack them. More than three hundred protesters gathered at First Baptist Church for what would be the largest sit-in yet.
Fearing what gangs of whites might do, the protesters appealed to the
Nashville police chief, Douglas Hosse, for protection, only to be asked
if all this was really "worth a twenty-five-cent hamburger." He told
the students that if there was trouble at the protests, he would arrest
them for disorderly conduct and trespassing.[22]

When Lewis entered Woolworth's, a group of whites were waiting. They started yelling "Nigger!" and "Get back to Africa!" As he
headed for the counter, they tried to block his way and struck at him.
The moment he sat down, he was knocked off his chair as the white
mob punched and kicked him.

At McClellan's department store, the sight of the white protester
Paul LaPrad seated between two black women enraged a gathering

white mob. They pulled LaPrad off his stool, beat and kicked him, and yelled "Nigger lover!" as he curled into a fetal position, desperately trying to protect himself. When the cops arrived, they arrested LaPrad for disturbing the peace. When another group of protesters moved to replace them on the empty seats, the police arrested them as well but continued to ignore the white bullies.

It was the same story everywhere downtown. Police arrested the young black protesters merely for taking seats at a lunch counter, but they ignored the gangs of thugs who yelled "Nigger!" kicked and punched protesters, and threw lighted cigarettes on them. By day's end, the Nashville police had arrested more than seventy-five protesters but not one of their antagonists.[23]

Lewis, one of those arrested, found the prospect of jail unnerving. For him, it was a powerful and frightening symbol of white power. An African American in jail was fully at the mercy of Jim Crow. Every black community in the South had its own cautionary tales about the absence of mercy in white justice. Going to jail also challenged the students' deeply ingrained ideas of what it meant to be a respectable citizen. "To go to jail was to bring shame and disgrace on [your] family," Lewis thought. As students, they worried that a criminal record might get them thrown out of school or hurt their chances of going on to graduate school or landing a job.[24] In their anxiety, these students were still very much children of the 1950s. In fact, this very moment, when a few young black Americans decided that going to jail was the only way to express the depth of their dissent, was when the 1950s ended and the 1960s began.[25]

In the end, Lewis found the arrest an oddly liberating experience. Slowly he realized that he was feeling not fear but exhilaration, the exhilarating independence of a free person. By accepting the idea of jail, he felt freed from the oppressive power of segregation. At that moment he came to believe more than ever that segregation could be toppled. No longer afraid, Lewis felt himself fully drawn into a "holy crusade," so that being arrested became a "badge of honor." There was no going back for him. He and the other protesters would refuse bail. They would stay in jail. To do otherwise would be to cooperate with a system they knew to be wrong. Several hours later Fisk's president, concerned about the safety of the students, convinced the police, still confused by this new and unusual protest, to release all those arrested into his custody.[26]

As she was handcuffed and hauled off to the station for booking, Diane Nash had felt the fear well up inside of her too. But as the police searched, photographed, and fingerprinted her, humiliation at being treated like a common criminal mixed with her fear. Looking around and seeing her friends also being processed gave Nash some reassurance, but still the humiliation lingered. Slowly, as she listened to the laughter of the white cops, the fear turned into anger. The policemen joked about the protesters' clothes, how they smelled, and their physical appearance. They ridiculed the fiery emotions and accents of black preachers. The idea that the cops were mocking her for the simple action of just trying to get a sandwich focused her anger. Anger then turned to resolve. She was absolutely certain that this was the right thing to do.[27]

A couple of days later a perfunctory trial found the students guilty. The judge gave them the choice of paying a fifty-dollar fine or serving thirty days in the county workhouse. Speaking for everyone, Diane Nash displayed her newfound confidence when she stood up and said to the judge, "We feel if we pay these fines we would be contributing to and supporting the injustice and immoral . . . arrest and conviction of the defendants." And with that they were led off to jail.[28]

The images of these neatly dressed, polite young people being taken to jail resonated powerfully across the country. Except for the color of their skin, they looked like ordinary middle-class college students. Telegrams of support—including one from Eleanor Roosevelt—poured in from all over the country. Meanwhile, other students carried on the sit-ins; another sixty-three were arrested the next day. The protesters' three days in jail had sent a powerful message to Nashville's white leaders: these students, hardly more than children, were willing to sacrifice themselves to bring down segregation. Confronted with the possibility of civic disorder and the erosion of Nashville's national reputation, the mayor ordered the release of Lewis, Nash, and the other protesters and appointed a biracial committee to study the situation.

The mayor stacked the committee with people sympathetic to the downtown businessmen. By offering an integrated and seemingly legitimate avenue of negotiation, the mayor hoped to isolate the students politically, cast the sit-ins as extremist, and defuse tensions within the city. On April 5, the panel announced that the downtown department stores had agreed to set up a three-month trial of "partial" integration—opening black-only sections in the lily-white restaurants. This flimsy repackaging of segregation won support from no one. Hard-core segregationists did not trust the committee to protect segregation any more than black activists trusted it to bring about integration.

On April 18, white supremacists bombed the home of Z. Alexander Looby, the lone African American on the Nashville city council and the protesters' lawyer. No one was killed, but five thousand black Nashvillians marched on city hall to protest. Mayor Ben West tried to calm the crowd with empty platitudes: "You all have the power to destroy the city. So let's not have any mobs." He concluded by reminding everyone, "We are all Christians together. Let us pray."[29]

Diane Nash stepped forward. Would West use his office to end racial discrimination?

"I appeal to all citizens to end discrimination, to have no bigotry, no bias, no hatred," said West.

"Do you mean lunch counters?" asked Nash.

"Little lady, I stopped segregation seven years ago at the airport when I first took office, and there has been no trouble there since."

Nash pressed on: "Do you recommend that the lunch counters be desegregated?"

"Yes," West finally conceded.

The crowd roared its approval. Nash had forced the mayor into trying to defend an undefendable institution, and he had caved. On May 10, African Americans sat down to their first legal meals at the city's downtown lunch counters. The students had taken on Goliath and won.[30]

In Atlanta, February 3, 1960, started out as an ordinary day for Julian Bond, a junior at Morehouse College. Since his father was a dean at Atlanta University, he lived at home, which allowed him both more and less freedom than his peers had. He had a quick bowl of cereal, went to his morning classes (math, English literature), and ran an errand. Late in the morning he headed over to the Yates & Milton Drugstore, a hangout for students from Morehouse and the four other black colleges that together made up the Atlanta University Center, for lunch. He had just settled into his usual seat in the back (so he could survey the whole joint) when Lonnie King, a football player he knew only by reputation (and who was not related to Martin Luther King), thrust a copy of that day's *Atlanta Daily World*—the city's African-American daily paper—at him.

"Have you seen this?" he asked.

"Yeah, you know, I read the papers," Bond replied sarcastically.

"What do you think about it?" King asked.

"Well, it's all right, pretty good stuff."

"Don't you think it ought to happen here?" King pressed on.

"It probably will."

Then out of nowhere King said, "Let's make it happen. You take this side of the drugstore and I'll take the other, and we'll call a meeting for noon today."[31]

Bond's first reaction was to try to figure out a way to wiggle out of helping King. (He later recalled ruefully that when Lonnie King said "Let's," he should have said, "What do you mean, *Let's*?"). But surprising himself, Bond started to recruit the students in the drugstore. About twenty people showed up for the first meeting, more the next day, and still more the next. And the Atlanta student movement was born.[32]

Lonnie King and Julian Bond made an odd team. King had come to college late, after a four-year stint in the navy. He was dark-skinned and thickly muscled, an ex-boxer with a checkered past. (He joined the navy after losing his job at an Atlanta YMCA for beating up a young patron.) He was full of angry determination to change the South. The light-skinned, slender, easygoing Julian Bond was a poet. Most people who knew him would have thought him an unlikely choice for a sit-in organizer. But in the last year a deepening curiosity in the burgeoning civil rights movement had challenged Bond's devil-may-care attitude. Emerging from his privileged cocoon, he was becoming more conscious of how segregation impoverished black Atlantans and robbed them of opportunity.[33]

Bond and King had little trouble recruiting students, but the movement evolved differently. Atlanta was not Nashville; indeed, it was different from any other city in the South. First, it was the corporate capital of the New South, home to many important businesses and financial service firms and to the South's largest and most powerful African-American business community. In the words of Mayor Ivan Allen, Jr., Atlanta's elites thought of themselves as "business-oriented, nonpolitical, moderate, well-bred, well-educated, pragmatic, and dedicated to the betterment of Atlanta." Atlanta was known as "the city too busy to hate." This image of racial moderation fed the vanity of white leaders, who liked to think of themselves as progressive, and of black leaders, who liked to think of themselves as influential. "Atlanta was a mercantile city," Bond recalled. "We weren't like Nashville, all motivated by religion."[34]

Bond and King turned to the presidents of the five Atlanta University Center colleges for advice. Playing on Atlanta's reputation as an exceptional city and on the students' vanity, the presidents expressed concern that the sit-ins might undermine white support (particularly financial) for their schools. Atlanta was not Nashville or Greensboro, they argued; here the students needed a different strategy. Dr. Rufus Clement suggested the students would impress the white business community if they wrote a statement explaining their grievances and suggesting solutions.[35]

Bond and another student spent more than two weeks writing "An Appeal for Human Rights," which appeared on March 9, 1960, in the city's major black and white newspapers (backed by money supplied by Dr. Clement). It read, in part:

> We do not intend to sit placidly for those rights which are already legally and morally ours to be meted out one at a time. Today's youth will not sit by submissively while being denied all the rights, privileges, and joys of life. We want to state clearly and unequivocally that we cannot tolerate, in a nation professing democracy and among people professing Christianity, the discriminatory conditions under which the negro is living today in Atlanta, Georgia—supposedly one of the most progressive cities in the South.[36]

With its ordering of legal rights before moral ones and democracy before Christianity, the "Appeal" reflected Atlanta's pragmatic, secular, commercial outlook. It also reflected the persistent influence and caution of their adult advisers. Instead of targeting downtown department stores, as in Nashville, the Atlanta group focused on public places such as bus stations and government buildings. In part, they did this as a favor to the college presidents who worried that the generous donations to their schools from downtown businesses would dry up. The students also were concerned about the legality of holding sit-ins on private property, such as department store lunch counters. Business owners argued they had the right to operate their stores any way they chose; on the other hand, many civil rights lawyers believed common law tradition compelled merchants to serve all equitably. But in 1960, neither the courts nor Congress had definitively settled this question.

On March 15, the first day of the Atlanta sit-ins, Julian Bond led about a dozen neatly dressed students to the City Hall cafeteria, while additional groups hit other targets. As they walked over, Bond jokingly predicted that they would be arrested within fifteen minutes.

When they arrived, they tried to help themselves.

The manager, a heavy-set white woman, challenged them. "What do you want?" she asked.

"We want to eat," replied Bond.

"Well, we can't serve you here."

"Well, the sign outside says the public is welcome."

"This is just for City Hall employees," she insisted.

"That's not true," Bond persisted. "You've got a sign outside saying the public is welcome, and we're the public, and we want to eat."

"I'm going to call the police," she said with finality.[37]

Bond's fifteen-minute estimate had been far too generous. They were in the cafeteria just five minutes before the employees called the police. The cops arrived quickly, hauling the students down to "Big Rock," the city jail. Bond assured the nervous students that it would take only a couple of hours for them to be bailed out.

As the day wore on and bail was not forthcoming, the others hassled Bond for his false optimism. In fact, they were not released until the early evening. They then inaugurated a movement tradition by heading to Paschal's, a prominent black-owned restaurant near campus, for a free meal of its legendary fried chicken. But as Bond recalled, the best came next: "We went over to Spelman, where we could be heroes, you know, among the women, and that was it."

The students would all plead not guilty. Later a grand jury would indict Bond on nine counts, including conspiracy, restraint of trade, and, most amazingly, violation of an anti-Klan law. Not until the mid-1970s would Bond get the indictment fully dismissed.

The Atlanta students prided themselves on running the best-organized protests in the South, drawing on the financial resources of Atlanta's black community. They employed two-way radios to coordinate, ran a shuttle service to get people downtown, made laminated signs that would not run in the rain, and wore special football coats with hoods to protect the women when whites threw spitballs and worse at them. Bond thought the protests were a blast; "We were hell," he joked.

The initial protests failed to produce any change. Despite its moniker as "the city too busy to hate," Atlanta proved as resistant as any southern city. Atlanta's white businessmen hoped that if city leaders stalled long enough, the protests would fizzle out with summer vacation. The willingness of the city's black elite to engage in negotiations and to see downtown integration as just one of a number of issues to be resolved—school integration, civic improvements in black neighborhoods, political representation—fed into the white strategy of delay.

In late March, the Atlanta students added sit-ins at downtown department stores. Circumventing the black leadership, they made a direct appeal to the middle class to "close out your charge account with segregation, open up your account with freedom." In April came the Easter weekend at Shaw and the formal birth of SNCC. When school started again in September, the Atlanta students restarted their protests and continued to draw wide support from the local African-American community. At one point, the students had more than five thousand dollars in the bank and four thousand black Atlantans picketing downtown. Even though the loss of black customers was economically painful, white businessmen continued to resist downtown integration. The popularity of the department store protests reinforced the mass appeal of the sit-ins' marriage of tactical innovation to a critique of black America's ambiguous place in the "affluent society."[38]

Despite the outward appearance of unity, the students and Atlanta's older black leaders bickered about strategy and tactics. When SNCC met in Atlanta the weekend of October 14–16, the students argued that if Dr. King got arrested at a sit-in with them, it would help the Atlanta movement and possibly influence the black vote in the upcoming presidential election. King, however, was under pressure from his father not to participate; Martin Luther King, Sr., came from the older, less confrontational generation. The younger King was already on probation for driving in Georgia with Alabama license plates; it was a trumped-up charge, to be sure, but an arrest would violate his probation and could land him in jail for several months.[39]

In the end, the students shamed King into joining them, questioning his commitment and courage. But his fears about his probation turned out to be justified; the judge sentenced him to four months' hard labor in a maximum-security prison, an unusually harsh sentence. Only intense public pressure from blacks across the political spectrum—Democrats like Harry Belafonte and Republicans like Jackie Robinson—and a blunt behind-the-scenes phone call to the judge from Bobby Kennedy secured King's release after a few days.

The Atlanta protests dragged on deep into the winter of 1960–61 as more than seventy stores temporarily closed in December, January, and February because of the decline in business. Finally, in March 1961, the white businessmen offered a compromise that would allow them to retain an illusion of control: they promised to integrate the lunch counters in September if the students would stop the demonstrations now. The students refused, calling the long delay unacceptable and demanding immediate integration. King felt caught in the middle. His father was part of the group of black leaders pushing for the settlement, but he himself was sympathetic to the students. As one of them observed, "He was trying to marry [the two sides] 'cause the thing was basically a young-versus-old split." The students had taken the initiative in leadership, and the older folks were "fighting" to get it back.

At a meeting to discuss the compromise, the crowd booed King's father and the other black elders. Then Lonnie King and Bond saw Martin Luther King, Jr., give "the best speech of his life." Speaking of the "cancerous disease of disunity," he urged the blacks to respect their elders while allowing the students to make their contributions. Ultimately King's speech tipped the crowd in favor of accepting the compromise.[40]

In September, the actual integration of the department stores and lunch counters further alienated Bond and the other students from the older generation. As Bond recalled, the older generation "came dressed in furs and all their finery to be the first to eat at Rich's. Sad. Sad. Sad . . . In fact they insisted that we send mixed groups, and by 'mixed,' I mean adults and students. Because the adults just wanted to be in on it when it happened."[41]

It is hard now, at a distance of fifty years, to fully appreciate the sensation created by the sit-ins, especially among the young. From Harvard to Berkeley and from Brown to Wisconsin, college students organized sympathy sit-ins and pickets of Woolworth's and other department stores, held rallies, and raised money for jailed southern protesters. Sympathy from white southern students was not unknown. The University of North Carolina's student paper, *The Daily Tar Heel*, offered an editorial in support of the sit-ins: "We hope they win. We hope they win BIG. We hope they win SOON." Student support was by no means unanimous, and passions ran high; at Princeton University students supporting and opposing the sit-ins came to blows.[42]

No one was more enthralled by the protests than a junior at the University of Michigan named Tom Hayden, who wrote for the school paper. His first editorial about the sit-ins appeared in early March 1960, five weeks after Greensboro. Hayden idolized the figure of the antihero, especially James Dean and Jack Kerouac, dressing in a white T-shirt and jeans and riding a motorcycle. A romantic rebel, Hayden was drawn to the sit-ins. He decided to spend the summer of 1960 paying homage to Kerouac's *On the Road* by hitchhiking across the country to meet other student activists and to observe the Democratic Convention in Los Angeles.

The editorials Hayden penned on his return to campus in the fall captured the excitement of the moment. The student activists he met on his trip were the first wave of a "revolution that would reduce complexity to moral simplicity" and "emotion to religion." In a world flooded with books critical of the atomization and bureaucratization of modern life such as David Riesman's *The Lonely Crowd*, Vance Packard's *The Hidden Persuaders,* and the William Whyte's *The Organization Man*, these students had shown how to create a "democratization of decision-making" that reconnected "the individual to the democratic order."[43]

Hayden was just one of many students at the University of Michigan inspired by the sit-ins and the founding of SNCC, which fired their imagination and convinced them that students could have a meaningful voice in politics. Students for a Democratic Society (SDS), which would become the most famous antiwar organization of the late 1960s, originated in Ann Arbor; as one early SDS member recalled of the sit-ins, "Here were people who were *doing* something."[44]

The young people's passion for the sit-ins surprised older Americans. *The New York Times*, echoing E. Franklin Frazier's point but in the larger context, observed: "The present generation had been accused of self-concern and a pallid indifference to social or political questions; this issue appears to have aroused it as few others." Operating under the assumption that prosperity bred complacency and viewing the world through the lens of 1950s conformity, the *Times* missed that the fusion of pop-culture images of youth rebellion and sophisticated social criticism in someone like Tom Hayden was the tinder for a broader generational rebellion. That fusion was generationally specific but racially inclusive. Hayden's synthesis of James Dean and William Whyte really drew from the same inspiration as Bond's poetry, with its mixed allusions to pop music and Du Bois.[45]

In 1960, the sit-ins revived a flagging civil rights movement with an innovation that sparked mass protest like nothing before. Even an act as seemingly modest as being able to eat lunch at a counter next to whites felt like a great victory, compared to the small pace of change in the previous decade. Much more than the tangible dismantling of such a visible piece of Jim Crow distinguished the sit-ins from other protests. The Montgomery bus boycott had essentially been a onetime event that was difficult to replicate; the sit-ins were truly a region-wide phenomenon, gaining momentum from one day to the next.

What set the sit-ins apart from other types of protest was their radically inclusive nature. In just a few short months, more black southerners participated in some form of direct action than they had over the previous decade. The sit-ins were wonderfully democratic as well; the distinction between leader and follower, between organizer and participant, collapsed during a sit-in, making each person responsible for his or her own protest.

The sit-ins were real, tangible, tactile protests. A court case like the *Brown* decision existed mostly as an abstraction, as an endless series of legal briefs, court hearings, and judicial decisions. The sit-ins, on the other hand, represented a direct and immediate challenge to Jim Crow. People were reaching out to grab hold of their freedom in the most direct way possible. Such open and defiant challenges to an institution that seemed so powerful and pervasive added to the thrill and excitement of participating in a sit-in.

The sit-ins were also highly visible. Judicial rulings made for often dry news copy, and lawyers standing in court made for boring news photographs. The sit-ins generated endless dramatic photographs that conveyed the deep African-American unhappiness with segregation. And at the center of those pictures was a new generation of black college students impatient for change and suddenly aware of a power they had not known they possessed.

4. MORE THAN A HAMBURGER

FROM STUDENT PROTESTERS TO CIVIL RIGHTS ACTIVISTS

The fall of 1960 was an awkward time, as the students found themselves caught between school and activism. A new world beckoned with excitement and a sense of importance, but they had not yet broken free of their conventional expectations. They were still students, with classes to attend, sweethearts to visit, and finals to study for. Many were looking forward to graduation just a few months down the road. Even with Ella Baker's inspirational speech that April at Shaw still ringing in their ears, most never imagined that SNCC would become a permanent organization. The students had no model to emulate, no historical examples to follow.

Only Baker had faith in SNCC's future, recruiting a student she knew at Union Theological Seminary in New York, Jane Stembridge, to run a small office in Atlanta. Actually, "office" is a bit of an exaggeration. All SNCC had was a desk in a corner of the SCLC offices. In the beginning, Stembridge spent a lot of time just trying to find out what was happening around the South. SNCC had no field operatives and could not even afford long-distance phone calls. Busy with school and their local protests, the students offered sketchy responses to her requests for information. As Stembridge noted at the time, "SNCC was not coordinating the Movement . . . We were not sure, and still aren't, what SNCC is."[1]

In Nashville, the initial fervor of the sit-ins receded when school resumed in September 1960 as Nash, Lewis, and the others returned to the regular rhythm of classes, dates, and college. A few of the students had stayed in Nashville to experiment with voter registration as a protest technique, signing up about four hundred new black voters.[2] The start of lunch-counter integration at the six downtown department stores temporarily halted the sit-ins. But the students planned a second round of targets, including restaurants, movie theaters, and hotels, for later in the fall.

No one yet contemplated dropping out of school to become a full-time activist. Lewis, a senior, began to think about what to do after graduation—more school, a job, maybe a year abroad. Nash began her junior year by breaking up with a boyfriend she'd met during the first sit-ins. Marion Barry had the most exciting summer, representing SNCC before the platform committee at the Democratic National Convention in Los Angeles and Republican National Convention in Chicago. The urbane Barry proved an effective lobbyist for SNCC, convincing the Democratic Party to issue a statement praising the "peaceful demonstrations for first-class citizenship." But then he followed through on his plan to move from Nashville to pursue his doctorate at the University of Kansas in Lawrence.[3]

The fervor did not recede entirely. With its well-organized protests and well-spoken protesters, Nashville drew a steady stream of media attention. Reporters found in these articulate and committed young people holding forth on Gandhi and integration an irresistible subject. When NBC filmed a documentary on the sit-ins, it focused on Nashville. Nash found the attention intimidating. Uncomfortable with the spotlight, she spent a couple of days avoiding broadcast journalists so she would not have to be interviewed on camera. SNCC leaders *did* accept many of the invitations they received to visit college campuses. John Lewis visited the Universities of Michigan, Wisconsin, and Minnesota. Traveling alone, staying in dorms and fraternity houses, he would arrive, tell stories about the sit-ins, perhaps lead a workshop on nonviolence, and try to raise some money for SNCC's work in Nashville.[4]

Julian Bond returned to Atlanta and school, but his heart was not in it. Extracurricular activism drew more and more of his attention as the 1960–61 school year progressed. He split his time among studying, organizing protests for the Atlanta student movement (known as the Committee on Appeal for Human Rights, or COAHR), and editing SNCC's newsletter, *The Student Voice*. His days were packed, and so were his nights; he frequented bars near campus, too jazzed up to sleep. It was the exhausting—and unsustainable—schedule of a young man suddenly caught up in the excitement of life.

Bond found his real passion in journalism. During the sit-ins, the students had become frustrated with the *Daily World*, the dominant black newspaper in Atlanta, when it attacked the protests as a misguided strategy. Such a stance demonstrated to them how the cozy relationship between the city's black and white leaders could slow the pace of civil rights change. A group of students and faculty from local black colleges founded *The Atlanta Inquirer* as a progressive alternative to the *World*. Bond quickly realized that by engaging in serious investigative journalism, the *Inquirer* could be an important weapon in Atlanta's civil rights struggle. He threw himself into the paper, breaking stories about dubious police shootings and white harassment of prospective black home-buyers in segregated neighborhoods.

Bond had also fallen in love with Alice Clopton, a Spelman student he met while producing *Sit-in Showdown*, a stage show the students put on to raise money. With the demonstrations, the *Inquirer*, school, and Alice, Bond was overextended, and his schoolwork suffered. At the end of the 1961 spring semester, he dropped out of Morehouse to devote himself to the *Inquirer*. His parents were unhappy. His father valued academic achievement above all else and worried that Bond "had thrown his life away." A few months later, on July 28, he and Alice eloped, something they also tried to hide from his parents. They sneaked off to rural Dallas, Georgia, to find a justice of the peace, figuring nobody would know them there. For the next six months, the two lived apart, trying to hide the marriage. None of Bond's work paid much money, and the newlyweds were afraid their parents would cut them off if news of the wedding came out. But when the couple finally came clean, they moved into an extra room in Bond's parents' house.[5]

If the Atlanta student movement generated less media attention than Nashville's, it attracted more than its share of gawkers, tourists, and romantics. Most proved more a hindrance than a help. Bob Moses was the one outsider who made a difference. After seeing pictures of the sit-ins on the evening news, Moses attended a rally in Hampton, Virginia, where he met Wyatt Tee Walker. Walker suggested that Mo-

ses help Bayard Rustin, a well-known activist in New York City, organize a rally in the city for Martin Luther King. Moses's intelligence
impressed Rustin, and he arranged for the young man to spend his
summer vacation (Moses taught high school math at the Horace
Mann School) working for the SCLC in Atlanta. Moses was thrilled,
imagining the SCLC's headquarters as a bustling hub of activists plotting demonstrations to bring down segregation.[6]

When Moses arrived at the SCLC's office in July 1960, he found
only a small suite staffed by three people: Ella Baker, who was about
to leave; Dora McDonald, Dr. King's personal secretary; and Jane
Stembridge. To compound matters, both Baker and King were away,
and neither McDonald nor Stembridge was expecting Moses. He
ended up stuffing envelopes and doing other office chores but struck
up a fast friendship with Stembridge, spending long hours debating
their shared interest in philosophy. It was through Stembridge that
Moses came to know Julian Bond, Lonnie King, and the other Atlanta
sit-in leaders. Eager to contribute something, Moses volunteered to
picket the downtown department stores. He was so eager, in fact, that
he spent hours walking the line alone.[7]

The Atlanta students did not know what to make of this strange,
intense man from New York City. Moses peppered his casual conversation with references to philosophers like Paul Tillich and attended
academic lectures in his spare time. A quiet, contemplative person,
he listened intently to others, paused to think before speaking, and
offered long, complex answers to simple questions. He spoke in a
soft, deliberate voice and exhibited none of the cocky enthusiasm of
the Atlanta students. These skills—along with his quiet authority—
would soon make Moses the most respected person in SNCC. But in
the beginning, he just seemed different, even eccentric. "We were immensely suspicious of him," Julian Bond recalled. "We thought he
was a Communist because he was from New York and wore glasses
and was smarter than we were."[8]

The Atlanta students' apprehensiveness about Moses stemmed
from their own lack of sophistication and maturity. They still did not
quite grasp the larger revolution that the sit-ins had started. Logistical questions dominated their conversations: How many protesters
should we send to this store? For how many days? What equipment
do we need? Moses, on the other hand, had already moved on to the

broader question of how the sit-ins could be part of the long struggle against segregation specifically and injustice generally.[9]

Martin Luther King didn't know what to make of Bob Moses either. King's politics and outlook were even more conventional than the students', and he expected others to follow his lead. Acting on his own, Moses had joined a protest sponsored by the Southern Conference Education Fund (SCEF), had been arrested, and then had been identified as an SCLC staffer in news accounts. SCEF was a favorite target of conservative southern politicians like the Mississippi senator James Eastland, who highlighted its supposedly subversive leanings to discredit its critique of segregation. As his fame grew, King disassociated himself from allies, even organizations like SCEF staffed with personal friends, who reinforced this charge.

King called Moses into his study at Ebenezer Baptist Church and insisted that he no longer associate with SCEF. King narrated the history of SCEF, its origins in the Southern Conference for Human Welfare, its links to Eleanor Roosevelt, the leftist politics of its founders, and the Senate Subcommittee on Internal Security's investigations into its allegedly Communist activities. It did not matter if the charges were or were not true, King explained: people thought they were, "and that's what matters." Whatever his personal feelings, King said the SCLC had to be pragmatic, and Moses should stay away from SCEF.[10]

Moses may have come to Atlanta to work for King, but he quickly gravitated to Ella Baker. Her idealized views rubbed off on Moses and reinforced his belief that the egalitarianism and inclusiveness of the sit-ins represented an entirely new approach to civil rights. Rather than see Moses waste his time stuffing envelopes in Atlanta, Baker and Stembridge arranged for him to travel through the Deep South during August, recruiting participants for the SNCC meeting to be held in October. On August 13, Moses left Atlanta armed with Ella Baker's list of contacts.[11]

The trip altered the course of Moses's life. In Cleveland, Mississippi, he met Amzie Moore, head of the local NAACP branch and owner of the Pan-Am Café, a combination gas station–restaurant–beauty parlor with the only bathrooms for black patrons along the 225-mile stretch of Route 61 between Memphis and Vicksburg. With the stout build of a football player and a bulldog-like face that signaled the tenacious determination of his personality, Moore had returned from World War II disenchanted by the federal government's indifference to segregation and appalled at the indiscriminate violence against blacks in his home state. Moore had been one of the few civil rights activists in the Mississippi Delta during the fifties, struggling to register voters and draw attention to lynchings. He was forty-nine years old in the summer of 1960 and had been waging a lonely fight for civil rights in Mississippi for fifteen years.[12]

Moore told Moses that neither the sit-ins nor the NAACP's legal strategy had done much for African Americans in Mississippi. Most black Mississippians were too poor to eat in a restaurant, whether it was integrated or not, and lawsuits were too slow and expensive. The best way to dismantle segregation, Moore believed, was to gain political power. In a state that was still more than 40 percent African American, registering voters was the most viable strategy for bringing about effective change. Even as Moses recruited Moore to come to the conference, Moore persuaded Moses that SNCC should come to Mississippi to register voters.[13]

Moses wrote Stembridge long, excited letters about his conversations with Moore, describing him as "dug into the Mississippi Delta countryside like a tree that's planted by the water." Moore's voter registration plan, he argued, was exactly the project SNCC should embark on. Before returning to his teaching job in New York City, he promised Amzie Moore that he would be back next summer—with help.

Moses thought Moore was the one person he met who grasped how the sit-ins had changed the calculus of civil rights activism; "it was if he had been sitting there in Cleveland watching the student movement unfold, waiting for it to come his way, knowing it had to eventually come, and planning on ways to use it." In Moses, Moore saw a kindred spirit, the kind of person who could connect with the local population. "I felt like if a man was educated, there wasn't very much you could tell him. I didn't think you could give him any advice." But, Moore recalled, "Bob was altogether different."[14]

In October 1960, Amzie Moore traveled to Atlanta for SNCC's fall retreat, in the hope of convincing the students of the value of voter registration. But with Moses back in New York, no one championed the proposal, and it failed to stir the students. James Lawson made a speech proposing that a strategy of "jail, no bail," flooding the jails with protesters to overwhelm the local bureaucracy, would make a bigger impact: it would play to the students' vanity by emphasizing their best moment so far, the sit-ins, and focus on the personal sacrifice and moral growth of each student. But it would not make the larger structural and political critique that Moses was beginning to articulate. Lawson's strategy continued to focus on middle-class impediments to equality—at lunch counters, bus stations, and public buildings—but offered no way to revive the flagging sit-in movement by connecting petty segregation to the pervasive economic, political, and educational inequality faced by black southerners.[15]

Much of the debate was underpinned by the jockeying for leadership between the Atlanta and Nashville groups. The Nashville students were the dominant ideological and philosophical influence, but the well-organized and well-funded Atlanta group had more resources. The election of South Carolina's Chuck McDew to replace Barry as chair was an attempt to find a balance between the two factions.

An argument about Bayard Rustin's participation highlighted the students' parochial concerns. After inviting Rustin to the meeting, SNCC then asked him to stay away, under pressure from the Packinghouse Workers Union, whose donation had helped fund the meeting. One of the great innovators and tacticians of the civil rights movement going back to the 1930s, Rustin was enmeshed in a web of left-radical organizations, including the Young Communist League and the pacifist Fellowship of Reconciliation. More damning still, Rustin was a homosexual who had been convicted of "sexual perversion" in California in 1953.[16]

As Bond recalled, SNCC members figured that if Rustin was "objectionable to people who are going to give us money, he's got to go."[17]

At the October meeting, the indifference to Amzie Moore, the enthusiasm for Lawson's speech, the jockeying between Atlanta and Nashville, and the casual abandonment of Rustin all revealed a student civil rights movement with only a limited sense of its role in the broader civil rights movement. To paraphrase Ella Baker: they were still about the hamburger.

In February 1961 the forces unleashed by the sit-ins snapped SNCC out of its lethargy. Students at Friendship Junior College in Rock Hill, South Carolina, had been staging sit-ins for a year. Fierce resistance from local whites had produced only a stalemate: local blacks boycotted segregated establishments, and whites refused to negotiate. A local judge had just sentenced ten protesters to a month in jail, and they decided to serve their full sentences, becoming the first group to implement Lawson's "jail, no bail."

Four SNCC members—Diane Nash, Charles Jones, Charles Sherrod, and Ruby Doris Smith—set out immediately for Rock Hill. They were quickly arrested for sitting in at a lunch counter and sentenced to either thirty days in jail or a hundred-dollar fine. Deciding they "could not contribute" to the funding of a segregated society, the four chose jail, hoping to revive the publicity that had tapered off since the previous winter's lunch-counter dramatics.[18]

Nash and the others served their full thirty-day sentences, marking the first time that anyone in SNCC had put Lawson's ideas to the test. The men did road work as part of a chain gang. Jones's local draft board, on learning he was in prison, tried to rescind his student deferment on the logic that he was no longer in school; only the intervention of the college president stopped him from being drafted. The guards banned books, telling them they were in prison, "not a damned school." The guards did allow visitors to bring in outside food, and local residents responded with hearty home-cooked meals. Good food was one of the great ironies of their stay in jail.[19]

The guards mostly left the women alone. Diane Nash found the relative peace and quiet of jail refreshing, giving her a chance to reread Gandhi and the Bible. Her cellmate, Ruby Doris Smith, also read voraciously, plowing through everything from Gandhi's autobiography to pop thrillers like Leon Uris's *Exodus*. The two fell into a routine: eat breakfast at seven, clean the cell, read, write letters, have lunch, read some more, debate politics, discuss books, exercise, and finish off with dinner around six-thirty. It had been almost a year since the first sit-ins in Nashville, and Nash's life had rushed forward. Jail gave her a chance to think.[20]

She used the time to reflect on what was happening, on what she thought the movement should be about, on where it was going, and on her role in that journey. The more time the young activists spent in jail, the deeper became their commitment to the movement and to one another. Jail time was both a logical extension of the sit-ins and a defiant rejection of all previous civil rights activism. The contrast between the passive withdrawal of the Montgomery bus boycott and the active disobedience of "jail, no bail" could not have been greater.[21]

After her release, Nash tried to return to the normal routine of a college student, but she now found "the Chaucer classes unbearable." Dropping out of Fisk, she went to work for the movement, becoming one of the first sit-in leaders to make the leap to full-time activist.[22]

Not everyone had yet come to the same realization. His graduation from American Baptist Theological Seminary only a semester off, John Lewis, unsure of what he should do, applied to spend two years abroad with the Quaker-run American Friends Service Committee (AFSC), building houses in Africa or India. As he was waiting to hear from the AFSC, Lewis came across a small notice in *The Student Voice*, SNCC's monthly newsletter. It sought volunteers for a "Freedom Ride" to test the desegregation of bus stations throughout the South. Having no firm plans, Lewis secretly applied. In early May (a few weeks before graduation), he left school for what he thought would be a ten-day bus trip from Washington to New Orleans.[23]

It was not the first Freedom Ride. In 1947 the Congress of Racial Equality (CORE) had held a Freedom Ride to test the Supreme Court's decision in *Morgan v. Virginia* that bus trips across state lines could not have segregated seating. The ride had mostly been a failure. The NAACP opposed it, and it came to an abrupt end in North Carolina, where police arrested the riders for breaking the state's segregation laws and jailed them for three weeks. Now, fourteen years later, CORE revived the idea of a Freedom Ride to test *Boynton v. Virginia*, a recent Supreme Court decision extending *Morgan* to include interstate bus stations.[24]

Lewis's Freedom Ride went smoothly until his bus reached Rock Hill, South Carolina—the same place where Nash and the others had been jailed three months earlier. When Lewis and Albert Bigelow, a retired naval officer in his mid-fifties, entered the white waiting room at the Rock Hill station, a half-dozen white toughs punched them as the local police looked on. The two teams of riders continued on through South Carolina and Georgia, arriving in Atlanta on May 13 without further incident. The easy part of the journey was over. Now they would pass through the Deep South—Alabama, Mississippi, and Louisiana.[25]

While in Rock Hill, John Lewis received a telegram from the AFSC: he was a finalist for the overseas project. The telegram contained money for a plane ticket and instructions to appear in Philadelphia in two days for an interview. That night Lewis struggled with what to do. The Freedom Ride was important; he already felt a bond with the other riders. On the other hand, the chance to go to Africa or India was a stunning opportunity for a poor black kid from rural Alabama.

In the end, he decided to go for the interview for the same reason he had submitted an application in the first place: he needed something to do after college. He did not feel ready for graduate school just yet, and he did not think of activism as a full-time option. Going abroad, he figured, would be a good transition experience. So on Wednesday morning, May 10, he left for Philadelphia. If all went well, he would rejoin the group a few days later on May 15 in Birmingham as the Freedom Riders headed for Jackson, Mississippi.[26]

He had the interview and headed back down south. On Saturday, May 13, he made a pit stop in Nashville, arriving just as students there had forced the integration of the city's movie theaters after three months of protests. He decided to stay for the victory picnic. On a beautiful Mother's Day afternoon, the Nashville students celebrated their success at a local park, laughing, joking, and dancing to a portable radio. Suddenly, a news flash interrupted the music and reported trouble for the Freedom Riders. Just past Anniston, Alabama, a white mob had forced the bus off the road, slashed the tires, and thrown a firebomb on board. The Freedom Riders were lucky to have escaped with just smoke inhalation.[27]

The party came to a halt as everyone gathered around the radio. Lewis felt momentarily paralyzed by guilt. Nash suggested they cancel the rest of the picnic in favor of an emergency meeting of the Nashville student group. James Bevel, the current head of the Nashville students, objected. To his mind, there was nothing they could do that afternoon about what was happening hundreds of miles away in Alabama.[28]

Nash pressed the point, joined by Lewis and Bernard Lafayette. How could anyone enjoy pie when their friends were in danger and possibly dying in Alabama? She scolded them for selfishness. If they had learned anything by this time, it was that the movement bound all activists in a common cause regardless of time or distance. They needed to help the Freedom Riders. Under Nash's relentless badgering, Bevel called an emergency meeting.[29]

As Nash and the others debated in Nashville, the second group of Freedom Riders pulled into Anniston about an hour after the first bus. Eight white toughs climbed onto the bus to taunt the riders. When two riders approached the bullies to talk, they were punched and kicked until they retreated. When the bus pulled out for Birmingham, the toughs were still on board to make sure nobody moved to the front.

In Birmingham, the Freedom Riders disembarked, and as they approached the white waiting room, a dozen whites shoved Charles Person and James Peck into an alleyway, then beat them with pipes. The Freedom Riders had paired off in interracial teams: Peck was white, Person black. Person managed to escape, but Peck was beaten unconscious. When he came to, Peck found himself in an empty alleyway, blood flowing down his face. He stumbled into the street, where he was spotted by another Freedom Rider. At the hospital, it took eight hours and fifty-three stitches to close Peck's wounds.[30]

All night the Nashville students huddled in the basement of the First Baptist Church, listening to radio reports about the violence in Alabama. Nash unsuccessfully tried to call James Farmer, the head of CORE. Late into the night, they discussed the situation. The willingness of the Freedom Riders to put their bodies on the line challenged the students to prove their own commitment and courage. Lewis recalled that a broad consensus emerged around Nash's insistence that allowing white violence to stop their lawful efforts at desegregation would only invite more violence. Disagreements centered on the practical: How would they go to Birmingham? Who would go? How would they pay for it?[31]

CORE, the sponsor of the Freedom Ride, was also trying to figure out what to do. In Washington, James Farmer favored canceling the rest of the Freedom Ride, fearing it had become too dangerous. But the Freedom Riders in Birmingham wanted to finish what they had started. At the bus station, every bus driver refused to take them on to Mississippi because of the danger. Disappointed, they made plans to fly to New Orleans for a symbolic finish at the May 17 anniversary rally for *Brown v. Board of Education*.

When the Nashville students found out that the Freedom Riders were flying to New Orleans, they decided to send a group of ten to Birmingham to complete the original bus trip. On Monday afternoon, Nash finally reached Farmer on the phone. Having only a vague idea who she was, he was taken aback by their plan. He told her that the students were proposing a "suicide" mission that could result only in a "massacre." Nash shot back, "We can't let them stop us with violence. If we do, the movement is dead." A reluctant Farmer gave his okay.[32]

The students in Nashville spent Tuesday picking the new Freedom Riders and raising money. Older blacks in Nashville, who had been supportive of the sit-ins, were reluctant to donate money for something so dangerous. Finally, after much persuading, the students convinced the Nashville Christian Leadership Council to donate nine hundred dollars for bus fare and other expenses. They picked a coed team of ten—two white and eight black, including John Lewis. Diane Nash would stay behind in Nashville to coordinate the effort and handle the phones; she volunteered for the ride, but her friends insisted she was too valuable as an organizer to risk injury. The new riders made out wills or gave Diane sealed letters for their families in the event they were killed.[33]

The attacks in Anniston had made international news, and officials in the Kennedy White House were now following events closely. Just two weeks earlier President Kennedy had made a strong speech in support of civil rights. Now a few determined Freedom Riders were trying to stretch his rhetoric into real support. The Freedom Rides in fact threatened to expose the soft underbelly of Kennedy's governing coalition as he simultaneously tried to retain the support of both African Americans and white southerners. Any support for civil rights would alienate white southerners, especially the powerful southern committee chairmen on Capitol Hill. But a failure to act threatened to alienate black and white voters outside the South, and no one in his administration felt comfortable sitting idle while people were beaten and possibly killed.

With the June 4 Vienna summit with the Soviet leader, Nikita Khrushchev, approaching, Kennedy desperately wanted to avoid a domestic crisis that the Soviets would exploit in their propaganda. But his aides argued that the White House had little power over local officials, who dodged Kennedy's calls. Some argued that the president had broad power, even under existing law, to intervene in the South, but Kennedy worried about the political costs of invoking the "Little Rock method," calling in the army or National Guard.[34]

Justice Department officials found out about the Nashville group's plans when a concerned observer in Nashville phoned them early Tuesday morning. They were as clueless about who they were dealing with as Farmer was. Robert Kennedy placed an urgent call to his aide John Seigenthaler, who had been dispatched to Birmingham to deal with the situation, telling him to get the students to stop. When Seigenthaler called Nash directly, she brushed him off forcefully. People will die, he warned. Then "others will follow them," she replied.[35]

The situation appeared less ominous when the new group arrived in Birmingham on Wednesday, May 17. The police let all the other passengers off the bus but kept the Freedom Riders on board for another three hours, taping over the windows to prevent the white mob outside from seeing in. As the Freedom Riders disembarked, a stout man with a round jowly face, white hair slicked back with Brylcreem, and old-fashioned black plastic glasses came up to them. It was Theophilus Eugene "Bull" Connor, the notorious Birmingham commissioner for public safety—the city's police chief. Not only did he look like a southern sheriff straight out of central casting—a malevolent Boss Hogg—but he had earned his reputation for using police violence to stop civil rights. Since taking over in the 1930s, Connor had used his authority with brutal efficiency to break up union meetings, stop racial activism, and enforce his ideas about morality (banning certain movies and comic books he disliked). With a little smile, he told the Freedom Riders they were being arrested for their own protection.[36]

Birmingham was already notorious. The *New York Times* writer Harrison Salisbury captured it best:

> No New Yorker can readily measure the climate of Birmingham today. Whites and blacks still walk the same streets. But the streets, the water supply, and the sewer system are about the only public facilities they share . . . Every channel of communication, every medium of mutual interest, every reasoned approach, every inch of middle ground has been fragmented by the emotional dynamite of racism, reinforced by the whip, the razor, the gun, the bomb, the torch, the

club, the knife, the mob, the police, and many branches of the state's apparatus . . . In Birmingham neither blacks nor whites talk freely . . . Birmingham is the Johannesburg of America.[37]

Two days after the arrests, Bull Connor and his henchmen loaded the seven African-American Freedom Riders into unmarked station wagons in the middle of the night. Connor told the young activists that he was going to personally escort them back to Nashville for their own protection. As they drove off, John Lewis wondered if this was what it felt like to be lynched. As they drove out of Birmingham, Connor tried to engage the students in friendly banter. Most of the students were too scared or confused to respond, though Catherine Burks, a Birmingham native, sarcastically invited Connor to breakfast in Nashville. When they arrived at the Tennessee border, the cars pulled by some railroad tracks as Connor, laughing to himself, kicked the students out. The Freedom Riders were alone in the heart of the Deep South in the middle of the night.

Fearful of being seen by unfriendly whites, the seven activists kept to the shadows as they hiked along the tracks. A little ways down the road, they stumbled on a pay phone, which they used to make a collect call to a surprised and relieved Diane Nash. She could send a car to drive them back to Nashville, or she could figure out how to get them back to Birmingham, where a second group of Freedom Riders was soon to arrive. Unsure what to do, the group promised to call Nash back soon and set off down the road.

About a mile farther on, they found a shack. The elderly black man who answered the door would not let them in, unnerved by the appearance of a group of well-dressed young African Americans on his doorstep at four a.m. After his wife berated him for rudeness, he relented. At daybreak, they sent the old man off with a few dollars for food because they had not eaten in the two days since leaving Nashville. After taking an unusually long time to return, the old man sheepishly admitted that he had gone to three different stores because he worried that whites might notice the purchase of an unusually large amount of food.

While they waited for breakfast, Lewis updated Nash. She told them she would send a car to pick them up, but where did they want go? Nashville or Birmingham? Back to Birmingham, the seven agreed. The car arrived, and as they began the drive, the radio reported their plans; word had leaked out. A large mob, maybe as many as three thousand hostile people, met the Freedom Riders at the bus station. While the Birmingham police held the crowd at bay, the driver announced, "I have one life to give and I'm not going to give it to CORE or the NAACP."[38]

Early Saturday morning Greyhound finally found a driver willing to take the nineteen Freedom Riders (their numbers had been expanded by reinforcements) to Montgomery. They were the only passengers on board, and they traveled escorted by state troopers, a police airplane, and a posse of reporters. When they reached the Montgomery city limits a couple of hours later, the plane vanished and the state police cruisers peeled off. The bus arrived at a deserted and strangely quiet station.

As the Freedom Riders stepped off the bus, people poured out of neighboring office buildings, out of side streets, and out of alleyways. In an instant, the hostile mob overwhelmed the riders. John Lewis saw "every makeshift weapon imaginable"—baseball bats, chains, pipes, bricks, even rakes. The mob jumped the first people they saw, in this case an NBC cameraman and a *Life* photographer. With the mob momentarily distracted, several Freedom Riders jumped a wall and slipped into the federal courthouse. The five black women in the group managed to pile into a cab with an African-American driver and speed off to safety.

Not everyone was so lucky. Jim Zwerg, one of the white Freedom Riders, was beaten unconscious. Even when Zwerg was out cold, one man still held his head up so men, women, and children could take turns hitting him in the face or kicking him in the balls. Someone smacked a wooden soda crate against John Lewis's head, knocking him unconscious. When he came to, he found the assistant state attorney general standing over him reading a state injunction banning the Freedom Riders for disturbing the peace.[39]

About fifteen minutes into the riot, the Montgomery police arrived on the scene but did little to break it up. Lester Sullivan, the police chief, had said that his officers had "no intention of standing guard for a bunch of troublemakers." The police watched as William Barbee, a young African-American divinity student who had volunteered to pick up the Freedom Riders at the bus station, was beaten unconscious, but they arrested an elderly white couple who helped some injured Freedom Riders.

Unexpectedly, Floyd Mann, the head of the state highway patrol, intervened to save Barbee's life. Holding the mob back at gunpoint, Mann called in sixty-five of his men to stop the riot; it would take them more than an hour to arrive. The cavalier and unprofessional attitude of the Montgomery police shocked Mann. When none of the city's white-owned ambulance companies would transport Zwerg, he used his own car.[40]

The next night, Sunday, the Freedom Riders gathered at Ralph Abernathy's church for a rally. Diane Nash, having spent a frantic few hours on the phone in Nashville trying to account for everyone's whereabouts, rushed to Montgomery for an emotional reunion. By early evening, the church was packed with almost fifteen hundred people. Outside stood a mob at least that large. The city and state police were conspicuously absent. Only the presence of a handful of federal marshals personally sent to the city by Bobby Kennedy kept the mob at bay.

The Reverend Solomon Seay, a well-known local minister, urged the people in the church to keep calm. The Freedom Riders led everyone in singing "We Shall Overcome." As they sang, they could hear rocks and bricks bouncing off the church's walls. Some were dipped in gasoline and lit on fire; one came crashing through a window. The marshals used tear gas to keep the mob at bay, and the smell filtered into the church. Some African Americans in the audience took out guns and knives.[41]

Meanwhile, Martin Luther King was in a basement office on the phone pleading with Bobby Kennedy, who could hear the white mob in the background. Kennedy promised that reinforcements were on the way, then pressed King to delay any further Freedom Rides. King was noncommittal, promising only to raise the issue with the other activists. Kennedy tried to lighten the mood with a joke, but King admonished him to remember the "bloody confrontation" that loomed.[42]

Diane Nash stood just outside the door, and she was pissed. Until this point, she had been the one dealing with the Justice Department. When King arrived, he had assumed the leadership position without hesitation. King's treatment of Nash reflected a mix of personal hubris, sexism, and general condescension toward SNCC. Certainly the White House preferred dealing with King, seeing him as an adult voice of reason to counter the militant students and as the clear leader of the African-American community. Nash felt that King and the SCLC, having done little for the Freedom Rides in the beginning, were now trying to take them over. She cared little about retaining credit for SNCC; she wanted to make sure King did not make any concessions that compromised the integrity of the Freedom Rides. Pushed out of the room and out of the decision-making process, she was reduced to shouting from the hallway, "What's going on?"[43]

King emerged to report on his conversation, hinting that he was inclined to support Kennedy's request for a temporary pause. Farmer leaned toward continuing but was noncommittal. Nash bluntly rejected any call for a halt: "We can't stop it . . . after we've been clobbered." Nash's determination stiffened Farmer's resolve, and he decisively rejected the offer. King agreed to tell Kennedy, but Nash sensed his reluctance.[44]

Just then the second set of federal marshals arrived. Tear gas meant to disperse the crowd forced the marshals, who lacked face masks, to retreat. The mob surged forward, throwing more rocks through the church windows. A growing panic gripped those inside the church. Tear gas drifted in through the open and broken windows. A few people had to be restrained from running out into the mob because of the smell. The body heat of fifteen hundred people quickly turned the church into a sauna. Fear and sweat mixed together. The mob reached the front door, trying to break it open, but the marshals pushed them back. Movement songs filled the air and broke the tension.[45]

In Washington, the Kennedy administration struggled with what to do. Justice Department officials worried about what would happen if the mob got inside the church. Floyd Mann asked the attorney general to send more troops. President Kennedy authorized a military deployment to Birmingham, but the president was spending the night in the Virginia countryside and the order had to be delivered by helicopter for his signature. The delay might mean the troops would not arrive in time to help the besieged church.[46]

In the meantime, the Alabama National Guard arrived at the church. Under tremendous White House pressure, Governor John Patterson, who had done nothing to discourage the attacks against the Freedom Riders, grudgingly declared martial law. The National Guard drove the crowd away from the church, possibly saving the lives of all inside, but ordered everyone to remain in the church. King appealed to the White House, asking what kind of society allowed peaceful churchgoers to be terrorized inside a church all night. President Kennedy pressed Governor Patterson. The governor said he could not guarantee King's safety, an argument the president dismissed out of hand. Finally, at four-thirty a.m., the White House and the Alabama National Guard worked out an agreement allowing the people trapped inside safe passage home.[47]

That evening more than twenty activists gathered to debate the next move. The publicity surrounding the Freedom Rides had drawn the movement's major players to the home of Richard Harris, a prominent pharmacist and one of the famed Tuskegee Airmen. As the meeting began, Nash, a heavily bruised and bandaged Lewis, and the other students sprawled on the floor as the older activists—Martin Luther King, his aides Wyatt Tee Walker and Ralph Abernathy, and James Farmer of CORE—sat among them on couches and folding chairs. Farmer, calling the Freedom Rides "my show" and insisting that CORE volunteers be the ones to finish the journey, rubbed the students the wrong way. "He talked loud and big," recalled Lewis, but Farmer "had no leverage." The CORE volunteers had not yet arrived in Montgomery—some doubted they ever would—and the sheer number of student riders who were already present (more than twenty) gave them control.[48]

Bolstered by advice from Ella Baker, Nash challenged King to join them on the bus to New Orleans. "Where is your body?" the other students murmured in assent, using SNCC's shorthand for a willingness to put oneself in harm's way. Ever since King had hesitated to join the Atlanta sit-ins for fear of arrest, many of the students had become disenchanted with him for claiming the mantle of African-American leadership without exposing himself to the same risks. King's lieutenants stepped in for him, arguing that King's high profile made him more valuable as a fund-raiser and speech-maker than as one additional person on the Freedom Rides. Wyatt Walker added that King had the more immediate fear of substantial jail time because he was on probation for an earlier arrest.

"I'm on probation," someone interrupted.

"Me too," added another student.

King held his ground. "I think I should choose the time and place of my Golgotha," he said, referring to the site of Jesus' crucifixion.[49]

The students shook their heads in disbelief at King's Jesus imagery—it was just the kind of self-aggrandizement they resented. Someone sarcastically called King "De Lawd," which quickly became SNCC's private nickname for him.[50]

The next day an expanded group of twenty-seven students, divided into two teams, left Montgomery by bus for Jackson, Mississippi. Governor Patterson ordered a convoy of National Guard jeeps and police cruisers—with reporters' cars, more than forty vehicles in all—to accompany the first bus. More than one thousand National Guard soldiers lined the highway. At the border, Mississippi state police and National Guard troops took over from their Alabama counterparts.

The Freedom Riders hated the armed escort. James Farmer derisively called it a "military operation." They thought it sent the message that the only thing that could protect African Americans foolish enough to challenge segregation was massive military force. When the Freedom Riders arrived at the bus station in Jackson, the local police promptly arrested them on trumped-up charges. Simultaneously, the police arrested another group of Freedom Riders arriving at the train station.[51]

Nash had recruited these new Freedom Riders from the Nonviolent Action Group at Howard University. NAG was one of the many student groups that had sprung up during that initial wave of sit-ins, and it had already conducted numerous demonstrations in Washington, which was still a segregated city. It was technically a "Friends of SNCC" affiliate, meaning it had not been represented at the original meeting in Raleigh; but over time it would contribute more than its share of important SNCC figures—Stokely Carmichael, Hubert Rap Brown, Cleveland Sellers, and Charles Cobb.[52]

Carmichael had picked up Nash's call at NAG's headquarters, and he promised to come as soon as he and the others could reschedule final exams. In fact, Carmichael was so busy cramming that he had missed all that had happened to the Freedom Riders in the week since Anniston. Having the group travel by train from New Orleans was a tactical decision, designed both to lessen the chance of attack by having people arrive from different directions and by different means and to dramatize the breadth of segregation.[53]

The arrests in Jackson were part of a secret deal between the White House and the governors of Alabama and Mississippi. Robert Kennedy got Governor Patterson and Governor Ross Barnett to agree to protect the Freedom Riders; in exchange for this promise, the attorney general agreed not to interfere when Jackson police arrested the

Freedom Riders, even though the laws under which they would be charged were constitutionally suspect. Kennedy simply wanted the Freedom Rides off the front pages so they did not harm the president politically.[54]

The students in Jackson, however, refused bail. The state framed its case narrowly, essentially charging the students with trespassing. Jack Young, the Freedom Riders' attorney, sought to make a larger point; as one Freedom Rider said, he wanted "to defend us as human beings having the right to be treated like human beings." In the courtroom, when he rose to make his statement, the judge turned his back. When Young finished, the judge issued a sixty-day sentence without saying another word.[55]

The riders' decision to accept jail time angered Robert Kennedy, who worried that it would derail his carefully negotiated agreement and keep the story in the news. The arrests actually did move the story off the front pages even as the Freedom Rides continued over the rest of the summer, revealing a dilemma that would confront activists time and again. Violent and dramatic confrontations generated media coverage that put public pressure on national politicians to intervene; but jail hid the Freedom Riders from public view, depriving the media not only of dramatic pictures but of personal contact with them. For the media, out of sight was out of mind. As the novelty of protest wore off, activists engaged in a difficult balancing act: to stage demonstrations that provoked a violent response from white segregationists, without allowing anyone to actually get killed.

The prisoners were sent to the city jail and then transferred to the Hinds County prison farm. After three weeks, twenty-two Freedom Riders were transferred to the notorious Parchman prison farm. Located in Sunflower County, deep in the heart of the Delta, Parchman was the inspiration for many of the Delta's most famous blues songs. Prisoners were subject to horrible abuse and forced to toil for long, hard hours in the prison businesses. The system was so successful that the prison actually turned a profit for the state. The transfer of the Freedom Riders there forced Mississippi officials to accept the uncomfortable truth that the publicity and arrests had actually increased the number of riders.[56]

As he stepped off the bus at Parchman, Stokely Carmichael came face-to-face with Deputy Tyson, "a massive red-faced, cigar-smoking cracker," who welcomed them by ordering them to strip naked. For two hours they stood naked in the processing room as the guards leered at them through the bars and made crude jokes about the size of their penises. They were marched down to communal showers and handed flimsy T-shirts and shorts. Only Bevel's humor broke the tension: "What's this hang-up about clothes? Gandhi wrapped a rag around his balls and brought down the whole British Empire!"[57]

The prisoners were segregated by race and confined two to a cell. Their only reading material was a small copy of the Bible. For many the isolation and loneliness of Parchman was the hardest part of the experience. As Lewis recalled, "The monotony was tremendous." Showering became a treasured ritual. "It was the only time we could actually see each other," remembered one prisoner. The trip down the hallway became a time to joke, to banter, and to raise one another's flagging spirits.[58]

The women were housed in a different wing, in circumstances both better and worse than the men's. The women's cells were more closely packed and on a day-to-day basis were less supervised by the guards, reflecting a sexism that assumed women were not as dangerous as men. The women used this relative freedom to hold long discussions about everything from the nature of nonviolence and politics to Greek and Roman history. They even managed to hold ballet lessons, shouting instructions across the way.[59]

When the guards and prison officials did turn their attention to the women, however, it exposed the unique vulnerabilities of female activists. The white women were peppered with questions about whether they slept with black men or wanted to marry them. Male guards watched them when they undressed and showered. The prison doctor conducted repeated and invasive vaginal examinations yet so ignored their basic health needs that one pregnant Freedom Rider suffered a miscarriage in prison. The harassment stopped short of actual rape but was designed in every other way to humiliate.[60]

They had little contact with the outside world, and were allowed to send only one (censored) letter a week. One week John Lewis used his to explain to his professors why he would miss graduation at the American Baptist Theological Seminary. Another week he had to write to the AFSC to explain why he planned to stay in the South instead of going to India.[61]

For Nash, the lack of information was a constant worry. Rumors abounded about the treatment inside the prison, but the careful control that Mississippi officials exercised over access limited publicity. Besides letters, the only news that outsiders heard from Parchman came from clergy (the only visitors allowed) and the occasional Freedom Rider who made bail and was released.

Very quickly, though, the Freedom Riders grasped that Governor Barnett had forbidden the guards to inflict serious injury or death. Once the young activists gauged the limits of the guards' physical abuse, they became bolder in their taunting and trash talking as the relationship between guards and prisoners evolved into a psychological battle of wills. The prisoners kept up a constant round of freedom songs to maintain solidarity and taunt the guards. When Deputy Tyson threatened to take away their mattresses unless they stopped singing, one prisoner thrust his mattress up against the bars and declared that Tyson could have the mattress but would never control his soul; a chorus of amens and the song "Aint' Gonna Let Nobody Turn Me Round" filled the jail. Stokely Carmichael and his cellmate, Fred Leonard, refused to relinquish their mattresses out of sheer stubbornness. The frustrated guards turned a fire hose on them and then made them sleep with the windows open.[62]

Virtually unknown to the students in Atlanta and Nashville before the Freedom Rides, Carmichael emerged as an important force within SNCC during the time in Parchman. Right away John Lewis noticed his skill at "starting an argument and winning it." And Stokely argued over everything. He argued with the Nashville contingent about nonviolence and the utility of hunger strikes, and he argued with the guards about their treatment of the prisoners. Carmichael was full of brio and swagger, always wanting to be the toughest activist, always projecting a larger-than-life personality. When the guards slapped the wrist-breakers—handcuffs with a T-shaped rod—on him and flipped him over and over, he did not give in.[63]

The inmates went on a hunger strike; Carmichael had opposed it and then vowed to be the last person to eat. At the end of seven days, when he had outlasted everyone, Carmichael announced:

My name is Stokely Carmichael. I'm in with Freddy Leonard. You may have heard of us. We're the youngest in here. Myself, I'm a very young man but I intend to be fighting the rest of my life so I'll probably be in jail again. So probably will some of you. That's why I want you to remember my name. Because if we are ever in jail again and any of you even mention the words *hunger* and *strike*, I'm gonna denounce you properly. I'll be the first to denounce you. You can tell everybody that. That if you are ever in jail with Stokely Carmichael, never ever mention anything about any hunger strike.[64]

Carmichael's attitude represented more than just macho posturing. The hunger strike and the mattress incidents revealed ideological and philosophical differences that lurked just beneath the surface. The Freedom Rides were attracting a new wave of students with only a casual knowledge of one another and competing notions of nonviolent protest. Carmichael and the others from NAG were disdainful of the "seminarians" from Nashville with their talk of "Christian love" and the "beloved community." They viewed nonviolence mainly as a tactic, useful in particular times and places, and preferred to think about the movement in terms of power and politics.[65]

On July 7, after twenty-two days in Parchman and forty days in custody, the Freedom Riders were released on bond. Unknown to the prisoners, CORE had paid their bond, in keeping with its strategy to maintain the possibility of appeal under Mississippi law. But bailing out the first batch of prisoners from Parchman did not change the Freedom Rides' dynamic. Volunteers continued to pour into Mississippi over the summer, at least twenty-five separate groups. More than three-quarters came to Mississippi—an inversion of the sit-ins, which had mostly occurred outside the Deep South. By the end of 1961, at least four hundred people had been arrested for participating in a ride; more than three-quarters were younger than twenty-nine.[66]

The Freedom Rides put SNCC back in the national spotlight and revived civil rights protest. A good gauge of the riders' appeal was the hero's welcome awaiting the Parchman prisoners. James Farmer and Stokely Carmichael stepped off a plane in New York City to be greeted by television cameras and a large crowd of supporters. Carmichael spent much of July convalescing at his parents' home and raising money for SNCC. The benefits often took place at the opulent apartments of rich supporters in Manhattan, and he never stopped marveling at the weirdness of standing in a posh apartment while telling "war stories" about his time in Parchman. "It was classic Americana," he thought, "shades of runaway darkies and Northern audiences."[67]

Much of the credit for the success of the Freedom Riders belonged to the indefatigable Diane Nash. No one did more to keep the rides going, to raise concerns about the prisoners in Parchman, and to focus the debate not on the legality of the arrests but on the immorality of discrimination. When the Freedom Ride Coordinating Committee met with Bobby Kennedy in early June, the attorney general pushed for a switch from the direct action of the rides to voter registration; it was Diane Nash who challenged him. The real issue, she told him, was the illegal arrests in Mississippi and the conditions in Parchman.[68]

She was King's conscience as well. By late June, many of King's advisers were openly questioning the value of the Freedom Rides, even going so far as to plant a story in *The New York Times* suggesting that movement leaders were planning to slow the flow of Freedom Riders to Mississippi. The ministers around King found the rides unsettling; they saw them as chaotic and out of control. They were much more comfortable with something like the Montgomery bus boycott, with its clear hierarchy and neat organizational structure. But they were also motivated by jealousy and a fear that SNCC and CORE would eclipse the SCLC in the public eye. After the *Times* story appeared, Nash berated King into disavowing the story and redoubling his public support for the rides.[69]

Ironically, the Freedom Rides also boosted the status of Martin Luther King. He may have played a small role in the drama, but he was still the face of the movement to the general public. The publicity surrounding the rides generated a huge windfall of donations for the SCLC. SNCC still shared space with the SCLC, and Julian Bond saw the mailbags arriving every day, full of small contributions from people all over the country inspired by the Freedom Rides. The SCLC kept most of the money, doling out only a small share to SNCC. The selfishness rankled Bond and other SNCC members.[70]

SNCC's inability to fully capitalize on the Freedom Rides showed how the summer drama masked the questions about its long-term viability. In fact, the excitement generated by the rides almost tore SNCC apart. The philosophical debates in Parchman between NAG and the "seminarians" about the utility of nonviolence manifested real divisions on the outside; one group emphasized direct action, like sit-ins and Freedom Rides, and another argued that SNCC should work to register voters, using the political system to leverage change. As the Freedom Ride drama unfolded over the summer of 1961, SNCC had a running debate at its monthly staff meetings—in Louisville in June, in Baltimore in July, in Nashville in August—about the right balance between direct-action protests and voter registration work. By August, the debate had become so acrimonious that it threatened to destroy the fragile coalition formed at Shaw.

Bobby Kennedy and others in his brother's administration were eager to channel the energies of civil rights activists away from direct action and toward voter registration, especially in the wake of the Freedom Rides. They thought this approach would lessen the hostility of white southerners to the president by getting the demonstrations off the front page and adding thousands of new Democratic voters to the rolls. They also hoped to unite the different civil rights groups—the SCLC, SNCC, CORE, and the NAACP—under one umbrella, where they would presumably be easier to control. The administration arranged for the Taconic and Field foundations to fund the project, the liberal Southern Regional Council to administer the funds, and the IRS to give the group, the Voter Education Project (VEP), tax-exempt status.[71]

Bobby Kennedy did everything possible to corral the major civil rights groups into joining the VEP. He sent his aides Burke Marshall and Harris Wofford to meet with not only King and Roy Wilkins, the head of the NAACP, but with SNCC leaders, like Charles McDew, who were not serving jail time. He recruited the singer Harry Belafonte, who had a personal relationship with both sides, to lobby for voter registration. In early June, Kennedy even met directly with Nash and a group of students to push his plan.[72]

Bobby Kennedy used all the tools at his disposal to get the students to go along with his plan. He leaked stories to *The New York Times* to make it seem as if the VEP were a foregone conclusion. He hinted at draft exemptions for those who worked with the VEP and extra legal aid for jailed protesters. Harris Wofford framed the choice bluntly as persecuted or prosecuted. The students could either help the Kennedys prosecute white officials for denying blacks the vote, or they could end up prosecuted themselves for violating local segregation ordinances.[73]

The Nashville group led the charge against the plan. Skeptical about the government's motives, Nash worried that the administration was trying to control the movement for its own purposes. But the Nashville group's objections ran deeper than that. As John Lewis noted, "We had gotten this far by dramatizing the issue of segregation, by putting it onstage, and *keeping* it onstage." Direct action was a powerful weapon because it exposed the immorality of segregation and offered the protester a sense of involvement and redemption not possible with voter registration. Those who saw nonviolence as a life philosophy, not just simply as a tactic, opposed the voter-registration plan for fundamental reasons.

Some Raleigh veterans, including Chuck McDew and Charles Jones, supported the idea. Working with national leaders on issues of common cause like voting rights, they believed, would further the overall movement, even if the two sides disagreed about the utility of direct action. It would give SNCC greater visibility, elevating it to the first tier of civil rights organizations. And the money would help it compete with the older, established civil rights groups, especially since SNCC was nearly broke, barely able to pay the rent on its one-room office.

Among the most vocal advocates of the voter-registration plan was Tim Jenkins, who in addition to being part of NAG was also the vice president of the National Student Association (NSA). The mostly white NSA had been involved in the student civil rights movement since the Greensboro sit-ins. Like Carmichael and others in NAG, Jenkins thought of the civil rights movement as a political struggle. Unlike Carmichael's, Jenkins's politics were conventional. He disagreed strongly with the Nashville group, which he thought was "addled by piety" and overly committed to a "pain and suffering" model of civil rights activism. One of Jenkins's main goals was to "nudge" people like Nash and Lewis "off that ethereal plane of the 'beloved community'" to consider the political realities.[74]

The Nashville group viewed the civil rights struggle as essentially a moral crusade. They thought about change in terms of personal growth—African Americans would overcome their fear, and whites would develop a sense of shame. In their idealism, they believed that ending segregation was about changing hearts. They believed that because they were willing to lay their bodies on the line, SNCC activists held a moral authority that outstripped crass political calculations. Human rights were not subject to negotiation. It was a conflict between youthful idealism and youthful ambition.

The debate came to a head at SNCC's August retreat in Nashville. Jenkins raised the money for the retreat from foundations connected to the White House, hoping to push SNCC toward his vision of political activism. SNCC organized the meeting like an academic seminar. "Understanding the Nature of Social Change" had an extensive reading list and mandatory class attendance, and everyone had to write a paper on the topic of their choice at the end. Prominent labor leaders, historians, psychologists, and other academics interested in questions of race led scholarly sessions. Ella Baker, Martin Luther King, Harris Wofford, and other public figures talked about their activism. The guest list reflected SNCC's high visibility in the aftermath of the Freedom Rides.

The style of the Nashville seminar incorprated SNCC's idealized notions of contemplative study and the style of participatory decision making inherited from Lawson's workshops and nurtured by Ella Baker. Study and debate were hallmarks of the SNCC style, something that both the idealists and the pragmatists agreed on. Everyone believed that one key component of success was knowledge, whether it was a thorough grounding in Gandhi before the first sit-ins or an in-depth analysis of the historic roots of segregation. "Once we decided we were going to make our move," Chuck McDew said, "we felt we were making it with the widest possible knowledge and information."[75]

Everyone had a voice in SNCC. Eschewing the hierarchy of the NAACP and the SCLC, the discussions sprawled across several days as every point of view received consideration. No idea or plan was too outrageous, especially in the heady aftermath of the Freedom Rides. One person suggested flooding the NAACP convention with SNCC supporters to try to take over the organization, arguing that SNCC could use the NAACP's money and membership base more effectively. Someone else suggested trying to take over the SCLC instead.[76]

The students had not felt this much enthusiasm since Raleigh. Many thought they were on the cusp of fundamental change, and in their youthful hubris and impatience, they were convinced they could make it happen quickly. "We talked in terms of five-year plans," McDew said, "like Mao in China." He and others believed that if they lasted longer than five years, they ran "the risk of becoming institutionalized and spending more time trying to perpetuate the institution than having the freedom to act." The freewheeling discussions mixed personal conversations about whether people were prepared to drop out of school for full-time activism with abstract musings on the nature of segregation and tactical debates about how closely they should cooperate with the White House.[77]

A few weeks later SNCC took one more stab at resolving its future during a retreat at the Highlander Folk School in Tennessee. "After four days in those mountains," Chuck McDew recalled, "the beloved community nearly fell apart because everyone was arguing so passionately." Nash wanted SNCC to focus exclusively on direct action, because she saw voter registration as a betrayal of the Gandhian ideal of the sit-ins. Charles Jones, who had been in Rock Hill with her, explained her logic: "Voter registration involves politics; politics is dirty; therefore voter registration is dirty and immoral. Nonviolence is truth and good; therefore to attempt to mix voter registration and nonviolence is immoral." The direct-action and voter-registration factions were equally divided, and McDew, SNCC's chairman, threatened to cast the tie-breaking vote in favor of voter registration. Nash was uncompromising, even hinting that she would quit to start a separate organization.[78]

Only the intervention of Ella Baker held SNCC together. She suggested that SNCC divide into two wings, one for direct action and one for voter registration. They would cooperate but stay focused on separate goals. Baker's imperfect compromise brought the students back together, and they elected Diane Nash to head the direct-action wing and Jones to head the voter-registration wing, with McDew as the overall chairman. James Forman, a teacher and sometime journalist, came on board as executive secretary, and the notoriety of the Freedom Rides opened the door to new sources of funding.[79]

Many SNCC members now considered themselves full-time activists. John Lewis and James Bevel were finished with school, so the decision was easy. But others, like Diane Nash and Julian Bond, had dropped out to devote themselves fully to the movement. Still others, notably Stokely Carmichael, were deeply torn. In the end, Carmichael, honoring a promise to his parents, returned to school in September, though he wavered every time he looked at a newspaper or listened to the radio.

Everyone again spun off in separate directions. Nash and Bevel headed back to Jackson to start "Move on Mississippi." Charles Jones set up shop in Albany, Georgia, where the Justice Department suggested a couple of promising targets for a voter-registration drive. Bond was back in Atlanta with James Forman, who would soon convince him to become SNCC's communications director. McDew and Barry headed to McComb, Mississippi, to join up with Moses.

With everyone headed in different directions, the Highlander meeting looked a lot like the Raleigh conference. But the eighteen-month gestation of SNCC that had started with the first sit-ins had come to an end. The tentative sense of group identity evident in Raleigh had blossomed into a tight-knit community of young activists. They were a "circle of trust" and a "band of brothers," they pledged.

Bob Moses made good on his promise to Amzie Moore and returned to Mississippi in the summer of 1961 to help with voter registration. C. C. Bryant, the NAACP head in nearby Pike County, read in *Jet* about the SNCC "voter-registration team" headed to the Delta and offered to host him. So Amzie Moore sent Moses—at this point the entire "team"—over to meet Bryant, and in July Moses opened a little office on the second floor of the black Masonic Hall in McComb. Quietly a new front in the war for civil rights had opened.[1]

Mississippi was not like the rest of the South. The depth of segregation, the rural poverty, the white population's ignorance, and the black population's illiteracy were all much greater. Whites retained nearly absolute control of the formal levers of political power. Only one in twenty black Mississippians was registered to vote; in Pike County, barely one in a hundred. A state that was 43 percent black had no black officeholders. With the exception of the Freedom Rides, the civil rights movement had hardly penetrated the state. The wave of sit-ins that had swept across the South in 1960 barely made it to Mississippi; the first substantial demonstrations came a year after Greensboro.[2]

There was no public debate to speak of. For the most part, the newspapers and television stations supported segregation. Mississippi's two senators—James Eastland and John Stennis—were considered the biggest roadblocks in Congress to the passage of any civil rights bill. African Americans who spoke out risked economic ruin at best, a lynching death at worst.[3]

Simply registering to vote was a challenge for black Mississippians. Aspiring voters had to fill out a twenty-one-question form. The "understanding clause" required applicants to be prepared to read and explain the meaning of any one of the 285 sections of the Mississippi Constitution. Complete authority rested with the local registrar. Those who passed these hurdles still had to pay a poll tax as long as eighteen months before the election to be eligible to vote.[4]

Moses saw his biggest challenge as simply getting local blacks to overcome their "deeply entrenched habit of deference to, as well as a genuine fear of, white power." As he started knocking on doors, he would introduce himself as "C. C. Bryant's voter-registration man" and ask if they were interested in trying to register. Most people shrugged him off: "Don't want none of that mess here, boy," or "Now y'all be careful foolin' around with white folks' business." Moses considered it a substantial victory just getting someone to make "the mental leap" to see voting as a real possibility.[5]

On August 15, he accompanied three local African Americans to the courthouse in nearby Amite County to register. The registrar was by turns belligerent and dismissive, dragging out the registration process from ten a.m. until after four p.m. As this was going on, whites—other county employees, citizens in the courthouse on business, the sheriff, and some deputies—kept peering in to see the African Americans' audacity. On the drive back to McComb, a highway patrolman who had been in the registrar's office pulled the car over; when Moses asked for the officer's badge number, he was arrested for interfering with the police.[6]

At the jail, Moses shrewdly used his one telephone call to ring the Justice Department, deliberately shouting the name and number to the operator so everyone in the station could hear. Moses had the number only because on his way out of Atlanta, Chuck McDew had slipped it to him for emergencies. Luckily, John Doar picked up the phone and agreed to accept a collect call. After Moses loudly relayed his story, the police offered to suspend his ninety-day sentence in favor of a five-dollar fine. He refused to pay and spent two days alone in jail.[7]

When an NAACP lawyer arrived to post bail, Moses made him wait as he pondered the ethics of the NAACP covering a fine that he refused to pay on moral grounds. The exasperated lawyer asked, "Boy, are you sure you know what you're about?" But Moses felt he might make a larger philosophical and tactical point about the limits of justice and whites' ability to instill fear by agreeing to serve his sentence. After some deliberation, Moses allowed the NAACP lawyer to pay his fine so he could be released.

A week later Moses brought another two black farmers to register. On the way to the registrar's office, three whites, including the sheriff's son and the son-in-law of the local state representative, attacked them. Billy Jack Caston, the son-in-law, bloodied Moses with numerous blows to his head from the butt end of his knife. After his attackers ran off, Moses continued on. The appearance of Moses at the courthouse—gashes on his head and blood all over his clothes—so freaked out the registrar that he simply closed the office on the spot.[8]

At a mass meeting that night back in McComb, Moses argued that black Mississippians could not let white violence intimidate them from exercising their right to vote. He promised to try again tomorrow. To hammer home the message that he was not afraid, Moses filed assault charges against Billy Jack Caston. No one in the county could recall a black man ever pressing charges against a white man. The fast trial ended in Caston's acquittal, but Moses had made his point.[9]

Moses's courage sparked the interest of the local teens Hollis Watkins and Curtis Hayes, who showed up at his door.

Peering in, Watkins asked, "Are you Martin Luther King?"

"No," replied a surprised Bob Moses.

"We heard he was here."

"I don't know anything about that. I'm here to teach Negroes how to vote," Moses explained.[10]

On the spot, the two decided to join SNCC. "The thing that really drew me to SNCC," Watkins explained, "was that here was a group of people that saw that a problem existed and said, 'Hey, we're going to go all out to do what we can.'" In contrast, the NAACP felt like a movement "in the closet."[11]

SNCC members converged on McComb as word of Moses's arrest filtered back to Nashville and Atlanta. Marion Barry and Charles Sherrod, another Nashville veteran, arrived on August 18 with instructions from Diane Nash to teach McComb's teenagers the nonviolence techniques they had learned from Lawson. In charge of SNCC's direct-action wing, Nash came up with the idea of "Move on Mississippi," a SNCC project to expand the confrontational nonviolence of the sit-ins and "jail, no bail" into a statewide campaign that would grind Mississippi to a halt. With Moses's arrest, McComb became the perfect place to test the strategy. By late August, more than a dozen SNCC members—now dubbed field secretaries—were in the area, and it became SNCC's first sustained organizing campaign.[12]

On August 26, Watkins and Hayes—who had attended every workshop since that first conversation with Moses—staged a sit-in at McComb's Woolworth's store, the first action of its kind in the county. They were promptly sentenced to thirty days in jail. Four days later, fifteen-year-old Brenda Travis and four others staged a sit-in at the bus station lunch counter. The four friends received eight-month sentences for disturbing the peace. Brenda was expelled from high school and sentenced to a year in juvenile prison.[13]

Bob Moses's view of direct action had evolved since he arrived in Atlanta; he now viewed these protests with ambivalence. As Amzie Moore reminded him, the right to eat at a restaurant meant nothing to those too poor to afford the hamburger. Moses was happy to see people "involved in something they were enthusiastic about," but he was developing a much more expansive vision of voter registration as something that could transform local communities.[14]

Unnerved by the newly aggressive African-American community, local whites responded with more violence. On another trip to the Amite courthouse, a group of them jumped Moses, severely beating Travis Britt, a SNCC member from New York. John Hardy, a veteran of the Nashville sit-ins, took a group of local residents to register in nearby Walthall County. The registrar told him to stop "messing" in other people's business and "go back to where you come from." Then—in a government office in public view—the registrar waved a gun at him to emphasize the point. As Hardy turned to leave, the registrar smacked him over the head with the butt of the gun and arrested him for inciting a riot and resisting arrest.[15]

Marion Barry found the transition from the relatively safe and predictable violence of the sit-ins to the dangerous and volatile protests of rural Mississippi frightening. In Nashville, the violence was confined to the sit-ins themselves, and the combination of their public nature and the relative professionalism of the city's police checked the whites' worst excesses. But in McComb, whites were so angry and primed that the violence was random and unpredictable. At night, white gangs, often armed with shotguns, cruised by the houses where

SNCC activists stayed, preventing Barry from getting a good night's sleep. The constant threat of attack was psychologically exhausting.[16]

Nothing revealed the brutal lengths to which whites would go more than the murders of Herbert Lee and Louis Allen. Lee, a farmer with nine children and a founder of the Amite County NAACP chapter, had been driving Moses around the county. Though he attended Moses's voter-registration classes, he had not tried to register. He caught the attention of white segregationists when they saw him writing down their license plate numbers as they spied on the registration workshops. In the late afternoon of September 25, Lee sat in his truck at a local cotton gin passing the time with a few friends, including Louis Allen, when E. H. Hurst, a state representative, drove up. The two men were about the same age and had played together as boys. Now Hurst waved a gun at Lee as he cursed his civil rights activism.

"I'm not going to talk to you until you put the gun down," Lee said from inside the truck.

As Hurst tucked the gun into his pants, Lee slid away to get out of the truck on the far side. Seeing Lee move, Hurst ran around the truck, pulled out the gun, and shot Lee once in the head, just above the ear.

Lee's body lay on the ground for several hours. No one in the small crowd dared to touch him. Worried Amite County authorities, when they summoned the McComb coroner, refused even to mention Lee's name over the phone.

Hurst claimed he shot Lee in accidental self-defense. He said that Lee had threatened him with a tire iron and that the gun had misfired when he tried to hit Lee with its butt. Both the black and white witnesses confirmed Hurst's story. A coroner's inquest the same day supported Hurst's story, and local authorities declined to file charges.

John Doar heard about the killing from Moses and promised to investigate. But by the time he got an FBI agent to go from New Orleans to McComb—there was no FBI office in the entire state of Mississippi—Lee was already buried, preventing a clean look at the bullet wound. Even with Doar's pressure, the FBI conducted only a perfunctory investigation.

A fearful Louis Allen confessed to Moses that he had lied at the inquiry and that Hurst had killed Lee in cold blood. Allen's revised testimony allowed Doar to convene a grand jury, but Justice Department lawyers believed the FBI had bungled the investigation so badly that no indictment was likely. Without an indictment, Doar told Moses, he could not provide Allen with federal protection. The two men were in the ironic and awkward position of offering Allen the same advice as Hurst's friends: Lie for your own safety.[17]

Even though Allen took the prudent path of sticking to his earlier lie, word leaked out about his offer to the Justice Department. Six months later a deputy sheriff confronted Allen about his FBI testimony, breaking his jaw with a flashlight as punishment. On January 31, 1964, while Louis Allen stood alone in his front yard, an unknown assassin shot him dead with three shotgun blasts.[18]

In the wake of Lee's murder, McComb's black teenagers were itching to act. On October 4, about a hundred students walked out of classes at the high school and over to SNCC's small headquarters looking for guidance. They wanted to march the eight miles to the county courthouse in Magnolia. Moses and McDew talked them out of it, pointing to the danger of arriving after dark. As a compromise, they got the students to agree to a prayer march in front of the McComb city hall. The students were excited and unruly, and the SNCC members had trouble restraining them. As McDew watched the students surge toward the city hall, he thought of Gandhi's words: "There go my people, I have to hurry to catch up with them for I am their leader."[19]

At the city hall, Curtis Hayes climbed the steps and knelt to pray. For this act, the city police arrested him. Then Hollis Watkins moved forward to pray, and he was arrested as well. Then the police decided to arrest all the protesters. As the scene unfolded, local whites, perhaps as many as several hundred, gathered to watch. The more they saw young blacks carrying signs with freedom slogans, defying the police, and willingly accepting arrest, the more agitated and angry they became.

They turned their fury on Bob Zellner, who had just joined SNCC as its first white organizer. People in the crowd hit Zellner, and someone started to choke him; it was another reminder that local whites saw white solidarity as crucial to the preservation of segregation. McDew and Moses pushed forward to help their friend and possibly saved him from being strangled to death before the police pulled them away. While the chief of police held Zellner, whites kicked him in the head, gouged at his eyes, and punched him. A handful of FBI agents on the scene stood idly by taking notes. When Zellner regained consciousness, he was in the city jail. The police hauled him into a car, drove him fifteen miles outside of town, and dumped him.[20]

The mass arrest of more than one hundred young people threw McComb into chaos. The local police, unnerved by the demonstrations, arrested C. C. Bryant, who had not even been at the city hall, simply because he was the head of the local NAACP. Then they rounded up every SNCC member they could find. Charlie Jones escaped the dragnet by disguising himself as a butcher in the shop below the SNCC office. Worried that those in jail might be lynched, Jones made two phone calls: to John Doar at Justice for legal help and to Harry Belafonte for bail money.[21]

Under pressure from local whites, the principal of the black high school told the arrested students that to return to their classes, they would have to accept a reduction in their grades and sign a pledge renouncing further demonstrations. When the students refused, the principal threatened them with expulsion. The next afternoon 103 students turned in their textbooks and left school rather than accept the principal's harsh terms.[22]

Moses and the others opened a temporary school nicknamed Nonviolent High, teaching about seventy-five of the expelled students in one big room. For McDew, trying to teach McComb's youth reinforced his understanding of the totality of white control. One student kept asking a puzzled McDew if his history class would cover "the War for Southern Independence." Finally it dawned on him that the student was talking about the Civil War. Nonviolent High ended when Moses and the other SNCC workers were sentenced to four months in jail for their role in the October 4 demonstration. SNCC convinced a school in Jackson to accept most of the students, while a smaller group accepted the principal's demands and reentered the local high school.[23]

In early November, McComb's entire SNCC staff entered the Pike County jail. Moses smuggled out a letter that SNCC workers passed around as an inspirational touchstone for anyone who had served or would serve jail time:

> I am writing this note from the drunk tank of the county jail in Magnolia, Mississippi. Twelve of us are here, sprawled out along the concrete bunker . . .

Later on Hollis will lead out with a clear tenor into a freedom song. Talbert and Lewis will supply jokes, and McDew will discourse on the history of the black man and the Jew. McDew, a black by birth, a Jew by choice, and a revolutionary by necessity, has taken the deep hates and loves of America, and the world, reserved for those who dare to stand in a strong sun and cast a sharp shadow.

In the words of Judge Brumfield, who sentenced us, we are "cold calculators" who design to disrupt the racial harmony (harmonious since 1619) of McComb into racial strife and rioting; we, he said, are the leaders who are causing young children to be led like sheep to the pen to be slaughtered (in a legal manner). "Robert," he was addressing me, "haven't some of the people from your school been able to go down and register without violence here in Pike County?" I thought to myself that Southerners are exposed the most, when they boast.

It's mealtime now: we have rice and gravy in a flat pan, dry bread and a "big town cake"; we lack eating and drinking utensils. Water comes from a faucet and goes into a hole.

This is Mississippi, the middle of the iceberg. Hollis is leading off with his tenor, "Michael row the boat ashore, Alleluia; Christian brothers don't be slow, Alleluia; Mississippi next to go, Alleluia." This is a tremor in the middle of the iceberg—from a stone that the builders rejected.[24]

After their release from prison in late December, Moses and the other SNCC workers retreated from McComb to regroup. On the surface, McComb seemed to have been a setback. SNCC had registered very few voters, Herbert Lee had been murdered, and more than a hundred high schoolers had had their education interrupted. Local whites had demonstrated the power of determined, illegal, and violent resistance. The federal government lacked the will and power to stop them.

Yet SNCC activists did not come away from McComb discouraged. The protests resolved the debate between direct action and voter registration by fusing the two. McComb marked an important expansion in SNCC's organizing from the small cadre of activists behind the sit-ins and the Freedom Rides. Here SNCC activists saw the power of mobilizing an entire community, especially its young people, in a protest campaign.[25]

Perhaps most important, McComb marked the emergence of Bob Moses as the most influential voice in SNCC. By the end of 1961, he commanded the respect of the members by connecting the personal courage necessary for organizing to the larger ethical and philosophical questions about the meaning of social and political equality. Unlike the Nashville seminarians, who turned the morality question inward to focus on personal redemption, Moses turned it outward on society to the morality of inequality. Unlike the politically oriented NAG faction, Moses saw political power not as an end in itself but as a tool for a more just society. And he did it with a style that was at once soft and commanding. "With Bob," Stokely Carmichael noticed, "it was as though he were not at all interested in impressing you with his brilliance or importance . . . In fact, quite the reverse, as if he were trying to transcend and efface his presence so as to concentrate on the problem, the idea. And get you to move beyond the superficial and focus on ideas too."[26]

Moses spent the winter of 1962 camped out at "Freedom House," SNCC's group home–headquarters in Jackson; he wrote Jane Stembridge that he had "left the dusty roads to run the dusty streets." The handful of people living there—Nash and Bevel, the Nashville veterans Paul and Catherine Brooks, and Bernard Lafayette—were trying to make Jackson the center of SNCC's efforts in Mississippi. In such a situation, as the journalist David Halberstam observed, "the bond of friendship becomes stronger than those the members have with any of their family members or previous friends."[27]

Nash and Bevel found romance, and in late 1961, they secretly eloped, surprising everyone. They seemed like an odd match. She was a pretty, self-effacing middle-class girl from Chicago; he was a fiery, charismatic poor boy from the Deep South. She was preppy; he wore a stylized skullcap as a fashion statement. She was methodical and disciplined; he was freewheeling almost to the point of being erratic. For all the outward differences between the two, however, they saw in each other mirror images of a committed young activist.[28]

The elopement revealed something about Nash's personality. In a crisis situation, she could be fierce and fearless—confronting Mayor West in Nashville, keeping the Freedom Rides going, standing up to Martin Luther King. But when it came time to take credit for her work, she would often slide into the shadows. These two sides reflected the uncertain role of women at the time, caught between the domesticity of the 1950s and the feminism of the 1970s. She was part of a generation of women coming into their own at a time when they were still expected to defer to men.[29]

After McComb, Nash and Bevel decided to focus their direct-action work on urban Jackson. With a black college and relatively large black middle class, Jackson was the part of Mississippi that most resembled the areas where the sit-ins had been effective. But the Jackson effort produced mixed results. They were great recruiters, especially Bevel, who had a natural rapport with young people, striking up a conversation on a street corner or a basketball court and winning the kids with tales of the Freedom Rides. But the Jackson police cunningly outmaneuvered SNCC. Rather than arresting demonstrators en masse—and creating a media sensation—or drawing the attention of the federal government with violence, the police arrested the SNCC organizers for "contributing to the delinquency of a minor." Bevel, Nash, and Bernard Lafayette were sentenced to three-year terms, though all temporarily stayed out of jail by posting bail.[30]

In April 1962, Nash, three months pregnant with her first child, dropped her appeal and presented herself to the court to serve her time. She said that she could "no longer cooperate with an evil and unjust court system." She specifically confronted the question of going to jail while pregnant. "I have searched my soul . . . and concluded that in the long run this will be the best thing I can do for my child. Since my child will be a black child, born in Mississippi, whether I am in jail or not, he will be born in a prison."[31]

Her action put the authorities in the uncomfortable position of either jailing a pregnant woman or looking weak by dismissing the charge. To avoid the embarrassing situation, the presiding judge actually pleaded with Nash to continue her appeal and, when she refused, sentenced her to ten days in jail for contempt. Nash's gambit made the Mississippi authorities squirm, especially after she released her own jailhouse letter, and they dropped all the charges.[32]

While Nash and Bevel were recruiting in Jackson, Moses expanded his contacts in the small community of Mississippi civil rights activists by traveling with Amzie Moore. During this time he forged a friendship with an NAACP organizer based in Jackson, Medgar Evers. A native Mississippian and World War II veteran, Evers was frustrated by his inability to register to vote after returning from Europe. In 1954 he became the first full-time NAACP worker in the state.

The two men recognized the need for cooperation among the state's civil rights groups. By 1962, SNCC, the SCLC, CORE, and the NAACP all had people in Mississippi. At the national level, these groups competed intensely, and not just for the media spotlight; they had real differences of philosophy and tactics and, of course, petty personal rivalries as well. But on the ground in Mississippi, these differences meant little. Amzie Moore was from the NAACP and worked closely with Bob Moses. Money to support Bevel and Nash's efforts came from SCLC funds, even though their tactics and relationships were rooted in SNCC.[33]

In August 1962, Mississippi's activists revived the Council of Federated Organizations (COFO), which had been founded to coordinate opposition to Governor Ross Barnett's program of massive resistance to any change in the racial order. In the basement of a church in Greenwood, Bob Moses and James Forman representing SNCC, James Bevel and Jack O'Dell for the SCLC, Dave Dennis from CORE, Amzie Moore and Aaron Henry for the NAACP, and Wiley Branton for the Voter Education Project agreed that COFO would coordinate voter registration and other protests to cut down on turf wars and the competition for funds. To placate the NAACP's national leadership, Aaron Henry was named the head of COFO. In a sign of SNCC's influence with ordinary Mississippians—and recognizing the importance of the McComb protests in linking voter registration and direct action— Moses was named program director for voter registration. Over the next several years, COFO would be the main coordinating civil rights organization in Mississippi, with SNCC contributing the most bodies to the cause.[34]

Charles Sherrod and Cordell Reagon arrived in Albany, Georgia, in late 1961, fresh from Mississippi, eager to spread the McComb-pioneered and grassroots-oriented combination of voter registration and direct action to other parts of the Deep South.

Just twenty-four and eighteen respectively, the two men were already veteran activists with long track records: the sit-ins, Rock Hill, the Freedom Rides, Parchman prison. Reagon had been the youngest participant in Lawson's nonviolence workshops.

But the young SNCC activists were still learning, and for every hard-won insight gained in McComb, Albany would offer a pessimistic rejoinder. Most important, Albany demonstrated how national media coverage and the ambitions of Martin Luther King, Jr., could complicate and undermine SNCC's grassroots strategy.

The city of about 56,000 was in the southwest corner of Georgia— the part that most closely resembled the Deep South because of its cotton plantations and peanut farms. One contemporary visitor observed that Albany's approximately 23,000 black residents "lived in a tightly segregated society from cradle to grave."

But a keen observer could see cracks in the edifice. Robust membership in the local NAACP branch had produced what one historian called "a small but significant" voting bloc. African-American civic groups lobbied the city government for integrated voting booths and civic improvements in the black neighborhoods. Albany thus represented an interesting mix of the near-complete white power of McComb and the political thawing that had made the Montgomery bus boycott possible.[35]

Albany also had Police Chief Laurie Pritchett, who turned out to be one of the movement's canniest opponents. Determined not to make the same mistakes as other sheriffs, he studied the movement carefully, reading King's books. He saw that nonviolent protest provoked a violent reaction, so he ordered his men to exercise restraint, and he prepared for "jail, no bail" by arranging to disperse arrested protesters over the surrounding area. If there was one law enforcement officer in the South ready for the movement, it was Laurie Pritchett.[36]

Sherrod and Reagon used the McComb strategy of recruiting from the young. High schoolers and students from the local Albany State College for Negroes gravitated to the two young men. Reagon, no older than they, cut an especially dashing and romantic figure, holding them in rapt attention with his personal story of the Freedom Rides. Gradually, the two won the trust of the town's teenagers and college students by casually hanging out with them on basketball courts and playgrounds.[37]

They held their first protest on November 1, 1961, to test the new federal regulation barring segregation in interstate bus stations. Sherrod, Reagon, Charles Jones, and Jim Forman took the bus from Atlanta to Albany. Ten Albany policemen met them at the terminal. Later in the day, when a group of Albany State College students entered the white waiting room, the police ordered them to leave. They complied and reported the violation of the Interstate Commerce Commission regulation to the Department of Justice.

It was the first civil rights protest of any kind in the Albany area. The SNCC organizers viewed it as an important psychological breakthrough. "From that moment on, segregation was dead," Sherrod reported back to his SNCC colleagues. The November 1 protest and the enthusiasm of the city's youth compelled wary black leaders to organize the Albany Movement, a coalition of seven local civic groups and SNCC. The Albany Movement's cautious founding statement called demonstrations "detrimental to the best interests" of the city and hoped that future protests would not be necessary, but its very formation underscored the quickening tempo of action.[38]

Soon after the founding of the Albany Movement, Pritchett arrested five local teens for sitting in at the bus station. On December 10, he arrested Zellner, Forman, and half a dozen others for sitting as an integrated group on a train through Albany. The arrests sparked mass protests among the city's young people, and SNCC members converged on Albany in support. At the trial of Zellner and the others in the first group, nearly three hundred high school and college students marched through the downtown. The police herded them into an alley for two hours before arresting them. The next day two hundred more demonstrators were arrested at a prayer vigil on the courthouse steps. The governor sent 150 National Guard troops to the city.[39]

A few days later Martin Luther King arrived at the invitation of the Albany Movement. The city's black leaders lacked confidence in themselves and in SNCC and believed that only King's presence would bring change. SNCC members had unsuccessfully opposed inviting him, arguing that Albany's mass movement was far stronger than one man. King led a group of more than 250 protesters to the courthouse, where they were arrested. He declared he would spend Christmas in jail rather than accept bail. He joined the more than 700 people arrested between Tuesday and Saturday, overflowing the city's jail and spilling over into surrounding counties.[40]

The large number of arrests marked a victory for Chief Pritchett's strategy. As the black community strained under the burden of the mass arrests, tensions between SNCC and local leaders grew. As one

SNCC member said, "We were naïve enough to think we could fill up the jails . . . We ran out of people before [Pritchett] ran out of jails."[41]

As SNCC had predicted, King's arrival shifted the focus from the mass movement to the great preacher. Unfortunately, King arrived in Albany after several months of whirlwind travel in Europe and America. Exhausted and jailed, he relied on his lieutenants to run things, especially the unpopular Wyatt Tee Walker. Local leaders, hoping for a breakthrough, were disappointed by the SCLC's disorganization. Having bought into King's myth, they were surprised to find that he did not have a plan or easy access to bail money. Walker's answer was to try to organize more mass demonstrations to force the Kennedy administration to intervene.[42]

But after receiving advice from James Gray, the editor of the *Albany Herald* and an old family friend, Attorney General Robert Kennedy told reporters the federal government would not intervene in Albany: "Real progress requires local leaders talk it out." The next few days were chaotic. While King was in jail, SNCC and the Albany Movement leaders called a press conference to criticize the SCLC's strategy and assert that local people controlled the movement in Albany.[43]

The combination of federal indifference, King's eagerness to free those imprisoned, and Pritchett's wily strategies pushed local activists to accept a deal. Confident that the federal government would not intervene, local whites took a hard line. They agreed to release King and all local prisoners without bail but insisted on high bail for SNCC members. But on the larger question of integration, white leaders offered only vague verbal promises to desegregate the bus and train stations and to appoint a commission to explore integrating lunch counters and other public facilities. And significantly, they would not commit to anything in writing. In exchange for these promises, the Albany Movement agreed to halt all demonstrations. Summing up SNCC's attitude to the deal, one activist said to another, "You curse first, then I will."

SNCC's skepticism turned out to be well-founded, as Albany's white leaders immediately backed away from the deal. King's departure from Albany diverted media attention, which returned to the city only when he came back in July 1962 to stand trial. The judge sentenced him to forty-five days in jail. King again vowed to serve his full sentence. Seeking to defuse national attention, white leaders secretly paid King's fine and then lied to the media that an "unidentified well-dressed Negro male" had paid it. A bewildered King had no idea what had happened.[44]

SNCC activists urged King to get arrested and go back to jail. McComb had demonstrated to them the importance of activists going to jail not as a moral statement but as a message to the community about their commitment to the local movement, and they urged King to make that point now through an arrest. King demurred, saying that bail money was lacking and that he needed to be free to raise money. SNCC pressed King, arguing that the local protests needed him to bolster their fading momentum and hopefully provoke federal intervention. King again demurred. "Ralph [Abernathy] and I have families," he said; "we are bound to be a little more conservative than you guys who have no responsibilities." SNCC went ahead with more protests anyway, shaming King into getting arrested again. As one SNCC organizer said, King "can't let a SNCC person be more willing to go to jail than himself."[45]

The hope that King's arrest would reinvigorate the protests by provoking federal intervention proved illusory. President Kennedy publicly urged negotiations but refused to commit federal resources to what he called a local matter. Local whites now had little incentive to negotiate in good faith, and the defiant segregationists held their ground. Civil rights activists strained to sustain the momentum and keep the community focused. On August 10, in a bitter concession, the Albany Movement suspended further demonstrations, trying to spin it as a "good-faith" gesture to promote new negotiations. The next day King and his staff left Albany. With King went most of the national media.[46]

Even though the national spotlight had moved on from Albany, SNCC continued to work with the local activists, staging protests and suing the city for harassment. Zellner and Sherrod staged a sit-in at the train station and further flouted segregation law by sitting together at their trial. Albany whites continued to couple violence with a dogged unwillingness to engage in any kind of good-faith negotiations with the city's African-American residents, holding changes in the racial order at bay throughout 1963 and into 1964. When a court ordered that the public library be integrated, the city removed every chair in the building. Instead of allowing African Americans to use the public pool, city leaders sold it to a private corporation that ran it as a whites-only private club.[47]

For SNCC activists, Albany demonstrated the challenges of sustaining a local movement in a national context and the dangers of relying on King's celebrity. Keeping the momentum required more money than either SNCC or the local black community could raise easily. Albany also underscored a new vulnerability: a determined and savvy white elite had pioneered a game plan for frustrating progress. Whites in Albany were no more committed to segregation than in other parts of the rural South, but Chief Pritchett taught them that if they kept the violence to a minimum—or at least out of sight of reporters—the protests would not become a national story and federal officials would have no credible excuse for intervention.

During 1962 and 1963, the alumni of the McComb and Albany protests spread out across the South, to Holly Springs, Laurel, Hattiesburg, Cleveland, Vicksburg, and Ruleville in Mississippi; to Terrell and Lee in Alabama; to Baton Rouge, Louisiana; and Danville, in Virginia. Impressed by Zellner's courage, Forman put him in charge of his own organizing project in Talladega, Alabama. The SCLC had more money and the NAACP had more members, but neither organization engaged in SNCC's kind of grassroots organizing and protest. By the measure of field activists, SNCC, with about fifty full-time organizers, was already the largest civil rights organization in the South.

Three things distinguished SNCC from other civil rights organizations: a willingness to set up shop in the rural Deep South, a focus on grassroots community organizing, and a capacity to flood the zone with activists when trouble arose. Bob Moses described SNCC's grassroots orientation as the bouncing-ball model of organizing: Hang out on a street bouncing a rubber ball, and kids will come talk to you. Eventually, the ball will roll under a house, and you'll start talking to the adults when you go to retrieve it. Such immersive total community organizing was time- and labor-intensive, but SNCC activists were convinced it was the only way to break the rural South's culture of segregation. SNCC had largely abandoned direct-action protests, like the sit-ins and Freedom Rides, in favor of community organizing that attacked deep-seated political and economic inequality. Many saw the moral theater of direct-action protests as a distraction from these substantive issues. When trouble did occur, as in McComb or Albany, SNCC would mobilize a large number of activists to sustain community interest, draw media attention, and increase pressure on segregationists, but such mobilizations were always in service to concrete local demands for political and economic opportunity.

SNCC's ability to run several operations across the Deep South at once was made possible by the increasing sophistication of its headquarters in Atlanta. Forman imposed order and discipline on SNCC's chaotic operations and set out to build a fund-raising program by opening satellite offices in six northern cities. Many of the students resisted, arguing that fund-raising would create the kind of bureaucracy that stifled the NAACP and distracted King. But by mid-1962, SNCC was over $10,000 in debt, and important foundations, like Field and Ford, hesitated to make direct grants to a bunch of kids, so Forman prevailed. The fund-raising initiative succeeded in doubling SNCC's income in 1963 to $309,000.

To aid in fund-raising and promote the organization, SNCC sold posters and buttons. The posters were a big hit. Based on photographs taken by Danny Lyon, a white University of Chicago student who became SNCC's first staff photographer in 1962, SNCC sold more than ten thousand of them for a dollar each, mainly to young people in the North, expanding SNCC's mystique. The most famous poster featured a picture of John Lewis and two other African Americans praying, with the caption, "Come let us build a new world together." Another famous one showed a menacing Mississippi state trooper with the question "Is he protecting you?"[48]

Fund-raising took SNCC's early leaders out of the field for extended trips. Those selected for fund-raising had an organizational position, as did Chairman McDew, or notoriety from the Freedom Rides, as did Lewis, or they were simply better at raising money than at field organizing, as was Barry. The fund-raising put SNCC on better financial footing but subtly changed the organization as well. Fund-raisers like Barry and Lewis reinforced SNCC's Gandhian public image even as that work deprived SNCC's field operations of some of its most passionate adherents of Gandhian protest.[49]

Julian Bond's savvy management of SNCC's communications office was equally important. In McComb and Albany, he realized, northern reporters had trouble covering the movement because they depended for information on duplicitous white officials and indifferent southern newspapers. Bond set out to establish SNCC as the one place to get the facts about what was going on. To ensure credibility, he set up clear guidelines. To the field secretaries, he emphasized the need to distinguish "between being shot at and shot down; between being hit with fists and beaten with blackjacks; between being taken into custody and being arrested; between city, county, and state police." Calls from field secretaries came in at all hours of the day and night; often they were fresh from confrontation, their reports unfolding in a first-telling rush on the phone. He told staffers to keep the emotion and interpretation out of their reports. Bond's credibility with reporters depended on him getting the facts right.[50]

Bond discovered he had a real talent for public relations. Editors tended to see SNCC's press releases as biased, he realized, and were reluctant to allow reporters to rely on them for news reports. So Bond pioneered the trick of first sending a telegram to the attorney general or president requesting assistance and then issuing a press release about how SNCC had contacted Washington. A telegram to Washington was news that editors felt they could report without appearing to have uncritically accepted SNCC's version of events. As SNCC spokesman, Bond had constant conversations with reporters and a steady stream of radio and television interviews, allowing him to develop a confident and polished speaking style.[51]

Bond also grasped the crucial role the main office could play in anchoring SNCC's spread-out operations. After much lobbying, he convinced Forman in 1963 to pay for two WATS (Wide Area Telephone Service) lines, which put SNCC on the cutting edge of 1960s communications technology. In the era of regulated phone service, long-distance charges were high. A WATS line allowed unlimited long-distance calling for a set fee. Each line cost SNCC the princely sum of $300 a month, but they soon proved to be worth every penny, allowing the far-flung local offices easy contact with Atlanta. The communications office had one unbreakable rule: one of the two WATS lines always had to be free so that if field operatives needed to reach Atlanta in an emergency, they would never get a busy signal. Bond established code names for every field office so that when they called collect, he would know who to call back after he declined the charges. The WATS lines ensured that SNCC members in danger were never far out of touch. Bond also used the WATS lines to record interviews with activists in the field, which he would in turn provide to radio stations to use in their news reports. Bond's assistant later said, "No WATS lines . . . ever got more use than SNCC's."[52]

In 1963 the husband-and-wife team of Bevel and Nash became part of the SCLC (Bevel officially, Nash unofficially), drawn in by King's continued preference for the kind of direct-action civil disobedience that SNCC increasingly eschewed. That some in SNCC's original core gravitated to the SCLC is not surprising. Bevel and Nash had always been the strongest proponents of using direct action to make a moral statement about segregation, and they had pushed King to adopt more of SNCC's confrontational style of nonviolence. They successfully pitched a plan for demonstrations in Birmingham that relied heavily on SNCC's early playbook of overwhelming the jails with protesters to focus attention on the immorality of segregation.[53]

Birmingham had a reputation as the most segregated city in America. Iron and steel production dominated the city's economy, whose highly segregated workforce was divided between skilled white workers and unskilled African-American ones. More than any other American city, Birmingham's tightly structured residential and economic segregation in an industrial setting resembled South Africa's apartheid. At a time when many southern cities had already begun the process of desegregating their downtown shopping districts and SNCC was engaged in rural voter registration, the SCLC's goal of ending the petty segregation of lunch counters and restaurants in Birmingham was a throwback to 1960. But changing Birmingham was just one of King's goals. Birmingham was the stage on which King could replicate the success of the Montgomery bus boycott, attract the attention of the federal government, and establish the SCLC as the preeminent civil rights organization.[54]

Shifts in white politics complicated the SCLC's plans. After the Freedom Rides riot, moderates in the city's white business community concluded that a polarizing figure like the public safety commissioner, Bull Connor, would threaten new business investment. Not by any measure were they integrationists; they were pragmatists. Negotiations and gradually controlled change offered the potential for more stability. In late 1962, these pragmatists engineered a successful referendum to replace the city's three commissioners with a mayor and city council. The April 1963 election accomplished the moderates' goal of putting one of their own in the mayor's office. But Connor would not go easily and challenged the results in court. Until a judge decided the issue, Birmingham would have two governments.[55]

This chaotic situation greeted King when he arrived on April 3. Earlier in the day, seven black activists jump-started the protests with a sit-in at a Woolworth's. The city's established black leadership of middle-class businessmen questioned the timing of the demonstrations, interpreting Mayor Albert Boutwell's victory as a signal that whites were ready to engage in negotiations. They viewed the Reverend Fred Shuttlesworth, the local head of an SCLC-affiliated civil rights organization, suspiciously; in the words of the city's black newspaper, he was a "non-responsible, non-attached, non-program 'leader.'"[56]

King confronted a much larger problem, though. Neither Shuttlesworth's group, the Alabama Christian Movement for Human Rights, nor the SCLC had adequately prepared for King's arrival, and fewer people than expected turned out for the first demonstrations. The black community had not been organized or trained in nonviolence. In fact, Shuttlesworth had tried to get King to arrive early to coordinate the nonviolence training. The lack of local preparation was a recurring problem for King and the SCLC, which—unlike SNCC—rarely got involved in the nitty-gritty of local organizing.[57]

To generate public support and test the legality of Connor's just-issued ban on demonstrations, King allowed himself to be arrested on April 12. Connor put King in solitary confinement; it was there that he wrote his famous "Letter from a Birmingham Jail." Ironically, few read the letter at the time, and it had virtually no effect on the protests. With King in jail, the campaign fizzled. President Kennedy called to offer Coretta Scott King moral support, but the Justice Department continued to claim that it had no legal basis to intervene. With its demonstrations losing momentum, and its coffers nearly empty, the SCLC needed to do something fast, before everything fell apart.[58]

Bevel urged King to recruit Birmingham's young people to join the protests, arguing that children old enough to participate in church should be old enough to protest. King, uncomfortable with the idea of putting children in harm's way, hesitated. Soon after his release from jail, he left Birmingham for two days to attend to other business. While he was away, Bevel organized a successful trial children's march. Many of King's aides were shocked by Bevel's insubordination, but the test run impressed King, who then gave the okay for the wide-spread recruitment of children into the marches.

As Bevel laid the groundwork for a children's march, Diane Nash peeled away to organize a memorial march for William Moore. A white postman from Baltimore, Moore had embarked on a quixotic one-man sympathy march through the Deep South wearing a bill-board that said "End Segregation in America" and was murdered along a highway in Mississippi. This was Diane Nash at her best and worst. For her, the moral power of civil disobedience and its tactical utility were inseparable. She saw segregation primarily as a moral problem: the purpose of protest was to expose its immorality. Protest was a religious experience in the truest sense of the idea, an act of re-demption for both the protester and the segregationist-sinner. Such a view fueled Nash's courage and her steely determination and gave her a sense of authority, which made her invaluable at times of crisis.

At other moments her moralism blinded her, and the Moore march was one such moment. Moore's death was a tragedy, but it was not then central to the movement's progress. He had not been testing a constitutional principle as the Freedom Riders were or testifying against a white murderer as Louis Allen was. Her organizing skills were needed in Birmingham, but to satisfy her personal sense of jus-tice, she neglected the larger strategic picture. Although her moral compass made her an admirable and compelling figure, her strategic myopia explains, in part, why she sometimes failed to translate that moral authority into tactical leadership.

On May 2, thousands of African-American children skipped school and gathered at the Sixteenth Street Baptist Church, in the center of the black community. Shortly after noon, they fanned out in groups of ten to fifty, some heading to city hall and others to the downtown shopping district. Given the situation, the mood was light. Onlookers could hear laughing, clapping, and singing. When the police came, the students surrendered quietly, some dropping to their knees in prayer, others breaking out in a freedom song. More than one thou-sand students were arrested that first day, but the child activists con-fused Connor. An officer on the scene remembers Connor "looking concerned, fidgety . . . desperate," as if he were thinking: "What the hell do I do?"

The next day some two thousand schoolchildren marched downtown. At first, the police arrested the young protesters, but the previous day's arrests had nearly filled the city's jails. Connor wanted to turn the 83,000-seat Legion Field into a makeshift jail, but he could not dislodge an ongoing track meet. This was exactly the kind of crisis Bevel and Nash had sought to provoke.

Connor panicked. He blocked key intersections with fire trucks and ordered the firemen to turn their high-pressure water hoses on the marchers. The force of the water sent some careening into the air and tore at exposed flesh. A crowd of African Americans on the side threw bottles, bricks, and other debris at the firemen. Connor loosed the police department's six German shepherds on the crowd. The dogs bit several people. As things veered dangerously out of control, movement leaders called off the demonstration at about three p.m.

A cyclone of activity swept Birmingham. Over the next few days, Connor and the protesters jockeyed back and forth. Activists rushed to the city. Forman and Zellner broke away from the Moore march; Ella Baker flew in from New York City; even the folk singer Joan Baez—piqued by the events—arrived. The press descended in droves—not just the American press, but reporters from around the world, more than 175. A suddenly worried White House sent the Justice Department official Burke Marshall.[59]

A brilliant tactical change by SNCC strategists on the fourth day brought the demonstrations to a crescendo. Rather than have the kids march downtown from a single direction in one large group, they would break them up into small groups, converging from multiple directions. Young people flooded the department stores and office buildings. Others stood in intersections and knelt in prayer. Central Birmingham ground to a halt.[60]

As protesters swarmed downtown, seventy-seven of Birmingham's leading businessmen gathered at the chamber of commerce, within earshot of the demonstrators. A vocal minority, led by the former governor Frank Dixon, wanted to declare martial law, bring in additional police, and arrest everyone. The majority, prodded by the group moderates, wanted to reach a settlement, fearing the chaos would hurt business. Faced with a complete breakdown in civic or-

der, the segregationist minority grudgingly agreed to the broad out-
lines of a negotiated settlement.

A group of black and white negotiators met secretly through the
night. It was an odd group, unrepresentative of either community;
neither Connor nor King was present. The whites represented the
moderate faction—moderate only in contrast to the hard-line attitude
of the die-hard segregationists—and while they were part of the business elite, they were by no means its most powerful or influential
members. The African Americans also included many who had been
on the periphery of the demonstrations—Birmingham's conservative
old guard of middle-class black businessmen, who had been skeptical
from the very start. They too were eager to reach an agreement, fearing that the demonstrations had turned chaotic. Only King's aide
Andy Young represented the demonstrators. The fate of the Birmingham protests rested in the hands of people on the margins of the dispute.[61]

The deal they reached reflected the negotiators' eagerness to bring
an end to the crisis rather than a genuine compromise involving all
parties. The white group agreed to end petty segregation and explore
the hiring of black clerks in department stores; in exchange, the African Americans agreed to immediately halt the protests. White leaders
refused to drop the charges against the arrested demonstrators, however, forcing the activists to come up with about $250,000 in bail
money. In rushing to reach an agreement and in doing so in secret, the
black and white leaders failed to prepare their followers for the compromise settlement and all but guaranteed that the raw feelings of
ordinary citizens would impede future progress.

Many activists reacted angrily to King's willingness to accept the
settlement. Fresh from the hospital, Shuttlesworth accused King of
abandoning the protesters just when they had whites on the defen-
sive. King, on the other hand, was eager to appease the Kennedy administration, especially after the White House persuaded the United
Auto Workers union to donate bail money. King thought the public
relations value of a "victory" and the goodwill of the White House
offset any weaknesses in the settlement. On Friday, May 10, with an
obviously angry Shuttlesworth by his side, King held a press conference, declared victory, and left Birmingham.[62]

Immediately, Birmingham's white businessmen undermined the
legitimacy of the settlement. The business leader Sid Smyer expressed

"the bitterness which every citizen must feel about these demonstrations" and claimed his group had acted only to prevent a "holocaust" provoked by the protests. In a note of smugness, Smyer patted himself and other members of the business community on the back for restoring "racial peace." From condemning the legitimacy of black demands to the suggestion that segregation equaled racial peace, Smyer's comments underscored how white elites eschewed responsibility for the violence and even the basic inhumanity of segregation and did nothing to prepare ordinary whites to accept the agreement. For years, white elites implied that defiance could prevent desegregation. With this agreement, ordinary whites confronted the hollowness of that rhetoric.[63]

Less than twenty-four hours after King declared victory, events on the ground pierced the charade of resolution. On the evening of May 11, about 2,500 whites attended a Ku Klux Klan rally in nearby Bessemer, where the Grand Dragon accused white businessmen of "selling out" white customers for "negro business." Later that night white extremists tried to assassinate King by bombing his brother's house and the Birmingham motel where he was staying. African Americans in black bars and nightclubs near the motel flooded into the street. When several cars of white policemen arrived, the crowd threw bricks and bottles at them, sparking a riot that lasted most of the night.[64]

The Birmingham demonstrations are best likened to an Impressionist painting. Viewed from a distance, they appear to be a great victory for the civil rights movement. They were the largest demonstrations since the start of the sit-ins, forcing concessions from white leaders in a city often considered the most violent and racist in the entire South. Yet the closer one moves to the picture, the more the image blurs. One sees a black community rife with conflicting opinions about the value of protests and divided between the local leadership and King. White hard-liners and pragmatists clashed over how to respond to the protesters. Finally, the politically cautious White House, fearful of alienating southern Democrats, neutered whatever federal power could have done to bring about a solution.

The tactical choices that rescued the protests—and King's reputation—from disaster bore SNCC's signature: the importance of young people, the use of confrontational forms of nonviolent direct action, and a calculated attempt to overwhelm Birmingham and its jail with protesters. King's mistakes in Birmingham—most notably his willingness to sacrifice the local movement for his own goals—came when he deviated from SNCC's approach. More than six years had passed since King had burst onto the scene and become the most famous black man in America, yet he had failed to re-create the success of the Montgomery bus boycott. Birmingham was the closest he had come to recapturing that magic. Ironically, its limited success was made possible only when King adopted SNCC's tactics and strategies.

In the wake of the Birmingham demonstrations, King seized on the idea of organizing a huge march on Washington in order to keep up pressure on the federal government and to rally support for Kennedy's just-introduced civil rights bill. The idea of a highly visible protest march on the capital was not new. Back in 1941, A. Philip Randolph, the head of the Brotherhood of Sleeping Car Porters, then the most powerful all-black union, had organized the March on Washington Movement to pressure President Roosevelt to provide African Americans with better job opportunities in defense industry factories booming with government contracts. In exchange for the Brotherhood's agreement to cancel the march, FDR established the Fair Employment Practices Committee to police the defense industry. Twenty-one years later, Randolph proposed another march to pressure President Kennedy to support vigorous equal employment legislation.[65]

Trying to head off the march, President Kennedy hosted a two-hour meeting with more than two dozen civil rights leaders at the White House. John Lewis, just one week into his term as chairman, represented SNCC. It was his first trip to Washington, and he found meeting President Kennedy and Vice President Johnson, and watching Bobby Kennedy bounce one of his daughters on his knee as he listened, intimidating. Afraid to speak, Lewis kept quiet as the other civil rights leaders refused to give ground.[66]

At a July 1963 organizing meeting in New York City, Lewis's insecurity about his youth was again on display. He was the youngest person in the room by a good decade and the newest leader. Though he was stunned when the NAACP head, Roy Wilkins, ordered some of the dozen or so activists present to leave the room, those who remained—Shuttlesworth, Abernathy, Rustin, Forman, and Lewis—quietly accepted it. Wilkins felt that the meeting should include only the "Big Six" who had been at the White House: Wilkins, Lewis, King,

Randolph, James Farmer, and Whitney Young from the Urban League, an ally of Wilkins.[67]

Privately Wilkins's behavior appalled Lewis. He felt a kinship with King and Farmer and respected Randolph's and Rustin's long history of activism. Lewis likened the attitude of Wilkins and Young to people who came "with an appetite to a meal that had already been prepared by others." Given the hard work that the SCLC, CORE, and especially SNCC had done on the ground in the South, Lewis thought Wilkins had "lost the moral authority" to lead the march. Still, he kept his reservations to himself. He was pleased that Wilkins even included SNCC in the Big Six, given the NAACP chairman's caustic attitude toward it. In situations like this, Lewis had a tendency to fade into the background, conscious of his country roots and darker skin, which distinguished him from Wilkins. Forman and Barry pushed Lewis to be more aggressive, Forman pointing out that in news photos of the planning group, Lewis always stood off to the side. "You've got to get out front. Don't stand back like that," he would tell him.[68]

Lewis's quietness also stemmed from the fact that he agreed that the march should be held, even though many in SNCC opposed it. He thought it would dramatize the struggle for civil rights and educate the country about the issue, and any form of action was a good idea. His basic endorsement put him at the moderate edge of SNCC's membership. Many others in SNCC expressed suspicion of a showy media event organized by what one member described as "the cautious, conservative traditional power structure of black America."[69]

Much of SNCC members' opposition to the march derived from their increasingly ambivalent feelings about federal intervention. In their most optimistic moments, they still saw the federal government as an ally and potential guardian, but experience had taught them that it was often a paper lion, acting in contradictory and unpredictable ways. The pending civil rights bill, they thought, was timid at best and inadequate at worst. It offered no additional federal protection for activists and did little to protect voting rights.

SNCC proposed a series of nonviolent demonstrations across Washington. The young activists wanted to stage sit-ins at the Department of Justice to protest its unwillingness to protect civil rights workers from the brutality of white policemen, to camp out on the White House lawn, and to swarm congressional offices on Capitol Hill. Shutting down Washington with the same kinds of protests used in the South, they argued, would be the most effective way to grab the attention of the White House and Congress. SNCC's suggestions fell on deaf ears.

In the end, SNCC acquiesced to King's vision, largely because of the support of Lewis and Forman. The march would be a huge rally on the national mall, with the podium erected on the steps of the Lincoln Memorial. Though they doubted that it would produce any concrete accomplishments, Forman and Lewis recognized the visual power of thousands of protesters standing in the shadow of the Great Emancipator as they made the case for civil rights. They worried that SNCC's absence from that picture would undermine its credibility among ordinary black southerners.[70]

The gulf between SNCC and the other major organizations boiled over on the night before the march. Bond and Courtland Cox learned that Whitney Young had circulated advance copies of his speech to reporters; they quickly ran off copies of Lewis's speech to guarantee SNCC its share of the media attention. Lewis soon received a phone call from Bayard Rustin asking him to come to his room to discuss a problem with his speech. A surprised Lewis headed downstairs, racking his brains to figure out what was wrong with it.[71]

The archbishop of Washington had seen the advance copy of Lewis's speech and said the Catholic Church objected to the description of patience as a "dirty and nasty word." A puzzled Lewis could not see why Catholics objected to criticizing patience. Rustin explained that their objection was theological; Catholics believed in the idea. Lewis, the former divinity student, could empathize with a theological objection (even if he did not quite agree with it) and agreed to strike the line. A minicrisis averted, he headed upstairs to try to get some sleep before the march. On the way out the door, though, Rustin warned Lewis that other objections might surface in the morning.[72]

As dawn broke, a constant flow of trains poured into Union Station, and officials braced for the biggest crowd since World War II. People came by car from Los Angeles, by train from Chicago, by bus from Mississippi. They came dressed in their Sunday best and their working denim; they carried signs attesting to their activism: "Martin Wilkerson—20 stitches, Emmanuel McClendon—3 stitches (age 67), James Williams—broken leg." When the unofficial program started at nine-thirty, more than 20,000 stood in front of the Lincoln Memorial.

An hour later the crowd had swelled to 90,000. Throughout the morning, an eclectic mix of entertainers and dignitaries kept the crowd entertained—the folksingers Joan Baez and Peter, Paul and Mary, the opera singer Marian Anderson, the pop star Bobby Darin, Jackie Robinson, and the well-known socialist Norman Thomas. The crowd was so thick by early afternoon—at least 200,000 people—that the organizers moved up the start of the central program an hour to one p.m.

Out of sight of the gathering spectators, a frantic meeting was taking place. The White House had read Lewis's speech and complained about his harsh criticism of the administration, and the other organizers wanted Lewis to tone it down. Roy Wilkins wagged his finger in Lewis's face, complaining about what he saw as (once again) SNCC's double crosses and its juvenile insistence on always being different. As the speeches started, the organizers deputized a small group— Randolph, King, Rustin, Lewis, and the Reverend Carson Blake of the National Council of Churches—to change the speech before Lewis went on.

The others made numerous objections. They wanted Lewis to strike a line comparing SNCC's activism to Sherman's march during the Civil War, and to soften passages questioning the federal government's commitment to civil rights, describing the civil rights bill as inadequate, and calling national leaders "cheap politicians." They wanted to curry favor with the administration, not alienate it. They found Lewis's speech too disrespectful, too angry, and too caustic for their tastes.

Lewis, Forman, and Courtland Cox huddled in a corner to mull the objections. They hated to make any changes. Lewis believed he was speaking not just for himself or for SNCC but for the thousands SNCC had enlisted in the movement. SNCC did more grassroots organizing any other group. They saw Lewis as speaking for ordinary African Americans, expressing their point of view. In the end, however, they concluded that the changes did not undermine the speech's message. So, tucked away in a corner of the Lincoln Memorial, with the early speeches already under way, Forman pulled out a portable typewriter, and they made the changes just in time for Lewis to go onstage.

John Lewis was the third-to-last speaker, followed only by a rabbi and then King to close. It was a coveted spot, considering the disdain the older civil rights establishment had for the young activists. Most SNCC members in on the planning were shunted aside to mundane tasks. Julian Bond spent the day ferrying Cokes to the dignitaries and celebrities on the stage. One can hardly imagine any of King's or Wilkins's chief lieutenants agreeing cheerfully—as Bond did—to do the same grunt work. Today, because of the subsequent attention given King's beautiful and moving words, few people know much about the other speeches given that day, but the inexperienced Lewis gave a terrific speech, one of the best of his young life. Only three years before, the shy young man had been hanging back, intimidated by his worldly peers in Nashville and slightly embarrassed by his simple rural upbringing. Now here he was, speaking before a crowd of perhaps 250,000 and a television audience of many millions. It was a remarkable journey, and the enormity of it hit him only when he finished, looked around, and drank up the atmosphere.

Even after the changes, though, Lewis's speech challenged the optimism of King's "I Have a Dream." He focused on the practical problems faced by activists in the field and the inability of the federal government to adequately protect them. King's speech rarely moved beyond abstraction to bring alive the struggle on the ground; Lewis pointed a finger at the southern congressmen who stymied civil rights bills in Washington and tolerated white opposition. King seemed to see it as less a political problem than as a need to change the hearts and minds of segregationist whites.

In closing, King seemed content to believe that dreams alone could bring about change. "When we allow freedom to ring, when we let it ring from every village and every hamlet, from every state and every city, we will be able to speed up that day when all of God's children— black men and white men, Jews and Gentiles, Protestants and Catholics—will be able to join hands and sing in the words of the old Negro spiritual, 'Free at last, free at last, thank God Almighty, we are free at last!'" John Lewis, on the other hand, concluded with a note of urgency and frustration. "By the force of our demands, our determination, and our numbers, we shall splinter the segregated South into a thousand pieces and put them together in the image of God and democracy. We must say, 'Wake up, America! *Wake up!*' For we cannot stop, and we will not be patient."[73]

. . .

Seventeen days later, on Sunday, September 15, 1963, a few parishion-
ers drifted into Birmingham's Sixteenth Street Baptist Church early
for the annual Youth Day Service. Down in the basement, four teenage girls had sneaked out of Bible class to primp in the bathroom.
They wanted to look nice since kids ran the main service on Youth
Day. Mamie Grier, the head of the Sunday school, poked her head
into the bathroom and told the girls to hurry upstairs.

Just as she arrived on the main floor, a huge explosion rocked the
building. A hidden bomb destroyed part of the church, burying the
basement in rubble. The four girls in the basement bathroom—Addie
Mae Collins, Cynthia Wesley, Carole Robertson, all fourteen, and
eleven-year-old Denise McNair—perished. Never had King's vision
seemed so remote, and never had Lewis's practical emphasis on the
federal government's failings seemed more prescient.

SNCC members rushed to Birmingham. In the two weeks since
the march, they had scattered around the South—Diane Nash was in
North Carolina, Julian Bond was back in Atlanta, John Lewis was taking a short vacation visiting family. They arrived to find a volatile and
chaotic situation. At the scene of the bombing, local blacks threw
rocks at police. Police shot a sixteen-year-old boy in the back for
throwing rocks at a pickup truck full of taunting whites. Two Eagle
Scouts on their way home from a pro-segregation rally shot and killed
a black teenage boy who stumbled across their path.

White officials offered inadequate responses to the bombing.
Mayor Boutwell denounced the "vile perpetrators of this dastardly
deed" but did little else. Birmingham police and the FBI blew the
investigation; not until 1977 would someone be convicted of the
crime. President Kennedy ignored requests by local civil rights leaders to send federal troops to stop the violence. Instead he sent the
former army secretary Kenneth Royall and Earl "Red" Blaik, the legendary West Point football coach. Predictably the two men concluded, "Birmingham will solve its own problems and does not want
outside help."[74]

Martin Luther King presided over a joint funeral for three of the
four girls. (The parents of the fourth girl could not bring themselves
to share their personal grief with the movement.) More than eight

thousand people came for the funeral, filling up every pew and spilling into the street. Some eight hundred clergy, both black and white, attended the service, making it the largest interracial gathering of religious leaders in the city's history. Not a single state or local elected official could be found among the mourners. Nonetheless, King reiterated his commitment to nonviolence: "We must not lose faith in our white brothers . . . You can bomb our homes, bomb our churches, kill our children, and we are still going to love you."[75]

Few in SNCC were that quick to forgive. The bombing of a church on a Sunday shocked the veterans of Rock Hill and the Freedom Rides and Parchman and McComb and all the other violent places of the movement. When Nash and Bevel first heard about the bombing, they indulged in violent revenge fantasies, egging each other on with talk about hunting down and killing the perpetrators. They figured with a little work and some money for bribes they could ferret out the killers. The kind of people who would do this thing, Nash thought, were the kind of people who would brag about it to sympathetic whites, which would make it possible to get them. When John Lewis and Julian Bond first saw the gaping ruin, they stared at it slack-jawed, trying to comprehend the horror.[76]

After the funeral, Bond, Lewis, Nash, Bevel, King, and a few others gathered at their motel, and the talk turned to how to respond to the bombing. Diane pushed for a massive nonviolent siege of Montgomery. The "Move on Alabama," as she called it, would try to paralyze Alabama's capital city by throwing wave after wave of protesters at voter-registration offices, bus stations, airports, and the state capitol. Their goal would be nothing less than to drive Governor George Wallace and other segregationist leaders from office. That night King was cool to Nash's idea, calling it unrealistic, but the SNCC members present liked it. After all, it was their vision of what the March on Washington should have been.[77]

In Mississippi, Bob Moses had similar thoughts, and he would soon propose that state as the ideal candidate for a large-scale campaign. But what Moses had in mind moved far beyond Nash's proposal. The March on Washington and the Birmingham bombing revealed the limits of relying on appeals to white conscience. Moses's Mississippi organizing had convinced him that civil rights were a political question and that African Americans needed real political power to bring about change. He grasped that in a place like Mississippi, where African Americans had been denied meaningful citizenship for so long, voting was also an act of personal redemption and the first step toward social transformation. He searched for a plan that would merge Nash's brilliant strategizing with his belief in the power of the vote to transform both a person and a society.

6. THE DREAMS THAT BREAK YOUR HEART

At the end of the summer of 1963, Bob Moses analyzed the situation in Mississippi in a memo to SNCC's executive committee. While SNCC had established "beachheads" up and down the state, gained the trust of "many" African-American community leaders, and provided the Justice Department with significant evidence of discrimination against black voters, Moses's overall assessment was pessimistic. Mississippi had endured the Freedom Rides, the integration of the University of Mississippi, and direct-action protests with few tangible changes in the state's racial order.

The use of state power and violence were the reasons for white Mississippi's success: "The full resources of the state . . . continue to be at the disposal of local authorities to fight civil rights gains." Whites stymied sit-ins with outlandish bail requests and punitive jail sentences. Local registrars rejected black voter applications with impunity, and state lawyers used every procedural trick available to slow the Justice Department's voter-registration suits to a crawl. Where state power failed, Moses noted, white violence filled the gap.

"What does the movement do?" Moses asked. He proposed bringing a thousand white college students to Mississippi for the following summer to force a voting-rights showdown similar to the federal-state clashes over school integration. Only a major confrontation would generate enough publicity and national media attention to embarrass white authorities and provoke federal intervention. Moses's proposal shows how much SNCC continued to rely on its original strategy of using confrontation to expose the gap between creed and commonwealth, between the ideals of America and the reality of American life, even as it shifted to voter registration. And even as SNCC changed its tactics and emphasis, a consistent thread of optimism was present. For even as he eschewed sit-ins, Moses clung to the belief that moral suasion and democracy could remedy America's failings.[1]

The Freedom Summer of 1964 would be the high-water mark of SNCC's efforts in the Deep South. It demonstrated black Mississippians' hunger for political equality, revealed the possibilities for true interracial activism, exposed the ugliness of white Mississippi's terrorism, and forced federal officials into action. For SNCC veterans, the dreams of 1960—that exposing injustice would end it, that personal redemption could come through activism, that a beloved community could be created where old cliques gave way to a circle of trust—seemed possible that Mississippi summer.

But Freedom Summer also revealed SNCC's ideological Achilles' heel. The fundamental premise of SNCC protests was the idea that Americans tolerated segregation out of ignorance. But at the end of the summer SNCC discovered that moral clarity did not always produce clear political change. When, in pursuit of a decisive electoral victory, President Johnson rejected the moral claims of black Mississippians for delegates at the Democratic National Convention for the political expediency of appeasing white southerners with a narrow reading of the rules, he smothered SNCC's optimism and made many of its members question the value of working within the system. As Julian Bond observed, "We didn't give up on liberalism; liberalism gave up on us."[2]

The idea for Freedom Summer emerged during the summer of 1963, when Tim Jenkins, now a Yale Law School student, brought some of his classmates down to Mississippi to see what—if anything—they could do to help Moses register more voters. Someone in Jenkins's group stumbled on an obscure eighty-year-old Mississippi law allowing voters to cast protest ballots in a primary. Mississippi had passed the law soon after the end of Reconstruction to allow potentially ineligible ex-Confederates to vote. The law students craftily suggested invoking the provision for African Americans denied a chance to vote by local registrars.[3]

In the August Democratic primary, about a thousand blacks cast protest ballots, which were simply thrown out by the Mississippi authorities. In the runoff election three weeks later, activists abandoned the protest ballots in favor of simply having black Mississippians cast unofficial "freedom votes" at churches and other black-run community gatherings; more than 27,000 African-Americans participated. Moses and the others quickly grasped that the Freedom Vote campaign's innovation minimized some persistent hurdles. From a practical perspective, using black institutions, like churches and civic clubs, as polling stations encouraged participation by insulating participants from white violence. Casting a ballot, even an unofficial freedom ballot, gave black Mississippians a tangible connection to the movement and a sense of accomplishment. Finally, the Freedom Vote established a clear record of the denial of black voting rights and made for compelling media copy. Moses and the others wanted to expand the idea for the general election in November.[4]

Allard Lowenstein, a rising young political activist in his early thirties, was an enthusiastic proponent of an expanded Freedom Vote campaign. A graduate of the University of North Carolina and Yale Law School and the author of *A Brutal Mandate*, a book about his travels in southern Africa, Lowenstein had cultivated close relationships with prominent Democrats, including Hubert Humphrey and Eleanor Roosevelt, while teaching at North Carolina State. Lowenstein told Moses he would recruit a large contingent of white college students to return in November to help with an expanded Freedom Vote.[5]

Lowenstein epitomized the naïveté and cockiness that many northern white activists brought with them when they came south. Rather than appreciate how much Moses had accomplished in the last few years, he focused on how little had been accomplished. He saw "a few SNCC kids holding out . . . but the people literally had no hope." With little real feel for the difficulties of grassroots organizing in the rural South, the brash Lowenstein thought he could change the course of the movement. His attitude, and his tendency to place himself and his ideas—not ordinary African Americans—at the center of the story, foreshadowed the tensions that would emerge between white and black activists during Freedom Summer.

While white activists like Lowenstein were part of the SNCC generation and shared its faith in the self-correcting ability of American civic democracy, they brought a "the best and the brightest" hubris to

social justice. Their hearts were in the right place, but they had a superficial understanding of the segregated South and of SNCC's commitment to developing local leadership. In their eagerness (and
hubris), white activists like Lowenstein often unintentionally pushed
aside local activists, failing to always appreciate that color and class
privilege allowed them to negotiate the white South with an ease that
was unimaginable to local blacks.

Mississippi whites reacted hysterically to the arrival of about one
hundred mainly white college students for the November 1963 Freedom Vote, but the mock election was a huge success. At least 70,000
and maybe as many as 90,000 African Americans cast freedom ballots. The vast participation demonstrated the pent-up demand for action among local blacks and exposed the white lie that blacks did not
vote because of laziness or indifference to the democratic process.
Voting made citizenship tangible and drew rural black Mississippians into the movement in the way the sit-ins engaged African Americans in the cities. The novelty of a protest election combined with the
presence of the white college students brought national attention to
Mississippi. While major publications including *The New York Times*
and *Newsweek* covered the Freedom Vote, college papers played up
the story, generating excitement and donations on campuses.[6]

Moses and Lowenstein wanted to follow up this success with an
even bigger effort during the summer of 1964, imagining perhaps a
thousand student volunteers. Such a large number of activists would
generate even more coverage; Moses believed national opinion would
swing decisively toward the movement if segregationists abused and
beat privileged white college students as they did local blacks.[7]

Many Mississippi-based SNCC members reacted coolly to the
plan, because of the tendency of the self-assured volunteers to push
aside local blacks. They advocated limiting the number of whites and
their activities to ensure the development of indigenous leadership.
The differences exposed a growing racial fissure within SNCC. In the
beginning, SNCC had been basically an all-black organization, save
for a few white activists like Bob Zellner. Now more and more whites
were joining SNCC, leading some to wonder if an African-American
freedom struggle needed to be led by African Americans. Newer and
younger Mississippi staff, mostly local kids, tended to have joined
SNCC after the first wave of sit-ins, and their work in Mississippi
made them less patient, less optimistic, than SNCC's founders.[8]

Older veterans like Lewis, Barry, and McDew took a pragmatic view of the plan. They thought SNCC would be foolish not to take advantage of any strategy that drew the nation's attention to the movement and that pressured the federal government to do more in Mississippi. By this time, though, these three were spending less time in the field and more time on the road doing fund-raising and publicity for SNCC. As SNCC had grown, responsibilities had become more segmented and the line between field work and office work more clear. Growth strained the intimacy and loose organizational structure of the earlier years, which had fostered a trust and camaraderie that made consensus easier.

People looked to Moses to resolve the dispute. He philosophically objected to the notion that whites should be excluded. "I always thought," Moses said, "that the one thing we can do for the country that no one else can do is to be above the race issue." Though not oblivious to the problems, he found the philosophical and pragmatic arguments more compelling. When Louis Allen, the lone witness to Herbert Lee's 1961 murder, was himself murdered in January 1964, Moses abandoned his usual reticence and pushed Freedom Summer as a way to draw attention to Mississippi's white terrorism. SNCC and COFO finally agreed to a plan for a large number of white volunteers.[9]

Even before the final okay, Lowenstein charged ahead, crisscrossing the East Coast during the winter, recruiting college students. One recruit marveled at how Lowenstein's rapid-fire, earnest pitch about the potential of an individual to make a difference "made you feel like you weren't doing enough and you weren't caring enough." But the headstrong earnestness that made Lowenstein such a great recruiter ultimately undermined his work on the summer project. For SNCC activists, consensus linked the everyday performance of democracy to the larger struggle for a more democratic politics. The emphasis on consensus frustrated the impatient Lowenstein.

The differences went beyond operating style. Lowenstein was a classic Cold War liberal, fusing a fierce anticommunism with a progressive domestic vision. He wanted SNCC to cut its ties to the left-leaning National Lawyers Guild and the Southern Conference Education Fund. SNCC, on the other hand, was willing to work with anyone or any organization that might help it advance its goals. The days when others could bully the young activists into cutting ties with Bayard Rustin were past. Lowenstein grew frustrated at SNCC's unwillingness to compromise with him. By the time the summer arrived, he had essentially cut his ties to the project, even going so far as to bad-mouth it to some donors.[10]

The friction between Lowenstein and SNCC is indicative of deeper fissures in American society coming into focus. For many SNCC members, the last several years of activism had eroded their faith in the possibility that Kennedyesque appeals to civic confidence could generate a centrist consensus for reform. The continuing ability of white southerners to stave off action with appeals to the value of political consensus had SNCC members wondering if justice and consensus were in fact compatible. During the early planning for Freedom Summer in the late winter and early spring of 1964, these doubts and questions bubbled up, but the practical concerns of organizing such a large project pushed them aside.[11]

More than twelve hundred students applied to join Freedom Summer. The applicants were the young and educated offspring of America's middle and upper middle class. Nearly half came from just three states—New York, California, and Illinois—and the great majority came from cities and suburbs, where the average income was far above the national average. White volunteers outnumbered African Americans by a five-to-one ratio. Students under twenty-one needed parental permission to participate, so the average age of the applicants was about twenty-three, and 20 percent had already graduated from college. Most had already had some involvement with the civil rights movement, generally on-campus activism or fund-raising. Summing up the group, one observer praised their idealism and optimism but worried that the combination of youthful arrogance, affluence, and the mood of the era created an inflated sense of "specialness and generational potency."[12]

The race and class background of the group is understandable, given the financial resources necessary for participation. Not only would the volunteers be making no money that summer, they would have to pay for their transportation to and from Mississippi, cover all their living expenses, and have access to an additional $500 for bail. One reason so few African Americans applied is that SNCC had trouble getting charitable foundations to subsidize volunteers' expenses.[13]

Before traveling to Mississippi the volunteers attended a training session at Western College for Women in Oxford, Ohio. The training included lectures on the history and politics of Mississippi, advice on what to do if arrested, and role-playing games simulating encounters with hostile whites and nervous African Americans.[14]

Most of the new volunteers stood in awe of the SNCC veterans, describing them with a cloying naïveté exemplified by one who wrote, "You can always tell a CORE or SNCC worker—they're beautiful." The veterans were ambivalent about being idolized. Consequently, many of the summer volunteers found them cold, aloof, and distant in person. One volunteer thought the veterans "looked down on us for not having been through what they had." The veterans, on the other hand, were not always sure the volunteers appreciated Mississippi's dangers. During the screening of a CBS documentary on the movement in Mississippi, a few volunteers laughed at what they saw as "ridiculous" pictures of a "big really fat . . . ugly" and "idiotic" registrar refusing to register black applicants with "incredible double-talk." A handful of veterans walked out of the screening because of what they saw as the volunteers' cavalier attitude. "Maybe you won't laugh when you meet these guys . . . and know that they are doing it every day with or without the Feds," said one veteran to the group.[15]

The intense media interest in Freedom Summer exacerbated these tensions. The press loved the story of clean-scrubbed white college kids joining the movement. In a letter home, a volunteer described *Look* magazine's search for "the ideal naïve northern middle-class white girl" to shadow throughout the summer. "For the national press, that's the big story." The volunteer presciently added, "And when one of us gets killed, the story will be even bigger." The veterans wondered how such scrutiny might have checked some of the violence of the last few years.[16]

More than anything the tensions between veterans and volunteers underscored the changes in SNCC's old guard. Four years ago they had been much like the volunteers: young, relatively carefree, optimistic about their future, and confident in their ability to end segregation. Now they were battle-hardened, weary from the pressure, unhappy with the federal government's impotence, and unsure anymore if America had the capacity to reform itself. They looked different as well. So many copied Moses's style of dress—white T-shirts and bib overalls—that it became SNCC's de facto uniform.

On Saturday, June 20, 1964, the first training session ended with a long overnight drive to Mississippi. A picture of a classic plantation and the slogan "Welcome to Mississippi, the Magnolia State" greeted them as they crossed the border, a spot they called "the point of no return."[17]

As the second group of volunteers settled into Ohio on Sunday, June 21, Mickey Schwerner, the project director in Meridian; James Chaney, a local staffer; and Andrew Goodman, a summer volunteer from New York City, made the forty-mile drive from Meridian to Neshoba County to investigate the burning of a black church. Neshoba was a rural county with a reputation as a rough place for civil rights activists; it was the South's South, the heart of the Mississippi Delta. Their plan that Sunday was to look into the burning, speak to a few local black residents, and return to Meridian by four p.m.[18]

Mickey Schwerner, along with his wife, Rita, had arrived in Meridian from New York City in January doing civil rights work for CORE. The couple formed a fast friendship with James Chaney, a twenty-one-year-old high school dropout. Other activists who knew them thought the two men made a good team—Schwerner's book smarts complemented Chaney's street smarts. The pair met Andrew Goodman, another New Yorker, at the training in Oxford. Impressed with his confidence and maturity, they invited him to join their work in Meridian.[19]

When the three did not report back on time, another summer volunteer in Meridian followed standard SNCC operating procedure by calling all the nearby local jails and homes of activists to see if they had been arrested or their car had broken down. They also notified the main summer project office in Jackson. A group of volunteers hung around the Meridian office waiting to hear news of the three. Finally, at ten p.m., after the three were six hours overdue, the volunteers in Meridian called the main SNCC office in Atlanta.[20]

Mary King, Bond's assistant in SNCC's communications office, took the call. With Julian in Oxford, she was in charge. Posing as a reporter from *The Atlanta Constitution*, she called the local jails in the surrounding area, starting with Philadelphia, the Neshoba County seat. Cecil Price, the deputy sheriff in Neshoba, and every other law enforcement official she spoke with denied having seen the group. She called the FBI office, but agents there told her that they were not sure a federal crime had been committed, and regardless, they were not prepared to do anything until speaking with headquarters in Washington in the morning. At one a.m. she called John Doar at home, who told her to call the Mississippi State Police and keep him posted. Mary King made the most difficult calls last: reaching Andy Goodman's parents in Queens, New York, and Rita Schwerner, who was still in Oxford helping with the orientation sessions, she let them know the group was missing.[21]

The call to Rita Schwerner roused Bob Moses and the other SNCC leaders still in Oxford. The group stayed up all night hoping to hear good news, but none came. Only hours before, Rita had been enthusiastically talking with friends at dinner about the plans she and Mickey had for the future. On Monday, Moses prodded federal officials, and the SNCC staff in Oxford, Atlanta, Jackson, and Meridian lit up the long-distance lines through the night trying to find the three. In the morning, Deputy Price altered his story slightly: he had arrested the three and released them during the night. After asking the volunteers to tell their parents and other family members to contact their congressmen to pressure the FBI to start an investigation, Rita Schwerner and Bob Zellner left for Neshoba County to see what they could find out.[22]

A subdued Moses, his exhaustion and worry plainly visible, bluntly addressed the anxious volunteers. The "ball game had changed," he told the group; the chance of finding the three alive was "almost zero." He asked them to think long and hard if they really were ready to go to Mississippi. No one got up to leave, which Moses found unnerving. Finally someone started singing, "They say freedom is a constant struggle." To Moses's relief, a few volunteers quietly left. Even years later the psychiatrist Robert Coles marveled at the "emotional power and support" of the moment.[23]

On Tuesday, the disappearance drew national attention. SNCC supporters flooded Congress with messages; McDew and Barry, in Chicago for fund-raising, led a sympathy sit-in at a federal building and were arrested for it. Outside Philadelphia, Mississippi, some Choctaw Indians found the smoldering remains of the missing men's station wagon in a swamp near their reservation. The picture of the burned-out station wagon soon appeared in papers nationwide. In a confirmation of the growing national interest, CBS News's Walter Cronkite, the highest-rated news anchor, hosted a prime-time special.[24]

Rita Schwerner and Bob Zellner drove through the night to arrive at the burned church in Philadelphia by dawn on Tuesday. They poked around for a few minutes but discovered nothing new. On their way out, they found the road blocked by several pickups full of white men with shotguns; they had to drive through a ditch to get away.

Back in Philadelphia, they went to the local hotel, looking for help from any FBI agents in town. All they found were a couple of reporters.

"Bob Zellner! My God, what are you doing here? Rita Schwerner! My God! What are you doing here? You'll get everybody killed," exclaimed one of the reporters.

The other reporter, Claude Sitton, a *New York Times* writer well liked by SNCC, hustled the nervous pair into his hotel room for a drink of whiskey before taking them to meet the FBI agents in town.[25]

Zellner and Schwerner asked the agents for help. The pickup trucks were now parked in front of the hotel. The agents said all they could do was ask Sheriff Rainey for help, but he declined. When Zellner and Schwerner decided to return to Meridian, they found their car damaged from a barrage of bricks, bottles, and buckshot. Luckily, the battered car made it back without breaking down.

From Meridian, the two SNCC workers went on to Jackson to lobby Governor Paul Johnson for help but were turned away at the capitol. They then decided to try to catch Johnson at the governor's mansion. As they walked up, they saw him getting out of a car with George Wallace, the infamous segregationist governor of neighboring Alabama, as the statehouse media gathered around the two men.

Zellner stuck out his hand, which Johnson reflexively shook. Zellner then grabbed the governor's arm with his other hand, pulled him close, and said, "Governor Johnson, this is Rita Schwerner here, and she wants to talk to you about her husband."

The governor squirmed.

"We feel it's reprehensible of you to joke about this situation at this time," Zellner added, referring to the governor's earlier cavalier comments suggesting the men were hiding out on a lark.

"That's the wife of one of those missing men!" a reporter shouted as state troopers hustled the governor away.[26]

SNCC conducted its own surreptitious investigation by sending in several undercover teams. On Thursday, four days after the disappearance, Stokely Carmichael and Charlie Cobb sneaked into the Philadelphia area pretending to be schoolteachers on their way to a Florida vacation—they'd filled the car with textbooks. As they passed through a small town on the way to Meridian, their car died. As they tried to fix the problem, a local police cruiser pulled up. Carmichael and Cobb told the police their cover story, but when the police saw that the car was not registered in either of their names, they became suspicious. The car had just recently been donated to SNCC, and Carmichael had misplaced a letter from the owner giving him permission to use it.[27]

The police arrested Carmichael on suspicion of auto theft. A further search of the car revealed a few stray civil rights leaflets, making the police even more hostile. Because Carmichael was driving, they threw him into a cell, but refused to arrest Cobb as well. This put Cobb in a quandary, as SNCC's rules called for the two to stick together. Posting bail for Carmichael in the dark of night felt "too much like what happened to the missing workers," but continuing to Meridian by himself would leave both alone and vulnerable. He tried to hang out inside the jailhouse building, figuring at least he would be safe from vigilantes, but the police kicked him out. Afraid and unsure, Cobb pulled the car up in front of the jail, grabbed the tire iron, locked all the doors, and prayed for a quick sunrise. It was the "loneliest, scariest few hours of my life."[28]

The next morning the police released Carmichael, and the two met up with the other SNCC teams in Meridian, who breathed a sigh of relief. They had spent a restless night worrying that Cobb and Carmichael had met the same fate as the other three.

The eight activists spent the next few days searching for their missing comrades. They searched only at night, traveling in the bed of a farmer's old pickup to hide from the police and Klan. As Cleve Sellers recalled, they walked through "swamps, creeks, old houses, abandoned barns," using long sticks to probe the ground for bodies. The "ominous hiss" of an unseen snake and the "hairy-legged" spiders that crawled down his shirt terrified Sellers. He felt "like a guerrilla in Vietnam or Latin America—or at least I imagined that I felt as they do." After several days of poking around, local blacks reported that the Klan had learned of their presence, and they reluctantly gave up the search.[29]

Federal officials felt the heat of public interest. On Tuesday—two days after the civil rights workers' disappearance and against the advice of some aides—President Johnson met with the parents of Goodman and Schwerner. LBJ assured them that the federal government would do all it could to find their boys, and his sincerity impressed Goodman's mother. Johnson's quick response and genuine empathy reflected subtle but important shifts in the White House's orientation in the seven months since John Kennedy's assassination. Driven by a mix of political calculation and real concern, Johnson proved more willing than his predecessor to involve the White House in the movement. He believed that extending strong support for civil rights would burnish his liberal credentials, establish him as Kennedy's natural political heir, and silence a challenge from the Left. Johnson's interest in civil rights represented more than crude opportunism; the protests of the last few years had convinced him that Jim Crow could not be sustained. In a July 1963 speech on the centennial of Gettysburg, he said, "The Negro today asks Justice. We do not answer him—we do not answer those who lie beneath this soil—when we reply to the Negro by asking 'Patience.'"[30]

The federal government became an active participant in the search for the three missing civil rights workers. By the end of June, the FBI had more than one hundred agents on the ground in Mississippi. J. Edgar Hoover personally presided over the July opening of an FBI office in Jackson, the very first in Mississippi. But Hoover remained suspicious of the movement, which he suspected of being rife with Communists, and while the Bureau investigated the murders, it never expanded the scope of the investigation to Mississippi's systematic white terrorism.[31]

The FBI's search stumbled over numerous *other* black bodies. Agents found the body of a teenage boy in the Big Black River wearing a CORE T-shirt. He was not identified for several years. After a fisherman reported seeing part of a black leg drifting in the Old River, about eighty miles from Jackson, the FBI dragged it. They pulled out the bodies of two students from Alcorn A&M University, an all-black school nearby. Local whites, convinced that Freedom Summer foreshadowed an armed insurrection by Black Muslims, had kidnapped and killed the two as the suspected ringleaders because one had lived in Chicago and the other had participated in a demonstration.[32]

With all the attention focused on the three missing activists, these victims of random, casual, unreported, and uninvestigated murders attracted little media attention. Nothing, however, better conveyed the dystopia of Mississippi life. The entire white population of Mississippi was complicit in the violence against African Americans. Few whites actively criticized the violence, and those who did were often shunned. White Mississippians might not bear collective guilt for the routine murder of African Americans, but they bore collective responsibility. The culture of violence and the culture of white supremacy could not be separated.

FBI agents in Neshoba County tried to break the community's insular silence, even bribing children with candy for information. In late July, the case broke open when one of the participants, for a $30,000 reward, revealed the location of the bodies. On August 4, after seven hours of digging, FBI agents discovered all three. One mystery was over, but another had begun: What exactly happened and who was responsible?[33]

At about three p.m. on Sunday, June 21, Schwerner, Chaney, and Goodman were headed back to Meridian when the Neshoba County deputy sheriff Cecil Price pulled them over. Exactly why they were stopped remains unclear. Price claimed the car was speeding, but their station wagon had suffered a flat rear tire just inside the Philadelphia city limits. It is just as plausible that Price stumbled on the three after the tire went flat.

While Price studied their licenses, another patrol car pulled up, and Price arrested the three men. The civil rights workers went along peacefully; in fact, as he got into the cruiser, Mickey Schwerner handed Price the handgun lying on the backseat. Price locked the three in cells and told them they would have to wait until the justice of the peace arrived before they could pay the speeding fine.

Price left the jail and met up with a group of local Klansmen. After six months of civil rights work in the area, Schwerner—nicknamed "Goatee" by the Klan for his scruffy beard—was known and hated by local whites. After learning of the arrest, Edgar Ray Killen, a thirty-eight-year-old sawmill operator, ordained Baptist minister, and head of the Philadelphia Klan, drove to Meridian to confer with its Klan. Over the next several hours, they hatched a plan to intercept the civil rights workers as they left the jail. Well known as a Klansman, Killen decided to get an alibi by making a conspicuous appearance at a local funeral.

At about ten p.m., Chaney paid the twenty-dollar fine for speed-ing and the deputy agreed to release all of them. As Price handed them back their wallets, he said, "Now let's see how quick y'all can get out of Neshoba County." The civil rights workers did not seem concerned as they left the jail. Price walked them to their car, parked a few blocks from the jail. The three piled into the station wagon, Chaney at the wheel, for the drive home. A police car pulled up to the vacant lot, and Deputy Price climbed in; the police followed the sta-tion wagon to the Philadelphia city limits, then turned around.

A few minutes later, Price kept a prearranged rendezvous with a carload of Klansmen, and both cars circled back to catch the station wagon. At first, Chaney tried to outrun the police car, but then he voluntarily pulled over. The three men surrendered to Price for a sec-ond time. The deputy ordered them into the patrol car, and when Chaney hesitated, he knocked him on the head with a leather club. Price drove off, followed by the blue station wagon, now driven by one of the Klansmen, and the other car of Klansmen.

The three cars pulled off the highway onto an unmarked dirt road. The men pulled Schwerner out of the police cruiser.

"Are you that nigger lover?" one of the Klansmen asked Schwerner.

"Sir, I know just how you feel," Schwerner answered cryptically.

The Klansman, Wayne Roberts, put his gun to Schwerner's heart and fired once. They grabbed Goodman out of the car next and shot him just above the armpit. Chaney recognized one of the Meridian Klansmen and pleaded for his life. They shot him three times—in the stomach, back, and head. Then, by prearrangement with the owner, the lynch mob buried the bodies in the newly constructed dam. It had been less than thirty-six hours since Mickey Schwerner, James Chaney, and Andrew Goodman had arrived in Mississippi from orientation in Ohio to start Freedom Summer.[34]

At the urging of Moses, SNCC temporarily moved its national head-quarters to Greenwood, Mississippi, for the summer. An in-state headquarters would draw even more publicity to the project and give SNCC greater influence within COFO. Headquarters was an old two-story barn that had been converted to ground-floor offices and a small lending library upstairs for local black kids who had no access to a public library. For fun they built a horseshoe pit outside the office, and when things got tough, they retreated to a little juke joint they nicknamed Blood's after the manager. It was a dingy black-owned café, barely lit by a few neon signs, with a few pinball machines and overwhelmed by the loud jukebox.[35]

Bond moved the communications office to Greenwood. With a wife and young children, Bond traveled less than his comrades, but he spent this summer shuttling between Greenwood and Atlanta. Sometimes he crossed paths with Lewis, who often passed through Greenwood as he crisscrossed the state, monitoring the different projects. Bond had two WATS lines (one national and one statewide) installed and a wireless radio control center to communicate with the two-way radios in SNCC's newly acquired fleet of twenty station wagons. He had somebody monitoring the phone and radio lines twenty-four hours a day to stay on top of trouble.

Most of the Greenwood staff bunked with locals who were poor but graciously shared their food and homes. Bob Zellner and his wife lived with the Greene family, two retired schoolteachers whose home became the unofficial local SNCC bunkhouse; Lewis, Carmichael, Bond, and other veterans all crashed there at some point. Harry Belafonte and Sidney Poitier even stayed at the Greene home when they visited Mississippi that summer (though it meant that Zellner had to sleep on the couch). For the veterans at least, Freedom Summer got everyone together and offered them the chance to reconnect and renew friendships.[36]

Carmichael and Zellner became close friends that summer, since both were permanently stationed in Greenwood. Carmichael was the project director for the whole second congressional district, and he put Zellner, who was hanging around Greenwood to be near his wife, Dottie, in the communications office, in charge of Greenwood. Zellner loved Carmichael's brashness: "He would call the sheriff a fat, tobacco-chewing white imbecile, cracker, redneck peckerwood. Any one of those might get him killed in certain situations, but Stokely was willing to die, and what he was doing of course with his great grin was delegitimizing them as a source of terror." In turn, Carmichael relied on Zellner to help him navigate the tricky world of white power. It was Carmichael's first extended stay in the Deep South since Parchman, and Zellner helped him "get his sea legs" by reminding him to temper his brashness so he would not end up "getting killed right away."[37]

For the young volunteers from outside the South, entering Mississippi, especially rural Mississippi, felt like entering a foreign country. "To see the place in the real is so different from seeing pictures of it," a volunteer confided in a letter. "The negro neighborhood hasn't got a single paved street in it. It's all dirt and gravel roads. The houses vary from beat-up shacks to fairly good-looking cottages . . . There are lots of smelly outhouses, and many of the houses have no inside water." Another volunteer in the Delta reminded a friend back home, "My views on rural fucking America are well known. Yet here I am living on a farm for the first time in my life—and enjoying it."[38]

Moments of levity sometimes broke up the stress. In the middle of the summer, a couple of volunteers got married in Greenwood. A local preacher involved in the movement opened his church to the interdenominational service (Christian-Jewish). Summer volunteers and SNCC leaders who were free came to the ceremony. The punch was spiked, cookies and potato chips were served, freedom songs were sung, and the dancing went on into the night. After the vows, Jim Forman called out from a back pew, "One man, one woman—two votes," cracking up the crowd. For a couple of hours they stopped being civil rights workers and were just a bunch of young people celebrating their friends' love.

Violence was a constant concern. The summer saw at least six murders, thirty-five shootings, thirty bombings, and eight beatings. A random excerpt from SNCC's running diary describes what the volunteers faced: "Aug. 2: Greenwood: Summer volunteer arrested . . . for assault with deadly weapon . . . released on $1,000 bond . . . Shortly after midnight, four shots fired at SNCC office . . . Aug 3: Columbus: Police arrest Negro volunteer for driving without a license and charge SNCC director for allowing him to do so . . . Batesville: SNCC project director Charles Weaver and summer volunteer Benjamin Graham arrested while trying to get the names of 25 potential Negro voters . . . Greenwood: white volunteer arrested on John Doe warrant for assault and battery. Jackson: Local volunteer arrested for vagrancy in front of drugstore near his home. He had a SNCC button on his shirt." One summer worker described the violence hanging overhead "like dead air—it hangs there and maybe it'll fall and maybe it won't."[39]

Danger could be erotic. As much as anything, the frightening and hostile soil of Mississippi gave birth to the sexual revolution. The conservative sexual mores of the 1950s remained strong in 1964, college dormitories were single sex, skirts came to the knee, boys wore ties to dances, and good girls didn't. But unmarried men and women rooming together in the Freedom Houses across Mississippi transgressed those norms. Breaking the taboo of interracial sex added to the charged atmosphere of Freedom Summer. Segregationist writings were rife with nearly hysterical rants about how the real goal of the movement was to allow black men to sleep with white women; they darkly warned of the creation of a single "mongrel" race. Cleve Sellers related a typical encounter. He had been pulled over by the sheriff of Marshall County with two passengers—a black man and a white woman. "Which one of them coons you fucking?" the sheriff asked the woman as a gathering crowd of whites shouted its approval. "Shit, I know you fuckin' them niggers. Why else would you be down heah? Which one is it? If you tell me the truth, I'll let you go."[40]

Summer volunteers did sleep across the color line. The reasons were varied. For some, it was the illicit thrill of violating such a powerful taboo. Some black men saw sleeping with white women as the most powerful assertion of their claim to equality, and some white women saw having sex with an African American as the ultimate statement of their commitment to an interracial society. More than one white woman commented that attention from African-American men represented a sexual coming-of-age for them. As one recalled, white men had told her she was "too large . . . to be attractive," but black men "assumed that I was a sexual person . . . and I needed that badly."[41]

Even among enlightened civil rights workers, the American past shadowed these relationships. SNCC's male leaders were not immune to the appeal of these encounters, but they worried that media attention would undermine public support. White women bore the brunt of this sensitivity, and a few were sent home by coed leaders. No white men were dismissed for the same reason. A black man sleeping with a white woman might be seen as asserting his independence and manhood, but other configurations could be controversial: with its overtones of white slavemasters taking advantage of female slaves, black men sometimes reacted negatively when a white man asked out a black woman.[42]

Nothing better captured the complicated internal dynamics of Freedom Summer than the relationships that developed among the participants. The America of 1964 was caught between the more con-servative 1950s and the more liberated 1970s, and the social scene of Freedom Summer tilted more toward *The Real World* than *Happy Days*. When the summer volunteers returned to their homes and colleges, they pushed to extend these personal freedoms, serving as an engine for the counterculture movement that would rise to prominence in the second half of the decade.

Half the summer volunteers worked on the Freedom Schools, the most innovative experiment of Freedom Summer. In Mississippi—where education (especially black education) was not valued, where there was no compulsory education law (it was the only state without one), and where the school calendar still seemed to revolve around the needs of agriculture—poverty, ignorance, and racism intertwined.[43]

Freedom School organizers fashioned an innovative pedagogy that emphasized student participation and the Socratic method. SNCC's educational experimentation was both a pragmatic response to limited resources—few textbooks, blackboards, and formal class-rooms—and a reflection of its philosophical commitment to put people in charge of their own lives. Organizers planned to open about forty schools for a two-month session, with a projected total of around a thousand students; by the time enrollment ended, more than three thousands students had signed up for Freedom Schools.[44]

The schools had a casual look to them that belied the determina-tion of staff and students alike. Classes took place outside, with stu-dents sprawled on the grass, on the steps of a church, inside crammed into the pews, in an abandoned school building, really anywhere that was available. The classes had an informal feel; students piped up with their opinions, and discussions often spun off on tangents. The work was serious though. One class read *Moby Dick*, another per-formed an original play, and a third pondered the different meanings of whiteness. The most popular electives were the foreign languages—French, German, and Spanish—because, one summer volunteer con-cluded, they "suggested other worlds and possibilities."[45]

So great were the needs of Mississippi's poor black residents that Freedom Summer expanded far beyond its original goals. Volunteers established community centers, secured federal grants, and helped local blacks navigate the welfare bureaucracy. Experienced professionals volunteered. Lawyers defended the volunteers and helped them negotiate the morass of Mississippi laws. The Medical Committee for Human Rights sent more than one hundred doctors and nurses to staff free clinics. The doctors were particularly useful. Not only did most local blacks have little access to health care, but white doctors often refused to treat civil rights workers.[46]

The Mississippi Freedom Democratic Party (MFDP) represented the most important endeavor of the summer. After the success of the November 1963 Freedom Vote, activists in Mississippi established the MFDP as an alternative to the segregated regular Democratic Party. Freedom Summer volunteers recruited people into the MFDP at the same time they tried to register them to vote. With the regular process usually blocked, SNCC believed the existence of the MFDP would demonstrate that the lack of black voters resulted from discrimination, not from a lack of interest in democracy. It would hold local, county, district, and state conventions to select delegates and nominate candidates to run for Congress and other offices. At the end of the summer, MFDP delegates would travel to the Democratic National Convention in Atlantic City to challenge the legitimacy of the Mississippi Democratic Party's segregated delegation.

The voter-registration campaign, which involved about half the summer staff, was the heart of Freedom Summer. Volunteers almost always got a friendly reception from local residents, with an invitation to sit for a glass of lemonade or some barbecue. Getting local residents to try to register was another thing. As one volunteer observed, they had to get local blacks to overcome both the "irrational fear of something new and untested" and the "highly rational . . . economic fear of losing your job, the physical fear of being shot at." Another volunteer used the example of road maintenance to bring home the importance of voting: "That man downtown in charge [of] roads doesn't have to listen to Negroes. He should be working for you." Registering voters was not a nine-to-five sort of thing. Volunteers were up early in the morning going house to house—often on foot—introducing themselves and explaining the summer project, and they worked into the night. Often they held mass meetings at night to build community support, to sing freedom songs, and to connect people to the movement. Not even the enactment of the Civil Rights Act in July distracted the volunteers from voter registration.[47]

When Johnson became president after John F. Kennedy's assassination, he made passage of a civil rights bill a central element of Kennedy's legacy. The new president invested substantial political capital in securing the bill's passage, buttonholing reluctant legislators and unequivocally stating his public support. By February 1964, his efforts had secured passage in the House of Representatives, 290 to 130. A difficult fight loomed in the Senate, where southern senators promised the longest filibuster in Senate history. Not until early June did Johnson secure enough votes; every southern Democrat save Ralph Yarborough of Texas voted no. On July 2, 1964, just hours after the final passage in Congress, LBJ signed the Civil Rights Act into law.[48]

The new law should have been cause for great celebration within SNCC. After all, its provisions reflected SNCC's early civil disobedience campaigns by outlawing segregation in waiting rooms, buses, restaurants, and other places open to the general public. But having shifted from direct action to voter registration, SNCC's policy in Mississippi was not to let tests of the new law distract its attention from Freedom Summer. Fears of segregationist violence, a desire not to force the few white moderates into a tenuous position, and a realization that enforcement depended on local, not federal, law reinforced the decision for a tempered funeral for Jim Crow.[49]

Local youths chafed at these restrictions. Two brothers from Greenwood, Silas and Jake McGhee, decided to test the new law right away by going to a movie at the white theater in Leflore. The agitated white crowd threatened them with violence, and the police took the brothers home. Zellner and Carmichael admired the boys' courage. Zellner called them "the bravest people I ever met in my life. They simply didn't take no shit." But SNCC could not let the boys' impromptu action undermine the voter-registration work. Zellner's combination of straight talk—"I said I'd behave nonviolently. I didn't say . . . how I'd feel" about it—and the example of his personal history of courage in McComb mostly kept the boys in check.

The two boys pointed out the hypocrisy of SNCC's counseling patience. Why, they asked, has "SNCC moved from a militant position to a rather subdued one"? The question put Zellner and Carmichael in the ironic position of arguing that "it depends on your definition of *militant*" and that registering voters was "one of the most militant things anybody could be doing." Carmichael admitted to feeling "uneasy" about restraining another's activism. Politics, he concluded soberly, requires patience, irony, and discipline to achieve larger goals, and the larger goal of registering voters demanded restraining other protests. The McGhee incident demonstrated that clear goals and a defined organizational structure could get Carmichael, for all his flamboyance, to subsume his own passion for the greater good.[50]

The hard work paid off. The summer volunteers registered more than eighty thousand African Americans with the MFDP, demonstrating the deep desire of Mississippi blacks to participate in the democratic process. Black Mississippians poured their hopes and dreams into the MFDP, essentially creating a political party from scratch in a just a few months. In the spirit of SNCC's belief that local people should control their own struggle, native Mississippians would control the MFDP; the local leaders were those who had gained confidence in their abilities by working with SNCC over the last couple of years.

More than one summer volunteer wrote home about how impressive it was to see these ordinary people—"housewives, unskilled workers, many but not all uneducated"—giving public speeches, holding serious debates about their community, and carefully selecting the best people to represent them at the next level. Stokely Carmichael said that it was at these precinct and county meetings that he really grasped Ella Baker's "unfailing confidence in ordinary people."[51]

The highlight of the MFDP effort in Mississippi was the state convention, which drew eight hundred delegates to the Masonic temple in Jackson at the start of August. The county delegations entered one by one, holding hand-lettered signs announcing themselves—Neshoba, Leflore, Amite, Sunflower, and the others. Reading the signs as the delegates entered, a wave of emotion flooded Stokely Carmichael as he thought of the sacrifices, the struggles, the pain, and the deaths behind each name. Barely forty-eight hours had passed since the FBI dug up the bodies of Schwerner, Chaney, and Goodman.[52]

Joe Rauh, the general counsel for the United Auto Workers union and an MFDP adviser, outlined the party's "eleven and eight" strategy for the Democratic National Convention in Atlantic City. It would need eleven votes on the credentials committee and the votes of eight states on the floor to force a roll-call vote of all fifty states on the legitimacy of Mississippi's all-white regulars. MFDP strategists hoped that a majority of delegates would be so uncomfortable publicly supporting the racist regular delegation that they would support the insurgent party. If the president remained neutral, Rauh told the convention, then "when states like New York, New Jersey, and Illinois [go] . . . before the television cameras, there's no doubt in my mind they will go with us."[53]

Having just taken charge of the MFDP's Washington office, Ella Baker gave the keynote address: "Until the killing of a black mother's son becomes as important as the killing of a white mother's son, we who believe in freedom cannot rest."

After Rauh's enthusiastic description of the strategy and Baker's moving keynote, spontaneous cheers and ovations broke out, and the delegates danced and sang. "It was the most wonderful thing I'd ever heard," remembered Rauh.[54]

If Freedom Summer was the apex of the movement, then the convention in Jackson was the apex of Freedom Summer. As the crowd sang and danced, hope and optimism enveloped them. The Civil Rights Act outlawing segregation in businesses and public places was a month old, and now activists seemed on the verge of achieving a major breakthrough against voting discrimination. Freedom Summer had worked beyond almost anyone's expectations. Black Mississippians crowded the Freedom Schools and rushed to join the MFDP. In less than four months, they had built a statewide political party and demonstrated to the rest of the nation that the only reason blacks did not vote in Mississippi was white racism. The MFDP also reminded the nation that citizenship and civic involvement were not the exclusive preserve of the rich and the educated. Given the chance, poor and illiterate Americans could be skilled political organizers and valuable civic leaders.

Anyone who looked around the convention hall carefully and thought about it would realize that this success had been accomplished through the efforts of a highly diverse group. Freedom Summer featured black and white, rich and poor, the educated and the unlettered, old and young, rural and urban, northern outsiders and southern natives, joined together. The coalition looked like a cross section of American life.

As the delegates celebrated, Stokely Carmichael stole a glance at James Chaney's mom, sitting with the Neshoba delegation. He reflected on the truth of Baker's words—that the backbone, the heart and soul, the strength of local organizing, was African-American women. Then he looked over to see Fannie Lou Hamer, the woman who would soon become the symbol of the MFDP and the movement in Mississippi, take the lead in a rousing rendition of "This Little Light of Mine."[55]

Fannie Lou Hamer's earlier life gave few hints of her emergence as an activist in the 1960s. The granddaughter of slaves and the twentieth child of sharecroppers, she left school in sixth grade to help out on the farm and care for her infirm mother. In 1961 she went into the hospital for a minor operation and was sterilized without her knowledge—something Mississippi did frequently to black patients. Hamer herself was a sharecropper, living on land owned by one of Sunflower County's most powerful white men, and if Mississippi was the center of the segregated south, then Sunflower was close to the center of Mississippi. At the turn of the century, it was the site of one of the most gruesome lynchings in Mississippi history. More important, Senator James O. Eastland, one the staunchest defenders of segregation in Congress, lived in Sunflower. In the two decades since Eastland arrived in the Senate in 1941, he had opposed every civil rights bill, voted against programs to help the less fortunate, and railed against the Communists he believed were hidden in every corner of American life.[56]

Hamer was already forty-four in the summer of 1962 when Diane Nash and James Bevel came to her hometown of Ruleville to talk about voter registration. Bevel's powerful sermon about the importance of voting inspired Hamer to become the first volunteer. Until then her life had embodied the unrealized potential of Mississippi blacks.[57]

Five days after Bevel arrived in Ruleville, Hamer tried to register but failed to convince the registrar that she "understood" a random clause from the state constitution and was turned away. The next day the owner of the plantation where she had lived for nearly two decades told her that if she wanted to stay, she would have to withdraw her application.

"I didn't go down to register for you," she told him. "I went to register for myself."

Dee Marlow, the plantation owner, gave her one more chance to return things to normal.

"That's what I'm trying to get out of now," she said. "Things be like they always was. I want some change."[58]

It quickly became clear to Bevel and Nash that Hamer possessed hidden strengths, and SNCC invited her to join them. She was a deeply religious person whose faith manifested itself in empathy for those like herself who lived at the margins of American life. Her faith made her, in the words of another activist, "a radical in the deepest sense of the word," trying to "understand, expose, and destroy the root causes of oppression." She was also a deeply curious person, asking questions about everything around her. She matched her religious faith with an equally strong secular faith in the power of the American creed to right the nation's wrongs. John Lewis recalled her saying, "Live up to the creed. Live up to the Declaration of Independence, to the Bill of Rights." Fannie Lou Hamer's life, indeed the life of every black person in Mississippi, was a stark reminder that the promise of the American creed remained elusive for many; nonetheless, she believed that its promises could improve her life.[59]

Hamer's singing voice drew people to her. The folksinger Pete Seeger, who knew her well, said trying to describe her voice was like trying to define jazz: "If you have to ask, you'll never know." Harry Belafonte marveled at "the *power* of her voice because there was a mission behind it and in it." It was, he concluded, "the voice of all of us." Hamer herself said singing kept oppressed blacks and movement activists going by bringing out the soul, revealing good works, and glorifying God. Her stirring rendition of "This Little Light of Mine" became famous.[60]

Between the summer of 1962 and the summer of 1964, Hamer worked closely with the student activists. Throwing herself into the movement, she traveled to Nashville, Charleston, and other big cities for SNCC seminars and training sessions. She got arrested integrating a bus station in Winona, Mississippi, and won a reversal of her arrest in a federal trial. She entered the 1964 Democratic primary as a candidate for Congress in Mississippi to draw attention to the racist positions of the incumbent congressman Jamie Whitten, and she participated in the Freedom Summer training sessions in Ohio. The statewide MFDP convention acknowledged her stature when it named her vice-chairman of the sixty-eight delegates who would travel to Atlantic City.[61]

Hamer and SNCC's young activists developed a mutual admiration that bridged the divide of age, education, and class. Many years later Charles McLaurin, a SNCC activist who worked in Mississippi full-time in the summer of 1962, recalls that meeting Hamer changed his view of the world. In return, Hamer acknowledged her debt to SNCC: "They treated me like a human being, whether the kids were white or black. I was respected with the kids and they never told nobody what to say, nobody . . . They brought every hope into the state of Mississippi." In short, "if SNCC hadn't come . . . there never would have been a Fannie Lou Hamer."[62]

Back in Washington, President Johnson caught some of the highlights of the Jackson convention on television and was determined to control or stop the MFDP. According to Rauh, Johnson told Senator Hubert Humphrey and the United Auto Workers president, Walter Reuther, "tell that bastard god damn lawyer [Rauh] . . . that there ain't gonna be all that eleven and eight shit at the convention." Johnson may have shared the broad concerns of civil rights activists, but the prize his eyes were fixed on was his reelection, and he was determined to prevent anything from getting in his way.[63]

Johnson's motives revealed the mix of ego, hubris, and altruism that often governed his actions. In August 1964 the major threads of the 1960s—civil rights, Vietnam, and the War on Poverty—converged on LBJ, and he tried to manipulate them all. On August 7, as the MFDP held its convention in Jackson, Congress debated the Gulf of Tonkin Resolution, which would give the president power to send more troops to Vietnam, as well as Johnson's War on Poverty legislation. Both proposals passed Congress, though the antipoverty bill, which LBJ imagined as the first in a series, made it through the House of Representatives only on a 228–190 vote. (The Gulf of Tonkin Resolution passed 418–0.) Worried that the coalition that passed the first antipoverty bill would not hold together for the next round of initiatives because of opposition from conservative Democrats—meaning southern whites—Johnson used the resolution to project an aggressive anticommunist stance in the hope of mollifying these critics. Johnson was eager for the appearance of a unified party at the convention to bolster his chance for a historic landslide in the general election. Seeing himself as the great and indispensable champion of African Americans and the poor, he resented criticism, confident that only his landslide victory would ensure the passage of more civil rights and antipoverty legislation.[64]

In the days leading up to the convention, MFDP strategists and LBJ both tried to gain the upper hand. The drama lay in the two sides' contrasting approaches to politics. MFDP strategists were masters of grassroots organizing, but Johnson was a master of backroom politics, an expert at using the formal and informal levers of power to undermine his opponents. While the MFDP was shaking hands and reaching out to the public, Johnson had his allies pressure state party chairmen and rework the rules of the credentials committee meeting.

On live national television, Fannie Lou Hamer, the NAACP head, Roy Wilkins, and Martin Luther King, Jr., all testified to the credentials committee in support of the MFDP. But the day belonged to Hamer. She talked about how she had first tried to register in 1962, how she was evicted from her home for trying, how she was shot at, how she was arrested, and how Mississippi state policemen ordered other prisoners to beat her. As her voice wavered and her eyes teared up, she concluded by saying, "If the Freedom Party is not seated now, I question America, is this America, the land of the free and the home of the brave, where we have to sleep with our telephones off the hooks because our lives be threatened daily because we want to live as decent human beings in America?"[65]

Unfortunately, her last words were not carried live. To distract attention from the credentials committee hearing, President Johnson called a sudden news conference. Because the networks thought LBJ might say something about his vice-presidential pick, they broke away from Hamer.

But by the end of the day, the MFDP's compelling story had clearly trumped LBJ's effort to manipulate the process. The major networks replayed her moving final words during the evening newscasts, where they reached an audience far larger than in the daytime. The Western Union office in Atlantic City received more than four hundred telegrams in support of the MFDP and only one against.[66]

Now the dispute shifted to the back rooms as both sides sought a negotiated compromise. Since Johnson controlled the Democratic Party, he had the upper hand in negotiations, but both sides had an incentive to reach a settlement: Johnson wanted to avoid the theatrics of an intraparty squabble on national television; the MFDP, uncertain whether it could win a floor fight, wanted something tangible. "You never take publicly your private position," Rauh observed some years later. Based on past precedent, the MFDP delegates were reasonably confident that the party would offer to seat both delegations with full voting rights, an imperfect but acceptable compromise.[67]

The Democratic Party's offer, however, fell far short of the MFDP's expectations. The vice-presidential hopeful Hubert Humphrey told Bob Moses that the regular Mississippi delegates would have to pledge their loyalty to Johnson before they would be credentialed as official delegates; that future conventions would disqualify segregated delegations; and that the MFDP delegates would be welcome at the convention as nonvoting guests. Moses and the others pushed Humphrey to agree to let MFDP delegates replace any regulars who refused the loyalty oath. Humphrey demurred but asserted that in the long run civil rights activists could not imagine a better situation than having him as vice president and a strongly reelected Johnson as president. The MFDP rejected the offer.[68]

The next day, Tuesday, August 25, Johnson sweetened the offer and turned up the pressure. Two MFDP delegates—Aaron Henry, head of the Mississippi NAACP, and Ed King, a white priest affiliated with Mississippi's all-black Tougaloo College—would be named at-large delegates with voting powers. Under pressure from Johnson, Reuther threatened to fire Rauh from his job at the United Auto Workers and told Martin Luther King he would withhold union donations to the SCLC unless it could get the MFDP to agree to Johnson's offer.[69]

In his hotel room, Humphrey met with Bob Moses, Martin Luther King, Bayard Rustin, Aaron Henry, and Ed King. With exaggerated rhetoric, Humphrey compared the proposal to increase the number of delegates to increasing the size of Congress and urged them to accept the compromise. When Ed King offered to withdraw in favor of one of the local black Mississippians, Humphrey cut him off: "The president does not want that illiterate woman to speak from the floor." In the middle of the meeting, Walter Mondale, then Minnesota's attorney general, Humphrey's protégé, and the chair of the credentials committee, appeared on television, preemptively announcing the revised offer as a final deal. Moses accused Humphrey of "cheating" the MFDP and walked out of the meeting.[70]

The next morning, August 26, civil rights and party leaders met one last time to discuss Johnson's offer to the MFDP. Humphrey and other party leaders once again pushed the activists to accept the compromise. Within the civil rights group, not everyone agreed on what to do. Those with close ties to or an eye on national politics leaned toward taking the deal. Martin Luther King, urging "pragmatism even in the most idealistic of situations," wanted the MFDP to take the deal. Roy Wilkins and Aaron Henry pushed hard for it as well. Wilkins got so frustrated with the opposition that at one point he actually called them "ignorant." Though they did not have specific evidence, Ella Baker and the SNCC leaders were so sure that Allard Lowenstein was trying to maneuver the MFDP into the compromise to please his friends in the Democratic Party that she had James Forman hover over Lowenstein during the meeting to prevent him from talking.[71]

Baker rejected any compromise. She derisively referred to the deal's supporters as the "save the country" group for identifying Johnson's victory with the success of the movement. She particularly disliked Lowenstein for his willingness to compromise the authentic democratic aspirations of the Mississippi activists. Ordinary black Mississippians in the MFDP delegation, like Fannie Lou Hamer and Victoria Gray, wanted no part of the deal. Hamer put it best: "We didn't come all this way for no two seats." Hamer and Baker's opposition reinforced SNCC's inclination to reject the offer.[72]

Moses spoke out against the deal. He resented Johnson's heavy-handed attempts to manipulate the MFDP, especially when he tried to pick the two at-large delegates. He particularly disliked Martin Luther King's attempt to have it both ways, to have solidarity with ordinary black southerners as well as influence with national party leaders. Moses launched a withering attack on King: "We are not here to bring politics into our morality but to bring morality into our politics." After Moses spoke, the MFDP delegates voted again to reject Johnson's compromise.[73]

Emotions were raw. The MFDP delegates returned their observer credentials en masse, singing "We Shall Overcome" as they marched toward the convention hall. When some of the MFDP delegates used borrowed credentials and guest passes to mingle on the convention floor with the official delegates, party officials had the state police and undercover FBI agents remove them. Still, Bob Moses and a few others managed to sneak onto the floor during Bobby Kennedy's

moving speech about his brother. Around their neck they hung photographs of the slain president framed in black with the quote "Ask
not what your country can . . ."[74]

For Johnson, it was an empty victory. Worried that the Deep South
would vote Republican in the general election, he had squeezed the
MFDP to appease white southerners. They abandoned him anyway.
Only three members of the regular Mississippi delegation signed the
loyalty oath. Other southern Democrats grumbled that two seats to
the MFDP were two seats too many.

For the activists of the MFDP, the wounds ran deep. They resented
what Aaron Henry called "the typical white man's mistake" of "picking black folks' leaders." The broader condescension of Democratic
officials further alienated the MFDP delegates. When Humphrey
blurted his comment about "that illiterate woman," he was giving
voice to an attitude that MFDP delegates sensed other party officials
held when they negotiated directly with African Americans they assumed led the movement because of their middle-class clothes and
diction. Yet as Bob Moses remarked, "the whole point" of starting the
MFDP was to give the "lowest sharecropper" the confidence that "he
knows better than the biggest leader what is required to make a decent life for himself."[75]

In the general election, Barry Goldwater, the Republican nominee,
carried the five Deep South states of Mississippi, Alabama, Louisiana,
South Carolina, and Georgia, including an astonishing 87 percent of
the vote in Mississippi. The Deep South embraced Goldwater, even as
the rest of the country embraced Johnson. The only other state Goldwater won was his home state of Arizona. Johnson received 61.1 percent of the vote, which remains the highest total in American history.
Johnson had devoted all his energy to appeasing those who had no
intention of supporting him anyway.

SNCC veterans joked about how easily the enthusiastic summer volunteers succumbed to "freedom high," the rush that came from challenging the conventions of society, the headiness of being involved in
something larger and more powerful than oneself. The joking was
partly wistful remembrance of a feeling the veterans knew well, for
they had experienced the excitement of the sit-ins, of the Freedom
Rides, and of McComb and Albany. And the joking was also partially

an ironic distancing from the naïveté of the volunteers and the veterans' earlier selves.

At its best, Freedom Summer captured the hopeful optimism of "freedom high." As one of the great grassroots-democratic insurgencies in American history, it demonstrated the ways in which ordinary people could take responsibility for their own affairs. Momentarily given the spotlight in Atlantic City, MFDP members showed themselves to be the equal of their leaders—articulate, smart, and capable. It was also a rare moment of genuine interracial possibility. In the midst of Mississippi's deeply segregated world, summer volunteers, SNCC veterans, and local residents not only worked hand in hand but lived and ate together as well, in a jumble of black and white, northern and southern, rich and poor. Less than twelve months after Martin Luther King spoke about interracial harmony as a distant "dream," SNCC was doing the hard work of building an actual interracial society.

More important, the veterans' joking about "freedom high" reflected how much Freedom Summer had changed them. SNCC had dramatically doubled in size, raising hard questions about its evolving personality and direction. Did being a member of SNCC still mean the same thing as it had two years before? Could it retain its ad hoc consensus-oriented structure going forward? With the passage of the Civil Rights Act but the MFDP's failure in Atlantic City, what was the relationship between moral suasion and black political power? These questions had no easy answers; until now the focus on the common enemy of white supremacy had masked some of the divisions within SNCC.

If SNCC members were unsure about what the organization was, they knew what it was not: it was not like the other civil rights groups. To their "us versus them" mentality, the civil rights establishment—notably Martin Luther King, the NAACP leadership, and the African-American middle class generally—had a very different view of the value of working within the system than did they. Men like King and the NAACP's Roy Wilkins viewed the situation pragmatically, believing that African Americans could prosper only within the larger Democratic coalition. SNCC veterans rejected this, believing it made blacks the patrons of Washington politicians and dependent on a white consensus to advance civil rights. They believed that to sacrifice justice for the expediency of pragmatism was to betray the very people they claimed to be trying to help.

For the first four years of its existence, SNCC held to an absolute belief in the power of creed and commonwealth to end segregation: moral appeals demonstrating the failure of the nation to live up to the American creed, combined with a savvy use of the mechanics of government, would produce victory. But at almost every turn they had been disappointed, and Atlantic City was the last straw. Many now lost faith in the ability of the political system to end segregation and solve the problems of poor black southerners. The lesson Cleve Sellers took from Atlantic City was that "never again" could SNCC be "lulled" into thinking that its mission "was exposing injustices so that the 'good' people of America could eliminate them." Another SNCC member bluntly articulated the extent to which Atlantic City undermined those beliefs: "Fuck it. We played by the rules, and look where it got us. So fuck the rules."[76]

Bob Moses's somewhat cool, aloof exterior and his tendency to intellectualize situations masked the warm heart of idealism and optimism underneath. For him, the MFDP had been not just a tactical response to white power; it had been an authentic expression of the American creed and a rare occurrence of real democracy. Perhaps somewhat naïvely, he believed the honest democracy of the MFDP would resonate with national Democratic leaders, who would side with the upstarts. Now no one was more bitter than he. "You cannot trust the political system," he said. "I will have nothing to do with the political system." John Lewis believed that the "cruel lesson" of Atlantic City exacted a punishing toll on his friend.

Freedom Summer, the Atlantic City convention, and the distrust engendered by LBJ's heavy-handed maneuvering set the stage for the growing opposition to the Vietnam War, the birth of a nationwide student movement, and the rise of black power. Many of the white volunteers, such as Mario Savio in Berkeley, returned to their campuses to ask tough questions about the war and to challenge college officials who tried to stifle those questions. For Savio, organizing Berkeley's Free Speech Movement was "another phase of the same struggle," likening California's suppression of student dissent to Mississippi's "organized violence" to suppress black political rights.[77]

For SNCC's veterans, 1964 marked not the cathartic release of protest but the end of an apprenticeship. Like high school, it had lasted four years, and its end signaled their coming of age. Unlike the summer volunteers new to the movement in 1964, the rush of protest—the freedom high—was no longer enough. In fact, to succumb to it was to signal one's own naïveté.

The youthful rush of optimism and hope that drove the SNCC generation from Greensboro to Atlantic City had come to an end. The original activists had lost some of their innocence. The harsh reality of Atlantic City had eroded their faith in the nation's leaders; it also liberated them from the conventions of political compromise and even the conventional rules of dress and sexual relations. They still held strong to a vision of a better, more just, more egalitarian world, but they were battle-hardened now. They understood that inequality could be eliminated only with significant strife and division, and that change had to be made regardless of the consent and comfort of Washington politicians and white public opinion. It was graduation day at Freedom High.

PART TWO

Shadows of Youth

As the summer of 1964 drew to a close, the young activists of SNCC felt as if they had been through a war. To Stokely Carmichael, the departure of the summer volunteers from Mississippi had the appearance of "a large army breaking camp," full of confusion, random movement, and debris. Tallying the movement's gains and losses took a backseat to overcoming exhaustion and contemplating the next move. "For the first time in my life," recalled Cleveland Sellers, "I understood how soldiers feel when they return from wars and have to grope unwillingly for answers to innocent questions such as 'How are you?'"[1]

With the signs of burnout everywhere, the actor Harry Belafonte offered a lucky ten SNCC members—including Bob Moses and his new wife, Donna; Julian Bond; the recently married Ruby Doris Smith Robinson; John Lewis; and James Forman—a free trip to Africa. When someone pointed out that the group included SNCC's leaders and none of the ordinary folk at the heart of Freedom Summer, they hurriedly added Fannie Lou Hamer as an extra eleventh. That the offer came from Harry Belafonte surprised no one in SNCC. The Harlem-born and Jamaica-raised singer was among the most famous African-American entertainers and also one of the most politically engaged, an enthusiastic supporter of King and cultural ambassador for Kennedy. Belafonte had a special fondness for the young firebrands of SNCC, admiring their fearlessness and supporting them with time and money. SNCC and Belafonte had clashed over his support for Kennedy's 1961 effort to use foundation grants to bribe SNCC to shift from sit-ins to voter registration. Still, all in all, it remained a close relationship, with Belafonte acting as mentor and big brother to SNCC.[2]

On September 11, 1964, the group left New York for Guinea, where Belafonte was friendly with President Ahmed Sékou Touré. As soon as the wheels left the ground, Lewis saw everyone "letting go and relaxing," wandering the aisles, joking, and swapping stories with a handful of Peace Corps volunteers headed out for their two-year assignments. When they switched planes in Dakar for an Air Guinea jet and encountered black pilots and black flight attendants, they knew they had entered a new world. Seeing a black crew for the first time heightened everyone's romantic image of Africa as an idyllic world of racial acceptance and black rule. It also underscored the group's naïveté. Only one of them had ever been to Africa before, and most of them had never traveled outside the United States.

Touré rolled out the red carpet for his American visitors, putting them up in luxurious government villas on the ocean. They spent their days wandering around the capital city, Conakry, a relatively new city built by the French colonial government on the Kaloum Peninsula, a strip of land jutting into the Atlantic Ocean, and their nights as the guests of honor at lavish dinners with extended after-dinner entertainment. Belafonte planned SNCC's visit around auditions he was conducting for an American tour of African artists, and the elaborate entertainment doubled as tryouts.[3]

The Africans were as curious about their American visitors as the Americans were about them. Just after they arrived, President Touré dropped in unannounced to meet his guests. Fannie Lou Hamer was taking a bath when Belafonte told her the president was in the hallway waiting for her. "You all playing a joke," Hamer said. "I'm having a bath." No, really, Belafonte persisted; President Touré is at the door. "I'm definitely not ready to meet no president," she yelled as she rushed to get dressed. When the meeting finally took place, Hamer cried, overcome with the emotion of meeting a black head of state. She explained to Touré that she had tried without success to meet her own president. Here was the president of this African country not only coming to meet her but welcoming her as a part of an extended family.[4]

Bond found the trip emotionally moving: visiting a black-run country stirred his spirit and made him eager to return home to finish the work of Freedom Summer. But it also left him feeling disoriented and strangely empty as he thought about how slavery robbed him of his heritage. "I could have come from here, for all I know," said Bond. "The tragedy is, you will never know, never have any idea."[5]

For Moses, the revelations were as much political as personal. Conversing easily in French with a government minister, he learned that the minister's relatively upbeat view of American race relations came from pamphlets put out by the American government and the text of a few King speeches. On the heels of Atlantic City, the American propaganda reinforced Moses's growing unease that SNCC's activism could be distorted and co-opted by political leaders. Bond noticed it as well: "There were all these pictures of Negroes doing things . . . judges [and] policemen. If you didn't know anything about America . . . you would think these were really commonplace things. That [was] the worst kind of deceit."[6]

After three weeks, most of the group returned to the United States. Bond and Bill Hansen detoured to Paris, and John Lewis and Don Harris stayed to explore more of Africa. They traveled through the Guinean countryside, to Ghana, Liberia, and other parts of West Africa, and then to Ethiopia and Zambia, soaking up the sense of possibility that was then sweeping the continent. Numerous colonies had become independent countries—Ghana in 1957, Guinea in 1958, and Zambia just a few weeks earlier. "We had been . . . speaking a great deal about one man, one vote," recalled Lewis, "but here in Africa people were making it real, making it happen." Most of what he knew about African independence had come from brief news accounts; actually being there gave Lewis "a sense of communion" with African freedom fighters who also "knew the insides of many jails." The global conversation on freedom had become circular: the American freedom movement inspired African struggles, which in turn inspired activists like John Lewis.

More than anything, Africans asked about Malcolm X, whose emphasis on building black institutions and on the connections between African independence and African-American civil rights resonated strongly; in comparison, SNCC's politics seemed moderate. It was just another disorienting effect of being in Africa—to be seen as moderate, after having just been dismissed by the Democratic Party as too radical.

The questions foreshadowed the strangest encounter of the trip. En route from Ethiopia to Zambia, Lewis's plane diverted to Nairobi,

Kenya, for emergency repairs. While waiting, Lewis and Harris were startled to see Malcolm X—on his own African sojourn—walk into their hotel café. Though Lewis had met Malcolm X before, this was their first—and it turned out only—in-depth conversation. They shared their impressions about Africa and debated the civil rights movement. Lewis found Malcolm X unlike the "angry . . . brooding" character depicted in the press. Malcolm X urged Lewis to begin "thinking globally" about the civil rights movement as part of a worldwide struggle for human rights and to recalibrate his aspirations accordingly.[7]

The Africa trip hinted at the transitions that SNCC members would wrestle with over the next few years. By privileging a few, the trip itself showed how the evolution of the movement differentiated its members, undermining the sense of shared experience that bound them together. The Africa trip sharpened their disillusionment with American democracy and propaganda, introduced an international dimension to their conversation about freedom, and forced them to reflect on their racial identity and the meaning of blackness.

In November 1964, with the presidential election over and Freedom Summer receding into the past, SNCC members gathered at a little resort on the Mississippi coast to grapple head-on with the strains in the organization. The Methodist church retreat in Waveland appeared to be the perfect setting for SNCC to renew the bonds of organizational fraternity, for friends to reconnect with one another, and for individuals to take stock of their lives. It stood in a grove of oak and pine trees overlooking the Gulf of Mexico, near Bay St. Louis, with dormitories right on the water. The pleasant temperatures of late fall made the simple wood structures tolerable, and at night the members would wander out to the pier with a few bottles of wine to enjoy the last whispers of the warm fall, to share their company, to laugh, and to joke.[8]

But the old esprit was becoming difficult to maintain. SNCC now had the largest ground operation of any civil rights organization in the South—at least sixty field secretaries, a dozen people working out of headquarters, and more than one hundred full-time volunteers. Many of the summer volunteers and local recruits clamored for permanent membership. SNCC had always operated loosely and informally, with membership fluid and decisions made by consensus. That organizational structure was possible, however, only so long as it remained a small and close-knit group with a unified vision.[9]

A review of the attendees illustrates SNCC's growing pains. The sprawling list included veterans and newcomers who were part of the ongoing programs in Georgia, Alabama, Arkansas, and Mississippi; headquarters staff like Bond and Forman; northern staffers from offices in New York and Washington; and "Friends of SNCC" volunteers and fund-raisers from Massachusetts and Michigan, New Jersey and California. Some of the fund-raising staff, like Barry, now stationed in Washington, and McDew, had been with SNCC from the beginning, but most were newcomers with little or no southern field experience. While acknowledging that most of these newcomers "were serious people with a long-term commitment," Carmichael also saw a number of "faddists getting on . . . the newest 'hot' political thing."[10]

The rapid expansion raised a difficult question about race in the movement. SNCC had always had a few white members, and one of its most respected veterans—Bob Zellner—was white. His relationship with SNCC went back to nearly the very beginning, and he had formed close friendships with Barry and Moses in the McComb jail, with Bond in Atlanta, and with Carmichael during Freedom Summer. Even among SNCC's veterans, Zellner's jail time and the beatings he had endured were legendary. For a group that accused King of being soft, with the refrain of "Where's your body?" Zellner's capacity to endure violence inoculated him against much criticism. But now, allowing all the northern volunteers to join SNCC would give it nearly as many white as black members. Older members, like Bond, Barry, and Moses, had always envisioned SNCC as an interracial organization, but they had imagined it remaining predominantly black.

Class anxieties mixed with questions of race. Most of the new members came from the opposite poles of American society—white college-educated northerners and rural blacks from the Deep South with little formal education. These new Deep South–reared African-American field organizers felt a sense of proprietorship over the movement, even lobbying (unsuccessfully) for a rule limiting SNCC's executive committee to southern-born African Americans without a college education.

The range of movement experiences exacerbated the conflicts. Some SNCC members were veterans of Freedom Summer only; some had spent a little time in jail; some had worked only in the Freedom Schools and others only in voter registration; still others had only raised money or participated in northern protests. A common set of experiences no longer drew SNCC members together.

Worries about money hung over the organization as well. SNCC had always operated on a shoestring, but working under the COFO umbrella during Freedom Summer had given it unprecedented access to the NAACP's and the SCLC's foundation and union donors. SNCC's larger size also brought about new costs. Lewis and Forman estimated that its expenses were now running about $40,000 a month, and the windfall of Freedom Summer money was drying up, in part because the group's intransigence at Atlantic City had scared away some donors. Late 1964 found SNCC with both more money and more money problems than ever before.[11]

Forman opened the Waveland meeting by arguing that the organization needed to adopt a new hierarchical and bureaucratic structure. He wanted SNCC to become "a strong centralized organization . . . moving toward becoming a mass organization" instead of the "limited cadre of organizers" trying to "catalyze" a mass movement but not become it. The tangible manifestation of Forman's views was the Black Belt Plan, essentially an expansion of Freedom Summer across the entire South. The key difference between the two projects was Forman's pragmatic reliance on a paid staff of college-age African Americans and local residents rather than on white volunteers.[12]

Forman found a receptive audience from two disparate factions—southern-born field-workers and the increasingly vocal NAG alumni, particularly Stokely Carmichael, Cleveland Sellers, and Courtland Cox. Carmichael supported Forman in principle but worried that "the devil was in the details." As far back as the Freedom Rides, Carmichael had argued that SNCC needed a dominant central office to set policy across the whole organization. The only way SNCC could retain its position as an important civil rights organization, he believed, was to become more disciplined and bureaucratic. But now that it had won a few important victories, he saw an even greater need for a reformed organizational structure that would help SNCC consolidate gains and push for more local political power.[13]

The field staff liked the idea of expanding the Freedom Summer project across the South, but they were wary of investing too much power in a central office. To the field staff, the NAG group represented everything they feared from a strong central office: aggressive, self-confident, and highly articulate intellectuals who overwhelmed local activists with their sophisticated arguments and fast talk. Because they were closer to the situation on the ground, they argued, they were better positioned to make policy decisions than someone far removed in the national office in Atlanta. They also argued that because the field staff was "closer in backgrounds" to the rural poor of the Deep South, they were more effective organizers than the college-educated staff of the central office.[14]

The southern-born field staff's views represented the catch-22 of SNCC's success. The organization had midwifed vibrant local movements by encouraging organizers to become part of the community, but once created, these local movements and the resident SNCC staff were increasingly difficult to control or even coordinate. Field staff, like Mississippi-based James Pittman, justified their position by drawing on Moses's ideas: "I think all people can make decisions no matter what kind of people they are."[15]

Aligned with them against NAG was a faction that Carmichael and Lewis both dismissed as the "freedom highs." The freedom high position was an unsteady cocktail of youthful exuberance and Bob Moses's organizing philosophy; it combined the existentialism of direct action—acting out one's beliefs through protest—with the emphasis on local leaders and local movements. The freedom highs saw SNCC as about ideas and conscience and balked at attempts to impose bureaucracy and hierarchy. The extreme version of freedom high advocated the complete elimination of a head office and no single leader.[16]

On the other hand, John Lewis saw the split in geographic and intellectual terms—the "northern intellectuals" of NAG arrayed against the southern field staff. Lewis worried that Carmichael and NAG were overly concerned with abstract questions about racial identity and veered too close to racial exclusivism. He sympathized with the southern-born organizer who dismissed the focus on Afros and demonstrations of blackness with the pithy retort, "We know we are black."[17]

Ideas of black consciousness were very much in flux, and many in the southern field staff advocated their own form of racial exclusion in calling for a mainly black organizing staff. Certainly, Carmichael was not the fan of the "freedom high" position that Lewis suggested.

The North-South division was never as strong as Lewis remembers. Many of SNCC's founders—Bond, Nash, and Moses—came from the North but did not adopt a separatist attitude. And many southern blacks fell under Carmichael's spell, flirting with a separatist position.[18]

The five days of meetings and debate were chaotic, the positions of different participants often murky, and the issues not always clearly defined. Some participants saw Forman and Moses as at opposite ends of the debate, a characterization fair to neither man. The two had worked out the basic details of the Black Belt Plan together. It would also be wrong to see the freedom high position as the embodiment of Moses's ideas. Moses wanted people to be their own leaders, but he also understood that organizing took patience and self-discipline. His organizing philosophy required maturity, self-control, and a willingness to subsume one's ego to the process. The freedom high position represented a shallow understanding of Moses's real ideas.[19]

The only thing that was clear was that the Civil Rights Act, Freedom Summer, and the events in Atlantic City had changed the civil rights equation. With the end of Jim Crow segregation, the direct-action protests that had sustained the movement for the previous four years seemed less relevant. The struggle for voting rights remained unfinished, but the tactics to achieve that goal were the subject of much debate. Neither direct-action-style protests nor attempts to work within the existing political system had produced the substantive change hoped for by SNCC activists.

Alongside the political debate, personal questions about the nature of activism contributed to the growing sense of burnout and fatigue. The students had come into the movement with the assumption that moral suasion and direct action could end segregation within a few years; they saw their activism as a temporary thing. Segregation did crumble quite quickly, but SNCC's work had taught them that the remedy to the underlying deep-seated inequality was the kind of sustained, all-inclusive community organizing that worked in Mississippi. The veterans now grappled with the idea of activism as a permanent position. Community organizing was hard and unglamorous work. Were they prepared to devote their lives to the cause, subsuming other, personal goals, and to do it while living in places like Greenwood, Mississippi, and Albany, Georgia?

SNCC was in the midst of an identity crisis, and the multiple personalities of its past, present, and future intertwined and clashed on the Mississippi coast. The freedom highs' emphasis on the personal and on the redemptive power of activism drew on the original ideas behind the sit-ins. The call for grassroots organizing and the creation of autonomous local activists reflected the influence of Ella Baker. The call for black-led activism and a more centralized organizational structure seemed grounded in SNCC's current need. At this moment SNCC was such a chaotic mix of overlapping and competing ideas that its future direction was unknown and unpredictable.

Many looked to Moses to unite these disparate voices into a coherent whole. After all, he had influenced SNCC's organizing strategies in the Deep South more than any other person. As Lewis conceded, he was probably the one person who commanded the respect of everyone. Forman recognized this by seeking his early support for the Black Belt Plan. Even Stokely Carmichael acknowledged Moses's deep influence on him and confessed his desire to "carry on" Moses's work.

But Moses hesitated to assert himself. The constant specter of violence—against himself and against those he brought to Mississippi—had taken an immense psychological toll, especially the murders of the three volunteers and Louis Allen. "It was as if all the strife of the entire movement was playing itself out inside his skin, inside his soul, and his head," observed Lewis. Atlantic City had shaken his faith in the American democratic system; the American propaganda in Africa had intensified his skepticism about government power. Moses had become deeply pessimistic about the ability of the United States to reform itself and about the prospects for authentic social change in the South.[20]

More important, he had become uneasy about his influence in SNCC. A profile of him at the time literally compared him to the biblical Moses. Forman described his "Jesus-like aura." The hero worship put Moses in a bind. The more he pushed people to find the leadership within, the more people admired him and deferred to him—the exact opposite of his intentions. As Moses himself complained: "Nobody would ever call me a motherfucker."[21]

He responded by retreating further into himself, staying silent in the hope that others would find their own voices. He refused to take a formal position on the Black Belt Plan or get involved in the debate about restructuring SNCC, hoping new voices would fill the vacuum.

Waveland marked Moses's last substantive involvement in SNCC policymaking, and he would drift further and further away from the organization over the next few years.

The depth of Moses's personal crisis became clear the next month. At a small SNCC gathering, he came into the room holding a bottle of wine and some cheese. He offered everyone a drink and a bite to eat. After a little while, he announced that he was dropping his last name and henceforth wanted to be known as Robert Parris, his middle name. So consumed was Moses by the movement and by the pressure of organizing in Mississippi, and so disillusioned was he by the events of Atlantic City, that he literally was trying to crawl out of his own skin. In extreme form, his personal and professional crisis embodied SNCC's general ennui. He had once said that time in the movement was compressed and that one month of Mississippi time was like a year of real time. Movement time was catching up with SNCC.[22]

As SNCC drifted in the months after Waveland, Martin Luther King seized the momentum of Freedom Summer and revived direct action as an effective civil rights strategy with a series of protests in Alabama. Even though he had pushed the MFDP activists to accept the Democratic compromise in Atlantic City, King understood that ending the South's discriminatory voting laws was crucial to further civil rights gains. In fact, Freedom Summer made clear to King the need for a real focus on voting rights. After all SNCC's work in Mississippi, fewer than one in fifteen black citizens were registered (up from just one in twenty). King decided to make 1965 the year of voting rights.[23]

The SCLC's campaign leaned heavily on the SNCC alumni working with it, especially Bevel and Nash, at a time when SNCC had all but abandoned direct action as a strategy. Since the 1963 Birmingham church bombing, Bevel and Nash had been working on their own in Alabama. In the beginning, Nash had stayed in Atlanta with their infant daughter, nearly stranded since Bevel had taken the family's one car. Eager to be involved in the movement again and lonely for her husband, she joined him in Alabama, where they spent the summer of 1964 organizing in Birmingham and Selma. Though still a firm advocate of direct action, Nash had come around to the importance of voter registration and staked much of the success of the project on blending the two strategies.[24]

When King looked for a place to dramatize the need for voting-rights legislation, Bevel and Nash's work offered Selma as the perfect starting point. With a segregated industrial workforce, a powerful white citizens' council, and a notoriously violent sheriff, Selma shared similar characteristics with Birmingham. During January 1965, Bevel and Nash prepared for King's imminent arrival, working closely with SNCC's Bernard Lafayette, a Nashville veteran, original Freedom Rider, and old friend of the couple. Lafayette had been in the city for most of the last two years leading a small voter-registration project. Like many, Lafayette oscillated between SNCC activism and a normal life, organizing in Alabama during 1962, returning to full-time college in 1963, and then moving back to Alabama in 1964. Tensions between SNCC's efforts to build a local movement and King's efforts to draw media attention complicated the planning.[25]

For the first month, the demonstrators and Sheriff Jim Clark jockeyed back and forth. White leaders pressured Clark to act with restraint, having concluded that a minimal response was the best way to counter civil rights protests. By keeping the police presence to a minimum, checking violence, and slowing the protests through bureaucratic methods in the registrar's office, white leaders hoped to exhaust the activists' patience and discourage media coverage. "If we can only get the bastards out of town without getting them arrested," concluded the editor of the local paper, "we'll have 'em whipped."[26]

Clark could not resist, though. Egged on by defiant segregationists and enraged by the sight of so many demonstrators, Clark ordered the arrest of hundreds of people—more African Americans, King claimed, than were registered to vote. But the sheriff especially hated Bevel. Spotting the young activist, Clark and a few deputies beat him unconscious. Bevel awoke alone in a freezing-cold jail in soaking-wet clothes. Clark had had Bevel hosed with cold water and opened the jail's windows in a cruel attempt to freeze the young demonstrator. Ironically, Nash's personal lawyer, seeking to serve Bevel with divorce papers, alerted the SCLC to his horrible conditions, possibly saving his life.[27]

The unsettled nature of an activist's life and Bevel's unique personality had taken a toll on their marriage. Nash found their nomadic existence ill suited to the demands of a couple with two babies. (A second child, a son, was born in 1964.) Often she was alone in Atlanta without a car; sometimes she would join him on the road, but that meant the near-impossible task of caring for the babies in a motel. Bevel also proved to be not much of a husband. The qualities that made him a good activist—fearlessness, personal magnetism, a single-minded devotion to the cause, and an indifference to material things—also made him a poor spouse.

In addition, Bevel applied his civil rights philosophy to sex and marriage, arguing that sexual freedom was a necessary element of political freedom. His cheating wore on Nash, who did not share these views. One time she even secretly followed him to see if he was meeting another woman. (He was.) When she confronted him with his indiscretions, Bevel reacted angrily, even striking her. By early 1965, the very forces that had brought them together now drove them apart.[28]

The Selma arrests prompted President Johnson to reaffirm his position that voter suppression "undermines the freedom of every citizen." But he hesitated to introduce his voting-rights legislation for tactical reasons. He feared that the protests and the premature introduction of the bill would scare away the support of the moderate southern congressmen he was carefully wooing. Two northern congressmen preempted Johnson's caution by introducing a pair of voting-rights bills in early February.[29]

On the ground in Selma, federal authorities remained ineffectual, constrained by the 1957 Civil Rights Act, which required a court order to intervene against the actions of local officials. White segregationists deftly used the legal process and the narrowest possible interpretations of legal orders to slow the protests. King concluded that only dramatic violence would rally local blacks and motivate Congress.[30]

Violence at SNCC-led protests in nearby rural Perry County galvanized the Selma protests. On the night of February 18, 1965, about five hundred people started on a short march from a local church to the Perry County jail when local police and several dozen state troopers jumped the group, indiscriminately beating and arresting people— more than eight hundred by the time the evening was over. At least eight people were hospitalized, including three white reporters caught in the melee. Jimmie Lee Jackson, a local man in his twenties, shielding his mother from a police beating, was shot twice in the stomach. He died eight days later.[31]

With Martin Luther King in California on a fund-raising trip, Bevel traveled to Perry to console Jackson's family. On the drive back to Selma, Bevel and Lafayette marveled at the resilience of Jackson's grandfather. "I've got nothing to lose now," he said. "We've got to keep going." Bevel hit on the idea of a fifty-four-mile march from Selma to the governor's mansion in Montgomery to honor Jackson. "I've got something to say to the governor about Jimmie Lee Jackson," Bevel announced to a large gathering of Selma-area activists the next day. "I want to say this to him personally, and I want to take my time to get what I say right, so I thought I would walk to Montgomery and tell the governor in person that the killing of Jimmie Jackson and the oppression of African Americans was wrong." As the crowd voiced its assent, Bevel shouted out, "How many of you will walk with us?"[32]

John Lewis wanted SNCC to participate in the march, scheduled for the following Sunday, March 7, especially now that King had agreed to participate. Over the last couple of years, he had drawn close to King and the SCLC staff, admiring its resources, seeing its hierarchical leadership as a virtue, and comforted by its continuing emphasis on the moral dimensions of the movement. In fact, he had been a member of the SCLC as well as SNCC since 1962. But Carmichael denounced the march as nothing more than staged—and needlessly dangerous—theater that promoted King and the SCLC's national goals at the expense of the local movement. Carmichael supported concrete activities, like voter registration, that would provoke arrests clearly linked to the denial of a particular right. SNCC's executive committee voted not to march.[33]

The day before the march, Lewis rushed back to Atlanta to make one final plea to the executive committee. Over barbecue at the ramshackle soul food joint that served as the organization's unofficial cafeteria, he pleaded his case. Invoking SNCC's creed of local autonomy, he argued that the march represented the authentic aspirations of local blacks. SNCC "had a moral obligation" to support them. Pragmatically, SNCC should also try to reap some of the huge publicity that the march would generate. But he could not sway his friends, who remained skeptical about the march's local roots and voiced tactical reservations about the marchers' safety. Lewis announced that he would still participate, but as an individual, not as SNCC chairman. At midnight, he started the four-hour drive to Selma, wounded by the lack of support. "I never imagined that my own organization, SNCC, would ever step aside and tell me to walk alone."[34]

Lewis interpreted the decision as a personal and political betrayal.

He clung to the idea that the march represented the aspirations of the local population; the thought that SNCC was "abandoning these people" hurt deeply: "The fact that those two could ever be separated—the people and SNCC—was something that I had never imagined." Lewis's melodramatic and self-absorbed analysis contained an element of truth: the movement was at a fork in the road. Lewis wanted to continue down the path of moral confrontations and federal intervention.[35]

From the other side, Carmichael and his supporters viewed Lewis's decision to participate in the march as an abdication of his responsibilities as chairman. No matter how much Lewis pretended to be participating as an individual, the press and most people saw him as representing SNCC. Carmichael believed Lewis had a responsibility to defer to the collective wishes regardless of his personal views. As the Alabama field secretary Fay Bellamy put it: "Maybe he was representing himself. But he sure wasn't representing us. He wasn't . . . participating on projects . . . Every time LBJ called, he'd rush his clothes into the cleaners and be on the next plane to Washington."[36]

Fast-moving events the next morning, in the hours before the march was to begin, left Lewis little time to dwell on the meeting. Governor Wallace issued an emergency order of dubious legality banning the march. King proposed a one-day delay because of death threats. In fact, King was not even in Selma, having returned to Atlanta to preach the Sunday sermon at Ebenezer Baptist Church. Neither Bevel nor Hosea Williams, another SCLC organizer, wanted to cancel, and many marchers had already arrived. In a series of hurried phone calls between Atlanta and Selma, Bevel, Lewis, and the others persuaded King to okay the march.[37]

At about four p.m. on March 7, Lewis, Williams, and about two thousand others set out. Organizers hoped to cover the fifty-four miles in six days. Planning had been haphazard; most marchers lacked the proper supplies or walking shoes, as if few actually believed they would make it all the way to Montgomery. Lewis worried about the lack of preparation but counted on the generosity of local blacks along the way.[38]

At the edge of Selma, the marchers reached the Edmund Pettus

Bridge, which spanned the Alabama River. The bridge rises slightly toward the middle, making it impossible for someone at either end to see straight across. Only when the marchers reached the bridge's apex did they see fifty state troopers in riot gear and a mob armed with sticks waiting for them.[39]

Lewis and Williams were met about fifty feet from the end by Major John Cloud, the state trooper in charge.

"This is an unlawful assembly," he said. "Disperse and go back to your church and homes."

"May I have a word?" asked Williams.

"There is no word to be had," replied Cloud.

Lewis looked around. Below him was a hundred-foot drop to the water. In front of him stood a hundred armed men. Behind him were two thousand innocent people. He did not want them hurt, but he could not retreat. We should pray, he thought, and the word went back through the group. People began to kneel down to pray.

Suddenly, Lewis heard a few rebel yells and a woman's voice yelling, "Get the niggers!" A trooper clubbed him on the head, fracturing his skull. As he fell to the ground, he could smell tear gas in the air. The mob plowed through the defenseless marchers, beating them, indifferent to whether they were men or women, old or young. Many had cattle prods, whips, or ropes. A dozen mounted police purposely trampled the fallen with their horses. Police sprayed tear gas at the marchers so it would stick to their clothes rather than disperse into the air. The road was littered with the detritus of the marchers—backpacks, blankets, shoes, and purses. Patches of vomit from people sickened by the tear gas dotted the ground. Lewis lay bleeding, but the police would not let anyone near him to provide first aid.[40]

The mob chased the crowd for a mile, back to the church where the march had begun. Some of the residents of the next-door housing project started throwing bottles and rocks at the white mob. A SNCC staffer caught in the church relayed what was happening by phone to the main office in Atlanta: "We have a problem—the guys here are not nonviolent anymore. They're ready to fight." Finally, the white mob retreated.[41]

From Atlanta, the SCLC announced that a second march was to take place on Tuesday, March 9. King rushed back to Selma, joined by hundreds of white clergy responding to the new call. The SCLC appealed to the federal judge Frank Johnson for an injunction against Wallace's ban. Johnson declined to issue an injunction without a hearing, asking the SCLC to postpone the march until after the hearing on Thursday. Johnson's decision threw Tuesday's march into doubt. John Doar pressured King to wait, promising federal support on the motion to strike down the ban. King was reluctant to violate a federal judge's order, but national attention was focused on Selma now, and he felt the need to seize the moment.

SNCC activists poured into Selma; their long-standing belief that the only response to white violence was more demonstrations had trumped their initial reservations. Forman spent several thousand dollars to charter a plane to fly a group from Atlanta; a caravan of four SNCC station wagons arrived from Mississippi. SNCC pressured King to follow through with the march, arguing that the morality of opposing violence outweighed the convenience of appeasing Washington.

With the start of the march just a few hours away, Judge Johnson issued a formal injunction against it. President Johnson followed with a statement urging obedience to the courts and in the middle of the night sent a personal representative to the scene, Leroy Collins, a former Florida governor, with orders to stop the march. When Collins saw that King intended to go forward, he proposed a compromise: King and the others would march back to the Edmund Pettus Bridge, symbolically challenging Governor's Wallace ban, but then turn around. If King did this, Collins promised he would restrain the police and state troopers. None of the marchers knew anything about the secret deal. Indeed, King had warned the marchers about the possibility of "beatings, jailing, and tear gas." But he would "rather die on the highways of Alabama than make a butchery of my conscience."[42]

When the group reached the bridge's apex, it faced the same tableau—a light blue sea of state troopers backed by a mob. A federal marshal stepped forward to read the text of the judge's injunction against the march. King moved the group ahead and down to the other side, just fifty yards from the police and mob. On the side of the road, a state trooper and John Doar narrated the scene over the phone to, respectively, Governor George Wallace and Attorney General Nicholas Katzenbach. After a prayer and the singing of "We Shall Overcome," King turned the group around. As he retreated, the state troopers parted, taunting the marchers. Confused marchers wondered, "What's going on?"[43]

Back at the church, angry SNCC members demanded answers from King. His explanation confirmed their worst fears about his deference to federal officials and his habit of assuming that his interests were the same as those of the broader movement. Some questioned his personal courage. The SNCC member Willie Ricks had been staging a series of small protests over the last few days to force a response from King and local whites; King lashed out at him: "I'm in charge here and I intend to remain in charge. You can't hurt me. Remember that. You are not Martin Luther King! I'm Martin Luther King. No matter what you do, you'll never be Martin Luther King."[44]

As news of King's secret deal became known, SNCC reacted by joining a series of protests at the capitol building in Montgomery. A few even staged a vigil at King's former church, Dexter Avenue Baptist, an open dig at the apostasy of his concessions. These angry and petulant protests did little to distract national media attention from King and the Selma march or to reinforce the local movement in Montgomery, only revealing the depth of SNCC's anger with King. SNCC believed that once again expediency had won out over justice, but coming from King, the betrayal was all the more painful.

For many in SNCC, nothing better epitomized the weakness of King's approach than the divergent deaths of Jimmie Lee Jackson and James Reeb. A few hours after the second march, James Reeb, a white minister from Boston, was walking back to his hotel when he was jumped by a gang of whites and beaten with baseball bats into unconsciousness. He died on March 11, two days later. Jackson's death had galvanized the local protests but generated little national attention. Reeb, on the other hand, was a white northerner whose attack had a marginal impact on local events but generated days of national coverage as he hovered between life and death. The president had phoned Reeb's family to offer support but had not phoned Jackson's family; Carmichael openly wondered if that behavior conveyed the message that a black life was less valuable than a white life. Such a conclusion was an unfairly harsh reading of Johnson's motives; however, SNCC's point was not without merit.[45]

As the rift between SNCC and King widened, the Selma protests reached an anticlimactic resolution. On March 17, Judge Johnson struck down Governor Wallace's ban on demonstations, calling them a "classic constitutional right." King scheduled another march for the twenty-first.[46]

On that day, more than three thousand people set out on the third Selma-to-Montgomery march. At the front of the mile-long line was a who's who of civil rights leaders—Martin Luther King and his wife, A. Philip Randolph, Lewis, Forman, Bevel, and Nash. Even Assistant Attorney General John Doar joined in. Strangely, someone produced a bunch of Hawaiian leis for the leaders to wear. Nearly four thousand soldiers, FBI agents, and federal marshals guarded the route as helicopters circled overhead. Despite the security, Judge Johnson had restricted the march to three hundred participants through the notoriously violent Lowndes County. By the time the group reached Montgomery, their numbers had swelled to at least twenty-five thousand, including a large Hollywood contingent organized by Harry Belafonte. The next day more than fifty thousand attended the final rally outside the governor's mansion as George Wallace hid inside, occasionally peeking out from behind the drawn curtains.[47]

It was the largest civil rights demonstration since the March on Washington, and it would be the last of its kind: never again would so many people participate in a civil rights demonstration. And never again would the leaders of the different civil rights organizations project such unity. Both the popular support and the unity shown at Selma were illusory. Selma became a protest carnival and a media event. Drawn in by the spectacle, people made a onetime commitment to protest. Few stayed in Alabama longer than the march itself. The unity of the civil rights leadership made for compelling imagery, but it, too, was superficial. Marching together did nothing to alleviate the underlying differences between the groups.[48]

The protests did accelerate the introduction of voting-rights legislation. Johnson had wanted to wait until the end of 1965, after Congress passed other parts of his War on Poverty program, the most ambitious federal effort to help the poor since the New Deal. But where the 1930s program had emphasized top-down reform emanating from Washington, the War on Poverty featured bottom-up initiatives. It embraced a SNCC-like vision that involved the poor in their own welfare through the Community Action Program; provided new educational opportunities with Head Start; and offered poor defendants lawyers through the Legal Services Program. Hoping the War on

Poverty would secure him a legacy next to that of Franklin Roosevelt as a great reformer, Johnson balanced voting rights against the passage of his whole agenda. But the northern congressmen had forced his hand by preemptively introducing their own voting-rights bill, which shared LBJ's goals even as it complicated his schedule.[49]

To Johnson's credit, he embraced the legislation, producing one of the finest moments of his presidency. On March 15—in the middle of the Selma demonstrations—he delivered to Congress the most honest and forceful acknowledgment of American racism ever by an American president. Since Emancipation, "every device of which human ingenuity is capable has been used to deny African Americans their full citizenship," he said. Civil rights must be the nation's cause "because it's not just Negroes, but really it's all of us who must overcome the crippling legacy of bigotry and injustice." Then Johnson startled the assembled crowd of congressmen, cabinet officers, and Supreme Court justices by closing with words from the best-known movement song: "And we shall overcome."

Johnson's call for voting rights was both the expedient move of a canny politician and the heartfelt affirmation of the true believer. He combined a white southerner's firsthand understanding of segregation with the moral passion of his hero, Franklin Roosevelt. More than any previous president, Johnson had a commitment to the cause of civil rights that was rooted in the simple proposition that racial discrimination had to be eliminated because it was wrong. "No other president has so completely . . . made the issue of equality . . . so frankly a moral cause for himself and all Americans," concluded *The New York Times*.[50]

Johnson's great flaw—one he shared with many white politicians involved in the civil rights movement—was an inability to cede control over the pace and timing of civil rights change. Many whites failed to understand that calls for patience, and arguments that sudden change would cause chaos, rankled African Americans. Whites had raised these arguments in one form or another in everything from *Brown* ("all deliberate speed") to the sit-ins (Atlanta's negotiated change) to King's "Letter from a Birmingham Jail" (in which he quoted white fears). African-American frustration arose from the implicit ways whites constructed black civil rights as something to be negotiated, while white civil rights were inalienable. Whites' efforts to determine the pace of civil rights change revealed how deeply they internalized the roles of benefactor and supplicant in black-white relations. For this reason, SNCC activists remained suspicious of Johnson even in his finest hour.

The final passage of the act—it cleared the House 328–74 and the Senate 79–18—gave the appearance of a broad national consensus for reform that obscured its limitations. The act did not establish a constitutional right to vote or consider voting inequality outside the South. National civil rights leaders remained mostly silent about its weaknesses as they joined Johnson at the White House to watch him sign the bill into law on August 6, 1965.[51]

Stokely Carmichael, for one, was excited that the passage of the Voting Rights Act signaled a transition for the civil rights movement from protest to politics. His experience with the MFDP had only reinforced his conviction that African Americans needed to acquire political power to influence events. So less than a week after the Selma protests, Carmichael found himself in Lowndes County, Alabama, in an agricultural community on Highway 80 between Selma and Montgomery. He was equipped only with a sleeping bag, a few dollars, and the contact information of a local activist but was ready to put into his practice his ideas about black political power.

Carmichael could hardly have picked a more difficult place to start. Lowndes County was so feudal, he said, that "it actually made the Mississippi Delta look advanced." It was the poorest county in the state; most black homes there lacked basic conveniences like running water and telephones. The eighty or so white families that owned 90 percent of the county's land had nearly absolute economic and political power. Though 80 percent of the county's fifteen thousand residents were African American, not a single one was registered to vote.[52]

Two days after the third Selma march, Viola Liuzzo (a thirty-nine-year-old white woman so moved by the events in Selma that she left a husband and young child in Detroit to participate in the third march) and Leroy Moton (a black man in his early twenties) passed through Lowndes County on their way back to Montgomery. Liuzzo was telling Moton about a favorite song lyric—"Before I'll be a slave, I'll be buried in my grave"—when a car with four whites pulled alongside and shot them. Viola Liuzzo died from multiple gunshots to her head. Moton survived only because Liuzzo's body partially screened him from the gunfire and because the crash after the shooting knocked him unconscious, fooling the murderers into thinking he was dead.[53]

Stokely Carmichael arrived in Lowndes County the next day. He and a small team from SNCC tried to register blacks to vote but made slow progress until August 1965, when the Voting Rights Act was passed and Lowndes became the first county thereafter to get a federal registrar. At the same time, Carmichael learned of an obscure Alabama law allowing the formation of independent county-level political parties and requiring election officials to put any party that received 20 percent of the primary vote on the general election ballot. So he and his team decided to form their own party and run candidates in the May 1966 primary election.

The ten months between August 1965 and the primary were an incredibly productive time for Carmichael and his small SNCC staff. The passage of the Voting Rights Act gave them more success in registering voters. They established the Lowndes County Freedom Organization (LCFO) to run candidates for local office. John Hulett, the head of the Lowndes County Christian Movement, became its head, formalizing the LCCM's shift from an initial SCLC-oriented approach to a SNCC-oriented perspective. When white landowners retaliated against black sharecroppers trying to register, SNCC set up a tent city on black-owned land to house them, complete with Freedom Schools—in essence, a miniature Freedom Summer project.[54]

To promote the new party, Carmichael and the others cast about for a symbol to represent it. After all, the national Democrats had the donkey, and the Republicans the elephant; the state Democratic Party had its own unique symbol, a white rooster, with the official slogan: "White Supremacy for the Right." The LCFO chose a panther because it was (in the words of Hulett) a "vicious animal" that would not back down and, the organizers' pitch went, "it sure can eat up any ol' white fowl too." They did not intend the black panther to symbolize racial separatism, but no local white person ever expressed interest in joining the organization.[55]

The establishment of the original Black Panther Party is best understood in the unique context of that moment. The LCFO did not represent a rejection of democratic politics, only of the Democratic Party. As one black resident observed, "It didn't make sense for us to go join the [state] Democratic Party, when they were the people who had done the killing . . . and beat our heads." After the MFDP conflict, SNCC organizers were uncertain about allying with the national Democratic Party, and the formation of an independent party represented a pragmatic response to the evolving dynamic. It also followed in the Ella Baker–Bob Moses tradition of nourishing the self-confidence and leadership of local activists.[56]

Even as Carmichael's faith in democracy remained firm, the months he spent living among the people of Lowndes County further eroded his faith in the universal value of nonviolence. Local blacks were deeply skeptical of the idea; living as an African American in the rural South could make you that way. Many farmers owned guns and were not afraid to carry them. "You turn the other cheek, and you'll get handed half of what you're sitting on," said one. Carmichael found himself swayed by this logic, especially as federal officials continued to eschew responsibility for the protection of local blacks. To engage locals in civil rights activism but then leave them exposed to white violence, he thought, would be unconscionable. Some SNCC workers began arming themselves as well.

Meeting with the Alabama staff, John Lewis criticized Carmichael's willingness to tolerate armed organizers. "We are not King or SCLC," Carmichael countered. "They don't do the kind of work we do" and "they don't ride the highways at night." The debate ended when Carmichael asked how many field-workers sometimes carried a gun and nearly everyone working in the Deep South raised a hand. It was another indication of evolving tensions within SNCC, the declining influence of the founding members and the rising influence of the Deep South field staff. Most of all, it revealed the staff's volatile mix of optimism and frustration—optimism that the Voting Rights Act would open the door to black voting, and frustration at the lack of state and federal support.[57]

In August 1965, Carmichael and a group of SNCC activists, including a white volunteer named Jonathan Daniels, who had joined the movement during the Selma march, were arrested for demonstrating in a rural part of Lowndes County. After spending a few days in jail, they were suddenly released with no explanation. No bail had been posted; nobody from SNCC was waiting to pick them up. When they hesitated to leave the jail, the sheriff and his deputies forced them out at gunpoint. Minutes later they were ambushed by gunfire that instantly killed Daniels.[58]

Daniels's death hit Carmichael hard. On the surface, the two men could not have been more different. One was a brash, cocky black man from New York City with a radical political perspective; the other was a quiet white man, a graduate of the conservative and traditional Virginia Military Institute, now training to be a priest. But they had liked each other immensely. "I appreciated his intelligence and his seriousness," Carmichael recalled. "In this he was a little different from the usual white activists you met. He was somewhat more thoughtful and analytic" and "didn't trot out glib slogans."

Carmichael traveled to New Hampshire to personally tell Daniels's parents about their son's death. He was so shaken with grief that he stopped in New York City to pick up his mother for emotional support. "I had never seen my son like that. Silent, grim, like a heavy weight had really hit him," she recalled. It was the only time during those years he ever asked for her support. They hugged and cried with Daniels's family. Carmichael remained silent for the entire drive back to New York, lost in his own sadness and sorrow. "I think this was the hardest thing my son ever had to do in the movement," she said.

For the first time, Carmichael really understood the pressure Bob Moses had felt the summer before, the burden of being responsible for people's lives. Daniels's death reinforced his growing doubts about using white organizers in the Deep South. For Carmichael, the choice was pragmatic. Whites were in some ways bigger targets than blacks. It was as if the South's violent white racists could understand why a black man would want civil rights, but a white activist—a race traitor, in their minds—infuriated them. SNCC organizers around Lowndes County voted to exclude white volunteers and to arm themselves.

Carmichael dealt with his grief by throwing himself into his work. In the May 1966 primary, the Black Panther Party easily got the necessary 20 percent of the vote, qualifying for the general election ballot. In November, white landowners essentially fixed the general election by driving their field hands to the polls and threatening to fire them unless they voted for the white candidates. Still, more than nine hundred people cast ballots for LCFO, a little less than half of the two thousand registered black voters. It was not enough for them to win office, but it was enough to sustain the movement, and within five years the party dominated local offices, including that of sheriff.[59]

After the success of the LCFO, Stokely Carmichael emerged as the most important of a new wave of SNCC leaders, partially filling the void left by Moses's withdrawal. A close-knit and loyal group of field-workers, many with ties to NAG, clustered in the southwestern part of Alabama near Carmichael. To them, the LCFO suggested a potential model for future SNCC projects rooted in some of Moses's basic ideas. But it was also controversial because it deviated from SNCC ideology in important ways. The Lowndes County project focused less on achieving personal redemption or the building of a new kind of community than on the acquisition and exercise of political power.

An unexpected visit from John Lewis and Martin Luther King to Alabama on the eve of the May 1966 primary election had showcased the growing tensions. Just as the LCFO was facing voters for the first time, Lewis gave a speech urging black Alabamans to vote in the Democratic primary. He believed the best strategy for African Americans was to work "within the structure of the existing Democratic Party to create a biracial alternative." He saw the LCFO as a rejection of that view, going so far as to use the unfair pejorative "segregated" to describe the local Black Panther Party. Carmichael and other SNCC staffers in Alabama had not even been aware of Lewis's visit until they read about it in a local newspaper, and they were angry. They could not believe that SNCC's chairman could so "knowingly . . . deliberately . . . publicly undercut our work."[60]

Many on the Alabama staff considered Lewis's act a personal betrayal. From a broader perspective, the incident was another sign of the unique perspective of local organizers. Leaders with a national perspective like Lewis and King thought in terms of what Congress and the president could do for black southerners; they believed that the Democratic primary—despite its limitations—was the best route to political power for African Americans. From the perspective of local organizers, however, the Democratic Party was a political manifestation of Jim Crow and should be avoided.[61]

This tension came to a head two days after the primary, during a SNCC retreat in Kingston Springs, Tennessee, to address the future direction of the organization and the status of its white members. One agenda item that had not been expected to draw much attention was the annual election for chairman. John Lewis had held the post for the past five years, and his reelection was normally a pro forma event. This year, though, Carmichael heard a lot of grumbling about Lewis's performance from the field staff, who pushed Carmichael to run.

Before the vote, staff members held a far-ranging and open-ended discussion about the future of SNCC. It was the kind of heated, passionate conversation that had been part of SNCC from the very beginning. Much of the criticism of Lewis focused on his decision to participate in the Selma march, his comments in Alabama, and the time he spent publicizing and fund-raising in the North rather than organizing in the South. The critics wanted to move away from the "vague" redemptive approach of SNCC's early years to focus on building community-based political power as they were doing in Lowndes County, creating black unity, and establishing an international program that linked the American civil rights movement to other struggles like the anti-apartheid effort in South Africa. The debate was a cathartic airing of grievances, and Lewis acknowledged the need for changes, supporting, for example, the establishment of an international bureau. Finally, around midnight, they reelected Lewis chairman.

Then that outcome fell apart. Worth Long, a former SNCC field organizer attending the gathering, wandered into the meeting and challenged the results, claiming that the voting procedure had not followed SNCC's constitution (a document so often ignored that most members had never lain eyes on it). Confusion reigned. Long was not even technically a member of SNCC anymore. Many drifted away to go to bed. But this was SNCC, so the discussion dragged on through the night. At five-thirty a.m., the Alabama staffers forced a revote among those who remained. Just like that, Stokely Carmichael was in as chairman; John Lewis was out. Years later Julian Bond regretted going to bed before the meeting had adjourned, and he regretted even more that he had not challenged the results when he found out the next morning what had transpired.[62]

Carmichael's victory signaled a fundamental shift from SNCC's founders to a slightly younger, more impatient, more militant generation. The new chairman was just twenty-four. Twenty-three-year-old Ruby Doris Smith Robinson replaced James Forman as executive secretary (Forman had much earlier announced his intention to leave SNCC), and twenty-one-year-old Cleveland Sellers came on as program secretary. Though just a few years in age separated these three from Bond and Lewis, they had been less involved in the original sit-ins and the founding conference in Raleigh and were less rooted in the philosophy of nonviolence. Whereas the founders believed that exposing injustice with appeals to conscience and creed would bring about reform, Carmichael believed that only the acquisition and exercise of real political power would improve the lives of African Americans.

When SNCC announced its new leadership, many in the national press saw it as indicative of broader shifts occurring in the civil rights movement; they equated the call for political power with a call for separatism. The *Los Angeles Times* called Carmichael one of SNCC's "most radical" leaders, and *The Atlanta Constitution* predicted a turn toward "black nationalism." *Time* thought Carmichael's plans for black political power would "only lead to even greater isolation" for southern blacks.[63]

The reaction reflected the press's increasing skepticism about the movement, especially SNCC. When movement leaders emphasized integration, two-party politics, humility, and patience, national press coverage was generally positive. But when movement leaders expressed frustration and impatience with the slow pace of change and contemplated reform outside the traditional two-party system, the coverage turned negative. In part, the shift reflected how Selma's appearance of a consensus for reform had quickly broken down as African Americans moved to exercise their new rights. In the second half of the 1960s, the press was often more critical of black impatience than of white intransigence, and it portrayed understandable efforts to overcome white opposition, like the LCFO, as betrayals of American ideals. Over the next few years SNCC's position would become more radical, but the press exaggerated its extremism long in advance of any real changes.

For Lewis, the immediate impact of his exit from SNCC leadership was personal, not political. Publicly, he endorsed the change, even supporting SNCC's withdrawal from a White House Conference on

Civil Rights, which he had previously favored. As a consolation prize, SNCC's central committee put him in charge of the new international affairs committee. The job had no real responsibilities, and he ended up hanging around Atlanta with little to do. Without his SNCC work, Lewis was at loose ends. He had kept a small apartment in the city for several years but had spent more nights away than not. He had few possessions—some clothes and books, mostly. SNCC had paid for all his travel, and supporters had housed and fed him when he was on the road.

Because his whole adult life to date had been structured around SNCC and the movement, Lewis's interpretation of events became a self-absorbed tale in which he cast himself as the martyr. He accused Forman of secretly plotting against him, of resenting his transformation from shy country boy to a self-confident national civil rights leader who no longer deferred to Forman's every bit of advice. His friends reinforced his sense of martyrdom. In the days following the vote, he received many tearful phone calls pleading with him to challenge it. Bond, who was away from Atlanta during much of this time, called and wrote as often as he could. In one letter he wrote, "The crazies are taking over," and confided that he was thinking about quitting SNCC as well. Tired after more than five years of activism, Bond, like many others, just gave up on SNCC.

In the two years following Freedom Summer, political and personal forces had unraveled SNCC. Atlantic City had forced a reevaluation of the strategies and tactics that had sustained the organization in the early 1960s. Tugging at the conscience of the nation did not always produce change, as the American capacity for civic self-reform proved far shallower than first imagined. Stokely Carmichael and John Lewis had very different visions of SNCC's future, one attracted to political power and one attracted to King's moral vision.

More important to SNCC's decline was that many of its long-serving members simply withdrew. Moses suffered the most profound and wrenching crisis of faith, but he was not the only one. Exhausted, Zellner retreated to graduate school at Brandeis. Barry, living in Washington as a full-time SNCC fund-raiser, drifted toward local politics. Bond (with four young children) and Nash (a single mother of two) had family obligations that pulled them away from SNCC and the movement. Lewis himself resigned from SNCC in

August 1966 to take a job with the Field Foundation of New York City. Only when he packed up his few possessions and set out for New York did the finality of it all hit him. "I had lived a lifetime in the past six years, and now the rest of my life lay ahead of me, without a map, without a blueprint."[64]

8. ANGRY YOUNG MEN IN THE SEASON OF RADICAL CHIC

THE BLACK POWER MOMENT

On the night of June 17, 1966, Stokely Carmichael stood on a rickety, makeshift stage in Greenwood, Mississippi, and looked out over a crowd of three thousand or so people. He had come to the rally straight from the local jail after being arrested for camping out on the grounds of the local black high school. Acknowledging the roar of the crowd, he raised an arm and a clenched fist as he started to speak.

Carmichael, along with Martin Luther King and many other civil rights leaders, had come to Greenwood for the Meredith March Against Fear. On June 5, James Meredith, the man who had integrated the University of Mississippi in 1962, set out to walk the 225 miles from Memphis, Tennessee, to Jackson, Mississippi, to protest the slow progress of black voting rights in Mississippi. Just inside the Mississippi border, a Ku Klux Klansman pumped Meredith full of buckshot (miraculously not killing him). At a hurried conference, the leaders of the five major civil rights organizations—the NAACP, the SCLC, SNCC, CORE, and the Urban League—agreed to continue the march. Initially, Carmichael did not want SNCC to participate, seeing the march as part of the tired strategy of meeting violence with nonviolence. In a compromise, Carmichael agreed to King's nonviolent interracial march in exchange for a strong statement criticizing the federal government's inability to protect southern blacks and supporting a new multiyear $185 billion antipoverty proposal made by A. Philip Randolph. (The proposed expenditure was more than twice the entire federal budget. In 1966, the government spent $56 billion on defense, $5.1 billion on required income support programs such as Social Security, and another $26.1 billion on discretionary domestic spending.) The statement's strong language drove away the NAACP and the Urban League, leaving King, Carmichael, Floyd McKissick of CORE, and several hundred marchers. Now Carmichael found himself back in Greenwood, just a stone's throw from the SNCC office that had been his home base during Freedom Summer.[1]

Addressing the crowd, Carmichael thundered, "This is the twenty-seventh time I've been arrested, and I ain't going to jail no more. The only way we gonna stop them white men from whuppin' us is to take over. We been saying freedom for six years and we ain't got nuthin'. What we gonna start saying now is black power."

As the crowd shouted "Black power!" back at Carmichael, Willie Ricks jumped onstage and yelled, "What do you want?"

"Black power!" the crowd responded.

"What do you want?" he asked again.

"Black power!" they chanted.[2]

Carmichael was not the first to shout "Black power!" a shortened version of a slogan used by SNCC's Alabama field staff: "Black power for black people." African Americans as diverse as the actor Paul Robeson, the writer Richard Wright, and Congressman Adam Clayton Powell had used the phrase in the 1950s when talking about politics, African independence, and the civil rights movement. A few weeks earlier Willie Ricks, a member of SNCC, had roused the crowd at a nearby church with the same phrase.[3]

When Stokely Carmichael said "Black power," though, the reaction was completely different. The media interpreted the phrase in the worst possible light, as a radical, possibly revolutionary, call for black separatism, contrasting its supposedly violent nature with a romanticized nostalgia for nonviolence. For the media, black power simply confirmed SNCC's new radical direction, and the negative coverage contributed to the wider public perception of black power as a deviation from the higher ideals of the civil rights movement. Indicative of the press coverage was *Time*'s description of black power as a "racist philosophy . . . of black separatism." *The Washington Post* ran a cartoon of an African American eyeing a menacing-looking genie materializing from a "black power" bottle.

Criticism from other civil rights leaders seemed to confirm that interpretation. The NAACP leader, Roy Wilkins, acknowledged that the term *black power* ultimately meant "anti–white power." The Urban League vowed not to work with any group that adopted "black power as a program." In part, the attacks stemmed from the other national civil rights organizations' long-standing jealousy of SNCC, but they had practical benefits too. In painting SNCC as extremist and themselves moderate, other organizations encouraged white political leaders to trust them. National political leaders took the bait. Vice President Humphrey suggested that black power was the moral equivalent to white segregation and urged Americans to reject both. President Johnson spoke of the dangers of black power and asserted that the only solution was "American democratic power."[4]

Martin Luther King, advised by his aides to attack Carmichael, nonetheless tempered his criticism. Partly, King's motivation reflected his deepening personal relationship with Carmichael. Despite the often harsh criticism he got from the younger SNCC activists, King saw himself as their big brother—especially of its two leaders, Lewis and Carmichael—listening to their concerns, tolerating their excesses, defending them to outsiders, and gently dispensing advice. Carmichael and King drew particularly close during the Meredith March, debating politics and the direction of the movement as they walked across Mississippi. King admired Carmichael's brashness, his uncompromising passion, and his ability to rally a crowd. In turn, Carmichael came to appreciate the man behind the icon for his easy humor, his quick mind, and his steady demeanor.[5]

The Meredith March occurred in the middle of King's own growing uncertainty about how to translate protest into political power. In refusing to sign a statement denouncing Carmichael, King emphasized the "dire need" for "this kind of legitimate power." He saw African-American enthusiasm for black power as an authentic emotional response to the "failure of white power" to tame the "monster of racism" hidden behind legal segregation. It also represented to King new energy that the movement could tap into for forthcoming campaigns. But King parted company with black power rhetoric by emphasizing the utility of engaging in the electoral process and the possibilities for change in a pluralistic society.[6]

. . .

In the summer of 1966, Carmichael attempted to define black power with a pair of essays. He saw black power as a political idea: the desire of African Americans to elect black representatives and to generate the political muscle necessary *"to force those representatives to speak to their needs."* It was part of the long process of political assimilation that the Irish, the Italians, the Jews—indeed, all ethnic groups in America in the twentieth century—had gone through, he argued. And it had to be understood in the context of the "specific historical experience" of the last six years: the fierce resistance of southern whites to black voting, the inadequate federal response to African Americans' needs, and the willingness of national leaders to value expediency over justice. To achieve true self-determination, the movement "cannot have the oppressor telling the oppressed how to rid themselves of the oppressor."

Integration, he pointed out, had long been a one-way process, in which blacks moved into white neighborhoods and sent their children to white schools; that reinforced the idea that white was better than black by definition. Black people moved from Watts to Beverly Hills and took their "energy and skills from the ghetto to white neighborhoods." He offered an alternative set of positive black values that highlighted the transition to an explicitly cultural assertion of liberation. "We are black and beautiful," he declared.

Carmichael took pains to stress that black power did not mean "Git Whitey"—he blamed the "sensationalism and race-war mongering" of some reporters for popularizing that myth. At the same time, he shifted blame for the failures of the movement back to whites. "White America" must stop "crying out against 'black supremacy,' 'black nationalism,' 'racism in reverse,'" and look inward. White critics, especially putatively sympathetic white liberals, needed to look at the problems within their own community. "Let them preach nonviolence in the white community," he wrote. "They come to teach me Negro history; let them go to the suburbs and open up freedom schools for whites. Let them work to stop America's racist foreign policy; let them press this government to cease supporting the economy of South Africa."[7]

Black power's departure from SNCC's earlier Jeffersonian vision of the American creed is clearly seen in the different books now cited as formative: Bob Moses had read Albert Camus' *The Rebel*; Stokely Carmichael read Frantz Fanon's *The Wretched of the Earth*. Moses had drawn a humanistic message from Camus' writings, warning activists against being overwhelmed by the struggle, advising them to "retain some glimpse of happiness within," and challenging them to move beyond victimhood without succumbing to the desire for revenge. Carmichael learned from Fanon to view the American civil rights movement as part of a worldwide struggle against colonialism. He also drew from Fanon the idea of a black colonial nation-within-a-nation in the United States, oppressed by the white establishment in the city and by hostile police and political leaders in the suburbs. In this context, Fanon argued that violence is sometimes necessary. Finally, Fanon warned activists to prevent revolutionary energy from hardening into complacency; he urged leaders to look for ways to continually renew the struggle.[8]

African students, particularly South Africans, were reading the same texts as Carmichael, not just Fanon but Kwame Nkrumah, Julius Nyerere, and other leaders of African independence movements. In South Africa, the young activist Steve Biko spearheaded the black consciousness movement, which like American black power grew out of the failure of liberalism to contain white violence. Founded in 1968, the South African Students' Organization broke with the multiracialism of the dominant SNCC-like National Union of South African Students with the slogan "Black man, you are on your own." The American civil rights movement and the struggle for independence in Africa fed off each other in such a way as to blur the original lines of inspiration.[9]

Malcolm X was another source of inspiration, even if black power advocates shied away from fully embracing his ideas. Like Fanon, Malcolm X used the language of colonization, oppression, and exploitation to describe the African-American experience. He saw black Americans as a distinct nation-within-a-nation and advocated solutions that fostered black political, social, and economic autonomy. SNCC members increasingly talked about black consciousness, which Cleveland Sellers defined as "the construction of a new, black value system" that would be "geared to the unique cultural and political experience" of African Americans. The ideas of black consciousness and black power gave SNCC members a new intellectual framework and a language for talking about the problems of African Americans as they moved away from the conciliatory language of the American creed.[10]

"No matter how many speeches we gave in order to set the record straight," wrote Sellers, "we were unable to convince most Americans that we weren't interested in sacking cities or dragging white women off." But the change in perception was also subtler than Sellers suggests. The very phrase *black power* challenged the American creed's assumptions of ideological consensus and assimilation into the majority culture. Black power suggested that all Americans did not have the same interests, and that American democracy was inadequate to the challenge of resolving those competing interests.[11]

Carmichael's public persona overwhelmed his efforts to claim a real intellectual footing for black power. He was the first SNCC person to rival King as a media sensation. He had a great sense of style—cool Chelsea boots, hip shades, a bracelet on one wrist, and a lean body built for the narrow-cut suits of the day. His look was a far cry from the SNCC "uniform" of a few years before—denim overalls, white T-shirts, and canvas sneakers, or the dowdy "Sunday best" suits worn by the movement's preachers. A friend described his style as the embodiment of revolutionary hipness. The slightly British hint in his accent—a residue of his Trinidadian youth—only enhanced his attractiveness, in an era when American youths of all kinds were beginning to idolize icons of exotic political radicalism. *Ebony* described him as a person who "walks like Sidney Poitier, talks like Harry Belafonte, and thinks like the post-Muslim Malcolm X."[12]

He had become a compelling speaker. *Esquire* said he dazzled with a "taut suppressed whisper" that flowed "musically" as he talked about the need for black power ("We have to be proud of our blackness") or criticized the war in Vietnam ("Ain't no Vietcong ever called me nigger"). With his mix of political radicalism and youthful cool, he represented both the new direction of the civil rights movement and the new student radicalism. His swagger and charisma captivated reporters. His quick wit and fiery rhetoric made for great news copy, and journalists flattered him with attention. For all his efforts to give black power a serious intellectual foundation, Carmichael reveled in the attention brought on by his theatrics.[13]

By the early winter of 1966, many in SNCC openly wondered if all the attention was going to Carmichael's head. Some called him "Stokely Starmichael" behind his back and poked fun at him for always seeming to have a microphone in front of him. Other staff members challenged him directly for "getting too much of the glitz." Ruby Doris Smith Robinson, who had replaced Forman as executive director, complained that to outsiders, "SNCC is only the organization that Carmichael has at his disposal to do what he wants to get done." SNCC's members had long criticized King for elevating fame and personality over grassroots activism, for putting the individual above the group. SNCC had always walked an uneasy line on this question. While its members emphasized the group over the individual in public statements, SNCC's own internal value system valorized the individual heroism of beatings and arrests as a marker of status.[14]

The contrast with the earlier Lewis-led and Moses-influenced SNCC was subtle but profound. Moses's rise to internal prominence had underscored that no matter how much SNCC members talked about the group, individual influence evolved naturally. In their own ways, both Lewis and Moses had realized that leadership required self-restraint and a willingness to defer to the group. Their shared experience, from the sit-ins through Freedom Summer, also worked to collapse hierarchy and check the power of the individual. But the Stokely-centric SNCC represented the founders' worst fears that an individual who gained too much power and influence could upset the fragile balance that had previously sustained the organization.

Carmichael's fame brought increased scrutiny from police and politicians. In September 1966, when a disturbance broke out in Atlanta over the shooting of a black man by a white policeman, city officials made Carmichael the scapegoat simply because he had arrived on the scene soon after the incident. Atlanta police raided SNCC's headquarters and arrested Carmichael on charges of inciting a riot. The police found it easier to blame his allegedly hotheaded rhetoric for inciting the crowd than to examine decades of tense relations between the city's white police and black residents. A month earlier, in Philadelphia, police found dynamite in an apartment used by a group of activists called the Young Militants. Since one of the four people arrested had ties to SNCC, Police Chief Frank Rizzo suggested (without any evidence) that the dynamite was evidence that Carmichael and SNCC were plotting a campaign of guerrilla warfare in northern cities. As the public face of black power, Carmichael—and SNCC more broadly—became an easy target for such persecution.[15]

On a more substantive level, Carmichael's fame further corroded the group-centered ethos of the old SNCC; never before had the organization been so closely associated with one person. Both John Lewis and Bob Moses tried to turn the spotlight back on SNCC whenever press attention came their way, but Carmichael always seemed to turn the spotlight back to himself. He also proved to be a poor day-to-day leader. By early 1967, SNCC was down to just ten functioning offices, many of which operated as nearly independent entities; staff members often had to go weeks at a time without pay because the financial situation was so grim.[16]

The rise of black power coincided with changes in the composition of SNCC's membership. Many veterans hated Carmichael's incendiary rhetoric, and the turn to black power drove them away from the organization. Lewis tried to hold his tongue, but when pressed by a reporter, he took a swipe at Carmichael: "We don't believe in sloganeering. We believe in programs." Charles Sherrod, who had been working as a field secretary in Georgia since 1961, proposed an interracial voting-rights project; when the main office rejected it, he quit. Diane Nash disliked the idea of black power so much that she cut her ties to SNCC.[17]

At a practical level, the departure of veteran activists drained SNCC of experience and institutional memory at an important moment. Talk of black power also opened a rift between SNCC and ordinary black southerners. As the Mississippi activist Joyce Ladner noticed, local activists defined *black power* as a concrete way to achieve their basic political and economic goals, in contrast to "cosmopolitans" like Carmichael who saw it as an ideology to "redefine 'black' and all that it symbolizes." The fact that new members increasingly came from urban areas and concentrated their work in cities widened the split. In Atlanta, Los Angeles, New York, Chicago, and Washington, SNCC-affiliated groups became activist centers in their own right by promoting black power. There "seemed to be an inexorable pull radiating from black power," Sellers observed. "Every SNCC program and every SNCC person was drawn toward the term's controversial vortex."[18]

The extent of the changes came into focus in December 1966, when SNCC gathered for a retreat at the Peg Leg Bates Country Club in upstate New York. SNCC's leaders hoped the remote location would give them the freedom to grapple with the impact of black power on the organization. The meeting was prompted not just by the overall decline of SNCC's operations but by the rise of the Atlanta Project, a community antipoverty project started by SNCC in 1965. Its members took issue with many of the group's founding principles, like the American creed–oriented critique of segregation, the belief in the redemptive power of protest, and Quaker-meeting-style consensus decision-making. Instead they argued for the existence of a distinct African-American worldview and called for black political and economic autonomy; its leaders barred white volunteers, even respected SNCC veterans, from their work in Atlanta's poorer neighborhoods.[19]

In early 1966, Atlanta Project organizers had circulated a paper to staffers calling for the expulsion of whites; no matter how genuine their commitment to the cause of civil rights, it argued, whites were part of "collective white America." White activists should devote themselves to the problem of white racism, and SNCC should be "black-staffed, black-controlled, and black-financed." When the Atlanta Project first released the paper, months before the toppling of John Lewis, few in SNCC subscribed to its extreme position. By the time the organization gathered in upstate New York on December 1, 1966, the situation had changed.[20]

The Atlanta Project staff hijacked the SNCC meeting. Bill Ware, the founder of the Atlanta Project, pushed for an end to white participation because "the cats on the corner do not dig having white people in the organization." More seriously, he argued, if people really understood the concept of black power, they would understand there was no place for white members in SNCC. The Atlanta group mercilessly pressed their case. When Fannie Lou Hamer spoke up in favor of a biracial SNCC, they mocked her and told her she was no longer relevant.[21]

Complicating the debate was the fact that, by late 1966, only seven whites were still active members of SNCC; the others had drifted away because of the rise of black power and the movement's changing dynamics. Those who remained, though, were among SNCC's most committed veterans. Chief among them was Bob Zellner, SNCC's first white member and Carmichael's running buddy during Freedom Summer. Since then Zellner had been absent from SNCC while pursuing a master's degree in sociology at Brandeis, but recently he had returned to Atlanta. However much the abstract question of a black-only SNCC might appeal to some, it was hard to contemplate such a step if it meant expelling Bob Zellner.[22]

For three straight days at the Peg Leg Bates Country Club, the hundred-plus participants debated the question of white membership. At the end of one long evening, at least forty left, worn out by the tense discussion. The Atlanta group continued to press the issue.

Finally, at two a.m., a vote was held. Twenty-four of the sixty-one remaining people abstained, including all the whites. The resolution passed by one vote, 19–18. Afterward, recalled one black SNCC member, "no one wanted to look at Bob." Immediately following the vote, the whites left the meeting.

The decision to expel SNCC's white members looked a lot like the vote to replace John Lewis six months earlier. Both occurred in the middle of the night after a long, exhausting debate that had driven away many participants. The actual vote was close and hardly definitive. No matter—the results were profound. The vote, along with the earlier position paper on whites, which had been leaked to *The New York Times*, reinforced the worst public image of SNCC as a radical, separatist organization. This image, however exaggerated, became self-reinforcing, as new members attracted to SNCC's black-only philosophy further radicalized it. At a practical level, the loss of the white veterans contributed to the erosion of institutional memory and organizing experience, further separating the new SNCC from its roots.

SNCC's radical image frightened away donors and made established civil rights groups even more reluctant to share money with them. For many months, SNCC could not even afford its already low twenty-dollar weekly wage for staffers. In Atlanta, the head office staff was sometimes forced to scrape together spare change to buy hot dogs and beans for a collective meal cooked on the little stove in the back.[23]

The burdens of trying to sustain SNCC's field operations, to resolve the deteriorating financial situation, and the possibility of significant jail time (from the trumped-up charges in Atlanta) weighed on Carmichael. Running a bureaucracy was not his strength, and he chafed under the restrictions he felt as SNCC chairman. He disliked having to run his public statements by a group and having his schedule dictated by the organization's needs. The ulcer he developed during Freedom Summer flared up. When his one-year term came to an end in June 1967, Carmichael announced he would not seek reelection—to the relief of everyone in SNCC.

Carmichael had come to power promising to solve SNCC's problems and had instead accelerated its decline. Managing its sprawling and fractious operations would have been a difficult task for anybody, but he lacked the patience to translate slogans into a program. Faced with the choice between doing the difficult work of building up SNCC's local operations or fulfilling the many requests for interviews and speaking engagements that followed the black power speech, Carmichael stepped into the limelight and became seduced by his own press clippings. He confused talking about action with action itself, and personal fame with institutional credibility.

Ironically, as SNCC's organizational effectiveness declined, its notoriety expanded, projecting a larger shadow across the mass-culture-mediated American scene. As SNCC was thrown into the limelight by the 1964 Atlantic City convention and the cry of black power, news profiles of the organization multiplied exponentially after 1965. *The Saturday Evening Post* and *Ebony*, paragons of the white and black establishments respectively, ran approving profiles. *Life* profiled Carmichael. *Esquire* proclaimed the emerging "Student Left" to be the "New Fraternity," announcing that "like most everything that has happened in the country the last five years, the Student Left owes its existence to the Negro sit-ins." The rise of the Student Left helps account for the expanded media interest in SNCC. With the emergence of the Free Speech Movement at the University of California at Berkeley and the growing youth-led opposition to the Vietnam War, reporters looked to explain these developments to their readers; they made it clear that SNCC, from the Moses-inspired consensual structure to the emphasis on grassroots organizing to the embrace of nonviolent rebellion, was an inspiration for much of what was happening among the nation's youth.[24]

Relinquishing the chairmanship of SNCC did nothing to diminish Carmichael's fame. If anything, his celebrity increased. Like SNCC itself during this period, the less he accomplished, the more the media treated him like an important figure. He spent the summer and fall of 1967 traveling around the world—going to London, Havana, Moscow, Beijing, Hanoi, and finally Africa. In London, he exchanged ideas with the famed Caribbean writer C.L.R. James. In Cuba, Fidel Castro took him on a jeep tour of the remote mountain hideaway where he had plotted the Cuban Revolution. In Moscow, he dined with the widow of W.E.B. Du Bois; in Vietnam, he lunched with Ho Chi Minh; in Algeria, he hung out with veterans of that country's war for independence. The Ghanaian leader, Kwame Nkrumah, offered him a job as his political secretary. These were heady experiences for a young activist barely twenty-five years old, much more fun than being SNCC's chairman.[25]

Carmichael's successor completed the ruin of SNCC. Hubert "Rap"

Brown, the new chairman, had become a full-time SNCC staffer only in 1966, though his roots went further back. His brother Ed, a field secretary, had joined SNCC in 1962 through NAG; Hubert had joined him in the South during high school and college and worked on voter registration during Freedom Summer. His nickname came from his unique ability to strike up a rapport with anybody. Rap Brown spoke the language of black political power, cultural autonomy, and urban discontent and promised to revive SNCC by moving it from "rhetoric to program" through a return to local organizing. He advocated the creation of a "freedom organization" to bring "jobs, power, and freedom" to poor communities in both urban and rural areas. But Brown's promises did nothing to arrest SNCC's decline. He proved an indifferent bureaucrat, with little interest in the nitty-gritty details of sustaining an organization. The larger problem was that the organization lacked both cohesion and camaraderie. Without a shared past as a compass, every member seemed to follow his own path.[26]

As with Carmichael, Brown's flair for fiery rhetoric undermined his efforts to rebuild SNCC's grassroots programs. Soon after Brown's election, when Carmichael was arrested at a protest in Alabama, Brown called it "a declaration of war" by a "racist white America." At a July 25 rally in Cambridge, Maryland, he told a crowd, "If America doesn't come around, we're going to burn it down." That night police and protesters exchanged gunfire, and then black protesters burned or looted more than fifteen buildings. Brown claimed he was not part of the violence, but he made it easy for the police to blame him. The FBI became involved in the case, and Brown was charged with arson. He spent the next few years fighting the charge and related legal troubles. He, too, stepped down as SNCC chairman after only a year's time. In March 1970, just before his trial was to start in Cambridge, two of Brown's close friends in SNCC died in a car explosion near the courthouse. The cause was never determined; the FBI claimed the men blew themselves up transporting a bomb, while SNCC claimed they were murdered. Brown fled to Canada. A year later he sneaked back into the United States. In October 1971, he participated in the armed robbery of a New York City bar and was sentenced to five years in jail.[27]

By the end of 1967, SNCC was only a shell of the organization it had once been, alienated from its original base of support among rural folk, ridiculed by the press, and scorned by whites.

. . .

The demise of SNCC as an organization did not halt the spread of the idea of black power. Once the phrase entered the public sphere, Carmichael and SNCC lost control over it, and its ambiguity made it the perfect slogan for a wide variety of groups. Probably the most famous was the Black Panther Party of Oakland, whose quick rise and fall exemplifies the morphing and splintering civil rights movement of the late 1960s. To fit the new circumstances, the Panthers challenged, reshaped, and remolded the methods and ideals that had made SNCC successful.

The seeds of the Black Panther Party predated the formation of the Lowndes County Freedom Organization and Carmichael's "black power" speech. Huey Newton and Bobby Seale, the two founders, met in early 1965 while they were students at Merritt Junior College in Oakland. Newton having been born in Louisiana and Seale in Dallas, they were both part of the century's twin great migrations— African Americans moving out of the South, and Americans of all colors moving to California. The two became friends through their work on the Soul Student Advisory Council, a student group lobbying for black history courses and black faculty. Eager to get involved in the community, they concentrated their energies on the North Oakland Poverty Center, an organization funded by one of President Johnson's new War on Poverty programs.

They were avid readers and self-taught intellectuals, embracing everything from W.E.B. Du Bois and E. Franklin Frazier to Mao Tsetung, Che Guevara, Jomo Kenyatta, and Kwame Nkrumah. Probably no book influenced them more than Fanon's *The Wretched of the Earth*. Even more than Carmichael, they found a language in Fanon's work that spoke to them. Fanon's description of the inequities of colonial Algeria—African underdevelopment nestled against white prosperity—resonated with their reality of urban poverty amid suburban affluence. To this insight they added Mao's ideas on organizational discipline and Malcolm X's emphasis on black identity.

In early October 1966, after a year of preparation, Seale and Newton formed the Black Panther Party for Self-Defense. Its platform was by turns an angry manifesto, a sophisticated political critique, and a paean to the American creed. Its core reflected mainstream progressive politics, calling for full employment, decent housing for all, and better schools. To it the Panthers added the perennial black national-ist demand for payment of the Civil War–era promise of forty acres and a mule. They advanced this program with national, even interna-tional, political rhetoric and gave close attention to grassroots social services. The group's first action was to successfully lobby for a traffic light at a busy Oakland intersection where several kids had been killed on their way home from school. During their heyday in the late 1960s and early 1970s, the Panthers organized programs to serve the community from cradle to grave, providing everything from free breakfasts for children to free ambulance services for the elderly.[28]

By framing their critique in racial terms, the Panthers frightened many whites and obscured the mainstream liberalism at the core of their work in Oakland. Their keen sense of the performative aspects of protest played into white fears, contributing to their extremist im-age. Their uniform—black leather jackets, black trousers, black berets, dark black sunglasses, often accompanied by a firearm—became an iconic symbol of black power, hinting at street gangs and paramili-tary groups.

Don Mulford, a California assemblyman, introduced a gun control bill aimed squarely at the Panthers' tendency to carry firearms. On May 2, 1967, during the debate on the bill in Sacramento, thirty armed Panthers (twenty-four men, six women) stood on the capitol steps: Bobby Seale read a statement from Newton attacking the bill for try-ing to keep "Black people disarmed" when "racist police agencies" terrorize and brutalize them. Then the group went into the Assembly's visitors' gallery. When television cameras and news photographers arrived, the group repeated their performance on the steps, then were arrested for disturbing the peace. The Panthers planned the protest for greatest effect; although it was provocative, it was also carefully choreographed, and planned out to the last detail; they had researched everything to minimize their legal exposure.[29]

The protest turned the Oakland Panthers from an obscure local organization into a national sensation by tapping into the oldest of white fears—that black Americans would reciprocate white violence in kind. Such fears stretched back to the slave conspiracies of Den-mark Vesey and Nat Turner and to John Brown's raid, and had their present manifestation in the frenzied coverage of the Black Muslims and armed civil rights activists. The Panthers' protest brought in-creased scrutiny from the Oakland police. The police circulated descriptions of Panthers and their cars; Panthers often found that police stopped them for little reason and gave them petty citations for things like spitting on the sidewalk. So on the morning of October 28, 1967, when an Oakland policeman radioed in that he was pulling over a "known Panther vehicle," it was not unusual. It turned out Huey Newton himself was driving the van. The police officers started to write out a traffic citation and ordered Newton to step out of the vehicle. As he got out, shooting started. When it was over, one officer was dead, another was seriously wounded, and Newton had four bullets in his stomach. He was charged with murder and kidnapping and denied bail.[30]

The Panthers turned the arrest and shooting of Huey Newton into the symbol of the new civil rights movement—urban and militant and focused on police harassment and the racial inequities of American justice. With its recruiting posters and buttons, SNCC had pioneered the idea of fusing youth culture and pop culture with protest, but the Panthers perfected it. Panther rallies in the Oakland area were well-coordinated performances that always featured a large contingent of Panther men and women uniformly decked out in leather jackets, Afros or berets, and dark sunglasses. The whole look was the antithesis of SNCC's early clean-cut, all-American image, a symbolic rejection of mainstream values, and a canny merging of a progressive political agenda with a consumer culture that defined people by appearances.[31]

The distribution of "Honkies for Huey" buttons and the like extended Panther support by making radical politics another element of a consumer culture. Easily the best-known example of the Panthers' astute grasp of revolutionary theatrics was the famous photograph of Huey Newton on his throne. It was supposed to be a simple photograph for the Panthers' newsletter. Eldridge Cleaver, another Panther, had sat Newton on a wicker chair (with a huge flowing back like a throne), arranged African-looking shields around him and a zebra pelt on the floor, and put a spear in one hand and a rifle in the other. It was a brilliant manipulation of symbols, and as much as they sometimes disdained the politics of cultural nationalism, the Panthers made shrewd use of it. The leather jackets were not just uniforms but fashion statements that conveyed a political message as well. What you wore and how you did your hair made a political statement that was easily understood by even a casual observer. As with the sit-ins, the fulcrum for this shift in the movement was youth. But where the early 1960s students had highlighted the gap between a supposedly inclusive youth culture and its reality of social exclusion to claim a larger political voice, the Panthers made that gap a substitution for greater political action.[32]

As the Panthers gained notoriety, Seale and Newton craved legitimacy, respect for their platform, and a seat at the table of major civil rights organizations. In late 1967 the Panthers approached Carmichael about speaking at some "Free Huey" rallies. All the other major civil rights organizations had turned their requests down. The Panthers saw Carmichael as their spiritual godfather; even though he was no longer chairman, he was still the most famous person in SNCC. For his part, Carmichael recognized the political differences between himself and the Panthers—primarily the Panthers' willingness to ally with white groups. But the Panthers appealed to his vanity, flattering him with an offer to become the "honorary prime minister" of the African-American Nation.[33]

The invitation to Carmichael sparked merger talks between the Panthers and SNCC. The Panthers thought a merger would give them access to SNCC's institutional competence and community organizing expertise—what Newton called the "bourgeois skills" necessary to run a large organization. If the older civil rights organizations saw SNCC as an annoying upstart on the radical fringe of American politics, the Panthers saw it as a mainstream organization that could provide access to established civil rights leaders. Many in SNCC, particularly James Forman, saw in the Panthers an updated urban version of SNCC at it origins—young African Americans at the vanguard of social change. They thought the Panthers could help them tap back into the spirit of youthful revolution that had once made SNCC so successful. A merger might help SNCC regain its own lost organizational youth and reclaim its waning influence.[34]

Both sides overlooked the serious hurdles to a successful union. Seale and Newton confused Carmichael's celebrity with real power in SNCC, and they imagined that the SNCC of 1967 was still the SNCC of 1964. For their part, SNCC members romanticized the Panthers, imagining them as the authentic voice of urban African Americans, and respected the Panthers' militant posture. As Willie Ricks bluntly put it, "The SNCC people were the bad niggers in town, and then the Panthers jumped up and started saying, 'We are badding you out.'" SNCC members let the theatrics blind them to the Panthers' own organizational deficiencies. Many of the urban young people who flocked to the Panthers were attracted by the performance of militancy more than to the Panthers' actual programs or any sophisticated analysis of the problems faced by African Americans.

But the Panthers rushed ahead with the merger idea, without the agreement of SNCC. At a February 17, 1968, "Free Huey" rally in Oakland, they announced a merger with SNCC and named Carmichael as "prime minister," Forman as the minister of foreign affairs, and Rap Brown as minister of justice. When Forman and Carmichael took the stage a few minutes later, they made clear that any talk of a formal merger was premature. Forman described the Panther-SNCC partnership as an alliance. Carmichael spoke out against the Panthers' willingness to align with white groups, in favor of a black-only stance.

The confusion at the rally foreshadowed the eventual collapse of the proposed merger a few months later. SNCC members balked at the Panthers' pressure for an immediate merger and their demand that SNCC accept all Panther political positions; the more aggressively the Panthers pushed SNCC to agree to the merger, the more SNCC resisted. Despite their rhetorical similarities, SNCC and the Black Panthers had very different organizational cultures. Both groups realized that the Panthers had tapped a genuine vein of anger among African Americans outside the South, but neither group could figure out how to translate SNCC's earlier southern successes to this new environment.[35]

Martin Luther King also felt compelled to respond to the legitimate issues raised by the Black Panthers and other advocates of black power. King, in fact, did more than just respond. Over the course of the three years separating the passage of the Voting Rights Act in August 1965 and his assassination in April 1968, his thinking changed. He sharpened his critique of the economic inequalities of American life, talked more than ever about the plight of the nation's poor—both black and white—and became an impassioned critic of the Vietnam War. He still spoke the language of the American creed, but the tone had changed. No longer did he start from the premise that the United States simply needed to live up to its basic ideals by including all. Now he openly wondered if the system was fair. As his rhetorical critique broadened, however, his tactical vision remained quite narrow, and like SNCC, he struggled to export his tactics outside the South.

James Bevel returned to the South from an April 1965 visit to Chicago determined to get King to make that city the target of a northern campaign against de facto segregation. With its highly segregated housing market, "the real estate dealers in Chicago," he concluded, "are the equivalent to Wallace and Jim Clark in the South." Bevel argued that King could apply the direct-action strategies used in Birmingham and Selma to the problems of residential and employment discrimination in Chicago.

In mid-1965, King told the press that Chicago could become the first "meaningful nonviolent movement" centered on "the ghetto." He readily conceded that Chicago presented a different set of challenges—fewer overtly unjust laws, issues not as "clear-cut" as in the South. But King and others in the SCLC tended to focus on Chicago's practical advantages of strong black community organizations, a powerful religious community, and a single political boss, Mayor Richard Daley, to negotiate with. They also had an exaggerated impression of themselves, deciding that the North suffered from a "bankruptcy of leadership" that could be remedied by their presence.

The exact goals of the campaign and how they would be accomplished remained uncertain as King vacillated between different approaches. He spoke mostly about the SCLC's objectives in general terms, saying the move north represented a shift in focus from "constitutional rights" to "human rights." At first, King suggested that the SCLC would focus on the city's schools to highlight the city's entrenched de facto segregation. Other SCLC officials pointed toward a large-scale voter-registration program. Bevel's hopes for the campaign were vague and idealistic. He spoke of "going for broke" in Chicago to "create a new city." He offered an even more simplistic—and cocky—description of the SCLC's plan: "We build people. People build organizations. Organizations move."[36]

The Chicago movement got off to a slow start. The mayor circumvented King's crusade by announcing a series of programs to improve ghetto conditions. Local blacks did not turn out in the numbers the SCLC anticipated. Recruiting young people, which had been Bevel's specialty, proved difficult in Chicago, with its well-established network of street gangs, which found King's message of interracial harmony and nonviolence hard to swallow. The biggest problem was King's inability to devise a protest that resonated with the public. It was difficult to frame the issue of ghetto poverty without pushing the debate outside safe political limits.[37]

A perfect example of these clumsy efforts was the SCLC's February takeover of a run-down apartment building. Arriving in work clothes, King announced that the SCLC was going to establish a "trusteeship" over the building and use the rent to improve it rather than to line some landlord's pockets. The SCLC spent about $2,000 on repairs but collected only $200 in rent when the city stopped the tenants' rent subsidy checks. In court, a federal judge described the SCLC's "revolutionary tactic" as "theft," ordering the return of the property. Opposing the sanctity of private property seemed to put the SCLC—not the ghetto conditions themselves—outside the boundaries of the American creed.[38]

Chicago was a near-total failure for King and the SCLC, though it is hard to identify a single cause as decisive. Dissecting the SCLC's day-to-day difficulties misses the larger problems. Long before tactical errors contributed to the failure of the Chicago protests, King failed to articulate a clear strategy that resonated with the public. As it moved tentatively from arguing for the inclusion of African Americans into civic and economic life to a more substantive activism requiring government intervention, the SCLC's campaign challenged the dominant public understanding of the movement's goals. The de facto discrimination dominant in Chicago resisted clear illustration through direct-action protest (of the kind that had worked so effectively in the South). The extreme residential segregation at the core of the city's racial inequality was a particularly difficult issue to bring to life.

Chicago changed King. He lashed out at critics and putative friends on all sides. When the 1966 civil rights bill, with its strong provisions for equal housing, went down to defeat in September, King decried the "hypocrisy" of Democrats who claimed to support equal rights but voted against the bill. His critique of American society sharpened. Now skeptical of capitalism, he was less sure that majoritarian democracy had the capacity to reform itself. The civil rights movement, he conceded, "did not defeat the monster of racism." The end of petty segregation only superficially changed American life. Real shifts required changes in the economic as well as the social arenas. "You can't talk about ending slums," he said, "without first seeing that profit must be taken out of the slums" by taking on "the giants of vested interest."[39]

King's views revealed the influence of SNCC and the Black Panthers. Yes, he used more soothing language than either, and he continued to frame the issues in less confrontational terms, but his critique of American capitalism as culpable for racial discrimination, his definition of the problem of the ghetto as essentially an economic one, and his conceptualization of African Americans as an interest group drew inspiration from the black power critique.[40]

The differences among civil rights activists were less analytical than tactical. Neither King nor Carmichael nor the Panthers offered—perhaps could not offer—new strategies for turning their critiques into viable action plans. Black and white Americans simply came to starkly different conclusions about the future direction of the movement. Economic injustice was ambiguous and difficult to illustrate with concrete examples that identified clear villains and victims. Designing a strategy for economic justice that did not challenge the fundamentally individualist and private-property-based notion of rights central to the American creed was therefore extremely difficult.

Before King had a chance to resolve these difficult questions, a lone white gunman assassinated him in Memphis on April 4, 1968. Violence broke out across the country in cities ranging from Tallahassee to Chicago, from Winston-Salem to Hartford. Breathless news accounts tended to overstate the urban violence, particularly in Washington. Stokely Carmichael received blame for Washington's violence when press accounts reported him telling local blacks to "go home and get your guns." Other articles mentioned "gangs of roving black youths" and government workers "fleeing" the city. Such reporting fit comfortably into the narrative of the last two years that simultaneously emphasized and delegitimized black anger by suggesting it was the product of Carmichael's demagoguery.[41]

The violence in Washington was scattered and random. Of the five deaths officially linked to the riots, two were the result of accidents and two took place far from most of the rioting, leaving only one that could really be so linked: Tom Wicker of *The New York Times* was one of the few reporters to recognize the riots' haphazardness. "The angry or vengeful actions of a few might have stimulated excitement in others and set them free of normal restraints," he wrote the day after King's death. "Most of the looters, far from appearing angry or mournful at the news from Memphis, appeared to be having a good time."[42]

When he learned about King's death, John Lewis was in Indianapolis with Bobby Kennedy, having just joined Kennedy's campaign for the Democratic presidential nomination. Many in SNCC believed that as attorney general, Kennedy had been more concerned with protecting his brother's political future than with the rights (and lives) of civil rights activists, but Lewis believed Kennedy had changed in the four and a half years since JFK's assassination. With his opposition to the war, his genuine embrace of racial equality, and his attention to the plight of the poor, Kennedy often sounded as if he could have stepped out of an early SNCC meeting. On Lewis's part, his embrace of Kennedy confirmed the continued relevance of SNCC's early embrace of the political process, an idea that ran from the sit-ins through Barry's speech at the 1960 Democratic National Convention to the MFDP, and now to a stage in Indianapolis. For a brief moment, the various threads of the 1960s seemed to converge—Lewis turning toward Kennedy and electoral politics as Kennedy turned toward the hope of SNCC's founding vision, and as both men grappled with the twin problems of violent white extremists and an impotent federal government.[43]

Kennedy himself was the one to inform those gathered for the campaign rally about King's death. The laughing, cheering, boisterous crowd grew immediately silent as he delivered one of the great speeches of his life without notes or preparation. He told them that King had died because of his dedication to love and justice. He urged them not to be angry at all whites, reminding them that a white man had killed his brother. The future would be difficult, he conceded, but he told them to remember that "the vast majority of white people and the vast majority of black people want to live together." He closed by paraphrasing an ancient Greek quote—"to tame the savageness of man and make gentle the life of this world."[44]

In a daze, Lewis traveled back to Atlanta for the funeral. More than sixty thousand people filled the sidewalks to view the cortege. There was no room inside the church for the ordinary people King had fought for. Dignitaries filled the eight hundred seats in Ebenezer Baptist Church—politicians like Bobby Kennedy, Richard Nixon, and Vice President Humphrey; celebrities like Diana Ross and Harry Belafonte; and civil rights leaders like Roy Wilkins and Whitney Young. Fifty senators, thirty congressmen, dozens of mayors, and religious leaders from every major denomination joined them at the funeral.[45]

Enough SNCC veterans came to almost make it a mini-reunion. Along with John Lewis and James Bevel, Diane Nash, James Forman, and Stokely Carmichael all came to pay their respects. But they came as individuals, not as representatives of SNCC. Absent were many of the organization's key figures (Bob Moses, Julian Bond, Ella Baker), and the only two current SNCC members present—Cleve Sellers and Willie Ricks—sneaked in without invitations.

King's transformation from controversial figure to revered American hero was instantaneous. President Johnson proclaimed Sunday a national day of mourning. Major League Baseball postponed opening day, and the NBA rescheduled an important playoff game between the Boston Celtics and the Philadelphia 76ers. But the memorializing presented only a limited picture of King, emphasizing his philosophy of nonviolence at the expense of his more controversial positions on economic inequality and Vietnam. Like the funeral itself, the eulogies did not dwell on the slow pace of civil rights change or the tricky question of King's critique of poverty, favoring instead an appeal for continued black patience and for white goodwill under the idea of nonviolence.[46]

Evidence of the limitations of this strategy was everywhere. Large numbers of white Atlantans ignored the day of mourning as stores and restaurants outside the downtown area remained open. Declining to attend the funeral, Governor Lester Maddox also tried to stop the secretary of state from lowering the capitol flags to half-mast. Governor Ronald Reagan of California framed King's death as a lesson in law and order: "We began compromising with law and order, and people started choosing which laws to break."[47]

As Reagan's quote illustrates, King's assassination confirmed for many whites the notion that the civil rights movement was out of control, responsible for its own violence, and outside the American mainstream. Rather than contemplate the political weaknesses that had exposed King to violence, Reagan's quote hinted at how whites seized on the rhetoric of black power to explain even King's assassination as a cultural failure rooted in the black community.

· · ·

From a different perspective, African Americans also turned to culture as a way of explaining the political and social limitations of the civil rights movement. The person with the most sustained influence on the transformation of black power from a political statement into a cultural one was the boxer Muhammad Ali. It is hard to overstate the importance of Ali as a transcendent cultural figure who shaped notions of blackness for both races in a country uncertain of what a post-civil-rights world would or should look like. His exploitation of the media culture crowded out the political elements of his message in favor of the cultural images of black pride, and by the early 1970s the transformation of the civil rights movement from one focused on politics to one focused on culture and personal identity was complete.

Cassius Clay, Jr., was a product of the complex social structures of the South, born in Louisville, Kentucky, on January 17, 1942. Clay Sr. was a sign-painter, but that job put the family solidly in the city's black middle class; they lived a comfortable existence. A white policeman got the young Clay involved in boxing as a diversion from the street, and he was good. At just eighteen, he won the gold medal in the heavyweight division at the 1960 Summer Olympics in Rome. When he returned home, the Louisville Chamber of Commerce presented him with a citation but could not find the time to hold an honorary dinner, as was the custom. Segregation was still in force, and when he tried to order a glass of orange juice at a local diner, he found himself kicked out. Local white elites sponsored Clay's pro career, providing the start-up cash for his training expenses in return for a cut of his earnings. They were motivated less by civic pride than the chance to make money. (One sponsor greedily calculated that his $2,800 buy-in would yield a $150,000 payout after a few fights.) But it would be wrong to see Clay as solely a captive of Louisville's power structure; his family rejected many of the syndicate's choices for managers and trainers, reminding them he was not just another docile Negro they could control.[48]

From the start, Clay was not an entirely apolitical figure. His entire persona—the bravado and swagger—challenged southern standards of behavior for a black man. Clay mixed patriotism ("I beat the Russian and I beat the Pole / And for the USA won the Medal of Gold") with a blunt acknowledgment that only his success allowed him such freedom. Without boxing, he observed, "I'd be poor and I'd probably be in my hometown washing windows . . . saying 'yes suh' and 'no suh' and knowing my place." In the four years following his Olympic victory, as he rose up the professional rankings, *Ebony* called him "a blast furnace of racial pride"—and not a pride masked with "skin lighteners and processed hair" but "scorched with memories of a thousand little burns."[49]

He upended conventional expectations. He was not a mainstream civil rights supporter like Floyd Patterson or Sonny Liston. He was not deferential like Joe Louis or overtly menacing like Jack Johnson. In fact, his combination of boyish good looks and aggressiveness in the arena gave him the same complicated sexual power as Elvis Presley. Talking quietly, he projected the same soft, nonthreatening, almost girlish look that Elvis had when being interviewed, but when both entered the arena to perform, they gave off a highly charged—and, to conservative whites, dangerous—sexual energy.

After defeating Sonny Liston to win the world championship in February 1964, Clay became even more controversial by announcing he was joining the Nation of Islam, sometimes known as the "Black Muslims." At the postfight news conference, one reporter asked if he was a "card-carrying" member of the Nation, underscoring its nefarious reputation. A few weeks later Clay adopted the Muslim name Muhammad Ali, further increasing his notoriety. *The New York Times* refused to recognize his new name and continued to use Cassius Clay in its articles. Ali's own father implied that the Nation had brainwashed his son. Jackie Robinson wrote a piece for the *Chicago Defender* critical of Ali's choice and arguing that African Americans would not embrace "Black Muslimism any more than they have embraced Communism."[50]

"I'm no troublemaker," Ali told the press as he ticked off the reasons white America should not be frightened by him. "I have never been in jail. I don't join any integration marches. I don't pay any attention to all those white women who wink at me." But he still found himself spurned by conventional civil rights leaders. In dismissing white expectations of the behavior of a black champion, Ali's independence made him an icon to young African Americans. Jackie Robinson might have been right that African Americans would not flock to join the Nation of Islam, but they flocked to Ali. Offering a new role model for being black, proud, and political, Ali paved the way for focusing on identity and culture as defining elements of civil rights.[51]

Ali's religious views might have remained nothing more than a controversial curiosity, but in 1966 the army tried to draft him. In 1964, the army had classified Clay as unfit for active service after its aptitude test suggested he had an IQ of 78. Ali was deeply embarrassed, but his low score illustrates the extent to which poor southern schools undermined African Americans. As the need for troops in Vietnam grew, the army lowered its qualifying score on the intelligence exam, reclassifying Ali as 1-A. Ali started learning about Vietnam, a subject to which he had previously not paid much attention; the more he learned, the more skeptical he became of what he saw as a white man's war. "Man, I ain't got no quarrel with them Vietcong," Ali famously declared to *The New York Times*.[52]

On April 28, 1967, Ali showed up at the Army Entrance Station in Houston, with H. Rap Brown at his side, to officially claim conscientious objector status on religious grounds. The World Boxing Association stripped him of his title, and the New York State Boxing Commission, one of the most powerful in the country, refused to license him, effectively putting a hold on his career. The well-known sports columnist Red Smith wrote, "Cassius makes himself as sorry a spectacle as those unwashed punks who picket and demonstrate against the war."[53]

To young Americans, however, he became even more of a hero; having the heavyweight champion of the world refuse to go to Vietnam energized the antiwar movement. Ali became a crossover icon, celebrated by black and white youth alike. But he was something of a curious hero. In addition to speaking out against the war, he expanded on his religious views, explained black nationalism, and argued the need for a separate black homeland. On lectures at college campuses, he criticized students for their drug and alcohol consumption and for premarital sex. But what resonated with students was Ali's fusion of politics and personal identity. His refusal to go to Vietnam on the grounds of personal conscience—as the only way to remain true to himself—seemed an act of self-definition and personal discovery. As such, Ali was a critical figure in the transition from defining civil rights gains in terms of external victories to defining them in terms of internal victories, in the development of personal identity and self-expression.

Ali's stand came at a price. He was banned from boxing until the

Supreme Court unanimously ruled in 1971 that the government had unfairly denied him conscientious objector status. It would take Ali another three years to regain his world title in the ring.[54]

By 1971, however, the transformation of black power from a political slogan to a cultural style was complete. The signs were everywhere: in the popularity of Afro hairstyles and dashiki clothes, in the music of bands like Sly and the Family Stone, and in blaxploitation movies like *Shaft*. Young African Americans sported "Black is beautiful" buttons and hung Huey Newton posters on their walls. It was the emergence of what the historian William Van Deburg called "soul style," the cultural manifestation of black power. Soul style encompassed everything from handshakes (the more complicated the better) to language (*dig* and *jive* became common slang) to food (not just traditional soul food like collard greens or catfish but anything cooked with "soul" and "feeling"). Soul music by such artists as Aretha Franklin, Marvin Gaye, James Brown, Barry White, Junior Walker, and Stevie Wonder provided the soundtrack to soul style.[55]

Much of soul style was not new; elements of it had deep roots in African-American culture. What was new was not just the way it all came together but the way it was commodified and marketed to consumers. One could mail-order "black on white" T-shirts emblazoned with "soul brother" or "soul sister" logos. (The same company also sold a "soul brother" vanity front license plate.) Wig companies introduced whole lines of Afro-style wigs supposedly made with "afrylic" or "afrilon" fake hair. A St. Louis–based company advertised "black and brown" trading stamps in *Proud* magazine as an alternative to the traditional S&H green stamps. Music consumers were urged to "buy this [album] and free yourself." Soul became a product, a thing that could be bought and consumed as an assertion of identity, a political statement, and a tool for empowerment.[56]

The commodification of soul had a powerful influence on the public perception of black power. Most important, it fused with the ongoing media coverage to complete the transformation of black power, and civil rights generally, from a political movement into a cultural statement. Civil rights now seemed to be about what you wore, what you ate, and what music you listened to. Black power became about black culture, not black politics, and if the mainstream image was slightly menacing, linked to the inner city, with whiffs of gangs and danger, that only widened the gap between black aspiration and the wider consensus once built around the American creed.

The strange career of black power stood as an ironic counterpoint to the story of SNCC, which had thrived by rejecting the hero worship and personality cult that surrounded King, only to find itself pulled apart by the attention given a single leader. It had burst onto the scene by harnessing the emerging cultural power of young blacks into a political movement, only to come apart when a new generation of activists turned that political energy back onto cultural questions. The story of black power thus throws into relief the struggles of SNCC to redefine itself, to build on its early achievements, and to define its place in an America that was both more open to and more wary of black action.

In 1970, the author and social commentator Tom Wolfe attended a fund-raiser for the Black Panther Party at the New York City apartment of Leonard Bernstein, the famous conductor. For Wolfe, the weirdness of the whole evening was summed up by the image of a Black Panther, decked out in a leather coat and sunglasses and with a huge Afro, deciding whether to eat a Roquefort cheese appetizer offered by a white servant on a silver tray. Wolfe marveled at the way New York City's upper-crust liberals flocked to attend parties for the Panthers, aping their clothing style, hanging on to every detail of their dangerous and vaguely criminal lifestyle. They vainly hoped that merely by association, and the occasional financial donation, some of the Panthers' cool would rub off on them. It was, Wolfe declared, "the season of radical chic."[57]

THE ENNUI OF VICTORY

Three successive summers of racial unrest in America's cities had driven the FBI director, J. Edgar Hoover, hysterical. He was sure subversive black activists threatened the country's stability. At Hoover's direction, the Bureau organized the "Black Hate Group" on August 25, 1967, to increase surveillance of civil rights leaders in the United States; its principal targets were Martin Luther King, Jr., and Stokely Carmichael, who particularly fascinated Hoover; he thought Carmichael was the only African-American civil rights leader with the "necessary charisma" to supplant King as the putative leader of the black community and to "unify the African-American community under a single nationalist ideology."

In response to the director's fascination, FBI analysts drew up wildly inflated estimates of Carmichael's influence. Bureau reports credited him with the rise of the Black Panthers and ominously warned that his haphazard organizing of the District of Columbia's poor represented a "long-term threat" to the country. In early 1967, the FBI put Carmichael at the top of a new "Rabble Rouser Index" as one of the "most radical and violent" black leaders. Hoover authorized the FBI to "expose, disrupt, misdirect, discredit, or otherwise neutralize" Carmichael and other black power leaders.

For as long as there had been a civil rights movement, the FBI had been spying on it. The Bureau opened a file on King shortly after the Montgomery bus boycott. Hoover sympathized with white southerners and was convinced that most movement activists were Communists. Begun in 1956, COINTELPRO, an acronym for Counter Intelligence Program, became the principal FBI program for monitoring the movement through surveillance, informants, and illegal wiretaps. Under Hoover's prodding, COINTELPRO analysts assumed that African Americans moved in lockstep and described black power as primarily the work of a few prominent individuals like Carmichael.[1]

FBI agents used every available tool to harass him. They followed him around. They opened his mail and listened in on his telephone calls. They hired informants to report on his activities and leaked stories to make him look bad. They whispered tales of his sister's marriage to a Jewish man and spread lies about how he and his new wife, Miriam Makeba, the South African singer, led a secret life in an opulent house in Washington. The Bureau even considered trying to discredit Carmichael by falsely leaking to the press that he was a CIA and FBI informant. To coax information from his mother, agents scared her with a fabricated tale about an assassination plot by the Black Panthers.

In her autobiography, Makeba wrote about what it felt like to be under constant surveillance. In lighthearted moments, she and Carmichael would joke about their "babysitters," but the surveillance did not always seem humorous. When she left her house, she would see "faceless white or black men in their suits" across the street observing them; when she arrived in a new city, she would see the same men speaking to the hotel clerk minutes after she checked in. She found the surveillance scary and "nerve wracking." She told her husband it felt like living in a prison, and she worried that the FBI had bugged their house and could listen to them making love. "This is really nasty treatment," she wrote, "from a country that is supposed to be free."[2]

Exhausted by the constant harassment, Carmichael and Makeba moved to Guinea in late 1968. Politically, he felt that he had reached the end of the road and that the current political climate precluded the development of black power in the United States. "Real black power requires a land base," he concluded. "The only place where we have a material basis for power is Africa." King's assassination tipped Carmichael over the edge, and he made his final decision to leave soon after the funeral. "I fought with him over going to Africa," remembered Cleve Sellers. "But SNCC was dying, the FBI was tracking him everywhere, and we had all gone through ten years with no break, and though nobody likes to admit it, you had to take your behind somewhere just to think."[3]

Carmichael accepted an offer from Kwame Nkrumah, the exiled leader of Ghana, to serve as his aide in Conakry, Guinea. He and his wife quickly established a new life for themselves. They were celebrities—the singer and the revolutionary. President Touré gave them open-ended use of a beautiful government villa and a car with a driver; they were overwhelmed with a flood of social invitations. Conakry was a hub of African intellectual thought and liberation movements, and Carmichael loved being at the center of it all.

Carmichael had struck up a fast friendship with Nkrumah during the former's 1967 Africa tour. He was soon meeting with foreign delegations, refining Nkrumah's revolutionary message, and training with a refugee Ghanaian military unit. His work focused on trying to return Nkrumah to power in Ghana. In fact, Carmichael was so obsessed with the idea that Nkrumah himself felt the need to rein in his protégé's "youthful impetuosity."

Both men, however, found the relationship beneficial. For Carmichael, being part of Nkrumah's entourage gave him a sense of power and legitimacy, and it brought speaking engagements around the world and meetings with famous leaders and revolutionaries. Nkrumah saw in Carmichael the possible future of Pan-Africanism, and the idea of this protégé spreading his message flattered the exiled leader's vanity. But Carmichael's dream of returning Nkrumah to power ended when the exiled leader died of a heart attack in 1972.

Carmichael's other passion during these years was nurturing and expanding the All-African People's Revolutionary Party (AAPRP), founded by Nkrumah and Touré in 1968. The AAPRP promoted a vision of a unified African continent with its own unique economic structure. Carmichael described Pan-Africanism as "the belief that all African peoples, wherever we may be, are one, and as Dr. Nkrumah says, 'belong to the African nation.'" The party's economic vision "is grounded in socialism which has its roots in communalism. Any ideology seeking to solve the problems of the African people must find its roots in Pan-Africanism." In practical terms, the AAPRP promoted its ideas, aided anticolonial movements across the continent, and established links with revolutionary movements around the globe.

The Pan-Africanist vision of a united continent that rejected the extremes of both capitalism and communism had grown out of the optimism of the postcolonial moment. Its adherents truly believed that a common African nationhood had been suppressed by the artificial lines drawn by European colonizers. The vision rejected Western political structures as alien to the African experience and Western economics as unsuitable. Democratic socialism would bring economic growth to Africa, without the social dislocation and wide disparities of wealth that had been key features of the colonial economy, and Pan-Africanism would unite the continent in a rejection of the national lines drawn by the colonial powers. It was a powerful imagining of the African future, a romantic vision of a continent transformed. While not everyone subscribed to the whole vision, the popularity of its specific elements among activists inside and outside Africa helped keep it at the center of continental political debate. In particular, the AAPRP's critique of the harsh inequities of colonial capitalism resonated with colonized people all over the world, and its socialism promised to reconcile the rapid growth and technological advancements of capitalism with the humanist values of precolonial societies. As a rallying cry, Pan-Africanism could be seductive; as a slogan, it could be powerful political shorthand.

At its core, the party's Pan-African democratic socialist vision was deeply flawed, representing a rejection less of European colonialism than of African history itself. The opposite of an Africa artificially divided by European colonizers was not a unified continent. Precolonial Africa had always been divided by differences of ethnicity and geography. Simply put, nothing really united Africans. The continent's history was too wide-ranging, and its people too diverse. Some African countries had been colonized in the 1600s, and others not until the 1880s; some had close links to the Middle East and Asia, others to Europe; some were long-established democracies and monarchies, others were loose confederations. People on the continent spoke hundreds of different languages, belonged to hundreds of ethnic groups, practiced everything from Islam to Christianity to animism. About the only thing that Africans shared was colonialism, and even there the response varied widely from place to place.

In the 1960s and 1970s, the birth of a United States of Africa was no more likely than the birth of a United States of Europe, and the notion of a united Africa never gained traction. Few leaders really embraced the idea of subsuming their national power to a continental organization. The differences among African countries—ethnic differences and legitimate differences of national interest—along with the ambition of various leaders thwarted that dream. In addition, the Cold War forced African nations to choose between Western-style democratic capitalism and Soviet communism. Both sides were suspicious of nations that deviated from the particular norm, so few countries really developed a third way. For a variety of reasons, including global economic forces, mismanagement, and outright corruption, the economy of most African states floundered in the 1970s, further eroding the credibility of the Pan-Africanist vision of democratic socialism.

The notion of a unified Africa mesmerized Carmichael, but he was more gadfly than powerful political player. The organizations in which he had the most influence—the AAPRP and the Organization of African Unity—had little power. They had no real political base. They were not political parties in the traditional sense. They could not translate ideas into reality. Carmichael spent most of his time writing, giving speeches, and meeting and greeting dignitaries in Conakry and abroad, communicating with such disparate revolutionary groups as the Irish Republican Army, the American Indian Movement, and the Palestine Liberation Organization. He gave fiery speeches denouncing Zionism that raised questions of anti-Semitism.[4]

His views were controversial within African society. Ordinary Africans coveted the Western things that Carmichael rejected—the clothes, the popular culture, and the consumerism. As his son Bokar (born in 1981 to his second wife, Marliatou Barry) observed, "My father's attempt to claim his African-ness alienated him in Africa. I think people have this idea of Africa being very African, culturally speaking. When you see my father, he's dressing up in African clothing and rejecting all things belonging to Western culture. But many people in Africa are trying to grasp Western culture."[5]

Carmichael attended the 1974 Muhammad Ali–George Foreman fight in Zaire. He dined with Fidel Castro when Castro visited Conakry. He changed his name to Kwame Ture in 1978 to honor his two African mentors, Kwame Nkrumah and Sékou Touré. He traveled the third-world revolutionary circuit as an ambassador for the AAPRP—to Syria and Iraq in the Middle East, to Liberia, Ethiopia, and Senegal in Africa, to Guyana and Jamaica. He got caught up in the vicissitudes of local politics, of coups and countercoups that followed the 1984 death of Touré, getting arrested for allegedly trying to overthrow the new government but essentially remaining on the periphery of Guinean politics.[6]

By the mid-1970s, Carmichael had become a political curiosity. He was a revolutionary celebrity, a sort of living Che Guevara T-shirt, all symbolism and no substantive power. His personality and politics seemed frozen at the moment of his greatest celebrity in the late 1960s. The brashness and audacity that had made him a notorious figure became more pronounced, and he became more ideological, strident, and dogmatic in his views. He seemed more intent on stirring up a firestorm with his comments than on making real economic and political progress in Africa. Charlie Cobb lamented that the "the old loose Stokely [became] completely consumed by the ideological Kwame." He was and would always remain the young rebel, the enfant terrible, the agent provocateur, unwilling or unable to see that speech-making was no substitute for the mundane and hard work of grassroots community development.[7]

The FBI harassment that drove Stokely Carmichael to Africa was the leading edge of a widespread law-enforcement campaign to harass and discredit SNCC leaders. Like the FBI, local law enforcement eschewed any complicated analysis of the late-1960s urban upheavals in favor of blaming a few individuals. In this context, the exaggerated rhetoric and flashy style of black power advocates made them an easy target. In February 1968, when a student protest at the all-black South Carolina State College in Orangeburg, over the city's failure to robustly enforce the 1964 Civil Rights Act, became unruly, police responded by shooting thirty-three demonstrators and killing three. Cleve Sellers, traveling to Orangeburg to offer advice to the student protesters, arrived just as the violence erupted and was shot in the left shoulder. Police later arrested him for inciting a riot, because, in the words of the governor's spokesman, "he's the biggest nigger in the crowd."[8]

The rise of black power rhetoric and the seeming breakdown in public order allowed police to redefine direct-action protests as riots and to blame protesters for any ensuing violence. For his alleged role in the Orangeburg demonstrations, a jury found Sellers guilty with a possible sentence of seventy-eight years. On appeal in October 1970, a judge reduced Sellers's sentence to one year in jail and a $250 fine. He spent seven months in prison, the only person to serve jail time for an incident in which the police killed three people.

The unraveling of SNCC left activists like Sellers alone to face such charges. It took SNCC nearly three weeks to raise his bail, and it offered no financial support during his trail and appeal. More important was the psychological isolation he felt while awaiting his appeal; he lamented the disappearance of "the sense of common cause and shared destiny." He had virtually no money, living an "uncertain hand-to-mouth" existence while sharing a run-down Atlanta apartment with Willie Ricks. Barely able to afford the cheap rent, they lit the apartment with pirated electricity and fed themselves on handouts. At the time, he wrote about his exhaustion, his hunger, and his lack of a personal life: "I am caught up in the strong current of a river of no return."[9]

Weariness and disillusionment gripped Bob Moses as well as he gravitated to the antiwar movement in 1965, giving speeches at rallies in Washington and Berkeley, and participating in a summer conference of antiwar activists. Moses saw opposition to the war as a moral issue, inextricably linked to the movement. He drew a direct connection between the federal government's failure to protect civil rights activists in the Deep South and its aggressiveness in Vietnam. "The rationale the nation uses to justify the war in Vietnam turns out to be amazingly similar to the rationale that has been used by the white South," Moses argued. A southern segregationist "condones murder in Vietnam for the same reason he condones it at home—he sees a threat to his civilization." Therefore, Moses believed, "Negroes better than anyone else are in a position to question the war, not because they understand the war better, but because they better understand the United States."

To illustrate the connection between the war and white racism, Moses brought a large group of African Americans from McComb to an August 1965 rally in Washington. A few weeks earlier a McComb resident who had participated in the earliest protests with Moses had died in Vietnam. The death prompted two McComb activists to issue a list of "five reasons why Negroes should not be fighting in any war for America." The list unleashed a firestorm of criticism. The editor of the *Delta Democrat Times*, Hodding Carter, who for a white Mississippian had been unusually supportive of the civil rights movement, said the list veered "close to treason."[10]

Moses also faced criticism from other African Americans, exposing the perennial divide between activists who saw the war as a moral issue and pragmatists who worried that foreign-policy dissent threatened to alienate white elites. The Mississippi NAACP head, Charles Evers, argued that "for Negro citizens to ignore the draft can only . . . destroy that which they have fought so hard to achieve." Most disappointing to Moses was the fact that John Lewis met with President Johnson on the very day that he brought the Mississippi group to the Washington rally.[11]

Moses never found a comfortable place in the antiwar movement. The rallies he spoke at drew mainly white crowds, less focused on the linkage between the immorality of white racism and the immorality of war. Media coverage in places like *The New York Times*, which tended to portray the antiwar movement primarily as a white hippie rebellion, only reinforced this image. Moses was also upset that black antiwar activists seemed to be subjected to harsher criticism. He complained bitterly about the criticism directed at the McComb protesters, pointing to a five-thousand-signature petition delivered to the White House on the same day. To Moses, the only real difference between the two groups of protesters was their race. Finally, the adulation that followed Moses everywhere he went continued to bother him. He may not have been the most publicly visible antiwar protester, but the leaders of the movement—many of whom got their start as civil rights activists—revered him.[12]

In late 1965, unsure of his place in either the antiwar or the civil rights movement, Moses traveled to Africa to represent SNCC at an Organization of African Unity meeting, then stayed to travel around the continent. He returned to the United States more disillusioned than when he left. The rhetoric of Pan-Africanism did not inspire him as it had Carmichael; rather, he saw that American propaganda successfully glossed over the reality of black life in America. The gap between image and actuality gnawed at Moses and hampered the hard work of organizing.[13]

On his return, Moses cut off contact with most whites and even some African Americans. Coming six months before Carmichael's black power speech, his further retreat from the spotlight reflected his increasing alienation from conventional politics and his distrust of white political leaders. At the time, John Lewis said, "I doubt seriously if he would speak to me today. I don't know. Maybe he would. But I understand he refuses to speak to any white person and selects the Negroes he likes to talk to."[14]

In 1966, Moses retreated to Amzie Moore's house in Mississippi, where he stayed for about four months, using Moore as a sounding board as he tried to figure out his next move. Perhaps if got back in touch with the ideas that originally motivated him, he thought, he would find a way to energize himself and the movement's flagging grassroots activism. Moore described Moses as "withdrawn," and not "speaking to anybody hardly." Many of his Mississippi comrades were unsure of his movements. In a 1967 interview, Fannie Lou Hamer admitted, "I don't know where he is now."[15]

The Vietnam War contributed to the breakup of Moses's marriage to Donna Richards. The two disagreed about the extent to which black activists should involve themselves in the antiwar movement; Richards believed antiwar protests distracted them from the ongoing struggle. Beyond those disagreements, the stress and uncertainty of their current situation added to the strain on their marriage. As with many movement couples, the very forces that had united them now seemed to be pulling them apart. Their shared commitment to ending segregation had brought Bob Moses and Donna Richards together; when the wandering and disillusionment of the late 1960s replaced the certainty of that crusade, fissures in their marriage appeared.[16]

In July 1966, Moses received a single thin envelope from the federal government that snapped him out of his lethargy: it was a draft notice. The U.S. government wanted to put him, at the age of thirty-one, into the armed forces. The army ordered him to report for induction in New York City on August 1, making him one of the 400,000 American men called for service that year.[17]

Bob Moses had first registered for the draft around January 23, 1953, his eighteenth birthday, and received a student deferment. Such a deferment, indeed any deferment, was not unusual in the quiet moment sandwiched between the end of the Korean War and the escalation of the Vietnam War. He had lost his deferment when he joined the movement full-time in 1961. Though he had passed the draft-eligible maximum age of twenty-six, his deferments rendered him still technically eligible to be drafted until thirty-five. He applied for conscientious objector status, citing his civil rights work, and attended a hearing before his draft board in New York in July 1962. He never received a definitive answer on his petition. In fact, he never heard anything more from his draft board until that letter arrived in 1966.[18]

Moses suspected FBI involvement; it would certainly explain the unusual decision to draft someone of his age. Though induction calls rose markedly in 1965 and the army tightened the requirements for deferments, the armed forces had little interest in men over twenty-six. After the January 1966 release of SNCC's antiwar statement, the twenty-six-year-old John Lewis had seen his draft status change from conscientious objector to 1-A. He, too, suspected political involvement. Lewis used his movement contacts to complain to Burke Marshall in the Justice Department. Subsequently, he received a 4-F deferment for being "morally unfit."[19]

The reclassifications of Moses and Lewis showed that the draft had become politicized. The rich and well connected got deferments; the poor and unlettered fought, and the politically dangerous could have their status changed at any moment. Intimidation of draft protesters was not unknown either. In October 1965, thirty-nine draft protesters had their student deferments withdrawn solely for their participation in antiwar protests. After appeals, all but six regained their student deferments, but the threat of reclassification hung in the air. Bob Moses, who occupied a pivotal symbolic and psychological place in the antiwar movement, no doubt attracted the attention of his local draft board and federal officials; the simple fact that he received a notice at age thirty-one strongly suggests that someone with power had intervened.

With his reporting date less than a month away, Moses faced the critical decision of what to do. Of course, entering the armed forces was out of the question. He mulled over the idea of refusing induction and going to jail. But that would have turned him into a martyr, exactly the opposite of what he wanted. On top of that, he did not relish spending even one more night in jail—he was tired of it. He never considered doing what Lewis did, getting a friendly face in the Justice Department to intervene on his behalf.

Near the end of July, Moses traveled to New York City. Instead of reporting for induction, he borrowed money from his brother and headed to Canada, becoming one of at least thirty thousand Americans to avoid the draft by leaving the country. For almost two years,

Moses worked a series of odd jobs in Montreal—night watchman, airline chef, telephone salesman—losing himself in the anonymity of menial labor and an assumed name, trying to figure out what to do next. While in Montreal, he became romantically involved with Janet Jemmott, a former SNCC field secretary, and they were later married. In the spring of 1968, they left Canada for Africa and traveled around the continent for almost a year before settling in Tanzania, where some friends from SNCC were already living.[20]

Tanzania had a thriving American expatriate community, with some eight hundred "Wa Negro" (black Americans) living in and around the capital city, Dar Es Salaam. Many came because of their admiration for Tanzania's president, Julius Nyerere, who embodied the optimism and hope of a continent newly emancipated from the constraints of European colonialism. Nyerere's mix of socialism and Pan-Africanism made him one of the continent's most important political leaders. His economic policies were mostly unsuccessful, but he nurtured liberation movements in Rhodesia, Mozambique, and South Africa (and in 1978 would help end Idi Amin's terrible rule in Uganda).

Dar Es Salaam was an intellectual and revolutionary hot spot. Nyerere provided refuge to, among others, South Africa's African National Congress and the Pan Africanist Congress, and to African-American draft resisters and Black Panthers running from the law. Leading revolutionary figures, like Malcolm X and Che Guevara, sought out Nyerere's counsel and stayed in the city for extended visits. The University of Dar Es Salaam housed some of Africa's leading intellectuals. By the time Moses arrived, the Tanzanian capital was already a mythical city where everyone and everything seemed to be happening at once, like London during the Blitz, Cairo in the early 1950s, or Prague just after the fall of communism.

Nyerere helped Moses and his new wife get settled, then got them jobs at a small school outside the capital, Moses teaching math and Janet teaching English. They lived in a small two-bedroom home out in the countryside with few neighbors but beautiful mountain views and wonderful open space all around. It was a quiet, anonymous life.[21]

In the quiet of Tanzania, Moses realized that part of the reason he had come to Africa was to start a family. "In SNCC we were in our early twenties. We didn't really have personal family responsibilities or personal job responsibilities except movement work." It had not seemed possible to balance both activism and family. "The real choice," he reflected, "was leaving and doing family versus staying and doing more movement. It would have been hard to stay and do family."[22]

Life was simpler in Africa, and Moses and his family thrived there. They had few visitors, and few people wanted to talk about his movement days, which suited Moses. But they were hardly recluses. They had a wide circle of friends, including government officials, local residents, and other American expatriates. Janet's mother visited often, sometimes staying for six months at a stretch. His close friend and fellow SNCC alumnus Charlie Cobb stayed for two years in Dar Es Salaam, covering Africa for American newspapers.

Moses focused on rearing his four children. His teaching job gave him plenty of time to be a hands-on father, changing diapers and cooking meals: "I've always felt it was a blessing. Tanzania turned out to be a good place to recuperate and also pay attention to family." He was also happy to avoid the political turmoil that engulfed the United States in the early 1970s. Tanzania gave him the perspective to realize that "the notion that you can fight everything is crazy."[23]

As Charlie Cobb observed, Tanzania was "a crossroads" where "a lot of us learned that political struggle was about more than color" and "about more than being against something. The essential discussion in Tanzania was about how human resources were mobilized." For Moses, these discussions focused on the differences between the American and Tanzanian approaches to education. Tanzanian schools were simple affairs, reminiscent of America's turn-of-the-century one-room schoolhouses; there Maisha Moses, his eldest child, carried a hoe with her books to work in the school garden. But simple was not simplistic. The Tanzanian schools were rigorous, serious places as well, and the students pushed themselves.

The student-centered Tanzanian schools inspired Moses. "For the first time," he recalled, "I felt what it was like to work in a school where the expectations of students drove the learning. There was purpose [and] motivation in day-to-day schoolwork." He thought the students could see the connections between their education and their futures—both as individuals and as a nation. By demonstrating how the bottom-up focus of the Freedom Schools blended with a rigorous traditional curriculum could yield impressive gains for students,

Moses's Tanzania experience cemented his belief in the centrality of education to expanded civil rights.[24]

Like Moses, Diane Nash briefly saw the antiwar movement as a place where she could recapture community and moral certainty. In 1966, she got involved with a group of about twenty-five female peace activists. That she worked with female activists was not an accident: her interest in the peace movement coincided with a rising feminist consciousness, influenced by her fellow activists and by a growing national conversation about gender. Her feminism also came from within. She had always been frustrated by how male activists overlooked the women in their group, and her rocky marriage to Bevel had made her think about the gendered expectations that governed SNCC's work. Becoming involved with a female peace group reflected both her long-standing morality and her growing sense of independence.

In December 1966, Nash and three other peace activists left America to get a firsthand look at the war from the perspective of Communist North Vietnam. They traveled to Hanoi via Moscow and Beijing, spending about two weeks assessing, among other things, North Vietnam's claim that the U.S. bombed civilian targets. The group paid its own way to Vietnam. Nash described the trip as a protest action because the State Department prohibited travel to North Vietnam and they theoretically faced legal sanctions for violating the ban.[25]

Nash's group was not the first or only group to make such a trip. The Hanoi run was a popular one among peace activists; some two hundred Americans made the journey between 1965 and 1975. Tom Hayden had made the first trip a year earlier, in December 1965, at the behest of Staughton Lynd, the Yale historian and a Freedom School organizer. But Nash's group was the first to link feminism, race, and the plight of the North Vietnamese.

Back in the United States, she spoke at a press conference in Chicago about her experiences. Her assessment of the Vietnam conflict as an "economic war with racial overtones" did not differ substantially from the views of the other women. What set Nash apart was her insistence that she speak only to African-American reporters. "I don't intend to have white reporters interpret to black people what I have to say" about the war, she said. Her suspicion of the press reflected the extent to which black power had broadly unsettled the racial terrain of the late 1960s. Even those who did not consider themselves black power advocates now echoed its ideas.[26]

Family responsibilities, however, curtailed Nash's further involvement in the antiwar movement. With her marriage over, she moved back her hometown of Chicago. During the Chicago campaign, Bevel tried to reconcile, but he was unwilling to alter his behavior. By 1967, Nash was a single mother trying to raise two kids all on her own. The only house she could afford was in a rough-and-tumble block on the South Side that she had to convert from apartments to a single-family home without help. But she put such care and effort into the work that later she was able to sell the house for enough profit to buy a new one in the better neighborhood of Hyde Park, where the kids could attend a better school.

Still, she struggled, later calling 1969–71 "the hardest years of my life." Money was always tight. Bevel contributed next to nothing in child support. She had to calculate the family budget down to the last penny, and any little deviation—someone's illness, a small splurge—could throw everything out of whack. Jobs were not hard to find, but for a black woman who had dropped out of college, good professional opportunities were. For a brief time, she worked at Western Union, where she organized black workers who had been passed over for promotions. Later she was an editor at *Muhammad Speaks*, the newspaper of the Nation of Islam. Finally, she worked at a local community service organization that helped the poor deal with corrupt landlords.

She found the jobs unsatisfying. She missed the sense of purpose she had felt in the movement, and the camaraderie. Even the work in community service organizations was unsatisfying: they were too bureaucratic, out of touch with the needs of the people they were supposedly serving, and staffed by people seemingly more interested in their own career advancement than the greater good.[27]

In 1972, her son's sixth-grade teacher invited Nash to speak for Career Day about her work at the newspaper. At first, the invitation stumped her. "I was employed at the paper," she thought, "but my vocation is liberation." She could not bring herself to talk about her daytime work, because to promote a job she hated would be to lie to the kids. So she talked about "my real profession—being a freedom fighter." Standing before the room of eleven- and twelve-year-old boys and girls, she told them she understood that "freedom fighter" deviated from the normal career aspirations of sixth-grade students—like doctor, lawyer, fireman, and teacher—but she tried to explain to them why it was a "vitally important" option to consider. She described the freedom fighter as someone who "loves people" but sometimes "carries weapons and fights." A freedom fighter was someone "who thinks for himself," organizes people, writes books, and raises money; someone who "does not stop until the changes are made," even if it means dying for the cause.[28]

Nash's description of herself as a freedom fighter is illuminating, especially her unwillingness to talk about her movement experience in concrete terms. Rather than inspire the middle schoolers with tales of the sit-ins and Freedom Rides and her intimate knowledge of Martin Luther King, she fell back on the abstraction of freedom fighter, which did not accurately describe either her past or her present. The self-identification as a freedom fighter offered a vague, romanticized sense of past heroism. More important, it underscored her current sense of alienation. Most obviously, she presented dual identities: the outward public self as a simple office worker, and the secret life as a revolutionary. By definition freedom fighters are outside the political system and have rejected electoral politics in favor of revolution. The description of her secret life, with its hints of underground revolution, also suggest the deeper personal pain of a woman disconnected from the community and camaraderie that had sustained her in SNCC.

Bob Zellner worked harder than almost anyone to carry on the spirit of SNCC's interracial grassroots organizing. Though bitterly disappointed by the 1966 vote to exclude whites, he and Dottie approached the organization a year later, in May 1967, with a plan for organizing white workers along the Mississippi coast near New Orleans under SNCC's auspices. They believed that SNCC's imprimatur would provide legitimacy and convey adherence to a particular set of values, especially to African Americans, and they requested to be reinstated to full membership.

In his letter describing his proposal, Zellner argued for its larger importance. African Americans could organize as a group without being considered racist, but white southerners organizing as a group would be seen only as racist. The first step to laying the groundwork for a new interracial coalition was to organize poor whites. For Zellner, the SNCC imprimatur would send an important signal to African Americans about the values and goals of project. It was going to be the kind of grassroots project that SNCC had specialized in. Even if Zellner was going to run it mostly by himself, he thought SNCC should get the credit and that the legacy of SNCC should live on in new projects.

Zellner touched on his and Dottie's long history in SNCC, but he wanted this project to be approved, he wrote, "not on the basis of our deep feelings about the years we have spent in SNCC, our length of service, what we feel to have been our contributions, and our emotional and personal ties." The project should be approved, rather, because interracial grassroots organizing represented the best hope for the future of the civil rights movement. But it would work best if he were a full-fledged member of SNCC again. He told the group that he would not accept any restrictions or special categories because of his race. "I am either a SNCC staff member or I am not."[29]

Zellner knew he was swimming against the tide. H. Rap Brown, newly installed as SNCC's leader, argued against the request. A few older veterans argued for some compromise position but were overruled. Even though Zellner had spent almost seven years with SNCC—compared to Rap Brown's two—the organization was now firmly in the hands of black power advocates, and it denied his request. As Cleve Sellers noted, the new SNCC had passed judgment not just on the "future membership of Bob Zellner" but "on the history of SNCC," as well.[30]

At first blush, it seems ironic that one of SNCC's white members had the greatest emotional attachment to the organization and fought hardest to preserve its legacy. But given the context, it is not surprising. By the late 1960s few opportunities remained for the kind of genuine interracial grassroots organizing that had been SNCC's hallmark. The space for African-American grassroots organizing had also eroded, but for whites it had essentially disappeared. The sense of loss and alienation that black activists like Nash and Moses felt was even more acute for white activists like Zellner, who saw SNCC as "the greatest thing that ever happened in my life."[31]

Bob and Dottie Zellner decided to go forward with the project even without SNCC's support. In 1967, they moved to Mississippi's Gulf Coast to establish GROW, or Grass-Roots Organizing Workers (also: Get Rid of Wallace). They also founded the Deep South Education and Research Center near New Orleans, a residential community workshop modeled on the Highlander Folk School and the Freedom Schools. They would bring in groups of white workers to teach them organizing skills. They focused on labor organizing but also pushed attendees to think about the way racism divided working people to their detriment.[32]

Zellner quickly dropped the idea of starting with just whites, to embark on a biracial organizing effort among Gulf Coast pulpwood workers. Such work—harvesting trees for paper manufacture—was a throwback to the southern economy of the early twentieth century. It resembled sharecropping in that agents furnished most pulpwood workers with tools and loans to get started and then resold the wood to the paper companies, insulating the larger corporations from responsibility for the working conditions and pay of the workers. It was low-paying, hard work. A pulpwood worker might get $75 to $100 for a load of wood, but the agent would deduct $25 to $40 in "stumpage fees" for the landowner and $2 to $10 in loan fees for tools and other things. Out of the remaining money, many would have to pay the two or three workers hired to help for the day. In a good week, he might clear about $100 for his work.

Since pulpwood workers were independent operators, they were vulnerable to exploitation and manipulation by unscrupulous agents. Race had historically complicated any attempt at cooperation. White workers believed that excluding blacks would reduce competition. Many were frank racists, and the Klan found a fertile recruiting ground. In the late 1960s, the paper producers squeezed the workers even more by changing the formula by which they calculated the load weight, effectively cutting wages even as the paper companies' profits increased. The economically squeezed workers started thinking about organizing to fight for better wages, and some even crossed the color line for tentative discussions. Zellner had heard about these meetings, which prompted him to offer his assistance.[33]

By encouraging that tentative interracial alliance, Zellner wanted to challenge black power's skepticism about the value of cross-racial alliances. Idealistic appeals to brotherhood no longer worked; anybody who was going to be moved by such talk had already accepted the changes brought on by desegregation. New converts could be won, he believed, mainly with pocketbook appeals. He would show white workers that allying with black workers actually improved their financial position.

Zellner succeeded. He organized the Gulfcoast Pulpwood Association to lobby for higher wages, and on September 1, 1971, about two hundred pulp workers, 40 percent of whom were white, refused to sell to the Masonite Corporation until they received a higher price for their wood. Over the next few weeks, the strike spread out over southern Mississippi until it included more than fifteen hundred strikers and affected operations at Scott and St. Regis, the two other large paper companies in the area.[34]

Some of the white recruits had Klan backgrounds, but that did not stop Zellner—he knew how to reach them. His grandfather had been in the Klan as well, and he had grown up in a Deep South area not all that different from the Gulf Coast. His message about economics over race hit home. Justin Pulliam, one of the white strikers, reflected Zellner's influence: "People are beginning to see that the rich people are out for just one thing—more money. The only way to stop it is for all the poor people to get together, no matter what the color of their skin is. Black and white is brothers."[35]

Masonite tried to break the alliance by accusing Zellner of being a Communist. The Southern Conference Education Fund, run by Carl Braden, had provided start-up money for the Pulpwood Association. White segregationists had been trying to tag Braden as a Communist ever since 1954, when he and his wife, Anne, bought a house in a white neighborhood for a black couple to integrate the community. SCEF and the Bradens were strong supporters of the civil rights movement, but the Communist charge had led some, notably Martin Luther King, to keep their distance. Zellner and the Bradens went way back; in fact, Zellner's initial salary at SNCC had been paid for by SCEF. The Bradens were not so much Communists as political progressives committed to a more just and fair South, and Zellner appreciated their support. Many of the white strikers saw the Communist charge for what it was. "We're just a bunch of poor people trying to a make a living," said one white striker. "They call us Communist. They're the Communists. Masonite, that's who's the Communist."[36]

The strike took place during a gubernatorial campaign in Mississippi. Charles Evers, brother of the slain Mississippi NAACP leader Medgar Evers, was running for governor. He gave strong support to the strikers, even flying to Washington to try to persuade federal officials to ease the qualifying rules for food stamps; by making it hard for strikers to get assistance, Mississippi officials had hoped to make it economically impossible for the strike to drag on. In return, Evers drew large crowds of whites to his rallies in towns with large numbers of pulpwood workers. Otha Lofton, a white pulpwood worker who voted for the arch-segregationist George Wallace in the 1968 presidential election, told a reporter that Evers "would do more for Mississippi than any man in the race."[37]

The NAACP also recognized the interracial character of the strike and donated $5,000 to a strike fund. As one local NAACP official put it, "This was not black and white. These were people who needed help." Some of the white pulpwood workers who received aid checks even joined the NAACP, though that was not a condition for receiving money.[38]

After more than three months, the strikers won. The three companies affected by the strike raised their payments on wood by two to three dollars a cord and restored the old measurement system. Trying to spin events in their favor, the companies claimed the increase came from market conditions. But Evers lost the election. Still, his defeat offered both hope and caution. He had attracted far more white votes in the areas hardest hit by the strike, surprising observers of Mississippi politics. As the first black Mississippian to run a serious campaign for governor, Evers's performance held out the tantalizing possibility of a truly interracial progressive coalition. His share of the white vote in other parts of the state, however, reinforced the difficulty that black candidates would have in attracting votes without the exceptional circumstance of the pulpwood strike.[39]

The strike victory made national news. Among the dozen speakers chosen for the 1972 "People's State of the Union" to rally opposition to President Nixon was a member of the pulpwood union, who spoke of the economic plight of his fellow woodcutters. Lost in the publicity about the strike was any sustained attention to what the interracial character of the union suggested about the future of Mississippi politics. Undertaken during the heyday of black power, Zellner's effort was at odds with that popular current. The whole debate about race had become framed around the idea of separate black institutions, about the need for black power of one kind or another; even civil rights organizers failed to see the possibilities in the pulpwood campaign, and the media ignored its interracial nature because it did not fit into the narrative of black power. What could have became a model for organizing in the 1970s instead become a curiosity, an interesting side note on what could have been.

The limited response to the success of the pulpwood campaign was a microcosm of the difficulties facing organizers who advocated interracial labor-based activism in the 1970s. Foreign competition and the tenuousness of the interracial political coalition hampered the Gulfcoast Pulpwood Association. Zellner found it difficult to generate sustained media interest or widespread public support for labor organizing. Labor strikes did not generate the same collision between individual rights and state power that had made the sit-ins and the Freedom Rides such morally compelling stories.[40]

On a personal level, the campaign foreshadowed a difficult decade for Zellner. Part of his goal had been to re-create the magic of SNCC by building a new band of brothers along the Gulf Coast. But beyond the collapse of SNCC itself, a combination of forces pulled black and white college students away from rural grassroots organizing. The antiwar movement drew attention and energy from other issues, especially on the part of white college students. With more African Americans now attending college, black students interested in civil rights tended to agitate for the establishment of African-American studies departments and the hiring of black faculty. The cumulative result was to fracture student activism by race, class, and issue. Without the support and camaraderie of a community of like-minded young activists, Zellner felt his work on the Gulf Coast lacked the spirit, the zest, and the sense of adventure that marked SNCC's early years.

In many ways, he resembled his friend Stokely Carmichael. The only identity either really had was as an activist. Zellner was more of a romantic than Carmichael, to be sure, as he lamented the loss of camaraderie more than anything. Still, neither wanted to—or could—move beyond the activist persona. To the old SNCC question of whether it would be possible to balance family and activism, their answer was no, and they shared a real lack of interest in family life. Zellner's marriage to Dottie broke apart during this time. A shared passion for the movement had drawn them together, but Zellner was unable or unwilling to move beyond that lifestyle, and there seemed to be no place for him in the 1970s, no community, no home like the one he had during the movement.

For many veterans, the collapse of SNCC resulted in a profound sense of ennui, where personal and political disappointments intersected. Discouraged by the slow progress of civil rights change, alienated by law enforcement's intolerance for protest, isolated by the loss of their community of activists, and saddened by the breakup of relationships, many felt adrift. Some turned to the antiwar movement or to new organizing efforts to recapture that old esprit, but cleavages of class, race, and ideology stunted those efforts. The young SNCC activists were getting older as well, and the desire to nurture families distracted them from the singular commitment necessary for sustained grassroots organizing. For some, like Carmichael and Moses, the solution to these disappointments was a literal exile to a foreign country; for others, like Diane Nash, the solution was a turn inward to family, a metaphorical exile from activism; and for still others, like Zellner and Sellers, the failure to find any safe harbor led only to depression and continued drift.

SNCC ALUMNI AND THE MAKING OF BLACK POLITICAL POWER

Hello, my name is Julian Bond. I'm running for the state legislature from this district. What do you want me to do if I get to the legislature?"

With that simple question, Bond launched his 1966 bid for the Georgia House of Representatives and inaugurated SNCC's transition from protest to politics. Media attention to the exaggerated rhetoric and posturing of black power often overwhelmed other news about the civil rights movement. Lost in the spectacle of black power was the power of the black voter. In the late 1960s and early 1970s, most African Americans believed that working within the democratic process offered the best chance to solidify the civil rights gains and that the Democratic Party, despite its flaws and legacy in the South, offered the best vehicle.

SNCC veterans like Bond, Lewis, and Barry played a crucial role in transforming black votes into real black power. Their notoriety as civil rights activists made them instant contenders for public office, and their mastery of grassroots-organizing tactics made them formidable candidates. Most important, they believed in the power of the ballot box, the value of political power to transform black communities, and they worked tirelessly to ensure other African-American victories as well.

In 1965 the combination of the Voting Rights Act and court-ordered electoral reapportionment gave black voters in Atlanta more influence by adding seats to the city's delegation in the state legislature, including a new district near SNCC's headquarters that was more than 90 percent African American. SNCC debated running one of its own for the seat, and many pushed Julian Bond to take the plunge. He was the logical choice because of his strong ties to the area, his family name, and the media skills he had honed over the last five years.

Bond hesitated until Howard Creecy, a black minister who represented Atlanta's cautious and accommodationist black elite, entered the race. "What has *he* done for Atlanta?" Bond would ask rhetorically as he mulled a campaign. Bond was not sure he wanted to be a politician, but he was sure that the new representative should represent SNCC's values, not those of the black establishment. He borrowed the $500 filing fee from his dad (who famously said he did not raise his son to be a mere politician), set up his campaign headquarters in the back of wig shop, and entered the race.[1]

Bond's campaign generated dissension within SNCC. Some were still angry about Atlantic City. They questioned the wisdom of having SNCC compromise its ideals to "play the political game" when the Democratic Party had proved so willing to abandon African Americans there. Members of the Atlanta Project criticized Bond's middle-class roots, arguing he was out of the touch with the district. When they saw Bond and his campaign staff dressed in pressed shirts and ties instead of the standard SNCC garb of white T-shirts and dungaree overalls, they said he had "sold out" to get elected.[2]

A core group of SNCC's old guard, especially Lewis, supported Bond's candidacy. For Lewis, it was "important in a city like Atlanta" to have "somebody who had been involved in the height of the student movement transfer some of this energy, some of the understanding, to the political arena." Bond and Lewis saw running for office as a logical extension of SNCC's work in registering voters and as an alternative to the theatrics of black power. The two men shared a belief in the efficacy of politics to solve problems. As Bond prepared to run in the fall of 1965, Lewis and others convinced a majority within SNCC to support his campaign.[3]

The newly created 136th legislative district was cramped and poor. Only about twenty blocks long and as little as two blocks wide, it ran through some of black Atlanta's poorest neighborhoods. Half of the men and a fifth of the women were unemployed. The only real business in the district was Paschal's, a black-owned motel, restaurant, and cocktail lounge, famous for its fried chicken and the steady stream of civil rights activists who passed through its doors. SNCC workers blanketed the neighborhood with leaflets, and Bond's mother held tea parties for the ladies of the district. But the key to Bond's strategy was to do more listening than talking. In fact, his campaign was classic SNCC. He simply walked around the district with his campaign manager, Ivanhoe Donaldson, knocking on doors to ask people what he could do to change their lives.[4]

Few people knew what to say. They had never had a state representative who actually represented their interests, let alone had a candidate come into their neighborhood. "At first it was confusing," Bond recalled. "We had to explain to people what it was a state representative did, and after we explained it, people began to tell us their problems were largely economic." Bond's campaign promises centered on the issues that mattered to his potential constituents—jobs, housing, and a minimum wage law for domestic workers.[5]

Bond's grassroots campaigning proved highly effective. He won 70 percent of the Democratic primary vote against Creecy, and in the general election more than 82 percent of the vote against a black Republican who was the dean of men at Atlanta University. What made the new state representative especially happy was that the 136th had the highest proportional turnout of any district in the entire state of Georgia.[6]

Just a few days before Bond was to take office in January 1966, an unexpected controversy transformed the new representative from a minor curiosity into a national sensation. When a reporter asked him to comment on SNCC's just-issued statement opposing the Vietnam War, Bond endorsed it. Under further questioning, Bond went on to offer an expansive discussion of his own antiwar views. "I would not burn my own draft card," he said, "but I admire the courage of those who do." A reporter tried to box Bond into a corner by asking if his opposition to the Vietnam War conflicted with the oath every elected official took to defend and uphold the Constitution.[7]

White Georgians reacted negatively. Lieutenant Governor Peter Geer said, "There is no way that Bond can take the oath of office . . . to honestly uphold the Constitution . . . in view of SNCC's subversive policy statement." Now that overt racism was less respectable in public discourse, segregationist whites jumped on Bond's antiwar views as a way to attack SNCC and the movement generally. Representative Jones Lane, who had invited George Wallace to address the Georgia House during the previous session, promised to lead the movement to expel Bond. *The Atlanta Constitution* fanned the controversy, running headlines in what newsmen call "second coming"–size type. The editor, Ralph McGill, insisted that SNCC's position was both anarchist and racist. McGill embodied a generation of elite white southerners whose advocacy of an amelioration of segregation during the 1930s and 1940s put them at the forefront of liberalism, but who now felt threatened by the rapid grassroots changes of the 1960s.[8]

The uproar caught Bond and his allies by surprise, but with the support of a handful of Atlanta's black establishment, they tried to head off the controversy. Leroy Johnson, the dean of Georgia's black politicians (by virtue of his having unexpectedly won a House seat in 1962), acted as a go-between with state officials, who despite the bluster generally wanted to avoid a full-blown confrontation. White leaders hoped to use the controversy to embarrass Bond, making him beg a little for his seat. House leaders told Johnson that if Bond would get the Speaker to recognize him before anyone was sworn in, put on his best aw-shucks face of youthful contrition, and apologize, everything would blow over. The group spent hours working out a statement that distanced Bond from SNCC's antiwar position without completely walking away from the organization.[9]

Bond was all set to go along with this plan until he had a chance encounter with Martin Luther King's best friend, Ralph Abernathy. When Bond confessed uncertainty about what to do, Abernathy told him to "just do something you can live with." Abernathy's advice struck a chord; for Bond it resonated with SNCC's emphasis on personal integrity and authenticity. Bond's youthful hubris also kicked in. He decided he was not going to cave in to the "arrogance" of these white politicians who "believe they had the right to tell me what to say."[10]

On the morning of January 10, 1966, Bond arrived at the Georgia capitol for the swearing-in ceremony. The clerk of the House had received five petitions requesting that Bond be denied his seat for committing "treason." As the other two hundred legislators rose to take the oath, the clerk motioned for Bond to remain seated. Bond slumped over, his chin resting on his hands like a bored schoolboy, as everyone else swore to uphold the Constitution of the United States and the laws of Georgia.[11]

The House immediately formed a twenty-six-member committee to interrogate Bond. He tempered his earlier remarks, saying he himself had not burned his draft card or counseled anyone else to burn theirs. But on the main issue he would not budge, maintaining his basic opposition to both the war and the draft. The committee recommended expulsion by a 23–3 vote. A little later the full House charged Bond with "disorderly conduct" and voted 184–12 not to allow him to take office.[12]

Three days later Bond sued the Georgia House of Representatives in federal district court for violating his First Amendment right to free speech, his Fifth and Sixth Amendment rights to be tried by an impartial jury, and his Thirteenth, Fourteenth, and Fifteenth Amendment rights as an African American to equal protection under the law.

This was murky constitutional territory. Historically, the courts had given state legislatures wide latitude to determine the qualifications of its members. As recently as 1919 the federal courts had allowed Congress to expel a legally elected Wisconsin congressman for declaring himself a socialist. But the Supreme Court's rulings in the reapportionment cases and its support for the Voting Rights Act offered Bond hope.[13]

The district and appeals courts both ruled against Bond. By a two-to-one vote, the appeals court claimed that Bond could not endorse SNCC's statement against the war and honestly take the oath swearing allegiance to the Georgia and U.S. Constitutions, asserting that free speech was a private right and was subject to limitation when Bond sought membership in the Georgia House. A powerful dissent from the chief judge of the Fifth Circuit asserted that Bond's expulsion "shocks not only the judicial, but the lay sense of justice." It pointed out that the Georgia Constitution listed only three causes for disbarment—being under twenty-one, being a felon, or not being a resident. To invent new criteria was to venture into "undefined, unknown [and] constitutionally questionable standards."[14]

While the Supreme Court considered Bond's appeal, Georgia held a special election to fill the now-vacant 136th District seat. Nothing prevented Bond from running again, so he did. No one ran against Bond, and he received 100 percent of the vote. But in late May, a House committee again barred Bond from taking his seat. With the regular election for the seat approaching in November, Bond announced he would enter the September primary. Malcolm Dean, his Republican opponent from the first election, ran as a Democrat, backed by a group of older middle-class blacks unhappy with Bond's position on the Vietnam War specifically and SNCC's turn to black power generally. Dean's attacks eroded Bond's popularity, and Bond won the primary by only fifty votes. Still, he managed to score a decisive victory in the November general election, making him the only person in American history to be elected to the same office three times without ever being officially sworn in. Only the pending Supreme Court ruling prevented the Georgia legislature from refusing to seat him for a third time.[15]

On December 5, 1966, the Supreme Court ruled 9–0 in Bond's favor, harshly criticizing the Georgia legislature for denying him his seat and marking the first time in American history that the Court had limited a legislature's ability to set the qualifications for its own members. It had been clear during oral arguments that the justices were extremely skeptical of Georgia's position. At one point, Justice Abe Fortas told the state's attorney general that he was "perilously close to saying that a person is unqualified . . . if he opposed the war in Vietnam." The unanimous opinion dismissed Georgia's contention that Bond's ability to speak as a private citizen was distinct from his ability to speak as a legislator. It noted that the rules required Bond only to swear an oath; they made no mention of sincerity or the obligation of the legislature to judge sincerity. Chief Justice Earl Warren argued that elected officials needed "the widest latitude to express their views." The opinion reinforced the legitimacy of the antiwar movement at a moment when the Johnson administration was vigorously attacking it.[16]

The Supreme Court may have forced the Georgia House to seat Bond, but it could not force his colleagues to treat him with dignity or respect. The slights came in small and large ways. When Bond entered the House chamber to take the oath of office, a handful of his colleagues walked out in protest. Others would not speak to him directly. Bond tried to keep a low profile, eschewing floor speeches or bold public stands, realizing that his support alone might doom a bill. He sometimes fantasized about trying to fool his colleagues by opposing something he really supported, but "they're not stupid."[17]

If Bond was a near-pariah to whites in Georgia, elsewhere in the United States he was a hero. The Supreme Court case made him the most famous state legislator and a highly sought-after speaker and fund-raiser. Finding himself at the nexus of both the civil rights and the antiwar movements, he tried to unite the two and influence the

1968 election by cofounding the National Conference for New Politics to encourage people in those two movements to participate in electoral politics. They shared a distrust of the Democratic Party establishment—one for its vigorous support of the Vietnam War, the other for its tepid support of the civil rights movement. Bond, however, believed it was still possible to work within the party to bring about change and to draw in a group of disaffected voters who were unhappy with the war and the general direction of the country.[18]

Race threatened to pull the fledging group apart. At a September 1967 meeting to plot strategy for the upcoming presidential election, black power activists demanded a 50 percent voting share, even though African Americans constituted about one-third of the delegates. White activists eventually caved in to this demand, while complaining that it violated democratic principles. The decision did not change the outcome of the meeting—the delegates voted to support a peace candidate but not necessarily to support a third-party candidate—but it revealed the difficulties of bringing together antiwar and civil rights activists to work for a common cause.[19]

Bond's work with the National Conference showed how he drew on his movement experience to forge a broad activist coalition within the Democratic Party. The group issued a platform calling for an end to the war, an expansion of the Great Society, and more support for civil rights from the federal government. Most important, the National Conference raised money for candidates. Since his own election, Bond had appreciated more than ever the importance of the less glamorous parts of politics to winning election. The National Conference's fund-raising activities created a broad donor base that Bond tapped to support grassroots voter-registration activities.[20]

Before the Democratic Party gathered in Chicago in August 1968 for its national convention, the collision between party regulars and youthful insurgents had already rattled the party. After the Minnesota senator Eugene McCarthy came close to beating President Johnson in the New Hampshire primary by emphasizing his opposition to the war, LBJ announced he would not seek reelection. Then McCarthy's candidacy faded as Vice President Hubert Humphrey (representing the party establishment) and the New York senator Robert Kennedy (representing the reform wing of the party) entered the race. Kennedy's ability to appeal to establishment Democrats, moderate antiwar activists, and civil rights activists made him the front-runner. His assassination on the night of the California primary, the last major primary, robbed the party of its presumptive nominee and threw the convention wide open. As the sitting vice president with control over the party machinery, Humphrey seemed to have the upper hand. But McCarthy and his supporters felt the war made it a moral necessity to challenge Humphrey, and they hoped to attract enough of Kennedy's supporters to derail the vice president.[21]

The 1968 convention became a legendary spectacle. Activists descended on Chicago, hoping to turn the nomination fight into a referendum on Vietnam. Chicago's mayor, Richard Daley, responded to the rumors of large protests by putting three hundred police in riot gear and calling up five thousand National Guard troops. He wanted the convention to showcase Chicago and was determined not to let the antiwar movement derail that dream.

The Yippies, a group of anarchist prankster activists headed by Abbie Hoffman, staged a "Festival of Life" spectacle in Lincoln Park near the convention, including a mock nomination ceremony for a pig. When the police tried to break up the festival, protesters responded with rocks, and the whole situation turned ugly. Police and National Guardsmen attacked demonstrators with tear gas and clubs as the latter chanted, "The whole world is watching. The whole world is watching."[22]

The situation inside the convention was nearly as chaotic, and Julian Bond was at the center of events. For civil rights activists, the important question remained the same as in 1964: Who really represented the Democratic Party in the South? Was it the nearly all-white delegations of questionable loyalty or the mostly black delegations promising 100 percent loyalty? Bond and other civil rights leaders questioned the slate of delegates handpicked by Governor Lester Maddox and the state Democratic chairman, James Gray, for Georgia. Bond's group, the Loyal National Democrats, pointed out that Gray had endorsed Barry Goldwater in 1964; it argued that many of the delegates were also unlikely to support the party nominee in this election.

A more complicated political situation than that of 1964 both aided and hindered Bond's efforts. The regular Georgia delegation was not made up solely of conservative white Democrats, as the Mississippi delegation had been. Instead, it featured among its 107 members seven African-American delegates and a handful of liberals and party

loyalists. But because Maddox and Gray had appointed the delegation and because of something called the unit rule, which allowed the
state chair to force the delegation to vote as a unit, the diversity of the
Georgia delegation was illusory. Segregationists like Maddox and
Gray retained control. Still, the challengers had advantages not available to them in 1964, chiefly the support of powerful allies like Eugene McCarthy and the absence of a single dominant power broker
like Johnson. The unit rule was also broadly unpopular among delegates, and in the wake of Atlantic City, they were generally more sensitive to the problems of using antidemocratic tactics to ram through
a nomination.

Bond and the Loyal National Democrats were not absolute
McCarthy supporters. They wanted to use him to make a larger point
about the continued underrepresentation of African Americans in
southern delegations. They planned on being in Chicago for only one
day. They thought their request to replace Maddox's delegation
would be turned down, but appearing before the credentials committee would generate publicity for their work.

But then a funny thing happened. After Bond and others in his
group made their appeal, they saw that members of the credentials
committee were still hanging around the conference room. They decided to schmooze them in the hope that a little one-on-one lobbying
would be effective. The lobbying, combined with the willingness of
the McCarthy allies on the committee to appease these potential supporters, led to a surprise vote awarding half of Georgia's delegates to
Bond's group.

The Loyal Democrats were in business, which presented a bit of
a problem for Bond. On the assumption that he was going to be in
Chicago for only one day, he had packed just one suit and booked
just one night at the YMCA. For the next few nights, Bond slept on a
couch in another delegate's room at the Hilton. Each night before bed
he would trudge down to the hotel's laundry room to sit wrapped in
a sheet while his clothes were cleaned.[23]

The Maddox forces immediately rejected the compromise, and
Bond found himself in the middle of a floor fight over the Georgia
delegation. The Humphrey forces were in a bind. Because of the
strength of the McCarthy forces, they did not have the power to ram
through a solution as Johnson had done four years earlier. In addition, Humphrey believed that the rising number of black voters na-

tionwide and the willingness of white southerners to abandon their party in the voting booth gave him little reason to appease Maddox. Over the continued objections of the regular Georgia delegation, the entire convention ratified the fifty-fifty compromise.[24]

It was a big victory, and Bond deserves much credit. Half the delegates, while still a compromise, was a much bigger share than the token representation offered the MFDP in 1964. More than anything, Bond's lobbying sold the compromise. Because he was already a hero to many in the Democratic Party owing to his court challenge, delegates cleared time on their schedules when asked if they would like five minutes with Julian Bond. A young lawyer working with the Loyal Democrats described Bond's importance:

> This delegation was unique, not only because it had a symbol, Julian Bond, leading it, but because it had the greatest sort of public relations going in this guy, whom the news people love and who is just extremely sharp and articulate: it could really capture the hearts of America. Bond was a Fannie Lou Hamer. A much different type, but Bond was the Fannie Lou Hamer of 1968. He became a television idol overnight; there was no one else on the delegation who could have done that.[25]

To thank the McCarthy forces for their help, Bond agreed to have the Georgia Loyal Democrats vote for McCarthy (though Humphrey had sewn up the nomination). McCarthy then asked Bond to be the person to officially second his nomination on the convention floor. The next night a Wisconsin delegate nominated Bond to be vice president, and Allard Lowenstein seconded the nomination, which had been designed as a publicity stunt to get Lowenstein, who was then running for Congress, the floor to make an antiwar statement. At twenty-six, Bond did not even meet the office's constitutional minimum age of thirty-five. The roar from the crowd for Bond surprised people, and he racked up an unexpected forty-nine votes before officially withdrawing his name. The nomination may have been a stunt, but it still made him the first black man in American history to be nominated for the vice presidency.[26]

Bond was now more famous than ever. *The New York Times* called him a national figure at the head of the youth, peace, and civil rights movements. Some suggested that he move to a northern city with a large black population where he could win immediate election to Congress; others touted Bond as a future vice-presidential candidate.[27]

Bond used his newfound prestige to raise money and support black candidates. He spent part of 1968 interviewing black elected officials for the Voter Education Project (VEP). The resulting pamphlet, *Black Candidates: Southern Campaign Experiences*, used the stories of twenty African-American officeholders to distill advice for prospective candidates. From his work with the VEP, Bond realized that the biggest hurdle for black candidates was fund-raising, so in 1969 he founded the Southern Elections Fund (SEF).[28]

SEF was the first political action committee devoted exclusively to black candidates. Working with Lewis, Bond recruited well-known black politicians like the New York congresswoman Shirley Chisholm and the Michigan congressman John Conyers to advise them. SEF held fund-raisers in the North to keep civil rights in the spotlight and fish fries in rural Mississippi to get local people involved. Donations came in big and small amounts, ranging from an anonymous $20,000 donation to the few dollars each that came from ordinary black citizens in Canton, Mississippi.

In the early years, SEF focused on little-known candidates running for local offices, working to build black political power from the bottom. While well-known candidates had little trouble attracting donations, SEF's support could make the difference between success and failure. The Mississippi NAACP leader, Charles Evers, could raise more than $100,000 to run for governor, but the $600 that SEF gave Zelma Wyche in the last days of his campaign running for sheriff of Tallulah, Louisiana, provided the margin of victory.[29]

It is hard to overestimate the importance of SEF during these years. One of its surveys found that most black candidates in the South dug into their own pockets for the majority of their campaign funds. With the decline of SNCC and the SCLC, SEF bridged the gap between northern donors and local activists. It also supplied campaign advice to candidates sorely lacking experience. Its work was not necessarily flashy but was necessary to transform the promise of the civil rights movement into reality, and perhaps more than anyone, Bond was the midwife to the first postmovement wave of southern black political leaders.

Bond and Lewis also put their energies into the task of registering new voters. In 1970, Lewis replaced Vernon Jordan as the executive director of the Voter Education Project and recruited Bond to join the board of directors. With the passage of the Voting Rights Act in 1965, VEP had begun to fulfill the vision of the Kennedy administration officials who had founded it and became a vehicle for transforming the Democratic Party in the South by adding scores of black voters. When Lewis assumed control, it had a staff of thirty-eight with operations in eleven southern states; it had helped register nearly a million voters since 1965 and would add almost 500,000 more over the next few years.[30]

Rather than confine themselves to office work, Bond and Lewis barnstormed the South in the early 1970s. Often they recruited friends like Fannie Lou Hamer, movement celebrities like Coretta Scott King, and rising political stars like the Virginia state senator Douglas Wilder to join them. They concentrated their work in the hundred or so black-majority counties of the Deep South, visiting small towns like Liberty, Mississippi, and Waterproof, Louisiana. In one eight-day stretch of eight-a.m.-to-midnight days, they visited twenty-five counties. Sometimes they would talk to a handful of local blacks outside a run-down café; other times they spoke at rallies of several hundred people. On the steps of the Tallahatchie County Courthouse—the same place where Emmett Till's killers had escaped justice—Julian Bond stood before a crowd of some five hundred and declared: "Whatever happens to us as black people from now on is going to happen to us because we want it to." That day the registrar's office in Tallahatchie had to cancel lunch to handle the flow of people eager to register for the first time.[31]

For Bond and Lewis, the voter-registration work harkened back to SNCC's earliest days. Together they registered more voters than SNCC had managed even in its heyday. The federal observers and legal tools of the Voting Rights Act made that possible, putting the federal government's failures to support SNCC in the early 1960s in even starker relief. Ironically, this success came from two veterans who had been only tangentially involved in SNCC's most prominent Deep South voter drives. Bond and Lewis had spent most of their time working in SNCC's main office, not out in the field. The 1970s, of course, presented different challenges: the hurdle now was not access but information and organization. The importance of grassroots activism had receded. Voter-registration campaigns depended on the long-term planning, fund-raising, and logistical skills of people like Bond and Lewis.

Both men found the work immensely rewarding. It was pure work—honest, authentic organizing, hard but fun. Bond and Lewis were about as different as any two people in SNCC—the poor country boy and the sophisticated city slicker—but they were the best of friends. Bond admired Lewis's courage and moral strength; Lewis admired Bond's easy charm and confident speaking ability. Bond, who loved to tease his friend, was one of the few people who could coax the shy Lewis out of his shell; Lewis was one of the few people who could get Bond to drop his glib facade to engage the serious issues at hand. Out on the road, unhampered by any of the other complications of life, the bond between the two men grew even stronger.[32]

African Americans made substantial political gains in the rural South as well. In 1968, there were just 400 black elected officials in the South; that figure rose to 1,847 in 1976, and 2,457 in 1980. In Macon County, Alabama, home of the Tuskegee Institute, local activists had been pushing for electoral power since the end of World War II. The Voting Rights Act allowed Lucius Amerson to be elected county sheriff in 1966—the first black Alabamian to hold that office since the 1870s. In St. Francisville, Louisiana, a place that had almost no black voters before 1965, Ledell Mackie won election as county commissioner in 1967. In Waterproof, Louisiana, a VEP-led effort increased black registration from fewer than one hundred to more than six hundred; Harold Turner, a local teacher, was elected the first African-American alderman in the town's history in 1970.[33]

Still, the Voting Rights Act provided assurances only that blacks would be able to register; it did not guarantee electoral victory. And the impediments to victory were substantial. Whites often voted in a bloc, especially where the African-American population was high but not a majority. Blacks were most successful when they made up at least 60 percent of the local voting-age population. Where they made up a quarter or less, white control was ensured, and blacks usually had only token representation. Where the African-American population was higher but was not quite a majority, whites employed a range of tactics to ensure effective control. Sometimes they tried to annex surrounding areas—as was the case in Richmond, Virginia—to beef up a white majority. Sometimes they gerrymandered districts to divide the black population among a series of white-majority districts. Sometimes they turned to at-large districts, so that even if African-American voters were 40 percent of the total and would have been a majority if there were single-member districts, the overall white majority still retained firm control.

The failure of whites to equitably share power forced African Americans to turn to the courts to resolve disputes. Recognizing that the courts were an imperfect vehicle, they did so reluctantly and only when white intransigence forced them. In the 1960s and early 1970s, African-American plaintiffs won a series of Supreme Court decisions that limited the ability of whites to use gerrymandering to dilute black political power. These victories were a logical extension of both the Voting Rights Act and the mid-1960s "one man, one vote" Supreme Court rulings. But the Court struggled to provide uniform rules. In every case that came before the it, African-American lawyers demonstrated that the effect of a particular policy diluted black political power. But the Court's rulings vacillated, sometimes upholding a policy, sometimes overturning it. Its indecision hinged on the question of whether the policies had to be implemented with a racist intent or simply had racist results. For example, the 1980 decision in *Mobile v. Bolden* suggested that intent should be the test for judicial intervention in electoral results, but two years later in *Rogers v. Lodge* the Court seemed to contradict itself by saying that the test was effect. The overall thrust of the decisions reinforced the Voting Rights Act and enhanced black political power, but the exact rationale for intervention remained in flux, sustaining the controversies about how to draw state and federal electoral districts in ways that kept the federal courts busy into the new century.[34]

As Bond and Lewis traveled through the South in the early 1970s, their old comrade Marion Barry led the way in the growth of urban black political power. Barry had moved to Washington in 1965 to head up SNCC's operations there, mainly fund-raising but also some organizing. For a few years he was on the periphery of SNCC's operations, concentrating on his doctoral studies in chemistry and joining protests in the South during summer breaks and holidays. But the movement tugged at him, and he returned to full-time work just before arriving in Washington.[35]

Almost immediately Barry became involved in the effort to get Washington an elected mayor, a position then appointed by Congress. Tensions between Barry and SNCC's main office simmered over his neglect of SNCC work in favor of the "free D.C." campaign. In 1967, he severed his ties to SNCC. That same year he started Pride, a job training and youth employment program. Secretary of Labor Willard Wirtz had met with Barry about federal efforts to help poor blacks in the city; at one point he became so annoyed with Barry's persistent questioning that he told Barry that unless he could do better, he should shut up. Two days later Barry showed up at his office with a complete proposal for Pride. Wirtz was so impressed that he gave Barry one month of trial funding, which he soon extended to a full year.

Pride was the perfect vehicle for Barry's growing political ambitions. He used the public works jobs that Pride supervised as patronage to build a political organization and the platform it provided to criticize the lack of economic opportunity in the city. Pride expanded into job training, college counseling, and continuing-education programs. Barry also founded several ancillary for-profit businesses under the Pride name, including a gas station, an advertising company, and management of an apartment complex. In 1968, he even commissioned a bust of Martin Luther King to sell as a souvenir to marchers during the Poor People's demonstrations. Technically, the nonprofit and for-profit businesses were separate, but Barry and his wife, Mary, controlled all of them out of a single headquarters building. Barry's blurring of the lines between the different enterprises and his disregard for federal rules made Pride the target of no fewer than six federal investigations in its first five years. In 1970, the government indicted thirteen Pride employees for misusing federal funds, eventually winning four convictions.[36]

Barry's troubles with the law did nothing to hurt his political career; in fact, he skillfully used his troubles to promote it. Casting the problem as a classic David and Goliath struggle, he brilliantly manipulated the symbols and pose of black power to his advantage. He donned a dashiki and in public affected a radical, aggressive black power posture. After a summer of riots in 1968, Barry said, "White people should be allowed to come back [to D.C.] only if the majority of the ownership is in the hands of blacks. That is, they should come back and give their expertise—and then they should leave."[37]

Few of his friends took the black power stance seriously. His SNCC colleague Charlie Cobb said, "I was probably more surprised to see Marion in the dashiki than when I saw him take it off." Nor did the city's white business leaders take Barry's rhetoric seriously, quickly learning that he could be a reliable ally in their push for business development.[38]

Barry's use of the theatrics of black power, combined with a mastery of the mechanics of building a political organization, propelled him to a seat on the board of education in 1970, to the city council in 1976, and finally to the mayor's office in 1978; he became the first SNCC alumnus, really the first grassroots civil rights activist, to lead a major city. His campaign manager and right-hand man was Ivanhoe Donaldson, who had run Bond's first campaign. Donaldson and Barry employed SNCC's grassroots organizing tactics and the strong-arm (and sometimes ethically questionable) tactics of classic urban political machines to fuse poor African Americans and middle-class whites into a winning majority. Barry embarked on the same door-to-door campaigning that Bond had used successfully in Atlanta, while Donaldson made sure that allies who delivered votes received patronage appointments and that white business leaders had help navigating the city's red tape. It was a winning formula. The only major constituency that did not support Barry was the city's large black middle class, who considered him—with his flashy clothes, Alabama accent, and rapport with poor folks—gauche and a bit of a hick. But these were the very qualities that made him attractive to the city's black poor. By 1980, Barry was probably the best-known black mayor in America, and his organization rivaled Chicago's old Daley machine for its power.[39]

The most interesting story about the growth of black political power took place in Atlanta, which stood at the nexus of several trends—changing urban demographics, the rise of the suburbs, the maturation of the civil rights movement, and the impact of the Voting Rights Act and "one man, one vote" decisions. By the late 1960s, it was clear to most observers that Atlanta would soon be a majority-black city. But the transition was not smooth. White officials did not include black officials in the decision-making process on such important projects as the new mass transit system and the urban renewal program. Black voters held up the transit proposal until their concerns were addressed and swung the 1969 election to Sam Massell when whites were divided between two candidates. African Americans were prepared to exert even more influence when the 1970 census confirmed the inevitable: they were now a majority of the city's population. In the next mayoral election in 1973, Maynard Jackson, who had been elected vice mayor in 1969, won 95 percent of the black vote and 17 percent of the white to garner 59 percent of the total and victory.[40]

African-American leaders in Georgia next set their sight on winning a congressional seat. Their best shot would be in the Fifth Congressional District, which combined with middle-class white suburbs the poor black neighborhoods that Bond had represented in the statehouse. As early as 1969, a number of black leaders thought about running. The district was still about 60 percent white, but many anticipated that the redistricting that would take place after the 1970 census would create a black-majority Fifth District. Ambitious black politicians were willing to lose in the 1970 election to position themselves as the front-runners in 1972.

Julian Bond was not one of those ambitious politicians. John Lewis thought he was the logical choice and wrote him a long letter urging him to run. Lewis knew that others, including his predecessor at VEP, Vernon Jordan, and the former King aide Andrew Young, were eyeing the Fifth District as well. Because of Bond's stand on the Vietnam War, his appeal to young and old voters, and most of all his belief in SNCC's original principles of humanism and local leadership, Lewis wanted Bond to run. Bond demurred. Despite Lewis's confidence, he was not sure he could win: the very forces that had propelled him to the national spotlight might also make him radioactive, too controversial to win a majority. A loss could also undermine his public standing and erode his speaking income. By giving speeches, Bond made many times over his salary as a state representative and he did not want to risk that income—he had a young family to support.[41]

Most of all, Bond could not decide whether he really wanted to be a congressman. There was an element of the accidental activist and politician about him. In this respect, he and Lewis were exact opposites: Bond struggled to find a life outside politics, while Lewis struggled to find one inside. Bond's goals had been stymied—by Stokely

Carmichael, by the deaths of his mentors Martin Luther King and Bobby Kennedy, and by his own insecurities about his background and campaigning skills. Being head of VEP had kept Lewis active in politics, but it was more like being a coach than a player. Lewis's letter to Bond can be read less as an effort to convince Bond to run for the congressional seat than to convince himself.[42]

So Bond shrugged off Lewis's recruitment efforts. Lewis then convinced Andrew Young to run. As expected, Young lost in 1970. Then came the redistricting: it did not create the black-majority district some had predicted, but Young still managed to win the Fifth Congressional District seat in 1972. Young was a similar candidate to Bond but without the political baggage of the antiwar cause. Handsome, with a patrician air about him, he had a smooth speaking style honed from years delivering speeches and sermons as a minister. African Americans admired him, and whites did not find him threatening. He won almost 100 percent of the black vote and about a quarter of the white vote (liberals attracted to his progressive stand on social issues) to get 53 percent of the total.[43]

When Young's Georgian friend Jimmy Carter, now president, named him UN ambassador in 1976, Lewis decided to run for the vacated congressional seat. He faced formidable opposition in the primary from Ralph Abernathy, King's closest adviser; from Wyche Fowler, a white politician popular in the suburbs who had challenged and narrowly lost to Young earlier in the year; and from nine other candidates. The primary was nonpartisan, with Republicans and Democrats running together. If no one got a majority in the primary, then the top two finishers would face each other in the general election. Lewis surprised everyone by winning several big endorsements—Martin Luther King, Sr., *The Atlanta Constitution*—and finishing second to Fowler. In the runoff, Fowler crushed Lewis by 62 percent to 38; each man got around 90 percent of his race's vote. Still, the election established Lewis as a serious political figure in the city, and four years later he won a seat on the Atlanta City Council.[44]

For Lewis, the moral certainty of the movement proved to be poor training for the compromises of urban politics. He made government ethics the central concern of his city council service, often publicly raising uncomfortable questions about how some councilors took legal and consulting fees from businesses vying for city contracts. He had a good point: the council lacked a strong official ethics policy, but

in this context the moralism that made him such an effective opponent of segregation sounded preachy and served only to alienate
other politicians. He was in danger of being seen as a gadfly rather
than as an effective leader. When the city council elevated several
freshmen members to committee chairmanships over the more senior
Lewis, he realized that his future in city politics was limited.[45]

In the early 1980s, Bond's career also stalled. In 1975, he had moved
from the Georgia House to the Georgia Senate, but despite the repeated urging of friends, he had never run for higher office. As the
years passed, Bond regretted the missed opportunities. "I've frittered
away a lot of power," he acknowledged. "I don't think I've ever done
what I could have done or should have done."

In October 1985, nearly a year before the next congressional election,
but as rumors already swirled around Atlanta, Bond met his old
friend Lewis for lunch at a Marriott Hotel downtown to discuss their
futures. Both men had their eyes on the soon-to-be open Fifth Congressional District seat. Wyche Fowler, the current congressman, was
trying to move to the Senate and out of a House seat whose district
had switched from majority white to majority black after the 1980
census.[46]

How many times over the years had they met like this to share
their lives?

Lewis made it immediately clear that this time was different:
"Senator, what are you going to do?"

"I'm going to run for Congress, Mr. Chairman," Bond replied,
teasing his friend with his old SNCC title, not sensing what was coming next.

"I'm running too," Lewis announced.

"Well, I'll see you on the campaign trail," Bond shot back.

And just like that, lunch was over.[47]

Though forty-six, both men were still relatively young to be making their first runs for Congress, but the musty smell of has-been was
beginning to replace the fresh scent of promise. Frederick Allen, a respected political reporter for The Atlanta Journal-Constitution, summed
up the prevailing wisdom in Atlanta: the race "is a last hurrah for two
men who were, just a decade ago, giants on the American landscape,
and who are now day by day diminishing in stature before our very

eyes." The winner, Allen suggested, would instantly move to the fore-front of America's black leadership, and "the loser will fall deeper into the shadows, perhaps never to escape."[48]

Bond was the prohibitive favorite. He had twenty-one years of experience in the state legislature and close ties to the city's three most powerful politicians—Mayor Andy Young, the city council president, Marvin Arrington, and the Fulton County Board of Commissioners chairman, Michael Lomax. He was graceful and articulate, a great storyteller, and a real charmer. Men jockeyed to hang out with him, and women swooned—no exaggeration—in his presence. Bond's appeal went beyond his boyish good looks—he simply exuded cool. Reporters struggled to capture him in phrases ranging from "dresses and speaks like a banker," to "the cool poet," to "still preppified at 46." These descriptions all missed the mark. A more apt comparison would have been to one of Bond's musical idols, Frank Sinatra. Neither man was movie-star handsome, but both shared a magnetic aura, a sense of style, and a swagger that just screamed cool without speaking a word.[49]

John Lewis, however, had a record that matched, even surpassed, that of Bond. He had another reason for running: to redeem his SNCC legacy. Still bitter about the midnight coup that had stripped him of the chairmanship, he always felt he had given up too easily, had not fought hard enough to save his job. In part, he blamed himself for SNCC's demise, sometimes believing that if he had stayed, things would have turned out differently. Losing the chairmanship had been a huge personal blow to Lewis.

In the 1985 congressional race, the press cast Lewis as the under-dog. Despite his accomplishments, he was still just a two-term city councilor whose one run for Congress in 1977 had ended in a blowout loss. An uncomfortable backslapper and an awkward stump speaker, Lewis was widely regarded as a poor campaigner and a weak politician. Because of his ethics crusade, he had few friends on the city council, a slim legislative record (no one wanted to work with him), and few endorsements.[50]

Lewis reveled in his image as an also-ran. He loved to reel off all the negative descriptions newspapers had printed about him, descriptions whose primary purpose was to imply negative comparisons with Bond. Among his favorites were "balding, dark, scowling," "short, squat, thick-necked," and "dogged, determined, pugnacious." Lewis now extended the underdog metaphor, casting himself as the one good man against the entire Atlanta political establishment, with Bond as their opportunistic poster boy. "A small group of influence-peddling and power-hungry individuals," he charged, were trying to "buy this seat." Most bothersome were the backroom efforts of some of the city's black elite—orchestrated, Lewis was sure, by Bond—to convince him to drop out of the race by promising him a lucrative private-sector job to fall back on.[51]

The move to force him out just fed Lewis's grandiose vision. To justify his own fierce ambition, he invested the race with the same moral imperative, the same us-versus-the-world mentality, that he had felt with SNCC. Taking on an old friend would appear less crass if the campaign had a larger meaning. In speeches and private conversations, he would compare the contest to the fable of the Prince and the Pauper, to the biblical clash between David and Goliath, and once, in an unusually naked moment of self-awareness, to Cain and Abel.[52]

From the very beginning, Bond and Lewis were conscious that their friendship defined the race. "I know things about John and he knows things about me," Bond pointed out, and "they're not campaign issues." Lewis agreed that his relationship with Bond should be secondary. "This is not a referendum on friendship," he would say. "It is not a referendum on the past."

But Lewis tried to make it about the past. He wanted it to be as much a referendum on SNCC's legacy as a vote for Congress. When asked about Bond's work with SNCC, he sniped that "in the early years, we had to bang on his door to wake him up and pull him out of bed to campaign," adding that Bond "worked for me." He dismissed Bond's work as simply writing press releases and sending out telegrams "back in Atlanta." In comparison, "I went on the Freedom Rides. I directed the sit-ins," he asserted, just in case anyone was unsure about his contributions.

Lewis seemed particularly galled about the credit and fame that came to Bond for speaking out against the Vietnam War. He wondered what all the fuss was about. "I spoke out against the war, and that's how Julian got known." In Lewis's telling of SNCC's history, he was the "headlight" and Bond the "taillight."

Lewis's aggressive campaigning crossed over from questioning Bond's contributions to SNCC to making mean-spirited personal attacks. He disparaged Bond's work ethic: "Some may want a pretty face, and some people may want someone who's going to get out there and work." The district needed a congressman, he would say, who has "a proven attendance record and the patience to attend to the tedious details of the legislative process."

The race also divided their wives. Almost since the day John first met Lillian in 1968, Alice Bond and Lillian Lewis had been close friends. Even before he met Lillian, Lewis always joked that he had been Julian and Alice's perpetual "third wheel." Even as John and Julian drifted apart, Alice and Lillian grew closer; Alice often used Lillian as a sounding board to vent her frustrations about Julian's inadequacies as a husband. In fact, John now learned more about Julian's life from his wife than he did from his friend. As the race wore on, however, the wives' relationship also frayed. On the eve of the primary, Lillian told one reporter that her friendship with Alice had been "irretrievably broken." Lillian was a fierce partisan for her husband, often badgering black local leaders about their lack of support, and she took any lack of support hard, seeing Andy Young's leanings toward Bond, for example, as a personal betrayal of their relationship, not as a political decision.[53]

Late one night Lewis picked up a ringing phone to find Stokely Carmichael on the line. The two had not spoken since that late-night coup in 1966 when Carmichael had orchestrated Lewis's ouster as SNCC chairman. That memory did not stop him from urging Lewis to get out of the race. "You're just dividing the Atlanta community," he said. Lewis was flabbergasted. Carmichael was the last person he would take advice from. Lewis was sure Bond had put Carmichael up to it in an attempt to rattle Lewis's cage by dredging up his most painful defeat. But it was unlikely Bond and Carmichael were in cahoots; Bond had only a marginally better relationship with Carmichael. More likely, it was Carmichael taking one more opportunity to mess with his old rival.[54]

Bond was genuinely hurt by his friend's disparaging words. In one debate, the only place they saw each other now, he looked Lewis in the eye and said: "We've been friends for twenty-five years. We went to Africa together, we were in Selma together . . . but never in those twenty-five years did I hear any of those things you are saying about me now. Why did I have to wait twenty-five years to find out what you really thought of me, to find out that you really don't think I amount to much?" Even if Lewis did not care to, Bond seemed determined to maintain the friendship. At a candidate forum less than a week before the primary, he squeezed Lewis's shoulder and pledged "not to let a six-month campaign separate me from a man I've been close to for thirty years."[55]

Lewis's harsh words revealed more about him than they did about Bond. The ill will and insecurities that had hampered Lewis since SNCC's early days lingered below the surface. He resented the attention others got—attention and praise that he thought he deserved. To top it off, Bond made it all look so easy, had joked about being lazy while coasting on his fame. Since the late 1960s, their public profiles had reversed. Lewis had gone from the spotlight of the Big Six to a city council seat that magnified both his bureaucratic strengths and his public-speaking weaknesses. Bond, on the other hand, had gone from behind-the-scenes work in SNCC's office to being one of the most famous black politicians. Why should glib charm and an accidental controversy get Bond a seat in Congress, when clearly Lewis was the more deserving choice?

Lewis's attacks brought into the open something that neither man had felt comfortable discussing privately: their friendship had changed since Lewis left the South for Washington in 1976 to work in the Carter administration. They had grown up, especially Lewis. Long gone were the days when he and Bond traveled across the South to register voters. It was not just that they had less time for each other; an emotional distance had grown up between them as well.

The contest gnawed at Lewis because the implication often seemed to be that if Bond ever got his act together, ever really applied himself, then he'd just sprint to the head of the line. There was, of course, some truth to Lewis's fear. Bond's campaigning was undisciplined. It was not just the posh (and expensive) campaign headquarters or the glitzy fund-raisers headlined by musical acts like the Temptations. Bond had a tendency to speak off-the-cuff around reporters; one time he agreed to the suggestion that "maybe he was a little bit lazy," or when rattling off the list of bills passed under his name, he would wink at the reporter when mentioning one that commended Lewis.

He told one reporter how he won over rural white audiences: "I go up to the biggest guy with a tattoo and tell him, 'I'm the only guy in this race with a tattoo.'"

Bond then unbuttoned his shirt to reveal a red rose tattooed on his left breast, the result of an impulsive whim at an NAACP convention in Denver three years earlier.

Nearby his press secretary was yelling at the top of his lungs, "THIS IS ALL OFF THE RECORD!"

This was Bond at his most infuriating: letting his adolescent disdain for convention and institutions undermine his stature and accomplishments as a serious public servant.[56]

As the campaign progressed, Bond struggled to project the blasé confidence of an incumbent: "If you want someone who doesn't need on-the-job training, send me to Congress." His campaign looked like that of a political insider, not someone making his first run for Congress, with not only the fancy campaign headquarters, but a huge organization and a couple of nationally known media consultants on the payroll. Bond ran on national issues like defense spending, taxes, American policy in Nicaragua, and the utility of sanctions against South Africa. By contrast, the dogged Lewis often sounded as much like a city council candidate as a congressional one. As so often happens in negative campaigns, Bond's efforts to talk about issues were ineffective; the press loved to focus on the titillating personal details.[57]

It was not just Lewis's attacks that distracted Bond. As the front-runner, he faced constant sniping from five lesser-known candidates in the race. Charles Johnson, a young black lawyer at a prominent downtown firm, attacked Bond ruthlessly. Johnson was an ambitious comer involved in numerous civic organizations. Here he let his ambition get ahead of his ethics, running ads accusing Bond of being antiwhite and of favoring "cop-killing."

The basis for the charge was nothing more than a couple of out-of-context and out-of-date quotes from Bond's 1972 book *A Time to Speak, A Time to Act*. Even more appalling, Johnson ran the ads on predominantly white radio stations in an attempt to frighten white voters away from Bond. Bond denied the charges and accused Johnson of race-baiting, but his support among whites slipped. Lewis, the prime beneficiary of Johnson's attacks, remained noticeably silent on the controversy.[58]

These sensitive and subtle questions of race and class were an undercurrent throughout the campaign. A black supporter of Bond argued that his candidate would win because "the black community basically sees this as sending somebody to Washington as its spokesman" and Lewis's weak speaking ability was a liability. Lewis countered by arguing that "style is more . . . than leaving off the 's' on the end of a word because you were brought up a poor southern boy."[59]

Heading into the August 12 primary, everybody wondered if Lewis had enough momentum to deny Bond an outright majority and force a runoff between the top two candidates. Every poll showed Bond with a comfortable lead in the low forties, Lewis second with about 15 percent, and no other candidate over 10 percent. Significantly, more than 30 percent polled said they had not yet decided whom to support. Though most public discussion of the election framed it as a symbol of emerging black political power, insiders were now saying that the district's white minority would decide the election, since the black vote would be so split.

This was where Bond's support was weakest. An informal poll of white voters by the Buckhead Business Association found Bond, with 7 percent support, trailing both Lewis, with 54 percent, and Charles Johnson, at 15 percent. As the pollster observed, Johnson's strategy had been "deadly effective in the white community."[60]

On election night, Bond seemed poised to get enough votes to win outright; but then a surge of late-reporting precincts went overwhelmingly for Lewis, and Bond dropped below the all-important 50 percent mark. Lewis jumped up on a chair. His voice, raspy and weak from the campaign, now rose thick with emotion as he shouted out:

"Go and tell Andy Young! Go and tell David Franklin! Go and tell Maynard Jackson! Go and tell Julian Bond here comes his old friend John! Here we come! Here we come!"[61]

In the end, Bond missed an outright victory by less than two thousand votes, winning 47 percent of the total in the smallest turnout in twenty-five years. The white vote had proved decisive. While Bond more than doubled Lewis's total in the district's black precincts, Lewis outpolled Bond two to one in white neighborhoods, where Lewis got more than half of his support.[62]

The results energized Lewis. His pollsters had convinced him that if he could keep Bond under 50 percent in the first round, he could ultimately prevail. Their polls also showed that Bond was a polarizing figure; people either supported him or disliked him. Lewis had virtually no negatives; those who did not support him did not know him well. Lewis thought 47 percent would be Bond's high-water mark.[63]

Lewis continued to attack Bond, accusing him of being more interested in furthering his own celebrity than in helping the residents of the district, and he attacked the black establishment for trying to rig the election. Bond "would be happy to spend the remaining fourteen days of the campaign in an air-conditioned studio with his feet propped up on a desk." Instead, Lewis would campaign "among the people," and he challenged Bond to "meet [him] in the streets." But this attack strategy had only been partially successful in the first round. It had done little to dent Bond's appeal with African-American voters, and Lewis's success with white voters owed as much to Johnson's harsh attacks as to his own appeal.[64]

Bond, too, embarked on a quixotic course, challenging Lewis to a series of debates. It violated a cardinal rule of politics: a front-runner never adds to his opponent's credibility by sharing a stage with him. The challenge did not come from a well-thought-out plan but was Bond's hotheaded response to Lewis's surprisingly personal and bitter broadsides. If Lewis was going to imply he was lazy and had not contributed much to the movement, then Bond was going to get on a stage with his opponent and show the crowd how much more polished he was as a public speaker. He imagined it as the Kennedy-Nixon debate all over again, with Lewis playing the role of a sweaty, uncomfortable, unattractive Richard Nixon.[65]

As Frederick Allen argued in *The Atlanta Journal-Constitution*, both candidates were pursuing the opposite of what they should. If Lewis was going to win, he needed to increase his margins in the white neighborhoods, but his one-eyed focus on "the streets" implied a struggle within the black community, where he had so far not attracted much support. Bond, on the other hand, was most hurt by the suggestion that he was too glib, too slick, too polished—all images that would be reinforced during televised debates. In addition, most political operatives had research demonstrating that televised debates mainly influenced middle- and upper-class white voters. Bond's support, however, was strongest in the district's poor and working-class neighborhoods. Allen was perplexed by a situation in which "a talker is hurt by talking and a walker is hurt by walking." Two friends turned rivals were trying to show each other up.[66]

At first, both men seemed uncertain about how far to push the personal attacks, but in the last two weeks, during the series of five debates, the ugliness grew. In the second debate, Lewis hinted at Bond's rumored illegal drug use by noting he recently took a drug test and suggesting Bond follow his lead. Atlantans had gossiped about Bond's playboy reputation and possible drug use for years, but it had never really been talked about publicly. Until now.

Bond refused to take a test, responding with a weak joke that Lewis's "jar wars" were as ridiculous as President Reagan's recently announced "Star Wars" plan. Bond got himself into more hot water later when, in placing Atlanta's drug problem in a national context, he seemed to suggest that the city did not in fact have a drug problem. It was a rare slip of the tongue that Lewis immediately exploited. "I don't know whether Mr. Bond is living in Atlanta," he said, simultaneously reinforcing the ideas that Bond took drugs lightly and that he spent too much time traveling around the country.[67]

Lewis thought the attacks were justified and was pleased that they seemed to rattle his old friend, but when Bond employed similar tactics, he was incredibly offended. Before one debate, Bond made a big production of asking an aide if he had a copy of Shirley MacLaine's autobiography ready, specifically asking about a passage that referred to Lewis being "stoned" at a SNCC party. As both Bond and Lewis knew, MacLaine was writing about two beers Lewis had drunk, but Lewis thought Bond was trying to rattle him. Even though he had done the same thing, Lewis was also galled that Bond would call into question his morality, when everyone in SNCC knew he was the straightest arrow in the group.[68]

In the final debate, both men crossed the point of no return. Halfway through, a questioner asked Lewis about a few small contributions from employees of a cable television company that had business before the city council. Was this not, the questioner asked, a conflict of interest? Lewis took it as an article of faith that there was no conflict. The cable contract had come up before he even arrived on the city council, and the vote on the contract had occurred early in his term, long before the contributions to his congressional campaign. He was sure that everyone would see there was no problem.

The questioner turned to Bond, who shrugged: "If it looks like a duck and quacks like a duck and waddles like a duck, then it must be a duck."

Lewis was dumbfounded. He could not believe that his friend, who knew he had done no wrong, would imply wrongdoing. Ironically, earlier in the debate Lewis had used equally flimsy evidence to question Bond's relationship with a city contractor. But in situations like this Lewis's thin skin made him politically tone-deaf, and he personalized the attack.

Lewis thought, "I'm not going to let this Negro get away with this."

Barely keeping a level tone to his voice, Lewis shot back his own challenge: "Mr. Bond, my friend, my brother. We were asked to take a drug test not long ago, and five of us went and took that test. Why don't we go step out and go to the men's room and take another test?"

The room went silent as Bond fumbled for a response. He made another joke about "jar wars"; he accused Lewis of McCarthyism, of "pandering to people's fears." He declined to take the test.[69]

That exchange crystallized all the nagging doubts Atlantans had about Bond that had arisen during the campaign: that he was more interested in having a good time, that he did not work very hard, that he was too slick, too smooth.

When the votes were counted on September 2, Lewis had scored an upset victory, trumping Bond 51.8 percent to 48.2 percent; but in a low turnout, that amounted to only 2,378 votes out of more than 65,000 cast. Bond's advantage in the district's predominantly black areas had narrowed, but he still outpolled Lewis by almost 8,000 votes in precincts at least 75 percent black. Lewis made up the gap by trouncing Bond four to one in precincts at least 75 percent white, winning 12,453 votes to Bond's 3,069.[70]

Lewis's victory was full of irony. He was the man of populist rhetoric, but it failed to resonate with black voters, and he had needed all the white votes he could muster to win. Bond, on the other hand, was supposed to be the smooth voice of black moderation, possibly the first black vice president, yet he could not convince white voters in his district to support him; in fact, his privileged upbringing and celebrity were clearly an asset with black voters. Bond had been the driving force behind the creation of a black majority district, only to see white voters decide the result. Strangest of all was the failure of these two men, who had probably done more than anyone else to register new voters, to get people to turn out for their election.

In many ways, Bond had only himself to blame. If he had run when the seat was vacant in 1970 or 1978, he probably would have won and definitely would not have had to square off against his friend. But by 1986, both the political landscape and the public perception of Bond had changed. In 1970, there had been few black elected officials in the South; by the mid-1980s, a whole new class of black politicians had moved in and built up their résumés. In comparison, Bond looked like he had rested on his laurels. No matter how hard he actually had worked, he had stayed in the Georgia legislature too long without seeming to accomplish much, especially since he had not assumed any leadership positions. In this way, Lewis's relative inexperience as an elected official actually served to his advantage. Bond had wavered for too many years. He had missed his window of opportunity.

Lewis was unashamed about his behavior in the campaign, seeing it as a necessary but unavoidable step. He recognized that "the days when Julian and Alice and Lillian and I had been inseparable, when we would vacation together at Disneyland or in Barbados, when we would stay up until three in the morning playing Scrabble, when we filled our scrapbooks with photos of the four of us laughing and sharing our lives together—those days were behind us now." Lewis accepted this outcome because in his mind the campaign was "about something bigger," something "beyond friendship," and to achieve victory, he had to "cut . . . personal ties." Lewis used this idea repeatedly to justify his actions, but he always left the larger issue unstated. No great philosophical divide separated the two men. What had been at stake was simply who would advance to Congress and who would not. Lewis, however, was uncomfortable with his own ambition. In order to justify his actions to himself and to preserve his saintly public image, he needed to convince himself that something larger than his own personal gain was at stake.[71]

The election was a clear reminder that the shadow of the movement followed both men. In a broad sense, the pressure that Bond and Lewis had felt to run was both understandable and unreasonable. If not for their youthful fame, both men would be considered rising political stars, not potential has-beens; the loser would still have had a future and would not be made to feel as if his career were over. The whole election was shaped by preconceived definitions of who they were, definitions rooted in the 1960s. It is a cliché to say they were boxed in by their fame, but in this case it was true.

On the Saturday following the runoff, almost one hundred black leaders gathered for a unity breakfast at Paschal's, the famed eatery that had been hosting gatherings like this since the 1960s, when move-ment activists would congregate there between protests to chow on homemade southern food and talk strategy. The mayor, the ex-mayor, and all the city councilors who had either explicitly or implicitly worked for Bond showed up to endorse the new nominee. Surveying the line of bigwigs going to pay homage to Lewis, reminiscent of the opening scene in *The Godfather*, the state representative Billy McKin-ney, one of his earliest supporters, observed, "Machiavelli said that to the victor goes the spoils. And we're basking in it." Bond, however, was conspicuously absent.

Bond was alone at his vacation home in Florida, stewing over his loss. He was angry, at his own failings as a candidate and especially at his friend's tactics. "We ran a high-level, first-class, up-front cam-paign, and we never have to be ashamed of one moment," he said in thanking his backers for their support in the face of "unprecedented negative campaigning." When asked by a reporter about his friend-ship with Lewis, he remarked dryly that the campaign had "put a real strain on it from my point of view."[72]

THE CIVIL RIGHTS GENERATION IN POWER

Ella Baker died on December 13, 1986. It was her eighty-third birthday. She had been in declining health for several years but still somehow managed to be engaged in an array of activist groups—women in the third world, the plight of Puerto Rico, labor organizing—until nearly the very end. A few days after her passing, her friends packed the Abyssinian Baptist Church in Harlem to celebrate her life. It was one of the largest gatherings of SNCC people since the Waveland retreat in the fall of 1964. The eulogists spoke about her authenticity and her humanity. "She wanted to know what people thought, but she mostly wanted them to think," recalled Anne Braden. Joanne Grant spoke about her friend as a *fundi*, a Swahili word for someone who passes a craft from one generation to the next. What Ella Baker had passed on was the lessons of grassroots organizing to the young people of SNCC, who in turn passed them on to the people of the Deep South. "We are all, no matter our color, her children," Grant concluded. At that moment, Bob Moses stood up from one of the pews and asked Ella's children to come forward. Hundreds of people in the audience stood up, crowding into the front of the church and linking their arms.[1]

SNCC's founders interpreted the idea of *fundi* in diverse ways, just as they had interpreted Baker's charge, nearly forty years earlier, to be about more than a hamburger in diverse ways. For some it meant holding tight to the past; for others, letting it go. Some accepted the compromises and limitations of electoral politics as necessary to securing the legacy of the movement, and some valued ideological consistency. *Fundi* could mean grassroots organizing or heading up a national organization or teaching or writing. The definition of *fundi* was as varied as their lives. Yet *fundi*, with its implication of a history, of a past, could be a burden as well as a gift. The ways in which SNCC's founders sought to pass on their knowledge hinted at their own struggles with their legacy. Were they seeking redemption? Power? Acclaim? Emotional succor? Their personal stories were so intertwined with the larger arc of American history that separating the two was not possible.

Just four weeks after Baker's death, Diane Nash found herself resurrected from historical obscurity by *Eyes on the Prize*, a six-hour documentary about the movement from 1954 to 1965 that premiered in January 1987. The public memory of SNCC had tended to focus on a few men in the public eye—Bond, Lewis, Carmichael, occasionally Moses. Aside from mentions of Rosa Parks, the story of women in the movement tended to jump to the late 1960s to look at how the movement inspired feminism, a tale usually more focused on white women. But in *Eyes on the Prize*, Nash was the unquestioned star of the segments on the sit-ins and the Freedom Rides. Her ability to project a sweet girlishness, even in middle age, combined with her passionate commitment to the moral importance of direct-action protest, made her interviews compelling television.

After the series aired, she started getting invitations to speak at colleges and to civic groups; she found she could make a living at it as well. She became an icon to a new generation of womens' and labor activists, supporting campaigns for workers' rights, for health insurance for the poor, and for women's rights. Her message was an update of her long-ago talk to her son's sixth-grade class, "What does a freedom fighter do?" She had always been better at articulating the philosophy of nonviolence than doing the nitty-gritty of community organizing, and her lectures dwelt on the idea of satyagraha and the importance of adopting nonviolence as a way of life. But she also found the lecture circuit comforting, frankly admitting to a reporter in the mid-1990s that she yearned for the sense of purpose and camaraderie of the early years of the movement.[2]

· · ·

History provided Bob Zellner with a place in the present as well. In 1991, he enrolled in the history Ph.D. program at Tulane University with the understanding that a memoir of his movement days would serve as his dissertation. Two years of coursework and writing led to a teaching job at Long Island University's Southampton Campus. While at Southampton, he organized a conference around the theme of "passing on" the SNCC experience. Out of that conference, he helped develop a "Freedom Curriculum" to teach social justice by connecting present-day problems to the civil rights movement. Teaching also led to opportunities to lecture on the history of the movement, and as he settled into his sixties, Zellner became a regular on the college lecture circuit.

Stokely Carmichael did not live to see his sixtieth birthday. In 1996, he was diagnosed with prostate cancer. His return to the United States for treatment brought an outpouring of support from his old colleagues. A thousand people, including Marion Barry and Cleveland Sellers, attended an April 1998 Friends of Kwame Ture dinner in Washington to raise money for his medical care and to celebrate his life. Even weak with cancer, he clung to his vision of himself as a revolutionary, opining on the possibilities for a socialist revival and switching from hospital garb to a dashiki for a news photographer. As Sellers observed, he "wants to be seen as a warrior for social justice. He doesn't want to be seen as a person who needs . . . well, I'll put a period there." Yet the dinner was clearly more eulogy than political rally. Neither the FBI (which had a large file on him) nor the Anti-Defamation League (which had followed him in the 1970s and 1980s because of his attacks on Zionism) took notice of his return. Seven months later, on November 15, 1998, Kwame Ture, the activist formerly known as Stokely Carmichael, died at his home in Conakry. At his memorial service, Bob Zellner was the only white person who delivered a eulogy. He was followed by Louis Farrakhan.

At the time of Ella Baker's death, Bob Moses had been back in the United States for ten years. On January 21, 1977, Jimmy Carter, in one of his first acts as president, offered amnesty to anyone who had left the United States to avoid the draft. The Moses family had had a good life in Tanzania, but when Janet got accepted to Harvard Medical School, they decided to take the opportunity to return. Moses resumed the Harvard graduate studies he had abandoned nearly twenty years earlier.

The family settled near both the medical school and the philosophy department. They wanted to enroll their children in public school, and their neighborhood school, Martin Luther King, Jr., Elementary, featured an innovative unstructured magnet program and a high degree of racial diversity. Their three children born in Tanzania (a fourth was born just after they returned to the United States) struggled with the adjustment. They spoke Swahili, not English; they found the fast pace of an American city disorienting, and all the white faces odd. One day their elder son, Omo, asked his mother, "Where did all the black people go?"[3]

For the next few years, Moses worked on his graduate studies and was a stay-at-home dad while Janet concentrated on medical school. Moses was unsure about his next move, and the combination of parenting and graduate school offered an ideal vantage point to contemplate the future. His life changed dramatically in 1982 when the MacArthur Foundation awarded him one of its $200,000 genius grants in recognition of his civil rights work in Mississippi. Since returning to America, Moses had been "fishing around for a movement" in which to invest his energies, but uncertainty about where his grassroots organizing skills might have the most impact, combined with his familial and financial responsibilities, had kept him from committing to a project. The unexpected five-year no-strings-attached MacArthur grant liberated him from some financial concerns, freeing him to pursue any project that interested him.[4]

Moses found his next great project at his kitchen table. In the spirit of his Mississippi work, he connected the ordinary ritual of helping his daughter with her homework to the larger educational inequalities in America. For several years, he had been nudging his elder daughter, Maisha, to study algebra with him. It was not offered at her school, but he thought higher math was necessary to succeed in college. Like any budding teenager, she rebelled. "Why do I have to do this?" she complained to her father. "No one else has to." He decided that if Maisha would not come to algebra, he would bring algebra to her. So with the economic cushion provided by the MacArthur Grant, he asked Maisha's teacher if he—Moses—could come into the school to teach algebra to her and three friends. All through the 1982–83 school year, Moses worked with the four in the back of the classroom, taking them through the basics of algebra in an informal seminar that seemed more a running discussion than a class. At the end of the year, his students became the first group from the King school to pass the citywide algebra test, qualifying them to move on to geometry and higher math in high school.[5]

When Maisha's teacher asked Moses if he'd like to continue the program, he readily agreed to expand it to a dozen seventh- and eighth-graders. During that first year of tutoring, he noticed that many of the worst math students were either poor or black or both, and he had been thinking about ways he might engage them. In the next year, 1984–85, the program, now dubbed the Algebra Project, opened to all seventh-graders. In the spring, the Cambridge School Committee made the Algebra Project an official part of the curriculum and the next year expanded it to include the sixth grade. By the end of the 1985–86 school year, 40 percent of the Algebra Project students placed into honors math classes in high school.[6]

Moses had successfully applied his ideas about grassroots organizing to the teaching of math. He thought most math textbooks disempowered students by making math an abstraction that was disconnected from their everyday experiences. To really teach math to fidgety sixth- and seventh-graders, teachers needed to connect it to the students' everyday world. Moses took his students onto Boston's subway to teach algebra, using the idea of a subway ride with its direction, starts and stops, and time to show how math was a language of the real world, not an abstract concept. Most of the kids were poor and relied on the subway for their routine transportation, so they knew the system better than Moses and the other teachers. He peppered them with questions that drew on their expertise: What's the quickest way to get from here to here? How long does it take? How many stops? If I want to go over there, how many times will I have to transfer trains? The students wondered what riding the subway had to do with math.[7]

Back in the classroom, Moses demonstrated the relationship between riding the subway and math. He divided the students into teams and asked them to sketch a map of their trip on paper; then he asked them to add numbers to the segments of the trip; and finally they worked to translate the questions (How long? How many stops?)

into mathematical equations. Moses summarized the Algebra Project method as five steps: Observe a physical event, make a pictorial representation of it, use ordinary intuitive language ("people talk") to describe it, turn intuitive language into structured formal language ("feature talk"), and finally translate that into the symbolic language of mathematics.

The Algebra Project continued to grow. The genius grant expired in 1987, but grants from the Hasbro Foundation, the Kapor Foundation, and other charities kept it afloat. Wheelock College, a small school primarily devoted to training teachers, offered Moses a job as an adjunct professor and office space. In 1989, with encouragement from the city's network of black ministers and social activists, it expanded into Boston's schools. The next year brought expansion to Chicago, Louisville, Milwaukee, and Oakland; to San Francisco, Indianapolis, and Los Angeles. By 1991, it had become so big that Wheelock could no longer handle its affairs, so the project rented offices in Cambridge.[8]

Moses promoted math literacy as the civil rights struggle of the twenty-first century. The political barriers to voting, he argued, had been superseded by economic barriers that restricted access to new technology and opportunity. More than half of the new jobs created each year require some science and math literacy, as does citizenship in an increasingly computer-based world. Algebra, Moses observed, is "the gatekeeper for higher math, and the priesthood who gained access to it, now is the gatekeeper for citizenship; and people who don't have it are like the people who couldn't read and write in the industrial age."[9]

His movement connections spread the Algebra Project southward. The Southern Regional Council (SRC), the group that had administered the Voter Education Project during the 1960s, invited Moses to do a presentation at a time when it was looking for ways to spend a Ford Foundation grant for improving education in the Mississippi Delta. His presentation convinced the SRC to fund a small pilot program of the Algebra Project.

Dave Dennis, who had done voter-registration work during Freedom Summer and was now a lawyer in New Orleans, came on board as the director of the new initiative. He had not seen Bob Moses for more than twenty years when a chance 1988 encounter in Jackson, Mississippi, brought them back together. The two men were in town for a panel criticizing *Mississippi Burning*, a fictionalized story of the

Schwerner-Chaney-Goodman murders that glorified the FBI. As they sat by the hotel pool, Moses told him about the Algebra Project. "It's the future" and the "legacy of our past," Moses told him. The project fascinated Dennis, and he stayed in touch. When the opportunity to work with his old friend came up, he jumped at the chance, closing his law practice and relocating his family to Jackson to head the new Delta Algebra Project.[10]

School administrators chafed at the experiential pedagogy and expressed skepticism at the ability of poor students to learn sophisticated math like algebra. After one presentation, a school superintendent told Dave Dennis, "If you were working in my district, I'd fire you now." To counter this, Moses and Dennis drew on their movement-organizing experience. They used teachers to recruit teachers. They organized meetings with parents and students to teach them about the project and to get them to pressure their local school systems.[11]

Moses devoted his time to teaching the Algebra Project in the Jackson, Mississippi, public schools. Dennis's willingness to assume many of the organizational and bureaucratic responsibilities for running the project freed Moses to do what he loved best—teach. Beginning in 1996, Moses would fly from his home in Cambridge to Jackson on Monday morning, teach at Lanier for the week, and then fly back to Cambridge for the weekend. As they got older, his three older children began working for the Algebra Project. Living in Mississippi for the first time since 1966, he reconnected with his activist roots. Once a week during the school year, Moses would make the ninety-minute drive from Jackson to McComb to visit C. C. Bryant. The trips had no political purpose; they were two old friends spending time with each other, helping Moses stay grounded. "When he comes here," Bryant said, "he's coming home."[12]

Despite the bureaucratic hurdles, the Algebra Project was successful in every school system that adopted it. In Weldon, the very worst-performing school district in North Carolina, over four years the Algebra Project nearly doubled the number of middle-school students achieving proficiency on the state math exam. In Bessemer, Alabama, a hard-hit steel town, the school with the highest percentage of poor and minority students achieved the highest math scores of any school in the city. By 2004, the Algebra Project had spread to include forty thousand students in twenty-eight urban and rural districts across the United States.[13]

For some students, the Algebra Project opened the door to political activism. In 2001, Baltimore Algebra Project students staged a student strike to protest cuts in the project's funding. Three years later they staged demonstrations outside the Baltimore city hall to force the governor to honor a ruling requiring the state to raise the level of funding in city schools to that of the wealthier suburbs. Chief Judge Joseph Kaplan, who was overseeing the lawsuit over school funding, was so impressed by the students' activism that he appointed one of them to participate in the settlement negotiations with state and city officials, union leaders, school leaders, and ACLU lawyers.[14]

In 1996, after working with the Algebra Project for several years, Moses's son Omo and several of the original Algebra Project alumni from Cambridge founded the Young People's Project (YPP). Originally, the YPP set out to expand the Algebra Project by training kids to act as peer tutors. But it had broader aspirations to use math literacy to teach leadership skills and give students the organizing skills to change their lives. In addition to training math tutors for the Algebra Project, YPP expanded to include a number of SNCC-inspired organizing projects, including Quality Education as a Constitutional Right, a grassroots effort to pass a constitutional amendment guaranteeing a good education; Finding Our Folk, a documentary effort on the impact of Hurricane Katrina on the Gulf Coast; and Training of Trainers, a series of workshops to teach high school students in the South the organizing traditions of the civil rights movement.[15]

The Algebra Project was not immune to criticism. Attracting parental support was difficult, and the results could be discouraging. Sometimes as few as a dozen parents would attend evening Algebra Project workshops designed to engage them in the process. The method itself was labor and time intensive, requiring patience and trust. Some found the workshops and organizing sessions meandering and inefficient, as Moses insisted on giving everyone in the room a chance to speak and held his own views mostly in check. Moses disliked fundraising and refused to schmooze wealthy donors, making raising money difficult.[16]

Moses recognized the criticism and ignored all of it. He'd heard the same things during the 1960s. He knew his methods worked and that they did not produce quick or easy results. He had patience, and experience had taught him to value incremental change. Fewer people than he had hoped might commit themselves to the Algebra Project, but those who did committed fully.

Both the Algebra Project and the Young People's Project built on and extended SNCC's legacy. Like SNCC in the 1960s, they connected a local problem, in this case poor math education in Cambridge's middle schools, to the larger problem of economic and social inequality. They were centered on areas—the inner city, the rural South—at the margins of the technological revolutions and economic booms of the late twentieth century. They were grassroots efforts to engage people often thought of as too uneducated, unsophisticated, or just plain slow to compete in the economy. Rather than change people's lives for them, they aimed to give people the tools to change their own lives.

The key to the Algebra Project's success was its ability to honor the past without being held hostage to it. By targeting math literacy, Moses acknowledged the evolution of the civil rights struggle. He framed the issue in ways that resonated with the teenagers he encountered every day in the classroom. He refrained from mythologizing his work in the 1960s, denigrating a hip-hop culture he did not fully understand, or moralizing about the failings of a younger generation. The key to success, he argued, was simply to listen to kids. "Really listen," he wrote. "It is a difficult thing for grown-ups to do— listen and pay serious attention to what young people are saying." Moses acknowledged that he sometimes struggled with this as well, but "it is the voices of the young people I hear every day, more than anything, that gives me hope."[17]

Bob Moses was at once the most and least surprising SNCC alumnus to return to grassroots organizing. He had, of course, been the earliest and most committed advocate of SNCC's grassroots strategies. On the other hand, his disillusionment had been the greatest and his fall the steepest. Few had internalized the failures of the MFDP as Moses had or turned away from friends in SNCC and the problems of the region with such abruptness. But from other perspectives, it's easy to understand Moses's return to organizing. In Mississippi, the day-to-day rhythms of organizing had always kept him focused, and as much as anyone in SNCC, he believed in Ella Baker's advice about the importance of local communities and the value of ordinary people in the struggle for social justice. The Algebra Project allowed him to pivot to become the Ella Baker to a new generation of activists. He was their *fundi*. A whole generation of kids who came of age in the Algebra Project could say, "We are all the children of Bob Moses."

Marion Barry became a cautionary tale for black politicians about the limits of urban political power. At first, Washington seemed to avoid the problems that plagued other American cities. Though the city's population dropped by 150,000 between 1970 and 1990, its tax revenues expanded dramatically. Much of the growth in revenue resulted from a real estate boom that added ten million square feet of office space during the 1980s. But in 1989, the real estate market collapsed, and with it the city's revenues. By this time, the crack epidemic was in full swing, and the city's murder rate exploded, going from fewer than two hundred a year in the mid-1980s to nearly five hundred a year in the early 1990s.[18]

By focusing on patronage at the expense of bottom-up economic development, Barry's policies produced a short-term boost for African-American residents that masked deeper problems. By 1990, the city bureaucracy was 40 percent larger than that of other cities its size. The economic development that Barry promoted relied on the construction of office buildings to house white-collar professionals. During the 1980s, the proportion of people commuting to work from the suburbs skyrocketed, and the unemployment rate for blue-collar city residents leaped upward. Barry's patronage machine helped ensure his continued reelection but was at odds with genuine grassroots democracy. The city's school and public health systems deteriorated, and his policies left many stuck in poverty.[19]

The press told it as a story of personal corruption, focusing on a few spectacular cases to make the point. In 1987, Ivanhoe Donaldson—who had moved with Barry from SNCC, ran his campaign, and then served as deputy mayor until 1984—pleaded guilty to stealing nearly $200,000 from the city. Smaller scandals involving city officials misappropriating thousands of dollars for personal use added to the image of a corrupt administration. Still, none of the scandals, not even the one involving Donaldson, personally implicated Barry. The larger story had less to do with Barry's personal morality than with the way he had used the organizations he controlled—going all the way back to Pride—to build a network more concerned with personal loyalty than with social justice.

But Barry's drug use overshadowed all other stories about him. Throughout the 1980s, Barry's hard-partying ways were legendary in Washington. In 1984, the rumors crossed into the public realm when an investigation by U.S. Attorney Joseph DiGenova suggested Barry used cocaine. Though Barry testified under oath that he never used it, rumors continued to dog him. The stories intertwined with a media obsession with Barry's mistresses. *The Washington Post* regularly reported on his alleged trysts—stories that almost always included allegations of cocaine use. In 1989, Charles Lewis, a friend and city employee facing conviction for a drug deal in the Virgin Islands, testified to federal officials that he had smoked crack with the mayor. The Lewis allegations sparked a federal probe that culminated on January 18, 1990, when Barry was videotaped smoking crack with a woman in a hotel room in downtown Washington. With charges hanging over him, Barry chose not to run for reelection that year, and in October he was sentenced to six months in jail for one charge of possessing cocaine.[20]

In the end, the things that brought Barry down were the very things that had made him an effective organizer and a successful politician. The personal courage he displayed in McComb became a reckless disregard for the legal consequences of his drug use. The concern for the poor expressed in the food drives in Mississippi and in Pride became patronage aimed at simply retaining office. The unease about the disparity in political access that motivated the effort to register voters and to win for Washington residents the right to elect their mayor devolved into the abuse of power.

John Lewis drew on the values of compromise, consensus, and working within the system that he had promoted from his earliest days in SNCC as he slowly climbed the congressional ladder. He entered Congress at a moment when the Democratic Party was in eclipse, especially the southern wing, because of sustained ridicule from canny agitators like his fellow Georgia congressman Newt Gingrich and the redistricting that further polarized majority-black urban districts and majority-white suburban districts. In 1994, just as Lewis gained a small measure of seniority, the Republicans gained control of Congress, though by the time the Democrats regained the majority in 2006 he was the senior deputy whip.

As he moved up the party hierarchy, Lewis proved willing to make the political compromises necessary for leadership. In 2006, he endorsed Joe Lieberman of Connecticut for reelection to the Senate despite Lieberman's unquestioning support for the Iraq War. Lewis also made the expedient choice by endorsing Hillary Clinton over Barack Obama in the 2008 Democratic presidential primaries. Only after Obama took the lead in delegates and his constituents expressed their deep disagreement did Lewis switch his endorsement. His legislative accomplishments were sparse. One Democratic staffer quoted in a sympathetic profile said that Lewis is "a big picture person" who "doesn't get as much into the nitty-gritty of legislative minutiae."[21]

Even as he made conventional political choices, Lewis's youthful civil rights work endowed him with a moral authority that defined his entire congressional career: "When someone walks out of the history books and takes the oath of office, that person carries a certain cachet and respect that the used-car salesman and the entrepreneurs don't command." Fellow congressmen sought his advice on issues dealing with race—even tangentially, like drugs and homelessness. He became the point man for an effort to build a museum of African-American history on the Washington Mall. Every profile of Lewis, every mention, referred to his SNCC years. After two terms in Congress, *The Washington Post* framed him as a "scarred survivor" bringing home "the lessons of the 60s." The media often referred to him as the "last living speaker" from the 1963 March on Washington. A 1996 *New Republic* profile cast him as the "strongest link in American politics between the 1960s—the glory days of the civil rights movement—and the 1990s" and the standard-bearer for a revived Great Society liberalism. The same piece detected a "deepening polarization of black politics," and lamented that Lewis's past contributions were "overlooked" in the attention given to more radical figures like Eldridge Cleaver and Louis Farrakhan.[22]

Lewis fell comfortably into this trap. His official congressional biography devotes more space to his accomplishments in SNCC than to his accomplishments in Congress. His 1998 autobiography essentially ends with his 1986 election to Congress, barely touching on his career in the House. As much as anyone, he loved reliving the old war stories, and he always found time to address schools or civic groups on the movement. Unfortunately, his invocations seemed more about nostalgia. A typical exchange with some Atlanta high school students in the early 1990s captures this problem. First, Lewis told the story of the first Freedom Ride in dramatic detail to try to make the point that the students, too, "have a contribution to make." When pressed by the students about how they could contribute to solving current problems in health care, housing, or education, Lewis invoked the emotionally charged history of the movement, offering nothing more concrete than the importance of voting. "Register and vote," he said. "People died to give you the right to vote." The very parts of SNCC's history that young people might find useful in dealing with these intractable problems—its youthful impatience, its unwillingness to defer to an older generation, the premium it placed on morality over political expediency—were left uncited by Congressman Lewis.[23]

Nothing better demonstrated the power and limitations of SNCC's past on Lewis than his autobiography, *Walking with the Wind*. Much of the book is a moving elegy to his unpredictable rise and displays his legendary courage. He recounts the first sit-ins, the Freedom Rides, and the Selma marches with an immediacy and power unrivaled by other accounts. Yet the very strength of the book is its undoing. The movement is presented as a mythical moment relatively unconnected to the present; 80 percent of the story takes place before 1968, and the transition from protest to politics is told in an uncomplicated fashion that offers little insight into its difficulties.

Lewis also used his autobiography to settle old scores and slights. As often as he used the story of the poor kid in Troy, Alabama, who baptized chickens and could hardly afford college to make his life an American success story, he railed against that imagery for diminishing him in comparison to more cosmopolitan SNCC leaders like Bond and Moses. After thirty years, he could barely contain his anger and resentment at Stokely Carmichael over the 1966 vote that cost him SNCC's chairmanship, speculating in minute detail on who was to blame and why. His version of the congressional campaign against Bond is notable for its lack of generosity to his old friend. He was obsessed with juxtaposing every negative press description of his own physical appearance with positive ones of Bond's looks. He belittled Bond's public career, casting him as a dilettante and unaccomplished legislator and describing his notorious request for a drug test as "not an entirely unreasonable request."[24]

The public had already fixed on an image of Lewis as a great moralist, so the public reaction overlooked the pettiness, just as it had excused his more calculated political endorsements. *The New York Times* praised Lewis's "consistent force of character" and his "faith in the Beloved Community . . . where people . . . reach across the barriers . . . in a spirit of love." *Time* magazine echoed this with admiration for Lewis's "moral consistency and power."[25]

Ironically, it was Bond who found the balance between protest and politics. After his bitter defeat, he retreated from public life for a while. Like others, he became a teacher of the movement. Friendships from the 1960s provided the connections. Virginia Durr, who had been Rosa Parks's friend and employer, had a son-in-law who was now the president of the University of Pennsylvania, and in 1989 Bond spent a semester there teaching a course on the movement. Other jobs at Williams College, Harvard University, and Occidental College followed; then, in the early 1990s, he secured permanent positions teaching at American University and the University of Virginia.

Forced to reinvent himself, Bond renewed his activist roots. Teaching helped pay the bills, but Bond's real passion was the NAACP. Soon after getting elected to the Georgia House in the late 1960s, Bond realized that the very things that SNCC disparaged about the NAACP—its large size, its appeal to the black middle class, its commitment to working within the system—made it a valuable political partner. Throughout the 1970s and 1980s, he worked closely with the Atlanta chapter, serving as branch president from 1978 to 1989 and becoming a member of the national board of directors.

In the early 1990s, after relocating permanently to Washington, he focused his energy on reforming the organization, which he thought had become out of touch and adrift. The leadership had become more focused on self-perpetuation than activism. For too many people, he thought, election to the board signaled the capstone of a career of service and not the start of a new chapter. The last straw came in 1992 when William Gibson, the chairman, proposed loosening the rules to allow himself to continue past the six-year maximum term. At

the same time, the longtime executive director, Benjamin Hooks, retired. Bond charged that Gibson wanted to consolidate too much
power in the chairman's office and turn the executive director, who
traditionally ran the day-to-day operations, into an "office manager."
Bond lost that power struggle, becoming the first board member in
more than a decade to lose a reelection bid.[26]

Three years later he organized a reform slate of candidates with
Myrlie Evers-Williams, the widow of the slain Mississippi NAACP
leader Medgar Evers. The problems in the organization had gotten
worse. The new executive director resigned over a sexual harassment
suit, the organization had a $2 million deficit on a budget of just $11
million, and corporate contributions had declined precipitously. The
reformers prevailed, Bond returned to the board, and Evers-Williams
replaced Gibson as chairman.

Working together, the two righted the organization. They turned
the deficit into a $5 million surplus and raised money for an endow-
ment. They reduced the power of the board of directors, which at
sixty-four members had become unwieldy and ineffective. Most important, they hired a strong executive director in the former congressman Kwesi Mfume and gave him power to run the organization. In
1998, Evers-Williams retired, and Bond replaced her as chairman.[27]

It was an ironic twist to have a former SNCC member at the head
of the NAACP, but Bond turned out to be a great choice and an effective chairman. He raised the organization's visibility. His SNCC past
actually gave the organization new credibility as an activist organization. With the financial crisis past, Bond pushed the organization to
return to its core commitments. By the early 1990s, many local NAACP
branches were as involved in social service issues, like teenage preg-
nancy, as they were in racial discrimination. Bond believed it was important for the NAACP to keep its eye solely on the question of racial
justice. "We want it to be a social justice organization," he said. "Our
mission is to fight racial discrimination and provide social justice. Social service organizations deal with the effects of racial discrimination. We deal with the beast itself. There are many organizations that
provide social services," Mr. Bond continued. "We say, 'Good for
them.' But we are one of the very few that provide social justice. It is
popular to say that we are in a post–civil rights period, but we don't
believe that."[28]

Bond's strategy gave the NAACP its greatest public influence in decades. While it had always been an important stop for presidential candidates, these visits now generated greater coverage in the press. More important, the NAACP's proclamations on housing discrimination, job discrimination, and bias in the criminal justice system received widespread attention. In pushing the NAACP's social justice mission, Bond also worked to broaden the "Colored People" part of the NAACP's name, highlighting discrimination against Asian Americans and Hispanic Americans. He also engaged the organization in the question of discrimination against gays and lesbians. Support for gay rights conflicted with the religious leanings of the NAACP's middle-class base, and many members tried to draw a distinction between discrimination based on sexual orientation (which they saw as a choice) and discrimination based on race (which they saw as a product of birth). Despite opposition from some members, Bond lent his name in support of gay marriage campaigns across the country and prodded the organization to come along with him.[29]

Some of the renewed public attention to the NAACP reflected Bond's willingness to be more overtly political than some of his predecessors. Because of its tax-exempt status, the NAACP was officially nonpartisan; throughout its history it had had strong ties to both Republicans and Democrats. The ties to the Republicans reflected the historical legacy of black Republicanism, which stretched back to Lincoln, and the fact that African Americans did not became reliable Democratic voters until the 1964 election. During the 1970s, Executive Director Ben Hooks balanced strong support from congressional Democrats with ties to the Nixon and Ford White House, even getting appointed to the Federal Communications Commission by President Nixon. While staying just shy of outright partisanship, Bond attracted considerable attention for his criticism of the second Bush presidency on a wide range of issues, especially his strident opposition to the Iraq War. During his first term, Bush became the first president since Herbert Hoover in the 1920s not to appear at the NAACP's national convention, and Bond used his absences to generate publicity and raise questions about Bush's racial policies. Finally, in 2006—his sixth year in office—Bush gave a speech at the national meeting.[30]

The journey of the civil rights generation began in the late 1930s, a time of swirling change both for the nation as a whole and for African

Americans in particular. To take jobs or to join the military, hundreds and thousands of African Americans moved out of the South, and the economic boom created a large and relatively prosperous black middle class. World War II expanded the conversation about race. African-American activists applied the rhetoric of liberty and democracy, used to justify American entry into the war, to critique race relations at home. Intellectuals transformed this rhetoric into the notion of an "American dilemma," the gap between an American creed that emphasized liberty and equality and the everyday reality of legal racism. This uneven mixture of prosperity, population shifts, and ideological self-examination set in motion a broad-ranging conversation about race in American life.

African Americans accelerated the debate about race in the 1950s. The Supreme Court's 1954 *Brown* decision declared school segregation unconstitutional but did not require any immediate integration. Constant debates over how *Brown* would be implemented kept the issue of school integration in the spotlight (even as few black children entered white classrooms). The visibility of civil rights increased again in 1956 with the Montgomery bus boycott and the emergence of Martin Luther King, Jr., as a national figure.

Still, at the end of the decade the shape and speed of civil rights progress remained murky. White segregationists exploited the law and leveraged their political power to prevent almost any school integration, and the courts were reluctant to force the issue unless absolutely necessary. The struggle for civil rights had not yet become a mass movement.

The sit-ins that began on February 1, 1960, inaugurated the era of mass protest, the most dramatic phase of the civil rights movement and a model for other protest movements throughout the 1960s and beyond. The first sit-in was a spontaneous event, but the idea quickly spread across the South, involving fifty thousand people in the first few months. In less than three months, the college students behind these protests formed the Student Nonviolent Coordinating Committee.

That SNCC was born on the campuses of the South's black colleges and universities was no accident. Young African Americans coming of age during the early 1960s were perfectly positioned to take a leading role in the civil rights movement. Born on the eve of World War II, they had known greater prosperity than previous generations and had an expanded sense of opportunity. They had finished elementary and high school in the shadow of the *Brown* decision, believing for the rest of the 1950s that integration was just around the corner.

They were also part of the first generation to think of themselves self-consciously as teenagers. The youth culture of the 1950s, especially the potent music- and movie-driven consumer culture, sent out a powerful message of generational unity that downplayed differences of region, class, and race.

At the same time, segregation and racism made young African Americans constantly aware of their inferior status. They grew incredibly frustrated at the contradiction between being first-class consumers and second-class citizens. Critics described the postwar generation as a self-absorbed, spoiled, and politically disengaged product of the new affluence, but these young Americans glimpsed the fact that the rapidly expanding powers of the American mass market could be harnessed to produce not apathy but activism.

In the five years from the sit-ins to the passage of the Voting Rights Act in 1965, these students stood at the forefront of the civil rights movement, leading demonstrations, registering voters, and organizing communities. No organization contributed more to the civil rights movement than SNCC. In breathtakingly few years, SNCC dismantled an institution—legal segregation—that had seemed as timeless and certain as the Mississippi River itself.

SNCC took the movement to the farthest corners of the Deep South, the places most resistant to change. It thrust civil disobedience into the forefront of movement activism with strategies like "jail, no bail," exposed the injustice and cruelty of segregation, and challenged Americans to consider the true meaning of an American creed that emphasized liberty and equality. SNCC believed in the ability of ordinary people to lead their own movements. Before there was a bumper sticker that said "Think globally, act locally," SNCC lived out the true meaning of this idea.

As an organization of young people, SNCC brought all the possibilities and passions of youth to its civil rights campaigns. Because most members were in college or just graduating, they had fewer obstacles to becoming full-time activists and were willing to live cheaply, on the edge of respectability. SNCC lacked the hierarchy and bureaucracy of older organizations, allowing it to respond to crises quickly.

In a broad sense, its organizational looseness made its members willing—even reckless—in their desire to challenge the most established authority in the South: segregation. In a narrow sense, it made them willing to experiment with any tactic or strategy that they thought would bring them success.

The initial protests were rooted in an optimistic, almost naïve faith in the capacity of the American democratic process to bring an end to segregation peacefully and in the power of moral suasion to achieve that goal. Many national politicians—President Johnson in particular—shared the basic goal of movement activists but balanced it against what they saw as the political realities of the possible. Increasingly frustrated by the willingness of politicians to value expediency over justice and uncertain of the American system's capacity for self-reform, SNCC members lost faith in the power of liberalism to solve the intractable problem of racism. What started as protests against the denial of consumer service became a far-reaching critique of the broad inequities of American society.

The great victories of the first half of the 1960s came at a price. A combination of factors—the weariness brought on by years of sustained activism, personal conflicts, the arrest or assassination of key leaders, the growing distraction of the debate over Vietnam, the lack of a national consensus on the next steps, and increased harassment from the police and FBI—drained the civil rights movement of its vitality. As quickly as the movement had achieved its key victories, it unraveled in the late 1960s.

The civil rights generation spent the rest of their lives grappling with their youthful activism, in a long reflective process that mirrored America's own unresolved feelings about the 1960s. The long shadow of that decade hovered over the rest of the twentieth century, serving as a Rorschach test for one's politics. Most of the movement's prominent veterans were barely thirty when SNCC collapsed; their only life experience during their formative twenties had been itinerant, urgent political activism. They searched for new challenges that would be just as meaningful as the old while they struggled to come to terms with the personal ramifications of having lived an unsettled existence where danger, even death, was a real and constant possibility.

In their adulthood, they elaborated on the gains they had fought for in their youth. Some worked in politics, quietly and more effectively continuing to register voters. But their lives reached far beyond politics. Many continued organizing the disfranchised as community activists and public advocates. One rose to head the very civil rights organization that SNCC had once criticized for being overly cautious and conservative. The civil rights generation sowed the seeds of victory in the 1960s and nurtured its fruit thereafter.

In the four decades since, the politics of race have played out in the shadow of the shining successes of the early and mid-1960s. The lightning-fast victories and the image of youthful activists dominated Americans' collective memory and established unrealistic expectations for the speed at which social change can be accomplished. The stagnant economy of the 1970s and early 1980s, combined with a misleading sense that the cultural expressions of "black power" represented the movement, obscured the great changes that took place in America.

Among the most powerful legacies of the civil rights movement was the election of large numbers of African Americans to political office and the flowering of the black middle class. In 1960 there were few black elected officials anywhere in the country and none in the South save for a handful of local officeholders. Twenty-six years later, Mississippi would have more African Americans in elective office than any other state in the nation.

Civil rights activists did not wholly anticipate the extent to which the middle class would disproportionately benefit from the end of legal segregation. As employment and education barriers fell, those who already possessed some skills, those in the broad middle class, were well poised to take advantage of these changes. The uneven distribution of the movement's economic gains was a predictable result of the choices that political leaders made to favor short-term gains over the most just and equitable solution. Indeed, the activists' inability to provide the poorest of the poor in the rural South with the modern equivalent of "forty acres and a mule" stands as the movement's great failure. The question of black poverty was not just about overcoming discrimination but also about making rural and urban areas economically viable in the face of the continued suburban consolidation of American prosperity. Rural poverty, in particular, proved to be deeply intractable. From the very beginning, SNCC activists had been concerned about the lack of economic opportunity in the rural South.

That even with the franchise and real political power, African-American activists made little headway in easing the problem of rural poverty was another reminder of the close link between political and economic freedom.

During the heyday of the movement, many activists thought of it as a "Second Reconstruction," a historical twin of the Reconstruction that followed the end of the Civil War. Like the first Reconstruction, the second erased a set of barriers that prevented African Americans from obtaining full citizenship. Like its historical ancestor, it also left unfulfilled the promise to link political and economic freedom. Depending on one's perspective, one could see the movement either as the triumph of a liberal vision of equality or as a minimal resolution that reinforced existing class divisions. These differences reflected deeper questions that remained unanswered: What should a truly integrated society look like? What is the meaning of democracy and equality?

The civil rights movement was also a third American Revolution. Like the original American Revolution and the Civil War—the second revolution—it benefited all Americans by expanding the notion of citizenship and advancing the idea of equality. It made a compelling argument that any restrictions on the franchise undermined democracy for all and that the United States was healthiest when most people participated in the process. The idea of "one man, one vote" powerfully linked equality and democracy and forced more than thirty-five states to more fairly apportion their legislatures.

The second half of the twentieth century mirrored the arc of the civil rights generation itself. Through the story of these remarkable young people—John Lewis, Julian Bond, Diane Nash, Bob Zellner, Stokely Carmichael, Marion Barry, Charles McDew, Bob Moses, and the others in the special band of brothers and sisters called SNCC— the organization they formed, the circle of trust they forged in difficult times, and their lives after those dramatic years, the arc of the civil rights movement takes shape. How this ragtag band with little money, no obvious power, painfully little help from the federal government, and the entire white South out to get them played a starring role in the demise of legal segregation is one of the great adventure stories of American history.

At the dawn of the twenty-first century, these activists enter the twilight of their lives. They should look back on those lives with great satisfaction. They devoted the best part of their youth to an idealistic and selfless quest to make the United States live up to the full meaning of its founding promise and their middle years to working out the implications of that vision in everyday life. Few generations can claim to have exerted as profound an influence on American life. This is the journey of the civil rights generation.

PROLOGUE

1. Charles McDew interview.
2. Zinn, *SNCC*, 18; Greenberg, *Circle of Trust*, 45–47.
3. Sellers and Terrell, *River of No Return*, 34–35; Bond interview in Hampton and Fayer, *Voices of Freedom*, 62–64.
4. Halberstam, *Children*, 215.
5. For background on Lewis, see Lewis and D'Orso, *Walking with the Wind*, 83–84; Halberstam, *The Children*, 145–47.
6. Carson, *In Struggle*, 21; Greenberg, *Circle of Trust*, 18–23.
7. Lewis and D'Orso, *Walking with the Wind*, 107–108.
8. Ibid., 83; Halberstam, *Children*, 219.
9. For background on Julian Bond, see Neary, *Julian Bond*.
10. Greenberg, *Circle of Trust*, 34. Ella Baker is the subject of two excellent biographies, Grant, *Ella Baker*, and Ransby, *Ella Baker*.
11. Hampton and Fayer, *Voices of Freedom*, 63.
12. Grant, *Ella Baker*, 122–23.
13. Ibid., 127.
14. For information on the planning of the Shaw conference, see the microfilmed Student Nonviolent Coordinating Committee Papers, 1959–1972.
15. Bond interview in Hampton and Fayer, *Voices of Freedom*, 61–65.
16. Sellers and Terrell, *River of No Return*, 36.
17. Bond interview in Hampton and Fayer, *Voices of Freedom*, 64–65.
18. This account of Baker's meeting with King is drawn from Grant, *Ella Baker*, 128–30.
19. Bond interview in Hampton and Fayer, *Voices of Freedom*, 64–65.
20. Zinn, *SNCC*, 33.

1. SURE BUGS ME

1. Lewis and D'Orso, *Walking with the Wind*, 43–44.
2. Kluger, *Simple Justice*, 133–38; Klarman, *From Jim Crow to Civil Rights*, 171–289; Greenberg, *Crusaders in Courts*, 54–92. The definitive account of the background to *Brown* is Kluger, *Simple Justice*, especially pp. 285–540.
3. Smith, *They Closed Their Schools*.
4. Kluger, *Simple Justice*, 702–10; Patterson, *Brown v. Board of Education*, 65–68.
5. The best analysis of the Supreme Court's internal debate is Klarman, *From Jim Crow to Civil Rights*, 290–320.
6. *Brown v. Board of Education*, 349 U.S. 294 (1955).
7. Lewis and D'Orso, *Walking with the Wind*, 43–44. For statistics on school desegregation, see *Statistical Summary of School Segregation-Desegregation in the Southern and Border States*. For a brief overview and a comparison of the Deep South and border states, see Klarman, *From Jim Crow to Civil Rights*, 344–63.
8. Olive Adams, "Time Bomb: Mississippi and the Full Story of Emmett Till" (1956 pamphlet), reprinted in Metress, *Lynching of Till*, 218–19.
9. Whitfield, *Death in the Delta*, 15–17.
10. Ibid., 15–17; Adams, "Time Bomb," and "Mamie Bradley's Untold Story," in Metress, *Lynching of Till*, 218–19, 226–35.
11. The account in this paragraph and the next is drawn from Huie, "Shocking Story," 46–49; Whitfield, *Death in the Delta*, 16–23.
12. The description of the scene at the funeral home is drawn from the recollections of Harry Caise, the mortician, and Mamie Till Bradley (at the time of the interview Mamie Till Mobley); see *The American Experience: The Murder of Emmett Till* (PBS television documentary).
13. Metress, *Lynching of Till*, 117.
14. Lewis and D'Orso, *Walking with the Wind*, 47; *American Experience: Murder of Till*, Sellers and Terrell, *River of No Return*, 13–15.
15. Carmichael and Thelwell, *Ready for Revolution*, 76.
16. King's quote is from his "Letter from Birmingham Jail," April 16, 1963, in King, *Why We Can't Wait*.
17. Thornton, *Dividing Lines*, 20–53. See also Parks and Haskins, *Rosa Parks*.
18. Thornton, *Dividing Lines*, 57–60.
19. Ibid., 61–64; Branch, *Parting the Waters*, 136–37.
20. Thornton, *Dividing Lines*, 63–67.
21. Branch, *Parting the Waters*, 138–40.
22. Thornton, *Dividing Lines*, 67–88; Branch, *Parting the Waters*, 155–59; quote from Raines, *My Soul Is Rested*, 61.
23. Thornton, *Dividing Lines*, 71–95; Fairclough, *To Redeem the Soul*, 20–22.
24. Fairclough, *To Redeem the Soul*, 37–56; see also Branch, *Parting the Waters*, 206–71, for King's struggles to build on the boycott and for the whirlwind of fame he got caught up in.
25. Fairclough, *To Redeem the Soul of America*, 11–36.
26. Lewis and D'Orso, *Walking with the Wind*, 48.
27. Rose, *Black Leaders Then and Now*; Raines, *My Soul Is Rested*.

28. Zellner radio interview; Zinn, *SNCC*, 168–71.

29. Bond interview; Kirk, *Redefining the Color Line*; Beals, *Warriors Don't Cry*.

30. Kirk, *Redefining the Color Line*, 108–12; Beals, *Warriors Don't Cry*, 34–35.

31. For a look at black activism in the 1940s and 1950s, see Kirk, *Redefining the Color Line*, 11–85. For regional comparisons, see Egerton, *Speak Now Against the Day*.

32. Ibid. For a brief account of events in Little Rock and a comparison of Arkansas with other southern states, see Bartley, *New South*, 187–260, especially 213–30 for an analysis of Faubus and Little Rock.

33. Bartley, *New South*; Jacoway and Colburn, *Southern Businessmen*; Kirk, *Redefining the Color Line*.

34. Kirk, *Redefining the Color Line*, 113–14.

35. Ibid., 116.

36. Ibid., 116–17.

37. Ibid., 117.

38. Ibid., 119.

39. Ibid., 120; Beals, *Warriors Don't Cry*, 134–230.

40. Beals, *Warriors Don't Cry*, 126–44.

41. Ibid., 249–311.

42. Kirk, *Redefining the Color Line*, 122–23; Beals, *Warriors Don't Cry*, 220, 238–39.

43. Beals, *Warriors Don't Cry*, 143–44, 192–93, 299–308.

44. Hampton and Fayer, *Voices of Freedom*, 51–52; Kirk, *Redefining the Color Line*, 123.

45. Kirk, *Redefining the Color Line*, 132–38; Bartley, *New South*, 241–48.

46. Frazier, *Black Bourgeoisie*.

2. GENERATION GAPS

1. Lewis and D'Orso, *Walking with the Wind*, 27–31.

2. Ibid.; Schulman, *From Cotton Belt to Sun Belt*, 90–91.

3. Lewis and D'Orso, *Walking with the Wind*, 38–40.

4. Ibid., 41–51.

5. Ibid., 51–53.

6. Halberstam, *Children*, 219–26; Barras, *Last of Black Emperors*, 103–104.

7. Honey, *Southern Labor and Civil Rights*, 177–78.

8. Halberstam, *Children*, 219–26; Barras, *Last of Black Emperors*.

9. Barry interview; *Washington Post*, April 26, 1987; Halberstam, *Children*, 219–26; Barras, *Last of Black Emperors*, 104.

10. *Washington Post*, April 26, 1987.

11. Barras, *Last of Black Emperors*, 104; Halberstam, *Children*, 219–26.

12. Barry interview; Rose, *Black Leaders Then and Now*, 47–58.

13. Rose, *Black Leaders Then and Now*, 58.

14. Barry interview. For an overview of Massie's career, see his obituary, *Washington Post*, April 15, 2005.

15. Barry interview; Rose, *Black Leaders Then and Now*, 47–58; *Washington Post*, April 26, 1987.

16. Barry interview.

17. Ibid.; *Washington Post*, December 11, 1978.

18. For accounts of black migration from the South to Chicago, see Grossman, *Land of Hope*, and Lemann, *Promised Land*.
19. Wynn, *Afro-American in Second World War*; Cohen, *Consumer's Republic*; Powledge, *Free at Last?*
20. For a portrait of black Chicago, see Lemann, *Promised Land*, 59–108.
21. Halberstam, *Children*, 146–48.
22. Nash interview.
23. Halberstam, *Children*, 146–48.
24. Nash interview.
25. Greenberg, *Circle of Trust*, 47.
26. Carmichael and Thelwell, *Ready for Revolution*, 100–101.
27. Ibid., 12–44.
28. Ibid., *Ready for Revolution*, 44–54.
29. Ibid., 55–82.
30. Ibid.
31. Ibid.
32. Ibid., 83–109.
33. Ibid.
34. Ibid.
35. Ibid., 95–99.
36. Ibid.
37. Ibid., 110–14.
38. Neary, *Julian Bond*.
39. Bond interview. Bond still has the "diploma" he received from Frazier and Du Bois.
40. Neary, *Julian Bond*, 42–45.
41. Ibid., 44.
42. Bond interview.
43. Ibid.
44. Ibid.
45. Zinn, *SNCC*, 35.
46. Neary, *Julian Bond*, 42–45.
47. "The Negro's New Economic Life," *Fortune*, September 1956.
48. Cohen, *Consumers' Republic*, esp. chap. 3.
49. *Newsweek*, September 16, 1957; *Life*, August 31, 1959; Cohen, *Consumers' Republic*, 318–19.
50. Mailer, "White Negro."
51. Ward, *Just My Soul Responding*, 26–27.

3. THE SIT-IN CRAZE

1. Chafe, *Civilities and Civil Rights*, 112–16.
2. Ibid., 112–16; Raines, *My Soul Is Rested*, 75–77.
3. Chafe, *Civilities and Civil Rights*, 116.
4. *New York Times*, February 2, 5, 7, 8, 1960; Chafe, *Civilities and Civil Rights*, 117–19; Raines, *My Soul Is Rested*, 78–82.

5. Southern Regional Council, "Special Report: Student Protest Movement, Winter 1960," April 1, 1960, Southern Regional Council Papers, 1944–68; *New York Times*, February 15, 21, 28, 1960; Chafe, *Civilities and Civil Rights*, 119–20.

6. Morris, *Origins of Civil Rights Movement*, 188–94.

7. Carson, *In Struggle*, 14–16; King, *Civil Rights and Idea of Freedom*, 138–43.

8. James Lawson interview in Hampton and Fayer, *Voices of Freedom*, 54; Halberstam, *Children*, 90–106; Lewis and D'Orso, *Walking with the Wind*, 90–111.

9. Carson, *In Struggle*, 22; Halberstam, *Children*, 11–50.

10. Powledge, *Free at Last?*, 203–204; Branch, *Parting the Waters*, 204–205; Carson, *In Struggle*, 22–25; Halberstam, *Children*, 11–50.

11. James Lawson interview in Hampton and Fayer, *Voices of Freedom*, 54.

12. Lewis and D'Orso, *Walking with the Wind*, 3–56; Halberstam, *Children*, 238–46.

13. Zinn, *SNCC*, 19; Halberstam, *Children*, 63, 224–26; Powledge, *Free at Last?*, 197–210.

14. Halberstam, *Children*, 60–89; Powledge, *Free at Last?*, 197–210.

15. Halberstam, *Children*, 60–89.

16. Lewis and D'Orso, *Walking with the Wind*, 85–92.

17. Ibid., 90–94.

18. Halberstam, *Children*, 2–10.

19. Ibid., 105–106.

20. Hampton and Fayer, *Voices of Freedom*, 57.

21. Lewis and D'Orso, *Walking with the Wind*, 95–96.

22. Halberstam, *Children*, 105–106.

23. Hampton and Fayer, *Voices of Freedom*, 57; Zinn, *SNCC*, 20–21.

24. Halberstam, *Children*, 138–40.

25. Lewis interview in Hampton and Fayer, *Voices of Freedom*, 58; Lewis and D'Orso, *Walking with the Wind*, 100–102; Halberstam, *Children*, 133–38.

26. Lewis and D'Orso, *Walking with the Wind*, 100–102.

27. Halberstam, *Children*, 133–35.

28. Lewis, *Walking with the Wind*, 102–103, 109–11.

29. Nash interview in Hampton and Fayer, *Voices of Freedom*, 66–68; Powledge, *Free at Last?*, 209–10; Halberstam, *Children*, 233–37.

30. Hampton and Fayer, *Voices of Freedom*, 66–68; Halberstam, *Children*, 234–37.

31. Bond interview; Raines, *My Soul Is Rested*, 84–85.

32. Bond interview; Raines, *My Soul Is Rested*, 85; Neary, *Julian Bond*, 54–55.

33. Bond interview; Raines, *My Soul Is Rested*, 84–85.

34. Pomerantz, *Where Peachtree Meets Sweet Auburn*; Kruse, *White Flight*.

35. Bartley, *New South*, 134–39; Raines, *My Soul Is Rested*, 83–93.

36. Bartley, *New South*, 134–39; Sitkoff, *Struggle for Black Equality*, 69–75; Raines, *My Soul Is Rested*, 83–93.

37. Bond interview; Raines, *My Soul Is Rested*, 86.

38. Bond interview; Raines, *My Soul Is Rested*, 86–87.

39. *New York Times*, October 20, 23, 1960; Garrow, *Bearing the Cross*; Branch, *Parting the Waters*; Raines, *My Soul Is Rested*, 86–93.

40. *New York Times*, March 8, 11, 12, 1961; Bartley, *New South*, 134–39; Sitkoff, *Struggle for Black Equality*, 69–75; Raines, *My Soul Is Rested*, 83–93.

41. Raines, *My Soul Is Rested*, 93.
42. Southern Regional Council, "The Student Protest Movement; A Recapitulation," September 1961, Southern Regional Council Papers, 1944–68; Miller, *Democracy Is in the Streets*, 36; Sitkoff, *Struggle for Black Equality*, 79.
43. Miller, *Democracy Is in the Streets*, 36–55.
44. Southern Regional Council, "The Student Protest Movement; A Recapitulation," September 1961, Southern Regional Council Papers, 1944–68; Miller, *Democracy Is in the Streets*, 36 and (for the origins of SDS) 21–156.
45. *New York Times*, March 20, 1960.

4. MORE THAN A HAMBURGER

1. Zinn, *SNCC*, 36; Carson, *In Struggle*, 25–26.
2. Halberstam, *Children*, 26, 366–67; Lewis and D'Orso, *Walking with the Wind*, 116–19; Agronsky, *Marion Barry*, 102–105.
3. Halberstam, *Children*, 366–67; Lewis and D'Orso, *Walking with the Wind*, 116–19.
4. Lewis and D'Orso, *Walking with the Wind*, 116–19; Halberstam, *Children*, 366–67; Agronsky, *Marion Barry*, 102–105.
5. Neary, *Julian Bond*, 61–65; Bond interview.
6. Carson, *In Struggle*, 46; Moses and Cobb, *Radical Equations*, 27–30; Zinn, *SNCC*, 62–64.
7. Moses and Cobb, *Radical Equations*, 27–30; Zinn, *SNCC*, 62–64; Moses interview; Raines, *My Soul Is Rested*, 105.
8. Sellers and Terrell, *River of No Return*, 41–42.
9. Ibid.
10. Moses and Cobb, *Radical Equations*, 30–31; Branch, *Parting the Waters*, 328–29; For the history of SCEF, see Klibaner, "Travail of Southern Radicals."
11. Moses and Cobb, *Radical Equations*, 29–36; Grant, *Ella Baker*, 125–45.
12. Moses and Cobb, *Radical Equations*, 37–42.
13. Ibid.; Branch, *Parting the Waters*, 329–30; Zinn, *SNCC*, 63–64.
14. Moses and Cobb, *Radical Equations*, 37–42; Branch, *Parting the Waters*, 329–30; Zinn, *SNCC*, 63–64; Payne, *Light of Freedom*, 103–106.
15. Carson, *In Struggle*, 25–30; Zinn, *SNCC*, 34–38; Branch, *Parting the Waters*, 380–89.
16. For a complete biography of Rustin, see Anderson, *Bayard Rustin*, or D'Emilio, *Lost Prophet*.
17. Sellers and Terrell, *River of No Return*, 43; Branch, *Parting the Waters*, 380–89.
18. Zinn, *SNCC*, 38–39; Carson, *In Struggle*, 32; Branch, *Parting the Waters*, 391–94; Halberstam, *Children*, 267–70; Powledge, *Free at Last?*, 246–50.
19. Zinn, *SNCC*, 38–39; Branch, *Parting the Waters*, 391–94; Powledge, *Free at Last?*, 246–50; interview with Charles Jones in Stoper, *Student Nonviolent Coordinating Committee*, 181–82.
20. Fleming, *Soon We Will Not Cry*, 74–77; Zinn, *SNCC*, 38–39; Halberstam, *Children*, 267–68.
21. Zinn, *SNCC*, 38–39; Carson, *In Struggle*, 31–33; Halberstam, *Children*, 267–68; Nash interview.
22. Powledge, *Free at Last?*, 262.

23. Lewis and D'Orso, *Walking with the Wind*, 128–29.
24. On the history of CORE, see Meier and Rudwick, *CORE*.
25. Lewis and D'Orso, *Walking with the Wind*, 130–39; Arsenault, *Freedom Riders*, 121–25; Halberstam, *Children*, 255–58.
26. Lewis and D'Orso, *Walking with the Wind*, 128–40; Halberstam, *Children*, 257–65.
27. Lewis and D'Orso, *Walking with the Wind*, 140; Branch, *Parting the Waters*, 424.
28. Branch, *Parting the Waters*, 424–25.
29. Ibid.
30. Peck, *Freedom Ride*, 123–27; Lewis and D'Orso, *Walking with the Wind*, 142–43; Arsenault, *Freedom Riders*, 140–59.
31. Arsenault, *Freedom Riders*, 179–80.
32. Farmer, *Lay Bare the Heart*, 203–206; Lewis and D'Orso, *Walking with the Wind*, 142–45; Branch, *Parting the Waters*, 428.
33. Nash, "Inside the Sit-Ins," 43–62; Branch, *Parting the Waters*, 430–31.
34. Branch, *Parting the Waters*, 433–39.
35. Arsenault, *Freedom Riders*, 182–83.
36. Lewis and D'Orso, *Walking with the Wind*, 147–49. For a brief biography of Connor, see Eskew, *But for Birmingham*, 89–98.
37. *New York Times*, April 12, 1960.
38. Lewis and D'Orso, *Walking with the Wind*, 147–49; Branch, *Parting the Waters*, 436–38; Arsenault, *Freedom Riders*, 197–200; Powledge, *Free at Last?*, 259–62; Raines, *My Soul Is Rested*, 117–21.
39. Lewis and D'Orso, *Walking with the Wind*, 154–58; Arsenault, *Freedom Riders*, 211–21.
40. Branch, *Parting the Waters*, 447–50; Arsenault, *Freedom Riders*, 211–21.
41. Branch, *Parting the Waters*, 447–50; Hampton and Fayer, *Voices of Freedom*, 91–92; Arsenault, *Freedom Riders*, 211–21; Halberstam, *Children*, 324–30.
42. Branch, *Parting the Waters*, 460.
43. Halberstam, *Children*, 324–30.
44. Branch, *Parting the Waters*, 459–65.
45. Hampton and Fayer, *Voices of Freedom*, 91–92; Branch, *Parting the Waters*, 459–65.
46. Branch, *Parting the Waters*, 459–65.
47. Ibid.
48. Ibid., 466–68.
49. Ibid.
50. Greenberg, *Circle of Trust*, 190; Raines, *My Soul Is Rested*, 123; Arsenault, *Freedom Riders*, 250–51.
51. James Farmer interview in Hampton and Fayer, *Voices of Freedom*, 91–92; Branch, *Parting the Waters*, 469–72.
52. On NAG, see Carmichael and Thelwell, *Ready for Revolution*, and Sellers and Terrell, *River of No Return*. Surprisingly, no scholar has written a separate history of NAG.
53. Carmichael and Thelwell, *Ready for Revolution*, 187–89.
54. Schlesinger, *Thousand Days*; Bauer, *Kennedy and Second Reconstruction*.
55. Fred Leonard interview in Hampton and Fayer, *Voices of Freedom*, 94.

56. On Parchman, see David Oshinsky, *"Worse Than Slavery."*
57. Arsenault, *Freedom Riders*, 326.
58. Ibid., 350.
59. Ibid., 360–61.
60. Ibid.
61. Lewis and D'Orso, *Walking with the Wind*, 170–72.
62. Carmichael and Thelwell, *Ready for Revolution*, 208–11; Arsenault, *Freedom Riders*, 349–52; Lewis and D'Orso, *Walking with the Wind*, 170–72.
63. Lewis and D'Orso, *Walking with the Wind*, 171.
64. Carmichael and Thelwell, *Ready for Revolution*, 195–98.
65. Ibid., 195–96.
66. For a complete list of Freedom Riders arrested that summer, see Arsenault, *Freedom Riders*, 533–87.
67. Carmichael and Thelwell, *Ready for Revolution*, 212–13.
68. Arsenault, *Freedom Riders*, 328.
69. Ibid., 424–526.
70. Bond interview; Lyon, *Memories of Civil Rights Movement*, 30.
71. Carson, *In Struggle*, 37–44.
72. Ibid.
73. Branch, *Parting the Waters*, 478–82.
74. Ibid., 480; Lewis and D'Orso, *Walking with the Wind*, 179; Carmichael and Thelwell, *Ready for Revolution*, 216–22.
75. Greenberg, *Circle of Trust*, 34–35.
76. Ibid.
77. Ibid., 34–40; Carson, *In Struggle*, 37–40.
78. Jones interview in Stoper, *Student Nonviolent Coordinating Committee*, 187.
79. Greenberg, *Circle of Trust*, 39–40.

5. HIGHWAY 61 REVISITED

1. Moses and Cobb, *Radical Equations*, 44–45.
2. For a comparison of Mississippi with other southern states, see Southern Regional Council, "The Student Protest Movement: A Recapitulation," Report 21, September 29, 1961, Southern Regional Council Papers, 1944–68. See also Payne, *Light of Freedom*; Key, *Southern Politics*; McMillen, *Dark Journey*.
3. Silver, *Mississippi*; Key, *Southern Politics*.
4. Key, *Southern Politics*, 533–618; Zinn, *SNCC*, 66.
5. Moses and Cobb, *Radical Equations*, 46.
6. Ibid., 46–47; Powledge, *Free at Last?*, 329; Dittmer, *Local People*, 103–106.
7. Forman, *Making of Black Revolutionaries*, 226–27; Branch, *Parting the Waters*, 495; Burner, *And Gently He Shall Lead Them*, 50–51; Zinn, *SNCC*, 68–69; Dittmer, *Local People*, 103–106.
8. Branch, *Parting the Waters*, 495; Burner, *And Gently He Shall Lead Them*, 50–51; Zinn, *SNCC*, 68–69; Dittmer, *Local People*, 103–106; Carson, *In Struggle*, 47–49.
9. Zinn, *SNCC*, 68.

10. Moses and Cobb, *Radical Equations*, 51–52; Dittmer, *Local People*, 103–106.
11. Powledge, *Free at Last?*, 325–29; Dittmer, *Local People*, 103–106.
12. Dittmer, *Local People*, 106–107.
13. Zinn, *SNCC*, 69.
14. Dittmer, *Local People*, 106–108.
15. Zinn, *SNCC*, 69–70.
16. Ibid., 145–47.
17. Dittmer, *Local People*, 108–10; Zinn, *SNCC*, 72–74; Branch, *Parting the Waters*, 499; Burner, *And Gently He Shall Lead Them*, 50–51.
18. Dittmer, *Local People*, 108–10; Zinn, *SNCC*, 72–74; Branch, *Parting the Waters*, 499; Forman, *Making of Black Revolutionaries*, 231.
19. Powledge, *Free at Last?*, 325–29.
20. Bob Zellner interview in Hampton and Fayer, *Voices of Freedom*, 143–47; Zinn, *SNCC*, 171; Dittmer, *Local People*, 110–11.
21. Charles Jones interview in Stoper, *Student Nonviolent Coordinating Committee*, 192–94; Branch, *Parting the Waters*, 518–23.
22. Branch, *Parting the Waters*, 518–23; Moses and Cobb, *Radical Equations*, 52–55; Zinn, *SNCC*, 75–76.
23. Charles Jones interview in Stoper, *Student Nonviolent Coordinating Committee*, 195–96; Zellner interview; Dittmer, *Local People*, 112–13; Zinn, *SNCC*, 75–76; Burner, *And Gently He Shall Lead Them*, 62–63.
24. Lyon, *Memories of Civil Rights Movement*, 17; Forman, *Making of Black Revolutionaries*, 233.
25. Powledge, *Free at Last?*, Carson, *In Struggle*, and Sellers and Terrell, *River of No Return* all echo this point.
26. Carmichael and Thelwell, *Ready for Revolution*, 310–12.
27. Halberstam, *Children*, 396–99; Burner, *And Gently He Shall Lead Them*, 67–68.
28. Halberstam, *Children*, 396–99.
29. Cagin and Dray, *We Are Not Afraid*, 175–78.
30. *Jet*, May 1, 1962; Branch, *Parting the Waters*, 487.
31. Arsenault, *Freedom Riders*, 480–81.
32. Ibid., 481.
33. Zinn, *SNCC*, 80; Moses interview.
34. Burner, *And Gently He Shall Lead Them*, 77–78; Carson, *In Struggle*, 78; Dittmer, *Local People*, 118–19.
35. Zinn, *SNCC*, 123–25; Hampton and Fayer, *Voices of Freedom*, 97–98; Powledge, *Free at Last?*, 341–51; Carson, *In Struggle*, 56–59; Dittmer, *Local People*, 85–87.
36. Powledge, *Free at Last?*, 353, 404–409; Carson, *In Struggle*, 56–59.
37. Zinn, *SNCC*, 123–28.
38. Ibid., 126–28; Branch, *Parting the Waters*, 527–28; Powledge, *Free at Last?*, 341–54; Carson, *In Struggle*, 56–60.
39. Zinn, *SNCC*, 126–28; Carson, *In Struggle*, 56–60.
40. Branch, *Parting the Waters*, 486.
41. Zinn, *SNCC*, 130–31; Carson, *In Struggle*, 60–61; Zinn, *SNCC*, 130–31.

42. Branch, *Parting the Waters*, 550–53; Garrow, *Bearing the Cross*, 181–87.
43. Branch, *Parting the Waters*, 555.
44. Zinn, *SNCC*, 130–35; Carson, *In Struggle*, 60–61; Fairclough, *To Redeem the Soul of America*, 86–109, esp. 103–104.
45. Fairclough, *To Redeem the Soul*, 86–109, esp. 103–104.
46. Ibid., 102–105.
47. Zinn, *SNCC*, 134–35; Fairclough, *To Redeem the Soul*, 105–109.
48. For Danny Lyon's story, see Lyon, *Memories of Civil Rights Movement*, a collection of his photographs for SNCC.
49. Forman, *Making of Black Revolutionaries*, 240–46; Davis, *Weary Feet, Rested Souls*, 161–62.
50. Neary, *Julian Bond*, 62–65; King, *Freedom Song*, 214–15, 231–36.
51. Forman, *Making of Black Revolutionaries*, 240–44; King, *Freedom Song*, 331–36.
52. King, *Freedom Song*, 216.
53. Charles Jones interview in Stoper, *Student Nonviolent Coordinating Committee*, 199; Halberstam, *Children*, 431–35.
54. Thornton, *Dividing Lines*; Norrell, "Caste in Steel."
55. Eskew, *But for Birmingham*, 152–53.
56. Ibid., 152–54.
57. Ibid., 214–15.
58. Branch, *Parting the Waters*, 734–37.
59. Eskew, *But for Birmingham*, 255–70; Thornton, *Dividing Lines*, 310–12; Branch, *Parting the Waters*, 750–67; Fairclough, *To Redeem the Soul*, 124–27.
60. Eskew, *But for Birmingham*, 277–83; Branch, *Parting the Waters*, 770–71; Fairclough, *To Redeem the Soul*, 127–28.
61. Thornton, *Dividing Lines*, 275–78, 313–23; Eskew, *But for Birmingham*, 278–86.
62. Thornton, *Dividing Lines*, 318–26; Eskew, *But for Birmingham*, 278–88; Fairclough, *To Redeem the Soul*, 127–29.
63. Eskew, *But for Birmingham*, 295–96.
64. Ibid., 299–303.
65. Carson, *In Struggle*, 159–61; Powledge, *Free at Last?*, 533–35.
66. Lewis and D'Orso, *Walking with the Wind*, 207.
67. Ibid., 202–204.
68. Ibid., 206–207.
69. Ibid., 204–205.
70. Forman, *Making of Black Revolutionaries*, 331–32.
71. Lewis and D'Orso, *Walking with the Wind*, 221–22.
72. Ibid.
73. *New York Times*, August 29, 1963.
74. Eskew, *But for Birmingham*, 322–23.
75. Ibid.
76. Halberstam, *Children*; Nash interview.
77. Branch, *Parting the Waters*, 492–93.

6. THE DREAMS THAT BREAK YOUR HEART

1. Dittmer, *Local People*, 198–99; Burner, *And Gently He Shall Lead Them*, 110.
2. Bond interview.
3. Chafe, *Never Stop Running*, 180–82; Carson, *In Struggle*, 96–98; Burner, *And Gently He Shall Lead Them*, 112; Dittmer, *Local People*, 200–207; Payne, *Light of Freedom*, 294–97.
4. Chafe, *Never Stop Running*, 180–86; Dittmer, *Local People*, 200.
5. For a full biography of Lowenstein, see Chafe, *Never Stop Running*.
6. Chafe, *Never Stop Running*, 180–82; Carson, *In Struggle*, 96–98; Burner, *And Gently He Shall Lead Them*, 112; Dittmer, *Local People*, 200–207; Payne, *Light of Freedom*, 294–97.
7. Carson, *In Struggle*, 98–99; Dittmer, *Local People*, 207–209.
8. Carson, *In Struggle*, 99; Lewis and D'Orso, *Walking with the Wind*, 246–52.
9. Carson, *In Struggle*, 98–101; Dittmer, *Local People*, 209–11.
10. Chafe, *Never Stop Running*, 180–86.
11. Chafe, *Never Stop Running*, 205–207. For a discussion of the tension between consensus and justice, see Chafe, *Civilities and Civil Rights*.
12. McAdam, *Freedom Summer*, 35–65; quote from 65.
13. Ibid., 35–65; Holt, *Summer That Didn't End*, 46.
14. Belfrage, *Freedom Summer*, 3–19.
15. Sutherland, *Letters from Mississippi*, 1–34; Carson, *In Struggle*, 112–13.
16. Sutherland, *Letters from Mississippi*, 18.
17. Belfrage, *Freedom Summer*, 30; Sellers and Terrell, *River of No Return*, 84.
18. Holt, *Summer That Didn't End*, 17–30.
19. Sellers and Terrell, *River of No Return*, 87–88. For an extended look at the background of the three, see Cagin and Dray, *We Are Not Afraid*.
20. Cagin and Dray, *We Are Not Afraid*, 41–44; King, *Freedom Song*, 378–79; Branch, *Pillar of Fire*, 361–62.
21. King, *Freedom Song*, 378–80.
22. Zellner interview.
23. Sutherland, *Letters from Mississippi*, 26–28; Zellner interview; Branch, *Pillar of Fire*, 362–63; Cagin and Dray, *We Are Not Afraid*, 44, 328–30, 352–53; Hogan, "Radical Manners."
24. *New York Times*, June 23, 1964; Branch, *Pillar of Fire*, 368–69; Cagin and Dray, *We Are Not Afraid*, 318–20, 352–53.
25. Cagin and Dray, *We Are Not Afraid*, 355; Zellner interview; Zellner interview in Kisseloff, *Generation on Fire*, 41–43.
26. Zellner interview; Cagin and Dray, *We Are Not Afraid*, 355–57; Zellner interview in Kisseloff, *Generation on Fire*, 41–43.
27. Carmichael and Thelwell, *Ready for Revolution*, 374–75.
28. Ibid.
29. Sellers and Terrell, *River of No Return*, 86–93.
30. Cagin and Dray, *We Are Not Afraid*, 331; Stern, *Calculating Visions*, 153–65.
31. Branch, *Pillar of Fire*, 367–74; Cagin and Dray, *We Are Not Afraid*, 369–73.

32. Cagin and Dray, *We Are Not Afraid*, 371–72.

33. Ibid., 391–95.

34. This version of the arrest and murder is drawn from Cagin and Dray, *We Are Not Afraid*, the definitive account of what happened that night.

35. Davis, *Weary Feet, Rested Souls*, 277–78.

36. Powledge, *Free at Last?*, 581–83.

37. Kisseloff, *Generation on Fire*, 44.

38. Sutherland, *Letters from Mississippi*, 40–41.

39. For a complete list of arrests and harassments, see Holt, *Summer That Didn't End*, 207–52; Powledge, *Free at Last?*, 281.

40. Powledge, *Free at Last?*, 581–83; Lewis and D'Orso, *Walking with the Wind*, 267.

41. McAdam, *Freedom Summer*, 105–109; Evans, *Personal Politics*, 77–81; King, *Freedom Song*, 463–65.

42. McAdam, *Freedom Summer*, 105–109.

43. Belfrage, *Freedom Summer*, 89–92.

44. Ibid.; Payne, *Light of Freedom*, 302–305; Carson, *In Struggle*, 109–10; Dittmer, *Local People*, 257–61.

45. Belfrage, *Freedom Summer*, 84–103.

46. Ibid., 97.

47. Sutherland, *Letters from Mississippi*, 64–89; Belfrage, *Freedom Summer*, 84–89.

48. Stern, *Calculating Visions*, 160–85; Dalleck, *Flawed Giant*, 111–21.

49. Belfrage, *Freedom Summer*, 170.

50. Ibid., 173–77; Carmichael and Thelwell, *Ready for Revolution*, 395–97.

51. Payne, *Light of Freedom*, 322; Carmichael and Thelwell, *Ready for Revolution*, 391–95; Carson, *In Struggle*, 117.

52. Carmichael and Thelwell, *Ready for Revolution*, 398.

53. Mills, *This Little Light of Mine*, 111.

54. Carmichael and Thelwell, *Ready for Revolution*, 398; Mills, *This Little Light of Mine*, 107–10.

55. Grant, *Ella Baker*, 163–64; Carmichael and Thelwell, *Ready for Revolution*, 397–98.

56. For a comprehensive biography of Hamer, see Mills, *This Little Light of Mine*, and Kai Lee, *For Freedom's Sake*.

57. Mills, *This Little Light of Mine*, 24; Branch, *Pillar of Fire*, 57.

58. Mills, *This Little Light of Mine*, 97–107.

59. Kai Lee, *For Freedom's Sake*, 23–31; Lewis and D'Orso, *Walking with the Wind*, 187–88.

60. Mills, *This Little Light of Mine*, 107–10.

61. Kai Lee, *For Freedom's Sake*, 23–60.

62. Mills, *This Little Light of Mine*, 107–10.

63. Dalleck, *Flawed Giant*, 163–65; Branch, *Pillar of Fire*, 457–67; Rauh interview in Hampton and Fayer, *Voices of Freedom*, 196–97, 200–202.

64. Dalleck, *Flawed Giant*, 163–65; Branch, *Pillar of Fire*, 430–55.

65. *New York Times*, August 23, 1964; Mills, *This Little Light of Mine*, 118–21.

66. Dalleck, *Flawed Giant*, 163–65; Branch, *Pillar of Fire*, 458–62.

67. Burner, *And Gently He Shall Lead Them*, 173; Carson, *In Struggle*, 124; Mills, *This Little Light of Mine*; Ransby, *Ella Baker*, 336–42.

68. Burner, *And Gently He Shall Lead Them*, 173; Carson, *In Struggle*, 124; Branch, *Pillar of Fire*, 462.

69. Rauh interview in Hampton and Fayer, *Voices of Freedom*, 196–97, 200–202; Lichtenstein, *Walter Reuther*, 392–95.

70. Branch, *Pillar of Fire*, 470.

71. Grant, *Ella Baker*, 173–76; Mills, *This Little Light of Mine*, 128–32; Branch, *Pillar of Fire*, 471–76.

72. Grant, *Ella Baker*, 173–76; Mills, *This Little Light of Mine*, 128–32.

73. Burner, *And Gently He Shall Lead Them*, 196–98.

74. Mills, *This Little Light of Mine*, 130–32; Branch, *Pillar of Fire*, 475–76.

75. Burner, *And Gently He Shall Lead Them*, 198.

76. Lewis and D'Orso, *Walking with the Wind*, 292.

77. Carson, *In Struggle*, 127.

7. UNRAVELINGS

1. Sellers, *River of No Return*, 112; Carmichael and Thelwell, *Ready for Revolution*, 415–16; Carson, *In Struggle*, 138.

2. Belafonte and Lewis interviews in Hampton and Fayer, *Voices of Freedom*, 204–207; Branch, *Pillar of Fire*, 480–81; Bond interview. On Belafonte's life story, see Gates, *Thirteen Ways*; Fogelson, *Harry Belafonte*.

3. Bond interview; Lewis and D'Orso, *Walking with the Wind*, 293–95.

4. Belafonte interview in Hampton and Fayer, *Voices of Freedom*, 205.

5. Neary, *Julian Bond*, 73; Bond interview; Belafonte interview in Hampton and Fayer, *Voices of Freedom*, 204–206.

6. Neary, *Julian Bond*, 73; Burner, *And Gently He Shall Lead Them*, 201; Carson, *In Struggle*, 135.

7. Lewis interview in Hampton and Fayer, *Voices of Freedom*, 206; Bond interview; Lewis and D'Orso, *Walking with the Wind*, 294–99.

8. King, *Freedom Song*, 448–52.

9. Bond, "The Movement We Helped to Make," in Bloom, ed., *Long Time Gone*, 16–17; Forman, *Making of Black Revolutionaries*, 411–32.

10. Carmichael and Thelwell, *Ready for Revolution*, 429.

11. Lewis and D'Orso, *Walking with the Wind*, 303–304.

12. Carson, *In Struggle*, 136–45.

13. Carmichael and Thelwell, *Ready for Revolution*, 428–35.

14. Carson, *In Struggle*, 143.

15. Ibid.

16. Carmichael and Thelwell, *Ready for Revolution*, 428–35; Lewis and D'Orso, *Walking with the Wind*, 301–304.

17. Carson, *In Struggle*, 151–52.

18. Lewis and D'Orso, *Walking with the Wind*, 307.

19. Carson, *In Struggle*, 133–52; Forman, *Making of Black Revolutionaries*, 433–38; Lewis and D'Orso, *Walking with the Wind*, 303–11; Carmichael and Thelwell, *Ready for Revolution*, 428–37.

20. Lewis and D'Orso, *Walking with the Wind*, 305; Carmichael and Thelwell, *Ready for*

Revolution, 435–37, 470. For an account of those events from Forman's perspective, see Forman, *Black Revolutionaries*, 430–502.

21. Carson, *In Struggle*, 139–40; Lewis and D'Orso, *Walking with the Wind*, 305.
22. Carmichael and Thelwell, *Ready for Revolution*, 310–12; Lewis and D'Orso, *Walking with the Wind*, 301–308; Sellers and Terrell, *River of No Return*, 137–39.
23. Fairclough, *To Redeem the Soul*, 208–13.
24. Halberstam, *Children*, 490–93.
25. Powledge, *Free at Last?*, 612–15; Thornton, *Dividing Lines*, 380–434; Halberstam, *Children*, 411–30, 499–500.
26. Fairclough, *To Redeem the Soul*, 226–31.
27. Ibid.; Halberstam, *Children*, 500–501; Branch, *At Canaan's Edge*, 12–13.
28. Halberstam, Children, 500–501, 535; Branch, *At Canaan's Edge*, 12–13.
29. Dalleck, *Flawed Giant*, 211–14.
30. Thornton, *Dividing Lines*, 479–84.
31. Powledge, *Free at Last?*, 623; Thornton, *Dividing Lines*, 486.
32. Thornton, *Dividing Lines*, 486; Fairclough, *To Redeem the Soul*, 240; Halberstam, *Children*, 502–505.
33. Carson, *In Struggle*, 157–59; Carmichael and Thelwell, *Ready for Revolution*, 445–50.
34. Carson, *In Struggle*, 158; Lewis and D'Orso, *Walking with the Wind*, 331–32.
35. Lewis and D'Orso, *Walking with the Wind*, 331–32.
36. Carmichael and Thelwell, *Ready for Revolution*, 481.
37. Fairclough, *To Redeem the Soul*; Thornton, *Dividing Lines*.
38. Lewis and D'Orso, *Walking with the Wind*, 331–32.
39. See the firsthand accounts in Hampton and Fayer, *Voices of Freedom*, 228–32.
40. Hampton and Fayer, *Voices of Freedom*, 228–32; Lewis and D'Orso, *Walking with the Wind*, 331–32.
41. Lewis and D'Orso, *Walking with the Wind*, 331–32; Lyon, *Memories of Civil Rights Movement*, 168–70, reproduces the transcript of the phone calls between observers and SNCC's Atlanta office.
42. Garrow, *Bearing the Cross*; 399–404; Fairclough, *To Redeem the Soul*, 243–51.
43. Fairclough, *To Redeem the Soul*, 246; Garrow, *Bearing the Cross*, 402–404.
44. Sellers and Terrell, *River of No Return*, 124.
45. Carmichael and Thelwell, *Ready for Revolution*, 452–53.
46. Fairclough, *To Redeem the Soul*, 249; Garrow, *Bearing the Cross*, 407–408; Lewis and D'Orso, *Walking with the Wind*, 349–56; Clark Olsen interview in Hampton and Fayer, *Voices of Freedom*, 232–33.
47. *New York Times*, March 21–23, 1965; Lewis and D'Orso, *Walking with the Wind*, 356–60.
48. *New York Times*, March 21–23, 1965.
49. For a good overview of Johnson's thinking and the War on Poverty, see Dalleck, *Flawed Giant*; Stern, *Calculating Visions*.
50. *New York Times*, March 16, 1965; Dalleck, *Flawed Giant*, 211–21.
51. Graham, *Civil Rights and Presidency*, 91–99.
52. Carmichael and Thelwell, *Ready for Revolution*, 457–63; Powledge, *Free at Last?*, 633–35; Carson, *In Struggle*, 162–66.

53. Hampton and Fayer, *Voices of Freedom*, 268–69; Powledge, *Free at Last?*, 633–35.

54. Carmichael and Thelwell, *Ready for Revolution*; 457–66; Carson, *In Struggle*, 162–66.

55. Carmichael and Thelwell, *Ready for Revolution*; 457–66; Hampton and Fayer, *Voices of Freedom*, 269–70.

56. Sellers, *River of No Return*, 152–54; Carson, *In Struggle*, 165.

57. Carson, *In Struggle*, 164–65; Carmichael and Thelwell, *Ready for Revolution*, 470–76.

58. Ruby Sales interview in Hampton and Fayer, *Voices of Freedom*, 272–75; Carmichael and Thelwell, *Ready for Revolution*, 468–69.

59. Carmichael and Thelwell, *Ready for Revolution*, 466–76.

60. Ibid., 477–79; John Lewis interview in Hampton and Fayer, *Voices of Freedom*, 280–81.

61. Carmichael and Thelwell, *Ready for Revolution*, 477–79.

62. Lewis and D'Orso, *Walking with the Wind*, 363–92; Carmichael and Thelwell, *Ready for Revolution*, 477–83; Carson, *In Struggle*, 199–204; Sellers and Terrell, *River of No Return*, 157–59; Forman, *Making of Black Revolutionaries*, 447–55.

63. Carson, *In Struggle*, 204–205.

64. Lewis and D'Orso, *Walking with the Wind*, 391–92.

8. ANGRY YOUNG MEN IN THE SEASON OF RADICAL CHIC

1. Sitkoff, *Struggle for Black Equality*, 194–99; Davis, *Weary Feet, Rested Souls*, 285; Joseph, *Waiting 'Til the Midnight Hour*, 132–46.

2. Sellers and Terrell, *River of No Return*, 166–67; Sitkoff, *Struggle for Black Equality*, 194–99; Davis, *Weary Feet, Rested Souls*, 285; Joseph, *Waiting 'Til the Midnight Hour*, 132–46.

3. Hampton and Fayer, *Voices of Freedom*, 292; Sellers and Terrell, *River of No Return*, 166–67.

4. Carson, *In Struggle*, 220–21; Fairclough, *To Redeem the Soul*, 319–21.

5. Sellers and Terrell, *River of No Return*, 65–66; Carson, *In Struggle*, 220–21; Fairclough, *To Redeem the Soul*, 319–21; Carmichael and Thelwell, *Ready for Revolution*, 511.

6. Fairclough, *To Redeem the Soul*, 319–21; Carmichael and Thelwell, *Ready for Revolution*, 511; King, *Where Do We Go*; Carson, ed., *Autobiography of King*.

7. Carmichael, "What We Want"; Carmichael, "Toward Black Liberation"; Carson, *In Struggle*, 216–18; Carmichael and Thelwell, *Ready for Revolution*, 527–37.

8. Self, *American Babylon*, 222–24; Carson, *In Struggle*, 192; Carmichael and Thelwell, *Ready for Revolution*, 527–37; Warren, *Who Speaks*, 92–94.

9. On Steve Biko and events in South Africa, see Woods, *Biko*.

10. Sellers and Terrell, *River of No Return*, 156–57.

11. Ibid., 171; *Life*, May 19, 1967.

12. Sellers and Terrell, *River of No Return*, 171; *Life*, May 19, 1967; *Ebony*, June 1966; *Esquire*, September 1965.

13. *Esquire*, September 1965.

14. Carson, *In Struggle*, 229–30; *Washington Post*, April 8, 9, 1998.

15. Sellers and Terrell, *River of No Return*, 174; Joseph, *Waiting 'Til the Midnight Hour*, 155–59; Carson, *In Struggle*, 225.

16. Carson, *In Struggle*, 229–35.

17. Ibid., 231–33.

18. Ibid.; Sellers and Terrell, *River of No Return*, 174.

19. Forman, *Making of Black Revolutionaries*, 475–81; Carson, *In Struggle*, 239–43.

20. Carson, *In Struggle*, 239–43; Forman, *Making of Black Revolutionaries*, 475–81.

21. Forman, *Making of Black Revolutionaries*, 476.

22. Carson, *In Struggle*, 231–32; Kisseloff, *Generation on Fire*, 46; Zellner interview.

23. Sellers and Terrell, *River of No Return*, 188–89.

24. *Life*, May 19, 1967; *Ebony*, June 1966; *Esquire*, September 1965.

25. Carmichael and Thelwell, *Ready for Revolution*, 572–606.

26. Carson, *In Struggle*, 252–56; Joseph, *Waiting 'Til the Midnight Hour*, 188–91, 222–24.

27. Carson, *In Struggle*, 252–57, 289, 297; Sellers and Terrell, *River of No Return*, 227, 246–47.

28. Self, *American Babylon*, 217–55.

29. Foner, *Black Panthers Speak*, 40–41, xxx–xxxi; Pearson, *Shadow of Panther*, 129–35.

30. Pearson, *Shadow of Panther*, 145–47.

31. Ibid., 150–68.

32. Ibid.

33. Carmichael and Thelwell, *Ready for Revolution*, 641.

34. Carson, *In Struggle*, 278–79; Forman, *Making of Black Revolutionaries*, 522.

35. Pearson, *Shadow of Panther*, 158–64; Forman, *Making of Black Revolutionaries*, 522–43; Carson, *In Struggle*, 278–85.

36. Garrow, *Bearing the Cross*, 432–49.

37. Fairclough, *To Redeem the Soul*, 288–89.

38. Ibid., 290; Garrow, *Bearing the Cross*, 465–66.

39. Garrow, *Bearing the Cross*, 502–32.

40. Fairclough, *Martin Luther King*, 324–31; Garrow, *Bearing the Cross*, 532–45, 567–68.

41. Sellers and Terrell, *River of No Return*, 229–39.

42. *New York Times*, April 5, 1968.

43. Lewis and D'Orso, *Walking with the Wind*, 405–407.

44. Ibid.

45. *New York Times*, April 9, 1968; Sellers and Terrell, *River of No Return*, 229–39; Lewis and D'Orso, *Walking with the Wind*, 409–11 .

46. *New York Times*, April 8–10, 1968.

47. Ibid.

48. For an overview of Ali's early years, see Remnick, *King of World*; Marquesse, *Redemption Song*.

49. Marquesse, *Redemption Song*, 48, 52–53.

50. Remnick, *King of World*, 211–12.

51. Marquesse, *Redemption Song*, 81.

52. Remnick, *King of World*, 285. Marquesse, *Redemption Song*, 173.

53. Marquesse, *Redemption Song*, 179–80; Remnick, *King of World*, 285–92.

54. Remnick, *King of World*, 285–92; Marquesse, *Redemption Song*, 234–38, 260–62.

55. Van Deburg, *New Day in Babylon*, 192–235.

56. Ibid., 192–235.
57. Wolfe, *Radical Chic*, 1–18.

9. EXILES

1. McKnight, *Last Crusade*, 22–40; Joseph, *Waiting 'Til the Midnight Hour*, 187–88.
2. Carmichael and Thelwell, *Ready for Revolution*, 665–73.
3. Sellers and Terrell, *River of No Return*, 266–67; Cobb, "From Stokely Carmichael to Kwame Ture," Africa News Service, October 21, 2000.
4. Carmichael and Thelwell, *Ready for Revolution*, 680–727; Cobb, "From Stokely, Carmichael to Kwame Ture, Africa News Service, October 21, 2000.
5. Bokar Ture interview in Blake, *Children of the Movement*, 158.
6. Carmichael and Thelwell, *Ready for Revolution*, 680–727; "From Stokely Carmichael to Kwame Ture," African News Service, October 21, 2000.
7. Sellers and Terrell, *River of No Return*, 206–28; Carson, *In Struggle*, 249–51.
8. Sellers and Terrell, *River of No Return*, 253–67.
9. *New York Times*, August 10, 1965; *Washington Post*, July 27, August 10, 1965.
10. Burner, *And Gently He Shall Lead Them*, 213–15.
11. *New York Times*, August 10, 1965; *Washington Post*, July 27, August 10, 1965.
12. Burner, *And Gently He Shall Lead Them*, 215.
13. John Lewis interview in Stoper, *Student Nonviolent Coordinating Committee*, 242.
14. Burner, *And Gently He Shall Lead Them*, 216; Stoper, *Student Nonviolent Coordinating Committee*, 307.
15. Burner, *And Gently He Shall Lead Them*, 219.
16. Cagin and Dray, *We Are Not Afraid*, 452–53.
17. Flynn, *Draft*; Burner, *And Gently He Shall Lead Them*, 217–19.
18. Lewis and D'Orso, *Walking with the Wind*, 366–75.
19. Cagin and Dray, *We Are Not Afraid*, 452–53; Lewis and D'Orso, *Walking with the Wind*, 366–75.
20. Maisha Moses interview in Blake, *Children of the Movement*, 37–45.
21. Ibid.
22. *New York Times*, February 21, 1993, Maisha Moses interview in Blake, *Children of the Movement*, 37–45.
23. Maisha Moses interview in Blake, *Children of the Movement*, 37–45.
24. Moses and Cobb, *Radical Equations*, 94–95; *Mother Jones*, May 1, 2002; *New York Times*, February 21, 1993.
25. Bevel, "Journey to North Vietnam," *New York Times*, December 17, 19, 1966, and January 11, 1967. On Nash's feminist consciousness, see Olson, *Freedom's Daughters*.
26. Nash, "What Does Freedom Fighter," 42–45; Halberstam, *Children*, 533–35, 629–35.
27. Nash, "What Does Freedom Fighter."
28. Sellers and Terrell, *River of No Return*, 193–97; Carson, *In Struggle*, 241–42; Zellner interview in Kisseloff, *Generation on Fire*, 46.
29. Sellers and Terrell, *River of No Return*, 193–97.

30. Carson, *In Struggle*, 302.

31. Zellner interview in Kisseloff, *Generation on Fire*, 46–47.

32. *New York Times*, February 11, 1967; September 24, October 20, 1971; January 2, 1972; June 30, 1974; Zellner interview in Kisseloff, *Generation on Fire*, 46–48; Zellner interview.

33. *New York Times*, September 24, October 20, 1971; January 2, 1972.

34. *New York Times*, September 24, October 20, 1971.

35. Zellner interview in Kisseloff, *Generation on Fire*, 47–48.

36. *New York Times*, September 24, October 20, 1971; January 2, 1972.

37. *New York Times*, October 20, 1971.

38. Ibid.

39. *New York Times*, January 2, 1972; Zellner interview; Zellner interview in Kisseloff, *Generation on Fire*, 47–48.

40. Ibid.

10. THE POWER BROKERS

1. Neary, *Julian Bond*, 76–77; Bond interview.

2. Carson, *In Struggle*, 167.

3. Ibid.; Neary, *Julian Bond*, 78.

4. Neary, *Julian Bond*, 78–79; Metcalf, *Up from Within*, 163–64.

5. Neary, *Julian Bond*, 78–79; Wilkins, *Bonds*, 217.

6. Carson, *In Struggle*, 167; Neary, *Julian Bond*, 79.

7. Metcalf, *Up from Within*, 164; Neary, *Julian Bond*, 93–97.

8. *New York Times*, January 12, 1966. On McGill's inability to evolve over time, see Kneebone, *Southern Liberal Journalists*, 175–212.

9. Neary, *Julian Bond*, 106–107.

10. Ibid., 107–108.

11. Ibid.

12. Metcalf, *Up from Within*, 167.

13. Ibid., 169.

14. Ibid., 170.

15. Ibid., 173.

16. *New York Times*, December 6, 1966; Bond interview.

17. Bond interview; *New York Times*, December 6, 1966.

18. *New York Times*, December 6, 1966

19. *New York Times*, September 7, 1966.

20. *New York Times*, June 10, July 7, 1966.

21. Neary, *Julian Bond*, 109.

22. Miller, *Democracy Is in the Streets*, 300–305.

23. Bond interview; Metcalf, *Up from Within*, 184–86; *New York Times*, August 26–30, 1968.

24. *New York Times*, August 26–30, 1968.

25. Neary, *Julian Bond*, 206.

26. *New York Times*, August 26–30, 1968.

27. Neary, *Julian Bond*, 206; Metcalf, *Up from Within*, 188.

28. Bond, *Black Candidates;* Bond interview.

29. *New York Times,* July 13, 1969; August 21, 23, 1970; June 9, November 1, 1971; August 29, 1973; *Ebony,* October 1971.

30. Lewis and D'Orso, *Walking with the Wind,* 434–35; *Ebony,* October 1971.

31. *Ebony,* October 1971.

32. Lewis and D'Orso, *Walking with the Wind,* 434–36; *Ebony,* October 1971.

33. Lawson, *Running for Freedom,* 155–58; *New York Times,* August 8, 1971; Bond, *Black Candidates.*

34. *Fortson v. Dorsey* and *Burns v. Richardson* invited more suits about discriminatory practices. See also *Gomillion v. Lightfoot, Whitcomb v. Chavis, Allen v. Board of Elections, White v. Regester, Mobile v. Bolden, Zimmer v. McKeithen, Rogers v. Lodge.*

35. Rose, *Black Leaders Then and Now;* Barras, *Last of Black Emperors,* 115–16; Agronsky, *Marion Barry,* 120–26.

36. *Washington Post,* September 10, 1972; Agronsky, *Marion Barry,* 135–44; Barras, *Last of Black Emperors,* 119–25.

37. *Washington Post,* September 10, 1972; January 2, 1979; April 26, 1987.

38. *Washington Post,* April 26, 1987.

39. *Washington Post,* September 10, 1972; January 2, 1979; April 26, 1987.

40. Lawson, *Running for Freedom,* 164.

41. Lewis and D'Orso, *Walking with the Wind,* 452–58.

42. Ibid., 429–33, 462; *Atlanta Journal-Constitution,* July 27, 1986; *Washington Post,* July 21, 1986.

43. Lewis and D'Orso, *Walking with the Wind,* 429–35.

44. Ibid., 441–45.

45. Ibid., 452–60.

46. *Atlanta Journal-Constitution,* February 2, 6, 9, 1986; Lewis and D'Orso, *Walking with the Wind,* 460–62.

47. *Atlanta Journal-Constitution,* July 27, 1986; Lewis and D'Orso, *Walking with the Wind,* 460–62; Halberstam, *Children,* 646–47.

48. *Atlanta Journal-Constitution,* February 2, 9, 1986.

49. Lewis and D'Orso, *Walking with the Wind,* 463.

50. *Atlanta Journal-Constitution,* May 15, July 27, 1986; *New York Times,* August 9, September 2, 3, 1986; *Washington Post,* July 21, 1986; Halberstam, *Children,* 647–48; Lewis and D'Orso, *Walking with the Wind,* 461–70.

51. Lewis and D'Orso, *Walking with the Wind,* 461–70; *Atlanta Journal-Constitution,* March 3, April 16, July 27, 1986.

52. Lewis and D'Orso, *Walking with the Wind,* 461–70.

53. *Atlanta Journal-Constitution,* July 27, August 23, 1986; *Washington Post,* July 21, 1986.

54. Lewis and D'Orso, *Walking with the Wind,* 464.

55. Ibid., 475–76.

56. *Atlanta Journal-Constitution,* July 27, 1986.

57. Ibid.; *Washington Post,* July 21, 1986.

58. *Atlanta Journal-Constitution,* July, 9, 11, 18, 1986.

59. *Atlanta Journal-Constitution,* July 27, 1986.

60. *Atlanta Journal-Constitution*, June 5, 22; August 8, 10, 1986.
61. *New York Times*, August 14, 1986.
62. *Atlanta Journal-Constitution*, August 12, 14, 1986.
63. Lewis and D'Orso, *Walking with the Wind*, 466–70.
64. *Atlanta Journal-Constitution*, August 14, 21, 1986.
65. Lewis and D'Orso, *Walking with the Wind*, 474–78.
66. *Atlanta Journal-Constitution*, August 24, 1986.
67. *Atlanta Journal-Constitution*, August 30, 1986.
68. Lewis and D'Orso, *Walking with the Wind*, 475–79.
69. *Atlanta Journal-Constitution*, August 30, 1986; Lewis and D'Orso, *Walking with the Wind*, 476–78.
70. *Atlanta Journal-Constitution*, September 3, 1986.
71. Lewis and D'Orso, *Walking with the Wind*, 473.
72. *Atlanta Journal-Constitution*, September 5, 6, 15, 1986.

11. IDOLS

1. Grant, *Ella Baker*, 226.
2. Halberstam, *Children*, 629–35.
3. Moses and Cobb, *Radical Equations*, 94–95; Blake, *Children of Movement*, 44–45.
4. Moses and Cobb, *Radical Equations*, 94–95; *Mother Jones*, May 1, 2002.
5. Moses and Cobb, *Radical Equations*, 94–99.
6. Ibid., 94–113.
7. Ibid., 102–105; *New York Times*, February 21, 1993; January 7, 2001; *Mother Jones*, May 1, 2002.
8. *New York Times*, February 21, 1993; January 7, 2001; *Mother Jones*, May 1, 2002; Moses and Cobb, *Radical Equations*, 91–122.
9. Moses and Cobb, *Radical Equations*, 14.
10. *New York Times*, February 21, 1993.
11. Ibid.; Moses and Cobb, *Radical Equations*, 136–51.
12. *Mother Jones*, May 1, 2002.
13. Moses and Cobb, *Radical Equations*, 152–68.
14. *Baltimore Sun*, April 9, 13, 15, 2004.
15. *New York Times*, January 7, 2001; *Mother Jones*, May 1, 2002; Moses and Cobb, *Radical Equations*, 172–87.
16. *Mother Jones*, May 1, 2002.
17. Moses and Cobb, *Radical Equations*, 191.
18. For an overview of Barry's tenure, see "Marion Barry: The Making of a Mayor," *Washington Post*, updated May 21, 1988, online at www.washingtonpost.com/wp-srv/local/longterm/library/dc/barry/barry.htm.
19. *Washington Post*, November 3, 1986; April 26, 1987.
20. *Washington Post*, January 21, 1990; "Barry: Making of a Mayor," www.washingtonpost.com.
21. Wilentz, "Last Integrationist"; *Boston Globe*, July 10, 2006; *Washington Post*, February 29, 2008.
22. Wilentz, "Last Integrationist"; *Washington Post*, March 6, 1990.

23. *Washington Post*, March 6, 1990.

24. Lewis and D'Orso, *Walking with the Wind*, 452–79.

25. *New York Times*, June 28, 1998; *Time*, June 22, 1998.

26. *New York Times*, February 19, July 11, 1992; March 31, 1993; August 17, 22, 1994; *Washington Post*, December 20, 1992; December 18, 1994.

27. *Washington Post*, May 21, 1998; *New York Times*, February 22, 1998.

28. *USA Today*, March 4, 2007.

29. *Washington Blade*, April 8, 2005; Bond interview.

30. *New York Times*, July 21, 2006; *Washington Post*, July 21, 2006.

BIBLIOGRAPHY

INTERVIEWS
Marion Barry
Julian Bond
John Lewis
Charles McDew
Bob Moses
Diane Nash
Bob Zellner

MICROFILM COLLECTIONS
Southern Regional Council Papers, 1944–68. Ann Arbor, Mich.: University Microfilms, 1984.
Student Nonviolent Coordinating Committee Papers, 1959–72. Sanford, N.C.: Microfilming Corp. of America, 1982.

NEWSPAPERS AND MAGAZINES
The Atlanta Journal-Constitution
Baltimore Sun
Boston Globe
Ebony
Fortune
Freedomways
Jet
Katallagete
Life
Look
Mother Jones
The New Republic

Newsweek
The New York Times
Time
USA Today
Washington Blade
The Washington Post

BOOKS, ARTICLES, AND TRANSCRIPTS

Agronsky, Jonathan. *Marion Barry: The Politics of Race*. Latham, N.Y.: British American Publishing, 1991.

Anderson, Jervis. *Bayard Rustin: Troubles I've Seen—A Biography*. New York: Harper-Collins, 1997.

Arsenault, Ray. *Freedom Riders: 1961 and the Struggle for Racial Justice*. New York: Oxford University Press, 2006.

Barras, Jonetta. *Last of the Black Emperors: The Hollow Comeback of Marion Barry in a New Age of Black Leaders*. New York: Bancroft Press, 1998.

Bartley, Numan. *The New South, 1945–1980*. Baton Rouge: Louisiana State University Press, 1995.

Bauer, John F. *John F. Kennedy and the Second Reconstruction*. New York: Columbia University Press, 1977.

Beals, Melba Pattillo. *Warriors Don't Cry: A Searing Memoir of the Battle to Integrate Little Rock's Central High*. New York: Pocket Books, 1994.

Belfrage, Sally. *Freedom Summer*. Charlottesville: University of Virginia Press, 1990.

Bevel, Diane Nash. "Journey to North Vietnam." *Freedomways*, Spring 1967.

Blake, John. *Children of the Movement: The Sons and Daughters of Martin Luther King Jr., Malcolm X, Elijah Muhammad, George Wallace, Andrew Young, Julian Bond, Stokely Carmichael, Bob Moses, James Chaney, Elaine Brown, and Others Reveal How the Civil Rights Movement Tested and Transformed Their Families*. Chicago: Lawrence Hill Books, 2004.

Bloom, Alexander, ed. *Long Time Gone: Sixties America Then and Now*. New York: Oxford University Press, 2001.

Bond, Julian. *Black Candidates: Southern Campaign Experiences*. Atlanta: Southern Regional Council, 1968.

Branch, Taylor. *Parting the Waters: America in the King Years, 1954–63*. New York: Simon & Schuster, 1988.

———. *Pillar of Fire: America in the King Years, 1963–65*. New York: Simon & Schuster, 1998.

———. *At Canaan's Edge: America in the King Years, 1965–68*. New York: Simon & Schuster, 2006.

Burner, Eric. *And Gently He Shall Lead Them: Robert Parris Moses and Civil Rights in Mississippi*. New York: NYU Press, 1995.

Cagin, Seth, and Philip Dray. *We Are Not Afraid: The Story of Goodman, Schwerner, and Chaney, and the Civil Rights Campaign for Mississippi*. New York: Macmillan, 1988.

Carmichael, Stokely. "Toward Black Liberation." *The Massachusetts Review*, Autumn 1966.

———. "What We Want." *New York Review of Books*, September 22, 1966.

Carmichael, Stokely, and Ekwueme Michael Thelwell. *Ready for Revolution: The Life and Struggles of Stokely Carmichael (Kwame Ture).* New York: Scribner, 2003.

Carson, Clayborne. *In Struggle: SNCC and the Black Awakening of the 1960s.* Cambridge, Mass., Harvard University Press, 1981.

———, ed. *The Autobiography of Martin Luther King, Jr.* New York: Warner Books, 1998.

Chafe, William. *Civilities and Civil Rights: Greensboro, North Carolina, and the Black Struggle for Freedom.* New York: Oxford University Press, 1980.

———. *Never Stop Running: Allard Lowenstein and the Struggle to Save America.* New York: Basic Books, 1993.

Cohen, Elizabeth. *The Consumers' Republic: The Politics of Mass Consumption in Postwar America.* New York: Alfred A. Knopf, 2003.

Dalleck, Robert. *Flawed Giant: Lyndon Johnson and His Times, 1961–1973.* New York: Oxford University Press, 1998.

Davis, Townsend. *Weary Feet, Rested Souls: A Guided History of the Civil Rights Movement.* New York: W. W. Norton & Co., 1998.

D'Emilio, John. *Lost Prophet: The Life and Times of Bayard Rustin.* New York: Free Press, 2003.

Dittmer, John. *Local People: The Struggle for Civil Rights in Mississippi.* Urbana: University of Illinois Press, 2003.

Egerton, John. *Speak Now Against the Day: The Generation Before the Civil Rights Movement in the South.* Chapel Hill: University of North Carolina Press, 1995.

Eskew, Glenn T. *But for Birmingham: The Local and National Movements in the Civil Rights Struggle.* Chapel Hill: University of North Carolina Press, 1997.

Evans, Sara. *Personal Politics: The Roots of Women's Liberation in the Civil Rights Movement and the New Left.* New York: Alfred A. Knopf, 1979.

Fairclough, Adam. *To Redeem the Soul of America: The Southern Christian Leadership Conference and Martin Luther King, Jr.* Athens: University of Georgia Press, 1987.

———. *Martin Luther King, Jr.* Athens: University of Georgia Press, 1995.

Farmer, James. *Lay Bare the Heart: An Autobiography of the Civil Rights Movement.* Westminster, Md.: Arbor House, 1985.

Fleming, Cynthia Griggs. *Soon We Will Not Cry: The Liberation of Ruby Doris Smith Robinson.* New York: Rowman & Littlefield, 1998.

Flynn, George Q. *The Draft: 1940–1973.* Lawrence: University of Kansas Press, 1993.

Fogelson, Genia. *Harry Belafonte: Singer and Actor.* New York: Holloway House, 1996.

Foner, Philip, ed. *The Black Panthers Speak.* Philadelphia: Lippincott, 1970.

Forman, James. *The Making of Black Revolutionaries.* New York: Macmillan, 1972.

Frazier, E. Franklin. *Black Bourgeoisie.* Glencoe, Ill.: Free Press, 1957.

Garrow, David. *Bearing the Cross: Martin Luther King, Jr., and the Southern Christian Leadership Conference.* New York: William Morrow, 1986.

Gates, Henry Louis, Jr. *Thirteen Ways of Looking at a Black Man.* New York: Random House, 1997.

Graham, Hugh Davis. *Civil Rights and the Presidency: Race and Gender in American Politics, 1960–1972.* New York: Oxford University Press, 1992.

Grant, Joanne. *Ella Baker: Freedom Bound.* New York: John Wiley & Sons, 1998.

Greenberg, Jack. *Crusaders in the Courts: Legal Battles of the Civil Rights Movement.* New York: Basic Books, 1994.

Greenburg, Cheryl, ed. *A Circle of Trust: Remembering SNCC.* New Brunswick, N.J.: Rutgers University Press, 1998.

Grossman, James R. *Land of Hope: Chicago, Black Southerners, and the Great Migration.* Chicago: University of Chicago Press, 1989.

Halberstam, David. *The Children.* New York: Random House, 1998.

Hampton, Henry, and Steven Fayer, with Sarah Flynn. *Voices of Freedom: An Oral History of the Civil Rights Movement from the 1950s through the 1980s.* New York: Bantam Books, 1990.

Hogan, Wesley. "Radical Manners: The Student Nonviolent Coordinating Committee and the New Left in the 1960s." Ph.D. diss., Duke University, 2000.

Holt, Len. *The Summer That Didn't End.* New York: William Morrow & Co., 1965.

Honey, Michael. *Southern Labor and Black Civil Rights: Organizing Memphis Workers.* Urbana: University of Illinois Press, 1993.

Huie, William B. "The Shocking Story of Approved Killing in Mississippi." *Look,* January 24, 1956.

Jacoway, Elizabeth, and David R. Colburn. *Southern Businessmen Against Desegregation.* Baton Rouge: Louisiana State University Press, 1982.

Joseph, Peniel E. *Waiting 'Til the Midnight Hour: A Narrative History of Black Power in America.* New York: Henry Holt & Co., 2006.

Key, V. O. *Southern Politics in State and Nation.* New York: Alfred A. Knopf, 1949.

King, Martin Luther, Jr. *Stride Toward Freedom: The Montgomery Story.* New York: Harper & Row, 1958.

———. *Why We Can't Wait.* New York: Harper & Row, 1964.

———. *Where Do We Go From Here: Chaos or Community?* New York: Harper & Row, 1967.

King, Mary. *Freedom Song: A Personal Story of the 1960s Civil Rights Movement.* New York: William Morrow & Co., 1987.

King, Richard. *Civil Rights and the Idea of Freedom.* New York: Oxford University Press, 1992.

Kirk, John A. *Redefining the Color Line: Black Activism in Little Rock, Arkansas, 1940–1970.* Gainesville: University Press of Florida, 2002.

Kisseloff, Jeff. *Generation on Fire: Voices of Protest from the 1960s, an Oral History.* Lexington: University of Kentucky Press, 2007.

Klarman, Michael. *From Jim Crow to Civil Rights: The Supreme Court and the Struggle for Racial Equality.* New York: Oxford University Press, 2004.

Klibaner, Irwin. "The Travail of Southern Radicals: The Southern Conference Educational Fund, 1946–1976." *Journal of Southern History,* May 1983, 179–202.

Kluger, Richard. *Simple Justice: The History of Brown v. Board of Education and Black America's Struggle for Equality.* New York: Alfred A. Knopf, 1975.

Kneebone, John. *Southern Liberal Journalists and the Issue of Race, 1920–1944.* Chapel Hill: University of North Carolina Press, 1985.

Kruse, Kevin M. *White Flight: Atlanta and the Making of Modern Conservatism.* Princeton, N.J.: Princeton University Press, 2005.

Lawson, Steven. *Running for Freedom: Civil Rights and Black Politics Since 1941.* Philadelphia: Temple University Press, 1990.

Lee, Chana Kai. *For Freedom's Sake: The Life of Fannie Lou Hamer.* Urbana: University of Illinois Press, 2000.

Lemann, Nicholas. *The Promised Land: The Great Black Migration and How It Changed America.* New York: Alfred A. Knopf, 1991.

Levine, Daniel. *Bayard Rustin and the Civil Rights Movement.* New Brunswick, N.J.: Rutgers University Press, 2000.

Lewis, John, and Michael D'Orso. *Walking with the Wind: A Memoir of the Movement.* New York: Simon & Schuster, 1998.

Lichtenstein, Nelson. *Walter Reuther.* New York: Basic Books, 1995.

Lyon, Danny. *Memories of the Southern Civil Rights Movement.* Chapel Hill: University of North Carolina Press, 1992.

Mailer, Norman. "The White Negro." *Dissent*, Fall 1957.

Marquesse, Michael. *Redemption Song: Muhammad Ali and the Spirit of the Sixties.* New York: Verso, 1999.

McAdam, Doug. *Freedom Summer.* New York: Oxford University Press, 1988.

McKnight, Gerald D. *The Last Crusade: Martin Luther King, Jr., the FBI, and the Poor People's Campaign.* New York: Basic Books, 1998.

McMillen, Neil R. *Dark Journey: Black Mississippians in the Age of Jim Crow.* Urbana: University of Illinois Press, 1990.

Meier, August, and Elliot Rudwick. *CORE: A Study in the Civil Rights Movement, 1942–1968.* New York: Oxford University Press, 1973.

Metcalf, George R. *Up from Within: Today's New Black Leaders.* New York: McGraw-Hill, 1971.

Metress, Christopher. *The Lynching of Emmett Till: A Documentary Narrative.* Charlottesville: University of Virginia Press, 2002.

Miller, James. *Democracy Is in the Streets: From Port Huron to the Siege of Chicago.* New York: Simon & Schuster, 1987.

Mills, Kay. *This Little Light of Mine: The Life of Fannie Lou Hamer.* New York: Dutton, 1993.

Morris, Aldon D. *The Origins of the Civil Rights Movement: Black Communities Organizing for Change.* New York: Free Press, 1984.

Moses, Robert, and Charles E. Cobb. *Radical Equations: Civil Rights from Mississippi to the Algebra Project.* Boston: Beacon Press, 2002.

Nash, Diane. "Inside the Sit-ins and Freedom Rides: Testimony of a Southern Student." In Matthew H. Ahmann, ed., *The New Negro.* New York: Biblio and Tannen, 1969.

———. "What Does a Freedom Fighter Do?" *Katallagete*, Spring 1972.

Neary, John. *Julian Bond, Black Rebel.* New York: William Morrow, 1971.

Norrell, Jeff. "Caste in Steel: Jim Crow Careers in Birmingham, Alabama." *Journal of American History*, December 1986, 669–94.

Olson, Lynne. *Freedom's Daughters: The Unsung Heroines of the Civil Rights Movement from 1830 to 1970.* New York: Scribner, 2001.

Oshinsky, David M. *"Worse Than Slavery": Parchman Farm and the Ordeal of Jim Crow Justice.* New York: Free Press, 1996.

Parks, Rosa, and Jim Haskins. *Rosa Parks: My Story.* New York: Puffin, 1999.

Patterson, James. *Brown v. Board of Education: A Civil Rights Milestone and Its Troubled Legacy.* New York: Oxford University Press, 2002.

Payne, Charles. *I've Got the Light of Freedom: The Organizing Tradition and the Mississippi Freedom Struggle.* Berkeley: University of California Press, 1995.

Pearson, Hugh. *The Shadow of the Panther: Huey Newton and the Price of Black Power in America.* Cambridge, Mass.: Perseus Publishing, 1994.

Peck, James. *Freedom Ride.* New York: Simon & Schuster, 1962.

Polletta, Francesca. *Freedom Is an Endless Meeting: Democracy in American Social Movements.* Chicago: University of Chicago Press, 2002.

Pomerantz, Gary M. *Where Peachtree Meets Sweet Auburn: A Saga of Race and Family.* New York: Scribner, 1996.

Powledge, Fred. *Free at Last? The Civil Rights Movement and the People Who Made It.* Boston: Little, Brown and Co., 1991.

Raines, Howell. *My Soul Is Rested: Movement Days in the Deep South Remembered.* New York: G. P. Putnam's Sons, 1977.

Ransby, Barbara. *Ella Baker and the Black Freedom Movement: A Radical Democratic Vision.* Chapel Hill: University of North Carolina Press, 2003.

Remnick, David. *King of the World: Muhammad Ali and the Rise of an American Hero.* New York: Random House, 1998.

Rose, Thomas. *Black Leaders Then and Now: A Personal History of the Students Who Led the Civil Rights Movement and What Happened to Them.* Garrett Park, Md.: Garrett Park Press, 1984.

Schlesinger, Arthur M. *A Thousand Days: John F. Kennedy in the White House.* New York: Houghton Mifflin, 1965.

Schulman, Bruce. *From Cotton Belt to Sun Belt: Federal Policy, Economic Development, and the Transformation of the South, 1938–1980.* New York: Oxford University Press, 1991.

Self, Robert. *American Babylon: Race and the Struggle for Postwar Oakland.* Princeton, N.J.: Princeton University Press, 2003.

Sellers, Cleveland, and Robert Terrell. *The River of No Return: The Autobiography of a Black Militant and the Life and Death of SNCC.* New York: William Morrow, 1973.

Silver, James W. *Mississippi: The Closed Society.* New York: Harcourt, Brace & World, 1964.

Sitkoff, Harvard. *The Struggle for Black Equality, 1954–1992,* rev. ed. New York: Hill and Wang, 1992.

Smith, Robert. *They Closed Their Schools: Prince Edward County, Virginia, 1951–1964.* Chapel Hill: University of North Carolina Press, 1965.

Southern Regional Council. *Statistical Summary of School Segregation-Desegregation in the Southern and Border States.* Atlanta, 1961.

Stern, Mark. *Calculating Visions: Kennedy, Johnson, and Civil Rights.* New Brunswick, N.J.: Rutgers University Press, 1992.

Stoper, Emily. *The Student Nonviolent Coordinating Committee: The Growth of Radicalism in a Civil Rights Organization.* Brooklyn, N.Y.: Carlson, 1989.

Sutherland, Elizabeth. *Letters from Mississippi.* New York: McGraw-Hill, 1965.

Thornton, J. Mills. *Dividing Lines: Municipal Politics and the Struggle for Civil Rights in Montgomery, Birmingham, and Selma.* Tuscaloosa: University of Alabama Press, 2002.

Van Deburg, William L. *New Day in Babylon: The Black Power Movement and American Culture, 1965–1975.* Chicago: University of Chicago Press, 1993.

Ward, Brian. *Just My Soul Responding: Rhythm and Blues, Black Consciousness, and Race Relations.* Berkeley: University of California Press, 1998.

Warren, Robert Penn. *Who Speaks for the Negro?* New York: Random House, 1965.

Whitfield, Stephen J. *A Death in the Delta: The Story of Emmett Till.* New York: Free Press, 1988.

Wilentz, Sean. "The Last Integrationist." *The New Republic*, July 1, 1996.

Williams, Roger M. *The Bonds: An American Family.* New York: Atheneum, 1972.

Wilkins, Roy. *Standing Fast: The Autobiography of Roy Wilkins.* New York: Viking, 1982.

Wolfe, Thomas. *Radical Chic and Mau-Mauing the Flak Catchers.* New York: Bantam Books, 1971.

Woods, Donald. *Biko—Cry Freedom.* London: Peter Smith, 1983.

Wynn, Neil A. *The Afro-American in the Second World War.* London: Elek, 1976.

Zellner, Bob. Interview by John Biewen and Kate Cavett in series *Oh Freedom Over Me.* American Radioworks, 1994. americanradioworks.publicradio.org/features/oh_freedom/interview_zellner.html.

Zellner, Bob, with Constance Curry. *The Wrong Side of Murder Creek: A White Southerner in the Freedom Movement.* Montgomery, Ala.: New South Books, 2008.

Zinn, Howard. *SNCC: The New Abolitionists.* Boston: Beacon Press, 1964.

ACKNOWLEDGMENTS

"Judge, I got debts no honest man can pay," sang Bruce Springsteen in "Johnny 99." I thought of that line almost every day I was working on this project.

My largest debt is to the men and women of SNCC who have shared their memories, especially Marion Barry, Julian Bond, John Lewis, Charles McDew, Bob Moses, Diane Nash, and Bob Zellner for sitting for interviews. I have tried to tell their stories straight and true and to honor their heroism with an honest take on their lives. Special thanks to Julian Bond for the use of two of his poems.

This book would not have been possible without the amazing work of the many historians who have come before me. I have been particularly influenced by Ekwueme Michael Thelwell's incomparably edited autobiography of Stokely Carmichael, Clayborne Carson's pathbreaking *In Struggle*, Howard Zinn's firsthand history, and Cleveland Sellers's moving memoir. Many people have done yeoman work collecting the life stories of movement activists, but no collection is as comprehensive, insightful, or interesting as the interviews collected by the late, great Henry Hampton and his team at Blackside Productions for the *Eyes on the Prize* series.

My agent, Jim Hornfischer, and my editor, Thomas LeBien, deserve special mention. Jim saw something in this project when it was just a two-page proposal. He helped me refine the idea and find the right publisher. At low moments, Jim's support sustained me. He gave me his loyalty before I'd really earned it, and I am humbled by that. It is hard for me to imagine a better editor than Thomas LeBien. His careful editing improved the manuscript at every turn, sharpening my thoughts and polishing the language. During a difficult personal time, Liz Maples guided me through the production process with a warm touch.

My old friend Jed Esty worked hard, harder than he thought, to help me conceptualize the story, shape the outline, and smooth out the writing. His fingerprints are everywhere. The keenest observations and most elegant turns of phrase came from him. Paige Meltzer read every word in this book more than once and saved me from more errors than I can count. Our daily phone conversations about everything from our work to our personal lives have been an anchor. Matt Lassiter and Doug Smith, my closest friends from graduate school, have listened to me spin this story for many years. Our shared fifteen-year conversation about modern American history has been the most rewarding intellectual experience. But the roots of my intellectual journey go back deeper—to Paul Gaston, who mentored me in grad school and whose influence on this book is everywhere; to Bob Engs, who introduced me to African-American history at Penn; and to Elliot Lilien, Dennis Cleary, and Jim Veitch, who nurtured my love of history as a teen.

I am deeply grateful for the institutions that supported this project. I was lucky to have the resources of a fellowship at the W.E.B. Du Bois Institute at Harvard University behind me during the months when I first outlined the book and prepared a full proposal. The next year, the Virginia Foundation for the Humanities offered me a semester-long fellowship to work on the project. While I was between teaching gigs, the University of Richmond provided research support, an office, and a community to call home. At Richmond, Cassie King went out of her way to help me track down information and to proofread early drafts. I was also lucky to become friends with a number of remarkable people during my years there—in particular, Don Forsyth, Matt Basso, Ed Larkin, Tom Shields, and Gary McDowell. My great friendship with John Marx is the best legacy of my time in Richmond. He often asked the kind of skeptical, probing questions that would send me scrambling back to my computer to articulate my thoughts with greater clarity and cogency. Most important, John and his partner, Beth Anderson, sustained my good cheer when my writing flagged.

Nearly every day I lived in Richmond, Woody Holton phoned to ask, "How much have you written today?" Far from being a nag, Woody was my friend, my confidant, and a model of intellectual rigor, scholarly productivity, and graceful writing. It is fitting that our books will be published in the same month. My time at Richmond was made possible in the first place because Woody and Juliette Landphair, the dean of Westhampton College at the University of Richmond and my dear friend, brokered a teaching position for me just as my fellowship at the Du Bois Institute expired. Joe Thorndike's unflagging support helped me through many a rough patch. And of course thanks go to the wonderful Megan Eliot.

I finished the book while teaching at Hamilton College. I was fortunate to make the acquaintance of a wonderful bunch of colleagues in the history department: Doug Ambrose, Maurice Isserman, Lisa Trivedi, Kevin Grant, Chris Hill, Jake Whitaker, Thomas Wilson, and Robin Vanderwall. I was especially lucky to have Phil Klinkner, a political scientist who shares my passion for the history of race relations, in the office next door to mine for my whole last year. And I made other remarkable friends at Hamilton: Chris Vasantkumar, Emily Rohrbach, Jean Burr, and Hye Seung Chung.

I have been fortunate to have a wonderful group of friends outside the academy whose support has helped me immensely in the writing of this book: Rob and Robyn Waldeck, Jay and Sue Cushing, Tony and Christine Salah, Jen Reingold, Pete Sheehy and Janice Min, Ira Gaberman, and Andrea Goulet. And thanks to my siblings, Liz and Neil; my nieces, Sophie and Ellie; and my brother-in-law, Nick, who have all thought that writing a book might have been a ruse simply to get out of doing dishes after family meals.

Finally, my mother lived long enough to see me finish the manuscript and to view a mock-up of the cover (which she loved). She died in February 2009, just as the manuscript was being completed. I had always intended to dedicate the book to my mom and my dad, but I was saving that news as a surprise. No words can adequately express what a parent means to a child. I hope this book is a testament to her enduring influence on me.

ANDREW B. LEWIS
March 30, 2009
Concord, Mass.